"This cutting-edge guide provides a comprehensive road map for understanding and implementing schema therapy as a truly integrative and dynamic therapeutic model. The reader is taken on a journey that interweaves conceptual underpinnings with cutting-edge theoretical advances, contextualizing it within the framework of second and third wave psychotherapy approaches. This book connects the dots of the schema therapy model. Its descriptions bring the powerful schema therapy techniques to life, while providing a clear pathway to guide the overarching process. This book is an indispensable text that will appeal to experienced clinicians, as well as those who are simply curious to learn more about this approach."

—**Susan Simpson, DClinPsych**, NHS Lothian, Scotland; department of psychology, University of South Australia

Contextual Schema Therapy

An Integrative Approach to
Personality Disorders, Emotional Dysregulation
& **Interpersonal Functioning**

Eckhard Roediger, MD
Bruce A. Stevens, PhD
Robert Brockman, DClinPsy

CONTEXT PRESS
An Imprint of New Harbinger Publications, Inc.

Publisher's Note

This publication is designed to provide accurate and authoritative information in regard to the subject matter covered. It is sold with the understanding that the publisher is not engaged in rendering psychological, financial, legal, or other professional services. If expert assistance or counseling is needed, the services of a competent professional should be sought.

NEW HARBINGER PUBLICATIONS is a registered trademark of New Harbinger Publications, Inc.

Distributed in Canada by Raincoast Books

Copyright © 2018 by Eckhard Roediger, Bruce A. Stevens, and Robert Brockman
        Context Press
        An imprint of New Harbinger Publications, Inc.
        5674 Shattuck Avenue
        Oakland, CA 94609
        www.newharbinger.com

Figure 1-2, "Photograph of feet in the sand at sunset," is reproduced with permission from the work of Angeles Hoffmann.

Cover design by Amy Shoup

Acquired by Tesilya Hanauer

Edited by James Lainsbury

All Rights Reserved

Library of Congress Cataloging-in-Publication Data on file

Printed in the United States of America

24   23   22
10   9   8   7   6   5

Contents

	Foreword	vii
	Introduction—Why This Book?	1
1	Conceptual Underpinnings	5
2	The Schema Model—Mapping the Badlands	25
3	Modes—In the Present Tense	39
4	From Past Tense to Present Tense—The Case Conceptualization	57
5	Harnessing the Therapy Relationship	83
6	Dealing with Child, Inner Critic, and Coping Modes	109
7	Building the Healthy Adult Mode	125
8	How to Bring Change	143
9	Imagery Techniques to Induce Mode Change	149
10	Mode Dialogues on Chairs	179
11	Behavior Change Techniques	197
12	Treatment Planning	215
13	Dealing with Difficult Clients	227
14	It Takes Two to Tango—Including the Client's Partner in Therapy	251
15	Therapist Schemas and Self-Care	259
	Epilogue—Training Opportunities and Resources	273
	Afterword	275
	References	277
	Index	289

Figures

FIGURE 1–1.	Basic emotions, coping styles, and self-expression	9
FIGURE 1–2.	An exercise in dual focusing	13
FIGURE 1–3.	A second exercise in dual focusing	14
FIGURE 1–4.	Attractors and the energetic landscape	15
FIGURE 1–5.	The emotional tolerance window	17
FIGURE 1–6.	Socialization and constitution of the self	20
FIGURE 3–1.	The mode model	41
FIGURE 3–2.	Connecting schemas, schema-coping styles, and coping modes in terms of learning processes	53
FIGURE 3–3.	Maladaptive coping modes and clinical symptoms	55
FIGURE 4–1.	Genogram for Joanne	61
FIGURE 4–2.	Mode monitoring form for Joanne	69
FIGURE 4–3.	Descriptive mode diagram for Joanne	71
FIGURE 4–4.	Mode map for Joanne	75
FIGURE 4–5.	Schemas, schema coping, coping modes, and ACT processes integrated into the behavioral analysis system	81
FIGURE 5–1.	Connecting the biographical, current life, and therapy scenes	84
FIGURE 5–2.	The dimensions of the therapy relationship	86
FIGURE 5–3.	Sitting positions to support emotional activation	87
FIGURE 5–4.	Therapist and client positions while reflecting on the process in a working alliance	90

FIGURE 6–1.	Chair positions according to the mode map	111
FIGURE 6–2.	Chair positions for empathic confrontation	116
FIGURE 6–3.	How to place the chairs when working with overcompensators	118
FIGURE 7–1.	The attention time line	130
FIGURE 7–2.	Two ways to consistency	134
FIGURE 7–3.	Values road map	142
FIGURE 8–1.	Emotional processing using the two-minds metaphor	144
FIGURE 8–2.	Steps for lasting change	148
FIGURE 9–1.	Working with the two systems of information processing in imagery (based on Schacter, 1992)	150
FIGURE 9–2.	The healing process in experiential work	173
FIGURE 10–1.	Chair positions in historical role-play	181
FIGURE 10–2.	Chair dialogue based on the mode map	185
FIGURE 10–3.	The vicious cycle of an alarm reaction, and how to escape	194
FIGURE 11–1.	Joanne's coping mode tracking sheet	202
FIGURE 11–2.	Joanne's schema-mode flash card (modified from Young, Klosko, & Weishaar, 2003)	205
FIGURE 11–3.	Joanne's talking-back diary	207
FIGURE 11–4.	Joanne's diary card	208
FIGURE 11–5.	Joanne's behavioral activation form	211
FIGURE 13–1.	Schemas and modes of a narcissistic client	229
FIGURE 14–1.	The maladaptive mode cycle of Joanne and Brandon	253

Tables

TABLE 1–1.	The two poles of human organization	7
TABLE 2–1.	Schemas, domains, need states, and resulting modes	27
TABLE 3–1.	The relations between schemas, schema-coping styles, and presented coping modes	51
TABLE 5–1.	Dropout rates in borderline personality disorder treatments	97
TABLE 15–1.	Possible mode cycles in the therapy relationship	260

Foreword

I could not be more delighted that my dear friends and colleagues Eckhard Roediger, Bruce Stevens, and Robert Brockman wrote this extraordinary book.

Contextual Schema Therapy will surely be an outstanding resource for any clinician's library. The authors are highly experienced and talented schema therapy practitioners and educators, having devoted many years to sharpening their clinical skills within each of their unique areas of expertise. They generously share a rigorous effort, resulting in a thoughtful and comprehensive body of work that offers the reader one of the most relevant psychotherapy guides for conceptualizing and treating a variety of challenging populations; and demonstrating how the use of schema therapy, an evidence-based model—with rich assessment tools and integrative treatment strategies—can lead to the healing of destructive lifelong patterns.

Informed by and following up on the instrumental *Schema Therapy: A Practitioner's Guide*, by Jeffrey Young, Janet Klosko, and Marjorie Weishaar (2003), Roediger, Stevens, and Brockman delve deeper into the schema therapy approach and bring us up-to-date on the latest developments for applying this evidence-based model with some of the most difficult cases.

The challenging work of helping those who have endured painful early life experiences fraught with loss, neglect, abuse, loneliness, and/or deprivation, along with the sustained core feelings of hopelessness, shame, inadequacy, inhibition; the need to be perfect; and the need to control or surrender demands a psychotherapeutic approach that thoughtfully assesses the client's autobiographical early experiences and consequential unmet needs; connects the dots between self-defeating life patterns, coping modes, and current activating conditions; and seeks to heal and correct biased emotional experiences that inform present-day emotional and sensorial systems, self-defeating beliefs, and maladaptive coping behaviors. The elegantly designed integrative treatment approach, founded in Jeffrey Young's schema therapy model, is exquisitely captured and elaborated in this beautiful body of work, as the authors illustrate the relationship between current and lifelong stressors and early life experiences—uncovering critical unmet emotional needs and temperamental factors that form personality. Schema therapy evaluates the *rigid truths*—that is, early maladaptive schemas and the coping reactions that get embedded in memory and become activated under familiar conditions throughout one's life span. The need for a sturdy, flexible, *real*, and attuned clinician is strongly proposed in the schema mode approach. The *realness* factor is a critical element for correcting the longstanding, biased emotional experiences, as you will come to appreciate in reading this book.

The authors are brilliant in making the model accessible through clear and colorful examples in almost every chapter, along with specific case vignettes, illustrating the comprehensive case conceptualization/assessment stage and the effective application of treatment strategies. The reader is sure to recognize both the unique and commonly shared challenges met in our treatment rooms in the examples shared by the authors.

The parallel process of client and clinician being triggered in the treatment room can lead to ineffective and frustrating outcomes, especially when an overwhelmed therapist ends up colluding with the client's avoidance or ends up giving in to entitled demands.

As I share in my book *Disarming the Narcissist*, about my work with narcissists, it is not unusual to be faced with a client who shifts between an emotionally distant mode and an angry or cynical mode; nor is it unusual to find myself having to stave off the urge to just give in and subjugate my rights and my voice (feelings triggered within the "little girl" mode in me), and to maintain my sturdy posture in order to meet the client's needs for trust, limit setting, accountability, and emotional connection.

The authors reveal how the integration of third wave therapeutic approaches, such as mindfulness and acceptance (to meet unmet emotional needs), along with the therapy relationship, serve to bolster the schema therapy approach to break through detachment; to confront harmful internal messengers; and to access, care for, and protect vulnerable modes, while strengthening the healthy adult mode in order to thwart self-defeating patterns in favor of healthier and adaptive responses.

I confidently recommend this exceptional book to anyone who wishes to gain more confidence and mastery for effective treatment outcomes, especially when it comes to facing the seemingly impermeable avoiders, narcissistic bullying and entitlement, and the hopeless forfeiters who surrender their needs and rights—marching to the beat of internalized critics and demanders.

You are about to be treated to a treasure trove of invaluable information, including conceptual and theoretical insights, along with clinical tools, tips, and strategies, in a keenly illustrated new book that is not to be missed.

—Wendy T. Behary, LCSW
Author of *Disarming the Narcissist*

Introduction—Why This Book?

Schema therapy brought a profound change to how we treat clients who suffer from chronic mental illness or a personality disorder. Building on the strengths of cognitive therapy, this approach provides a comprehensive map of personality using eighteen schemas, adds experiential change techniques, and uses attachment and developmental understanding to address maladaptive schemas arising from childhood neglect and trauma. Randomized controlled trials have demonstrated its effectiveness.

Time doesn't stand still, and we saw a need to provide an update on schema therapy. *Contextual Schema Therapy* is a comprehensive practitioner manual with clear principles and guidelines illustrated with clinical examples. We incorporated theoretical advances into its pages, so the book is cutting edge. Its innovative and integrative presentation is very much in the spirit of schema therapy.

Since its inception, schema therapy has been highly integrative. In 1990, Jeffrey Young outlined its parallels with and differences from major therapies, including Beck's "reformulated" model, psychoanalytic theory, Bowlby's attachment theory (especially internal working models), and emotion-focused therapy. There have also been contributions from gestalt, transactional analysis, and psychodrama (Edwards & Arntz, 2012). Schema therapy, in contrast to most cognitive therapies, has a greater emotional focus and willingness to explore the childhood and adolescent origins of psychological difficulties. Current problems are seen in terms of whole-of-life patterns that we call *schemas*. All this is integrated into a cognitive information-processing mode theory of personality. Additionally, schema therapy's breadth, applicability, and ease of understanding encourage broad application.

We believe that this integrative spirit has been a key to the success of schema therapy. Young introduced the original schema model in 1990, and the second step was the mode model that was developed about ten years later (Young et al., 2003). *Modes* are activated schemas. Since they are present in the here and now of therapy, modes are easier to track and to target with interventions. While in the United States, the basic schema model is still widely in use, schema therapy has been developed further in the Netherlands and Germany (Arntz & Jacob, 2013), where the mode model has been center stage for both research and treatment. All of the successful randomized controlled trials of schema therapy to date have used this model (Jacob & Arntz, 2013).

Schema therapy is one of the key evidence-based treatments for people suffering from personality disorders. Research indicates that features of personality disorder are very common in the general population. Only 23 percent of people are relatively free of such symptoms. According to Yang, Coid, and Tyrer (2010), more than 70 percent have some degree of personality disturbance. For this reason, it is essential to consider maladaptive personality traits in any comprehensive theory of change. There is already some evidence base suggesting that schema therapy can effectively treat clients with borderline personality disorder in both individual (Giesen-Bloo et al., 2006) and group settings (Farrell, Shaw, & Webber, 2009). A review of five schema therapy trials (three of them randomized controlled trials; Jacob & Arntz, 2013) showed an average effect size of 2.38 (95% CI 1.70–3.07). Compared with other specific borderline personality disorder treatments, dropout rates are low. Further studies have demonstrated the effectiveness of schema therapy with dependent, avoidant, and obsessive-compulsive personality disorders (Bamelis, Evers, Spinhoven, & Arntz, 2014), and antisocial individuals can be helped to change as well (Bernstein et al., 2012). There are also indicators that schema therapy is more cost-effective than other treatments (Van Asselt et al., 2008). For a more detailed overview, see Bamelis, Bloo, Bernstein, and Arntz (2012).

Recent advances in schema therapy derive from its capacity to straddle both the second and third waves of behavior therapy. The application of the mode model is in line with the second wave cognitive behavioral therapy (CBT) approach because schema therapy seeks to obtain change by shifting the *content* (in terms of meaning) deriving from negative early maladaptive schemas through experiential change techniques. Since Tara Bennet-Goleman (2001) introduced mindfulness to heal schemas in 2001, the ensuing years saw further evolution of the model, including the integration of the concepts of mindfulness and acceptance (Cousineau, 2012; Parfy, 2012; Roediger, 2012; Van Vreeswijk, Broersen, & Schurink, 2014). We call this book *Contextual Schema Therapy* because the model has been revised in light of contemporary contributions and understandings from third wave therapies. Schema therapy now balances the focus on change in schema *content* with an approach to building a healthy version of the self through changing the way people *relate* to their experiences and deal with them.

We argue that schema therapy can do more than change coping reactions to schema activations: it can help people become mindfully aware, disengage from unhelpful patterns of relating to past experiences, and strive for healthy and well-balanced behavior in general. In Germany, for example, schema therapy is already seen as a third wave therapy (Roediger & Zarbock, 2013).

The healthy adult mode is one of the key modes in schema therapy. It represents psychological health, maturity, and good judgment. This mode maps well onto the construct of psychological flexibility (Brockman, 2013) and can be largely described and addressed using the concepts and strategies of acceptance and commitment therapy (ACT; Hayes, Strosahl, & Wilson, 2012). Our comprehensive approach in this book incorporates the basic principles of ACT on a practical level and merges the more cognitive focus of ACT with the largely emotional focus of schema therapy. Thus, schema therapy becomes a contextual therapy (Hayes et al., 2012) while balancing second and third wave approaches, making it even more flexible and effective. However, we do not claim to provide a comprehensive theory. Jeff Young and colleagues' *Schema Therapy: A*

Practitioner's Guide (Young et al., 2003) remains foundational to our approach. We continually draw connections from their pioneering insights.

Schema therapy was developed from cognitive therapy with the intention of helping hard-to-treat cases by being open to innovation and alternative perspectives in terms of what Messer (2001) called "assimilative integration." This describes how therapists incorporate attitudes, perspectives, or techniques from another therapy into their primary approach based on a consistent conceptual framework. This systematic approach goes beyond technical eclecticism and is "truly integrative" (Young, 2008). Our framework is still the schema therapy model. We see this book as one way to develop schema therapy so it is further in line with the integrative spirit of its founder. Like Young, we use techniques derived from other therapeutic approaches in a very specific way based on the case conceptualization, and embed the techniques into the schema therapy relationship. In this way, schema therapy has become more than the sum of its parts. According to Young (2008), schema therapy has three hallmark elements:

- A case conceptualization based on the schema mode model
- A specific therapy relationship called limited reparenting
- An intensive use of experiential techniques, such as imagery rescripting or chair dialogues (in almost every session)

The schema model is easy to grasp and close to a "commonsense" psychology. Overall, this book has a practical focus. The clinical questions are "What works?" and "What works with the most difficult cases?" These represent the acid test for any therapy. We will help you to make comprehensive dimensional case conceptualizations according to the alternative dimensional model in the *Diagnostic and Statistical Manual of Mental Disorders*, fifth edition (DSM-5; American Psychiatric Association, 2013). Our goal is to provide therapists with a kind of road map to plan interventions and then tailor them in a specific way, using powerful techniques embedded in a caring relationship. Schema therapy calls this *reparenting*, which feels natural because it is what good parents do with their children!

We hope you find this book both illuminating and inspiring—a worthy tool to help you develop and implement schema therapy successfully.

A few words about organization. Self-reflection is pivotal in schema therapy. Thus over the course of the book, we invite you to take a self-reflective stance with prompts under the "Reflect" heading. In the spirit of self-reflection, let's start with the first one now: How long have you practiced psychotherapy? What changes have you noticed? What have been the most important therapeutic advances you can identify? Can you see parallels with schema therapy?

We also use the "Principle" heading to identify key principles to guide your work. In addition, we offer precise tips ("Therapist Tip") to help you to learn clinical skills for schema therapy. Finally, we alternate references to gender in this book in order to be as inclusive as possible.

CHAPTER 1

Conceptual Underpinnings

Why do we start this book by linking the schema therapy model with theory and by basing its development on current research findings in various fields? While we seek to condense the essence of rational therapies into one consistent and comparatively simple approach, we do not dare present a unified theory. Nevertheless, having an idea of the theories behind schema therapy deepens therapists' understanding of the processes involved, enabling them to develop the model beyond a purely practical "cookbook" approach and tailor their work to individual clients. Young and colleagues (2003) indicate these underpinnings but do not describe them in detail. We try to do so here.

This approach is intellectually challenging and complex. The content we present is very condensed, and understanding it requires some basic knowledge. Especially for those who are familiar with neurobiology findings, the rationale of schema therapy will become clearer with an understanding of this material. In the long run, having this knowledge will give you a fundamental understanding of change processes in general, helping you to adapt your approach to any targeted problem. However, if you are eager to get straight to the model, you might skip this chapter and jump directly to chapter 2. Maybe as you read through the book your interest in the theoretical background will grow, and later you can refer to this chapter when we connect our practical approach with the theory to underline its foundation in current research findings.

The Emotional Core Needs, Basic Emotions, and the Autonomic Nervous System

Needs are fundamental. Schema therapy is centered on the concept of core emotional needs (for a review, see Lockwood & Perris, 2012). Needs are universal and nonnegotiable. A very large body of research indicates that the ongoing frustration of core emotional needs detrimentally affects childhood development and leads to immediate and long-term impacts on physical and psychological well-being (Vansteenkiste & Ryan, 2013; see Ryan & Deci, 2017, for comprehensive coverage of this issue). There are several systems of needs.

Systems of needs. Maslow (1970) outlined a pyramid of needs, reaching from basic biological needs (such as food and water) through to the need for self-actualization.

More recently, researchers investigating self-determination theory have found evidence for the key role played by three basic emotional needs in human well-being and development: autonomy, competence, and relatedness (Ryan & Deci, 2017). In their original writing on the subject, Young and colleagues (2003) named five core emotional needs, including limit setting for the child. Unlike other practitioners at that time, Young took a developmental view of core needs, that of a child's perspective (for details, see chapter 2). For Young, needs satisfaction leads to healthy schemas, and needs frustration leads directly to the development of early maladaptive schemas.

We tried to keep the number of needs to a minimum in order to reduce the complexity of the model presented in this book. This led us to reduce the three needs described by Ryan and Deci (2017) to two irreducible ones, which are regarded as poles in a dimensional construct of attachment orientation (or connection/relatedness) and assertiveness orientation (including autonomy, competence, and control). These need-poles are embedded in a complex orientation of the organism as a whole (see table 1–1). They have an inverse relationship with one another: the more you strive for attachment, the more you have to sacrifice assertiveness and autonomy, and vice versa. However, you can aim for a good and flexible balance between them.

Principle: The needs for attachment and assertiveness are poles in the physiological, psychological, and social orientation of the whole organism.

The Attachment Pole

Interpersonal connection is essential for the survival of humans. Compared to the young of other animals, human babies are born in a very immature state and require great care while they mature. In order to guarantee survival, human beings have an inborn biological urge to form groups and cooperate. Thus we feel more safe in groups than going it alone (Gilbert, 2010). When we feel we are secure in a group, our emotional activation subsides and we shift into a healthy parasympathetic state. Our heart rate oscillates when we breathe in and out, as a sign of emotional flexibility. Heart-rate flexibility is a predictor of good health. Being in an ongoing activated state leads to a loss of heart-rate flexibility and an increased morbidity risk (Porges, 2007).

The physical and mental effects of loneliness, isolation, and social rejection are known to be severe (Hawkley & Cacioppo, 2010). Eisenberger, Lieberman, and Williams (2003) showed that rejection "hurts" by activating almost the same insular cortical areas that are activated when we experience physical pain. It is common to hear people describe emotional rejection as "a kick in the guts" or "a stab to the heart." In contrast, people with stronger social relationships have a 50 percent higher chance of survival than those with weaker social relationships (Holt-Lunstad, Smith, Baker, Harris, & Stephenson, 2015). Prosocial behavior directly activates our dopaminergic reward system (Van der Meulen, Ijzendoorn, & Crone, 2016)—just as drugs do!

Table 1–1. The two poles of human organization

Feature	Assertiveness	Attachment
Activated autonomic system	Sympathetic branch	Parasympathetic (vagal) branch
Focus of attention	Outward directed	Inward directed
Physiological reaction type	Activation of the alarm system	Calming down, recreation
Social tendency	Autonomy and competence	Connecting, relatedness
Type of breathing	Into the chest	Into the belly
Metabolic tendency	Exhaustion	Regeneration
Motoric tendency	Expansive activation	Receptive reaction
Social tendency	Self-centered, being dominant	Prosocial, seeking harmony
Tendency to react	Fight or flight	Cooperation up to submission
Active child pole if threatened	Angry child pole	Vulnerable child pole
Direction of inner critic modes	Directed to others	Directed to self
Direction of action	Externalizing	Internalizing
Coping style (Piaget, 1985)	Alloplastic	Autoplastic
Parenting mode (Lockwood & Perris, 2012)	Paternal (trains self-soothing)	Maternal (soothes directly)

The Autonomy, Control, and Assertiveness Pole

The autonomy, control, and assertiveness pole, based on the activities of the sympathetic nervous system, enables us to fight or flee and is the "second leg" that we stand on: the need for assertiveness and autonomy. In this more self-centered state, we tend to be self-reliant, and we are able to act dominantly and achieve a higher status in the social system.

Principle: Following the attachment need and taking a cooperative stance is essentially prosocial. Doing so makes us welcome in a group, which increases our chances of survival. However, being able to fight or flee is important in order to survive as an individual.

Alarm System

When we feel individually threatened, or when our attachment needs are constantly frustrated, our alarm system gets activated, providing us with the energy to fight or flee. If we are energetic and strong enough, being excluded or dominated can create a secondary anger, driving us to stand up for our rights. Thus we can try standing on our assertiveness leg in order to get the situation under control again. Successful social interaction is based on a good and flexible balance between these two poles of human behavior (see table 1–1).

How Are Needs and Basic Emotions Connected?

Ekman (1993) originally described a system of basic emotions based on transcultural facial expressions. He has since (Ekman, no date) described five basic emotions: the negatively tainted emotions of fear, sadness, disgust, and anger, and the positive emotion of joy. The four negative basic emotions operate like red lights on a dashboard, indicating that something is wrong. Primarily, frustration of the attachment need leads to feelings of fear or sadness. Disgust or anger indicate frustrations of the need for assertiveness or control. Joy indicates that the alarm system was successfully downregulated and that all needs have been adequately met.

Reactions to needs frustration. How can we deal with a threatening situation to downregulate our alarm system? The animal model (Cannon, 1915) described four general ways to escape the threat and calm down. In schema therapy, we call these basic reaction tendencies *coping styles*:

1. *Fight*, if we see a chance to win and become "top dog." We call this the *assertiveness way* to gain autonomy, control, dominance, and respect.

2. *Flight*, as an active escape. In the human model, this means overt avoidance and self-soothing activities.

3. *Freeze*, or passively withdraw by emotionally detaching, numbing, or dissociating.

4. *Follow*, or if the opponent appears stronger, in order to remain part of the group. Among humans, we call this the *attachment way* to achieve harmony, resonance, and a loving connection.

Needs frustration and coping styles. Anger drives us to fight. Disgust makes us turn away and care for ourselves (flight). When feeling sad, we tend to withdraw (freeze). Fear pulls us more to the submission side (surrender). The downside of these solutions is that they can become unbalanced when we overuse them and neglect the other pole of the needs spectrum, leading to needs frustration and the maintenance of schemas. Only when we are able to find a flexible solution with mutually changing roles do we feel balanced and gain the possibility of experiencing positive affect. Figure 1–1 puts all these pieces together in a complex framework that includes needs, levels of activation, spontaneous reaction tendencies, and the balanced way to joy and relaxation. This is the theoretical bedrock that we base our interventions on.

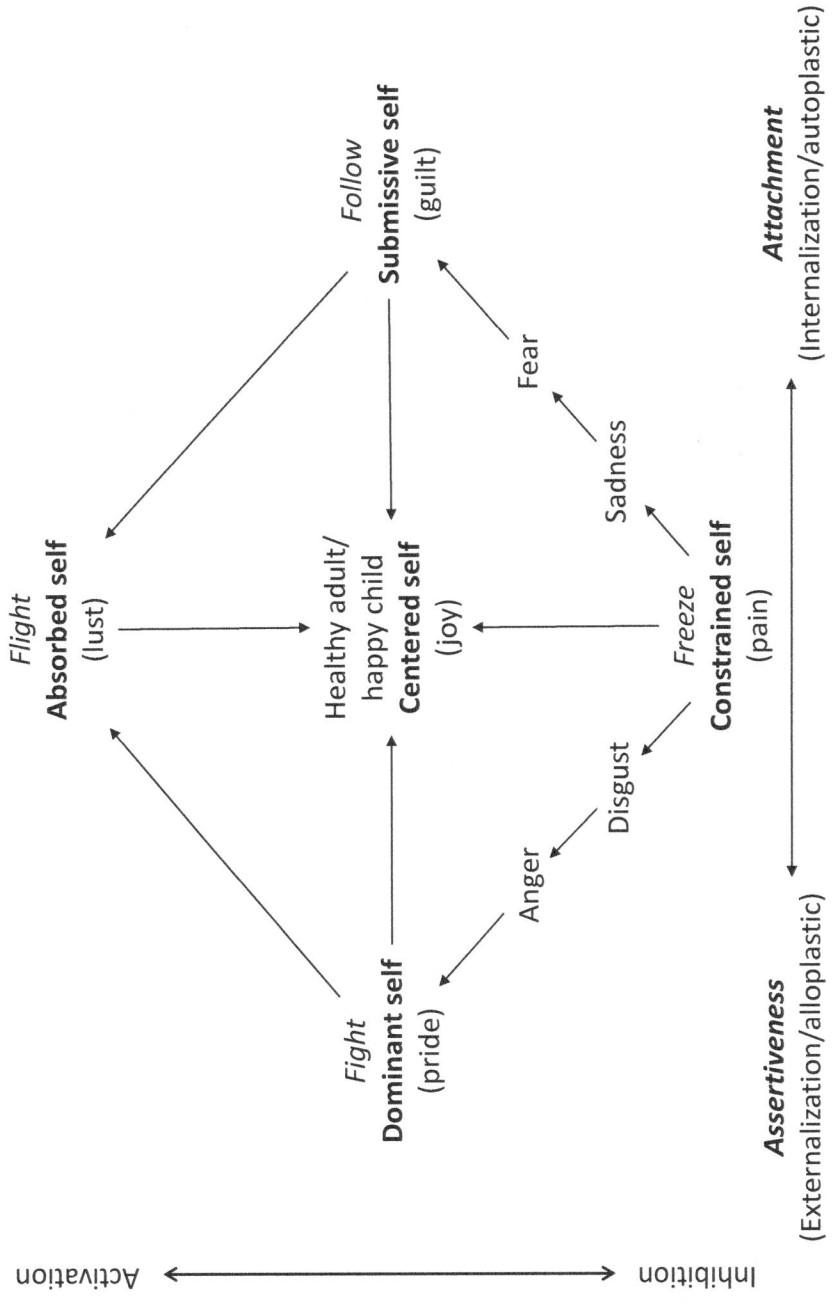

Figure 1–1. Basic emotions, coping styles, and self-expression

On Attachment

The need for attachment is biologically entrenched. Panksepp (2011) and, earlier, Bowlby (1969) described an attachment system acting in resonance with a caretaking system within the nurturing person as the neurobiological underpinning of our need to connect with other people and care for them. So what we perceive as "love" to a great extent is based on biology.

> *Principle:* The attachment and caretaking systems are the glue in our social system.

To survive, it is essential for the child to be able to induce goodwill in her caregivers. In everyday language, the child must make us like her. When watching Edward Tronick's video of his "still face" experiment, people usually react with a painful feeling to the deterioration of the child's mood following the rupture of this interpersonal resonance (Tronick, 2009). Being reconnected allows the child to calm down and get back into a parasympathetic (or vagal) state again. But not only does the child calm down, so too does the adult. Even we observers do! These feelings are connected with the release of oxytocin—the attachment hormone.

Oxytocin is the prosocial hormone par excellence. It supports trust in people, induces intimacy, and keeps young couples together (Kosfeld, Heinrichs, Zak, Fischbacher, & Fehr, 2005). After a nasal application of the hormone, people on the autistic spectrum are able to look into another person's eyes for twenty minutes (Buchheim et al., 2009), for as long as the drug acts. This is not a very romantic message, but a great deal of oxytocin underlies the activities we do for "love." These feelings of empathy are probably based on a system of so-called mirror neurons (for an overview, see Bargh, 2014).

Mirror neurons bridge the gap between our perceptions of ourselves and others (for an overview, see Gallagher & Frith, 2003). Unfortunately, these neurons are not preinstalled, but have to be trained by stimulation. Stern (1985) argued that a key role of caregivers in the development of an infant's self-regulation is their capacity to communicate affect attunement to the child. Caregivers, mostly at an unconscious level, undertake a range of gestures and behaviors that reflect some essential aspects of the baby's behavior and presumed emotional state. These mirroring acts of the caregiver constitute consistent states within the child.

Affect attunement helps to create for the baby a kind of preverbal feeling of being understood, setting the scene for the infant to develop self-regulation and identity (Winnicott, 1958). Beyond that, it lays the tracks to understand what's on other people's minds (Siegel, 1999; see "Mentalization and the Theory of Mind" in this chapter).

Insecure attachment. If resonant connection fails, this leads to an insecure attachment, an entangled attachment style, and an overexcited child (Ainsworth, Blehar, Waters, & Wall, 1978). However, the child manages to reconnect with the mother by controlling her. If the mother does not react at all, that leads to severe deprivation and life-threating stress for the child. This is why extended time-outs or not talking to a child over days is so detrimental. To cope with this stress, the child detaches or self-soothes, leading to an avoidant attachment style. Activation hardly subsides and becomes the precursor of many psychiatric and psychosomatic disorders (Hayes et al., 2012; for details, see chapter 3). Withdrawn partners use this innate vulnerability to punish others by stonewalling.

The self-compassion approach of Gilbert (2010) points in a similar direction. In his model, the activation of a compassionate self based on the attachment system is the key to moderating the activations of both the alarm (fear-based) system and the reward system. He sees the oxytocin-driven attachment system as essential for developing emotional regulation. He names "warmth" as the core agent to calm the basic emotions on both poles (the defensive and the greedy sides) and to open us up for a compassionate connection.

In therapy, the therapist acts as a role model, being present, mindful, accepting, and warmhearted. If necessary, the therapist first soothes the client directly in a maternal mode (Lockwood & Perris, 2012). Later, the therapist induces an internal representation by speaking to the client in an encouraging way. Thus, the client learns self-soothing in a kind of inner role-play between a caring mental representation and the activated emotional state. This helps to build a so-called acquired (secondary) secure attachment style (Pearson, Cohn, Cowan, & Cowan, 1994). Self-soothing capacity reduces dependence on other people, mediates autonomy, and makes well-balanced, flexible relationships much easier (see chapter 14). In chapter 7, we describe how we try to integrate self-compassion into schema therapy.

The Neurobiological Perspective and the Attractor Model

Memory storing and neural networks. Life is for learning. From a neurobiological perspective, learning means building up internal representations within neural networks and storing current experiences for later retrieval. Hebb (1949) described how cells that fire simultaneously become wired together, forming tighter synaptic connections. Bliss, Lomo, and Blane (1973) coined the term *long-term potentiation* to describe a process in which connected neurons increase their reaction to a stimulus in a lasting way. Similarly, the reverse process—long-term depression—produces a long-lasting decrease in the strength of those connections. Thus, our modern understanding of neuroplasticity was born. The flexible flow of neural activation is directed into more or less fixed and rigid pathways. Those pathways can be changed, but change requires a serious and deep impact reaching the bedrock of neural networks.

The attractor model. The attractor model is another approach, derived from physics, to describe these processes (Haken, 1983). A system of neural connections organizes itself out of chaos around so-called attractors. They work like a footpath on a lawn: once a few people have walked a certain route and the grass is worn down, a kind of pathway starts to emerge, making it more and more likely that other people will take the same pathway. Eric Kandel (1989) was honored with a Nobel Prize for demonstrating that the repetitive stimulation of neurons leads to more intense synaptic connections between cells, building up these pathways. "Schemas" is another word for these rigid connections that tend to stabilize in a given state. In this way, it is much easier for us to be led by automatic patterns of activation. The attractor model underlies constructivist theories of self-organization (Maturana & Varela, 1998). In its essence, the model infers that, on the one hand, neural systems always tend toward low levels of energy or activation, just as water runs downhill. On the other hand, being in an unstable state of fluctuation induces feelings of discomfort. Once our mental process finds an interpretation for the current situation, the level of activation goes down again. Mentally, we perceive this as a positive feeling of relaxation or relief.

Consistency theory. If we have a perception but there is no attractor in our brain (or mind) representing it, or if the perception does not match an existing attractor, this creates an inconsistency. This leads to increased activation (perceived as stress or emotional tension) until the information is assimilated into the existing structure or the system has to adapt by changing. Piaget (1985) called the latter process to gain consistency "accommodation." One way or another, the system tries to overcome the inconsistency. Ongoing high levels of inconsistency (and associated emotional activation) lead to a persisting stress reaction (Selye, 1936), exhaustion, and, finally, disorders. Ongoing stress leads to changes in the hypothalamic-pituitary-adrenal axis and finally to a reduced expression of corticoid receptor genes as an epigenetic change (Meaney, 2001). These changes are currently regarded as an important mediator of many disorders (Weaver et al., 2004).

Schemas. In schema therapy terms, an attractor is a schema. The neurobiological model thus gives a unique perspective on schemas (or attractors) at a deeper level of analysis, and in this way, many of the findings of neuroscience may be related to schema therapy. In the schema context, learning can be viewed as building up new attractors (or schemas) and thereby creating alternative states or pathways. But moving from one attractor (schema) to another requires energy to overcome the "energetic hills" between them. The "energy" that a therapist brings to therapy by way of technique (for example, through imagery work) or the therapist's presence (limited reparenting), or both, supports attractor-state changes within the client that he would otherwise not be able to manage by himself. The therapist (and later the client's healthy adult mode) acts like a catalyzer in a chemical reaction. Since this sounds rather theoretical, we invite you to try a little experiment by doing the following exercise.

How Attractors Work

As a therapist, you are trained to have a double focus of attention: first, you watch your client; second, you observe your own activations. Let us try that together now. Please note your current level of activation and then look at figure 1–2. If you want, you can use the subjective units of distress scale (SUDS) to rate your amount of stressful activation from 1 to 10. When you look at the figure, note the changes in your level of activation while you try to discover the content of the image in a dual-attentional focus. Once you realize what you see, read on.

Figure 1–2. An exercise in dual focusing

How did your level of activation change when you started looking at the picture? You probably perceived an initial rise in activation that quickly dropped after you identified the content. This drop indicates that you built up an attractor about the content of the picture. Getting out of the activation state is a powerful driver of our mental processes because the brain tries to save energy. Your mental process forces you into this interpretation. You became a slave of your autopilot. Hard to believe? You will see! Let us now examine the content of what you first saw.

You probably saw feet in the sand. We assume that most of you saw elevated feet coming out of the sand, as if they had been carved out of it, correct? Okay, let us get rational now. How probable is it that somebody made the effort to carve these feet out of the sand? And the footprints of the seagulls, too? Watch your level of activation. Is it rising again? Well, we seeded some inconsistency between your automatic perception process and your rational mind. This inconsistency leads to increased activation. Do you find yourself trying to find some justification for why the feet are carved out of and not printed into the sand? A fairly normal reaction! The attractor (or the schema) fights for its "life" and tries to avoid getting back into the fluctuation state.

From the person who took the picture, we know that these are footprints on a beach in Brittany, close to sunset. So with this in mind, you should be able to see the feet as being printed in the sand. Some of you probably can. How about your level of activation? Try to change your perspective now. Not possible? Then you are probably not trying hard enough! Please, try a bit harder!

And how about your level of activation? Are you starting to feel a bit bothered or annoyed by us being pushy? This is the normal reaction coming from your assertiveness need. Clients feel the same when we get too demanding. Now, reparenting comes into play. Look at the heel of the foot on the right. Can you see the sunlight streaming in from the right side across the sand, forming the edge where the heel is pressed into the sand? The footprint creates the shade at the right edge. Further to the left, the sunlight lightens the footprint in the sand. Did this instruction work? Great! Is your level of activation dropping again? Are you a little happy and proud that you passed the test? This feeling indicates that you built up a second attractor. Now you have two interpretations of the picture. Your mind has broadened; you have gained flexibility.

How about those of you who still failed to shift your perspective? Your tension probably still remains high. To give you some relief and bring the experiment to a successful end (as in every schema therapy session), take a look at figure 1–3.

Figure 1–3. A second exercise in dual focusing

You can surely shift perspective now. But watch yourself carefully when shifting from the faces to the vase (or back). Can you feel the little "bump"? There is not a smooth shift but a kind of tipping point. This is why these kinds of pictures are called *tilted* images. The little bump indicates the attractor change and a short transitory state of fluctuation. Finally, note your decrease in activation now. Figure 1–4 summarizes the changing level of activation and the resulting attractors, or schemas.

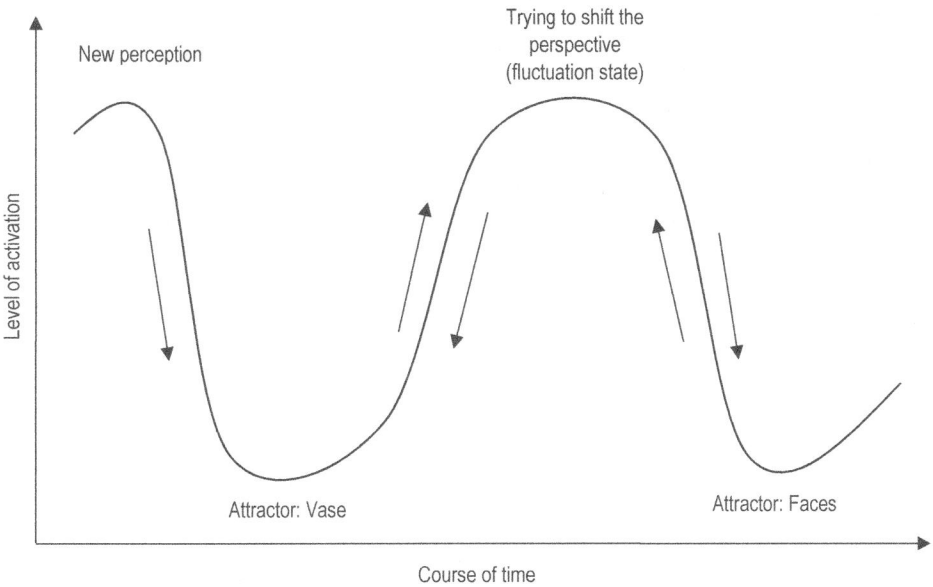

Figure 1–4. Attractors and the energetic landscape

Traveling the road from good intentions to actual behavioral change often takes time, patience, and ongoing effort (for details, see chapter 8). The therapy relationship is a powerful tool for connecting with clients and supporting them as they climb the energetic hills between two attractors. Inducing change takes three major steps that may occur throughout therapy:

1. *Building up motivation* and showing the client that there is another road he or she might take. Often, this will occur by identifying with the client what a healthy schema or a healthy adult response looks and feels like.

2. *Inducing corrective emotional experiences* to give the client access to adaptive information and to build up an alternative attractor state. In schema therapy, the therapist usually achieves this using a combination of experiential (for example, imagery rescripting), relational (limited reparenting), and behavioral techniques (behavioral experiments).

3. *Training* a capacity for mindful self-awareness in order to increase the client's awareness of old, maladaptive, schema-driven patterns and the possibility of choosing alternative adaptive responses.

In schema therapy, the organizer or conductor of this change process is called the healthy adult mode. We describe in detail in chapter 7 how therapists can explicitly train this mode to clients in therapy.

Emotional Learning

Joseph LeDoux (1996) described two major pathways for processing incoming information:

- The so-called lower (but faster) pathway in the limbic system, driven primarily by precognitive (basic) emotions
- The slower pathway, including more cognitive procedures, in the cortical areas of the brain

Brain processes and modes. The autonomic responses of the lower pathway reflect the older stage in the development of the brain. This pathway is needs based, driven by contingencies, and still present as the lowest level of functioning once we become intensively emotionally activated. We experience these precognitive emotions as if in a "child" mode, sometimes in a preverbal state (Stern, 1985). During the development of speech, symbolic representations of the world outside get stored in cortical areas in terms of cognitive relational frames (see "The Contextual or Third Wave Perspective" in this chapter). They help us to develop a set of display rules (Fuster, 2002) that we later experience as beliefs or what are called inner critic modes in the schema therapy context. The anterior cingular cortex provides a convergence zone to merge emotional and cognitive input (Botvinick, Braver, Barch, Carter, & Cohen, 2001), preparing the executed behavior (coping modes). With maturation, the skills of self-control emerge in conscious procedures of the working memory in the lateral prefrontal cortex (LeDoux, 1996); we call this the healthy adult mode. We will go into the details of the modes in chapter 3. This brief summary is only meant to roughly outline the relationship of the modes to underlying brain processes.

Changing schemas. Since schemas are like footpaths in the neural structure of the brain, they cannot be deleted or healed in the sense of undoing them (Hayes et al., 2012). However, by developing additional pathways, we can build up a superposing network, for example, by building up inhibitory synaptic connections. This kind of overlearning weakens the attractors and makes changing into more functional attractor states easier. In the footpath metaphor, that means consciously taking a new road and not following automatic pilot. According to the control theory of Power (1973), doing this requires influencing the existing system from a higher level of functioning. In the beginning of therapy, this influence is the therapist. Later, the healthy adult mode of the client is strong enough to take over. Thus, the "good parent" model of the therapist is internalized by the client. Unlike a rewarding contingency, this structure does not fade but becomes a mental competence for the client to utilize in order to take the lead in emotional processes (Lewis, 1990).

This executive function of the healthy adult is systematically trained in the experiential techniques introduced in chapter 8. The impact that psychotherapy has on the process of decision making is visible in functional magnetic resonance imaging (fMRI): while drugs directly affect the amygdala, psychotherapy acts indirectly by building up inhibitory circuits, starting in the prefrontal cortex and leading to a secondary downregulation of amygdala activities (DeRubeis et al., 2005). It is probable that all kinds of psychotherapy work by increasing prefrontal activities and dampening limbic activation (DeCharms, 2008).

The Emotional Tolerance Window

Our chances to learn something new depends very much on our level of emotional activation. The learning curve follows an inverted U shape (Yerkes & Dodson, 1908; see figure 1–5). If the level of activation is too low (for example, due to drowsiness), no learning happens. The neural processes remain stable and unchanged. Mindfulness enhances learning, but if the level of activation rises too high, the alarm system gets activated, shuts the brain activities down at a level of emotion-driven, automatic processing, and new information is shut out (this is called emotional hijacking; Goleman, 1995). No change occurs in this state either. Only when the level of activation stays within the so-called emotional tolerance window is new information processed, inducing changes in information storage and building up new attractors. Intensive prefrontal activities help with refocusing (this is called cortical override; Siegel, 1999).

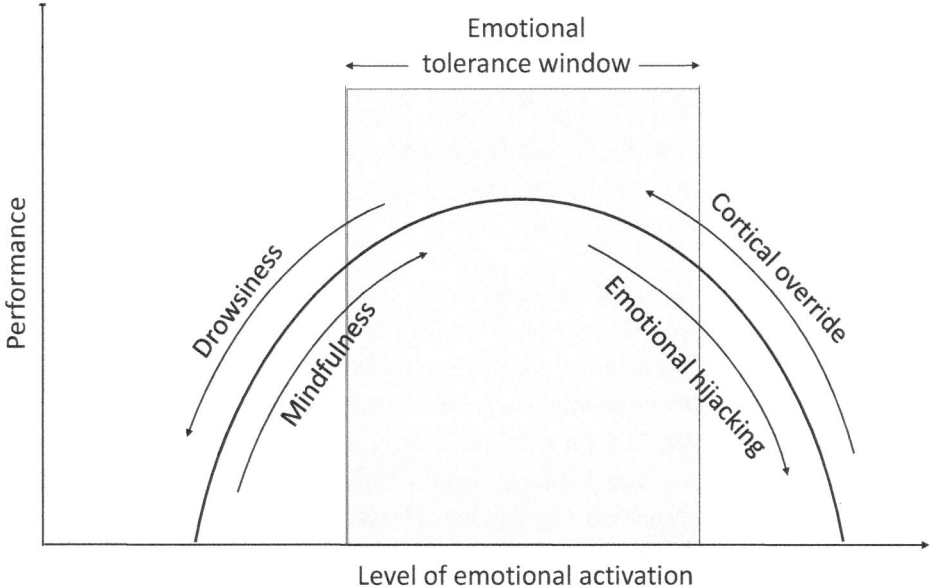

Figure 1–5. The emotional tolerance window

Conceptual Underpinnings

Learning means building up new attractors, depending on the level of emotional activation (intensity or frequency, or both). Emotional-detaching drugs administered before an experiment lead to reduced memory consolidation (Cahill, Prins, Weber, & McGaugh, 1994). These facts have two important consequences:

1. Every intensive emotional experience in childhood leads to imprints in the evolving neural networks of the child and builds up schemas. This is especially relevant for the first two years of life, when most of the cortical anatomical structures are built. Traumatic childhood experiences lead not only to bad memories (in the "software") but to a lasting deformation of the brain development (on a "hardware" level) down to an epigenetic programming (Heim, Shugart, Craighead, & Nemeroff, 2010). We have to accept our schemas, which carry our emotional wounds.

2. Schemas have to be activated to be transformed and reconsolidated in a different way (Nader & Hardt, 2009). In therapy, we have to create adequately intensive experiences to build up new attractors. This can hardly be achieved through purely cognitive interventions (Hayes et al., 2012) but can be done with imagery work when emotions get readily activated (Arntz, 2012). Corrective emotional experiences lay the neural tracks (in terms of positive schemas) for new paths to take on a behavioral level. Good intentions need a neural bedrock to be able to lead to new behavior. This is why experiential techniques and behavior experiments are pivotal in therapy.

Principle: The therapist is in charge of keeping the level of activation high enough so key schemas get activated, but low enough to prevent the client from shutting down.

The client's emotional wounds, or schemas, can remain latent for years unless a triggering event activates the "sleeper." Only the combination of schema activation and controlled schema reprocessing within the emotional tolerance window allows clients to integrate schema activations into their life history and to cope with them. For illustration, here's a case vignette:

Sally was admitted to the hospital with dramatically increasing panic attacks that started after the extraction of a wisdom tooth under narcosis. With each panic attack, the symptoms became more severe. In an imagery session with her therapist, she visualized the wallpaper of her childhood bedroom, together with the fear of dying. Then she remembered that her parents once told her that when she was two years old they had found her unconscious in her bed, having almost been strangled by a cord that affixed the cover of her bed. Now Sally and her therapist could identify the feeling of fainting as part of the scene in the bed, the onset of the narcosis, and the dizzy feeling at the beginning of the panic attacks. Each panic attack activated the schema connected with the deadly fear resulting from the childhood scene. After she discovered this connection, it was much easier for her to connect her panic feelings with the schema, distance from them, and remain in an adult coping mode focused on her current activities.

Mentalization and the Theory of Mind

During the "decade of the brain" early in this century, biological determinism was overemphasized. Mental activities were regarded as emerging solely from brain activities (see, for example, Metzinger, 2000). Now the pendulum is swinging back again and we are observing a renaissance of the "theory of mind" perspective (Leslie, 1987). The brain is seen as a "social organ" (Adolphs, 2003) developing in a mutual interaction with its environment. The self creates itself in a social world (Eisenberg, 1995) by connecting internal activations with the reactions of others. In a first step, on a preverbal level we experience separate representations (modes) of a fragmented core self (Stern, 1985). In a process of self-reflection (or in schema therapy terms, mode awareness) we build up a sense of a conceptual self (Hayes et al., 2012), integrating the parts (modes) into a coherent self (Siegel, 1999) expressed in a self-narrative. We organize our autobiographical self in a canonical, semantic manner that is culturally acquired. The resulting "story" makes us the person we believe ourselves to be—both to ourselves and others (McAdams, 2001). We finally relate to values to define our place in the social world (right-hand column in figure 1–6).

Getting connected. On a parallel conceptual track, Fonagy, Gergely, Jurist, and Target (2004) described a mental activity they called "mentalization" that connects our internal mood states and their mental representations. Besides looking into the world from the inside, through maturation we develop the skill to look at ourselves from the outside (observer stance). Mentalization also enables us to understand what goes on in other people. We integrate their comments, facial expressions, and nonverbal signals into our understanding of the scene. This social scaffolding organizes our way of experiencing and creates individual symbols that we calibrate with the collective symbols of our society. We become part of a social system and learn to follow its display rules (left-hand column in figure 1–6). Mentalization is a second prosocial connection with others, alongside our sense of belonging that is based on the oxytocin effect. In terms of the "extended mind" concept (Clark & Chalmers, 1998), mentalization helps us to distance from our internal impulses, matching them with the needs of our social environment. In therapy, role-plays and changing to a third-person perspective are based on mentalization skills.

Principle: Mentalization connects our needs-driven, internal states with the social world around us.

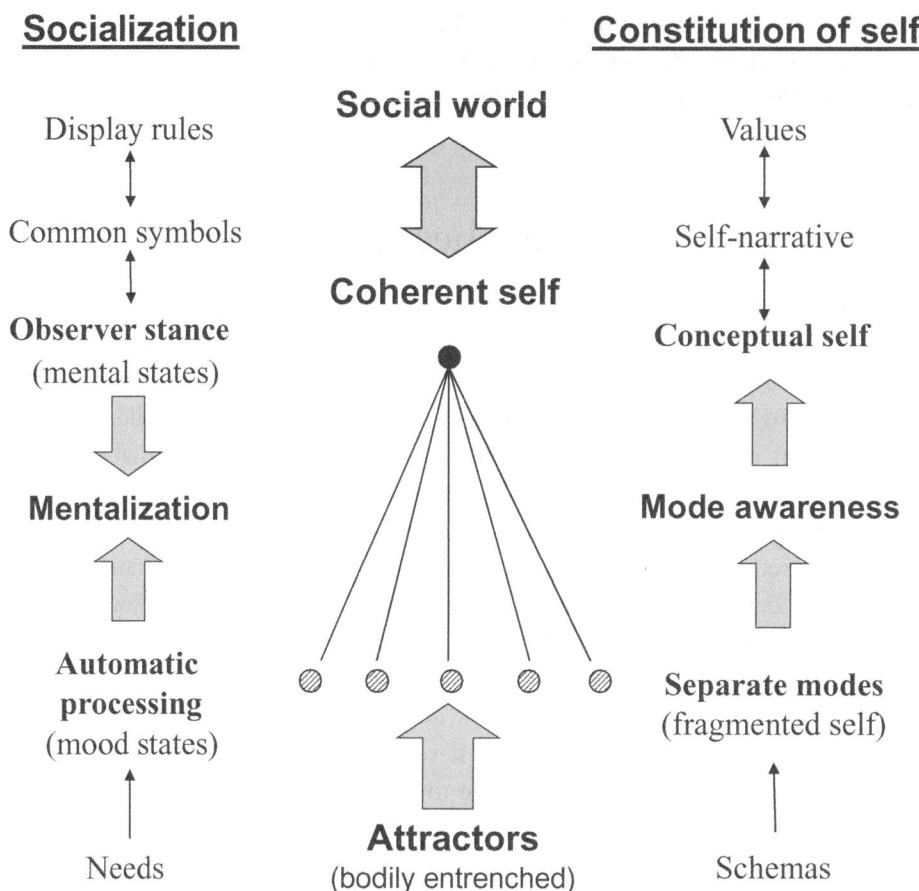

Figure 1–6. Socialization and constitution of the self

Becoming vulnerable. Mentalization connects us with others, but it also makes us vulnerable to their impact on us, which can invade our developing self. We develop our sense of self based on how others react to us. Winnicott (1958) described how a baby who is not mirrored by her mother does not build up her own self but internalizes the mother's picture instead. This is an example of how external objects become part of the inner world. Thus, an abuser's voice later feels like an inherent part of the self. A child cannot protect herself against these influences. The identification with social expectations and the appraisals of others poses the risk of us having internal conflicts with our biologically entrenched self-centered impulses—for example, our assertiveness needs.

Integration is fragile. Finally, the process of developing an integrated self remains fragile and reversible. When we are tired, sick, intoxicated, demented, or in a state of rage, mentalization breaks down, and our sense of a coherent self falls apart. Parts of the self can become dominant, and we might later flip back to another state; for example, trauma clients sometimes operate with a fragmented self (Yehuda & McFarlane, 1995). In schema therapy, we call these rapid shifts *mode flipping* (Bamber, 2004).

The Contextual, or Third Wave, Perspective

From second to third wave. So-called second wave cognitive therapy initially emphasized direct change, from maladaptive *content* ("I am defective") to more healthy and adaptive content ("I have worth"). While this emphasis has been quite successful, contemporary behavior therapies focus on changing the way one *relates* to internal experiences (thoughts, feelings, urges) as being an important route to well-being (Hayes et al., 2012).

Principle: Third wave therapies shift the focus from the content and the intentions to the context and the actual effects.

During the past fifteen years, this change in emphasis has led to the development of a range of approaches that loosely fall under an umbrella of "third wave CBTs" that includes such therapies as acceptance and commitment therapy (ACT; Hayes et al., 2012), mindfulness-based cognitive therapy (Segal, Williams, & Teasdale, 2002), compassion-focused therapy (Gilbert, 2010), metacognitive approaches (Wells, 2009), and functional analytic psychotherapy (Holman, Kanter, Tsai, & Kohlenberg, 2017).

The influence of Buddhism. Inspired by Buddhist psychology, most third wave therapies teach clients to distance from automatic thinking by looking at the thinking process itself from a mindful observer's perspective. As an overarching label for all third wave–oriented therapies, Hayes and colleagues (2012) suggested the term "contextual therapies." Meanwhile McKay, Lev, and Skeen (2012) have connected ACT techniques with schema therapy, while van Vreeswijk and colleagues (2014) have added mindfulness to it.

The schema therapy model remains intact even with mindfulness integrated into it, but increasingly the role of the schema therapist is to help the client not only to build more adaptive schema content, but also to be able to build mode awareness as a core mechanism of change (Farrell & Shaw, 2018). Some initial research (Brockman, 2013; Lazarevic, Hough, & Brockman, 2013) suggested that there is considerable overlap between third wave models and the schema therapy model, and that techniques from third wave models have already been successfully integrated into the schema therapy model.

Relational frame theory. Hayes and colleagues (2012) outlined an underlying theory of contextual therapies called relational frame theory. We do not claim that this theory fully encompasses the background of schema therapy, but its view on cognitive processes on a practical level contributes to a more detailed understanding of functional (healthy adult) behavior.

For those not familiar with relational frame theory and the core therapeutic processes derived from it, we offer a brief description. Our mental process constantly tends to relate two (or more) objects if they appear simultaneously. Hayes and colleagues (2012) call this cognitive connection a *relational frame*. Once the relational frame is established, if one part is triggered, the whole frame (or network) will be activated. Fear networks, described by Foa and Kozak (1986), are a typical clinical example of this kind of generalized activation.

Thinking in terms of creating relations between objects is a double-edged sword. On the one hand, it enables humans to extract rules and anticipate events. We can learn from our own experience as well as that of other people in what Sterelny (2003) calls "downstream engineering." This relating is the source of our cultural development. The resulting structures in our thought operations are attractors, or schemas.

On the other hand, attractors bias our thinking procedures onto given pathways and tend to reduce our flexibility to react in the here and now. Relational frames can lead to prejudices that limit our chance of learning. For example, if a child has a bad experience with a dog, she might tend to regard all dogs as dangerous and will never have one. If an aged woman living alone reads in the newspaper about the increasing number of robbers and hears a scratching noise at her door, she might call the police. Fear dominates perception. We extend, or project, our inner world into the world around us. Hayes and colleagues noted that "our minds begin to warn us with alarms about past and future psychological states rather than only alarms about external threats…with toxic results" (2012, p. 18). They compare this to "a kind of allergic reaction to our own inner world" (p. 19), calling these self-restricting thinking procedures "cognitive fusion." Those thinking procedures trap us in our own "ontological networks" (p. 30), and we don't even realize it.

The six pathological processes leading to psychological rigidity. Many clinical disorders show signs of fused thinking, such as thought rumination in depression or general anxiety disorder, or thoughts anticipating disasters (phobias, obsessive-compulsive disorder, hypochondria, paranoia). Hayes and colleagues named six underlying pathological core processes that lead to the wide range of disorders in the DSM-5 and represent "excesses of normal behaviors and cognitive processes" (2012, p. 10):

1. *Cognitive fusion:* The "dark side of the mental power" (p. 19) creating relational frames

2. *Experiential avoidance:* "Attempting to avoid, suppress or eliminate unwanted private experiences" (p. 22); the "behavior comes to be more under aversive control rather than appetitive control—more dominated by avoidance and escape than natural attraction" (p. 23)

3. *Inflexible attention:* "A problem-solving mode of mind is restricted, future- and or past-oriented, sometimes rigid, judgmental and highly literal" (p. 57)

4. *Attachment to the conceptualized self:* Being absorbed and identified with one's story of self

5. *Disruption of values* while being absorbed with everyday hassles

6. *Inactivity, impulsivity, or persistent avoidance* as self-focused autopilot behavior

The six functional processes for psychological flexibility. Hayes and colleagues identified six core processes they regard as capable of being used to regain psychological flexibility in order "to control the whole show of symptoms or syndromes" (2012, p. 60):

1. *Defusion:* Disentangling from the automatic (fused) processes of the mind by developing the "skills to shift out of a fused problem-solving mode of mind into a descriptively engaged mode of mind" (p. 21)

2. *Acceptance:* As "the preferred alternative to experiential avoidance" (p. 23); this includes accepting upcoming thoughts instead of "not thinking something, thinking less of something or thinking only in one way" (p. 50)

3. *Present moment/mindfulness:* "Learning to be consciously aware of one's thinking as it occurs" (p. 23) in a mindful and flexible way

4. *Self-as-context:* Seeing the self in a "changeable stream of events," including "history and situations as they relate to behavior" (p. 33) in a functional context; "true is what works" (p. 33)

5. *Values:* "All therapeutic interactions are evaluated as they relate to the client's chosen values and goals and the issue is always workability" (p. 34)

6. *Committed action:* Keeping the attention focused to "build successively larger patterns of effective value-based actions, just as is done in traditional behavior therapy" (p. 66)

These six functional processes describe three healthy response styles: being open, being centered, and being engaged.

Schema therapy as a contextual behavioral therapy approach. The core features of ACT as a contextual approach are wholly consistent with schema therapy, making it a good candidate for being a contextual therapy. We believe that schema therapy will benefit from having an explicit focus on these contextual processes. First, the centrality of needs in the schema model means that there is no inherent truth in terms of schemas. Rather, a schema is adaptive or maladaptive depending on context and the capacity for that schema to help the person experience needs satisfaction in that context. The schema approach is thus a functional-contextual model in which needs satisfaction is the proxy for context.

There are four big implications for the schema therapist from this contextual point of view:

1. Schemas and behavioral patterns are functional (that is, they ultimately serve some function) and must be uncovered.

2. One must understand context in very broad terms, from current situational triggers right through to the developmental antecedents of schemas (such as childhood trauma).

3. Altering aspects of context, be it in the therapy room (such as by creating defusion) or in the person's life (creating needs satisfaction), can lead to therapeutic change and is thus a significant therapeutic target.

4. The ultimate aim of therapy is to build a healthy and flexible self that is concerned with the longer-term, value-based fulfillment of needs satisfaction.

Summary

In this chapter, we briefly outlined the well-accepted theoretical concepts on which we base our extended schema therapy model. We feel this information will contribute to a deeper understanding of our intentions about refining the therapy relationship and applying the techniques. We will add some theoretical details later to underline how schema therapy can be further developed as a contextual therapy without losing its roots. In chapter 7 especially, we will integrate the functional ACT processes seamlessly into the building up of the healthy adult mode.

CHAPTER 2

The Schema Model—Mapping the Badlands

In this chapter, we look carefully at the dynamic quality of schemas. There are currently eighteen schemas, which fall into five domains. We distinguish between core and compensatory schemas. Then we look at the "fate" of schemas in terms of coping styles, because these determine how schemas appear in therapy. Finally, we get practical with the important clinical skill of schema attunement.

What Are Schemas?

Aaron Beck (1967) introduced the idea of schemas to cognitive therapy. He used the term to refer to clusters of negative beliefs, and this understanding has continued (see, for example, Wright, Basco, & Thase, 2006). Jeff Young and colleagues (2003) added an understanding of schemas as being the result of toxic childhood experiences relating to unfulfilled needs. Schemas "sleep" in the background until they "wake up." A current situation that is similar to a defining childhood experience may trigger or activate a schema. If a schema is activated, the past intrudes into present awareness:

Beatrice has nagging worries about her weight. When she was young, her parents monitored her weight, and she became highly self-conscious. Later, as an adult, she went to a fashion show and reacted to the stick-thin models. She said to a friend that she felt "bloated, like a beached whale" and was determined to go on another fad diet. Kent, her husband, was exasperated by what he called her "diet merry-go-round."

Beatrice's case provides an example of schema activation and a poor coping strategy. In this example, an event (going to the fashion show) triggered an emotional reaction in Beatrice. She was flooded by feelings of being defective. This also led to a somewhat questionable plan of action.

It is important to grasp the idea of schema activation. It is the result of a trigger, so activating a schema can be compared to stepping on a land mine. Schemas are like short video clips storing memories along with scenes of intense emotions and bodily reactions. Once a schema is activated, a person will seem to travel back in time to childhood. This means seeing the world through a child's eyes. Another way of saying this is that schemas are essentially a bodily-entrenched tendency to react. Note that the action is a resulting step but not part of the schema itself.

Principle: Schemas are hidden. They do not reveal themselves unless activated. They distort perception and thus become disruptive in adult life.

Reflect: What causes you to overreact? Can you identify a trigger for the activation of one of your schemas? Everyone has schemas, but we hope that we, as therapists, are aware of ours.

Robbie had a disadvantaged childhood, shifting from one foster family to the next. He was never any trouble, being a shy and withdrawn child. Though he never caused problems, on the inside he was untrusting, suspicious of almost everyone, and socially isolated. He saw a therapist who recommended that he join a therapy group. Robbie found this experience excruciating: "All those strangers talking about the most intimate things." Gradually he began to notice that being in a group made him feel unsettled, as he had been as a child, moving from one family to the next and having nowhere that was safe.

Frustrating interpersonal experiences such as Robbie's are carved into the child's developing memory, serving as an early blueprint about the self, others, and the world. This developmental perspective is not unique to schema therapy. There are concepts quite similar to schemas discussed in the therapy literature, such as the developmental model of the child's self (Stern, 1985) and the internal working model (Bowlby, 1969).

Jesse Wright and colleagues (2006) noted that people typically have a mix of different kinds of schemas, including some that are positive and adaptive. Lockwood and Perris (2012) contributed a list of positive schemas to strive for in therapy. Even people with severe symptoms or profound despair have adaptive schemas that can help them cope. To allow us to understand the difficulties of our clients, a schema therapy case conceptualization (described in chapter 4) focuses on the early *maladaptive* schemas. Nevertheless, to make progress in therapy we also make use of *adaptive* schemas.

Therapist Tip: When we think about our clients, their weaknesses are usually obvious. While it is helpful to identify limitations, we should never forget an individual's capabilities. Progress comes more easily when based on preexisting strengths.

Identifying and Understanding Schemas

The schema list in table 2–1 has been revised over the past two decades and has shown good overall validity (Lee, Taylor, & Dunn, 1999). For a detailed description of the schemas, see Young and colleagues (2003); Rafaeli, Bernstein, and Young (2011); and Arntz and Jacob (2013). Young groups them in five categories called domains, determined by the frustrated need that leads to a particular group of schemas.

Table 2–1. Schemas, domains, need states, and resulting modes

No.	Schema	Domain	Need State	Mode
1. AB	Abandonment (instability)	Disconnection and rejection	Frustration of attachment	Vulnerable or angry child
2. MA	Mistrust-abuse			
3. ED	Emotional deprivation			
4. DS	Defectiveness-shame			
5. SI	Social isolation (alienation)			
6. DI	Dependence-incompetence	Impaired autonomy and performance	Frustration of assertiveness and control	Vulnerable or angry child
7. VH	Vulnerability to harm or illness			
8. EM	Enmeshment (undeveloped self)			
9. FA	Failure (to achieve)			
10. ET	Entitlement-grandiosity	Impaired limits	Lack of self-control	Impulsive child
11. IS	Insufficient self-control (or self-discipline)			
12. SU	Subjugation	Other directedness	Sacrificing assertiveness and control	Submission (driven by inner critics)
13. SS	Self-sacrifice			
14. AS	Approval seeking (recognition seeking)			
15. NP	Negativity-pessimism	Overvigilance and inhibition	Sacrificing attachment and joy	Overcompensation or detachment (driven by inner critics)
16. EI	Emotional inhibition			
17. UR	Unrelenting standards (hypercriticalness)			
18. PU	Punitiveness			

First Domain: Disconnection and Rejection

The person in this domain shows problems with attachment. What is missing is any expectation of reliability, support, empathy, and respect. In childhood, the person may have been treated in a cold, rejecting manner. Emotional support, perhaps even basic care in extreme cases, may have been lacking. Caregivers were unpredictable, uninterested, or abusive.

1. *Abandonment (instability):* The person expects to lose those with whom she has an emotional attachment. Important others appeared unreliable and unpredictable; all intimate relationships will eventually end.

2. *Mistrust-abuse:* The person is convinced that others will eventually take advantage of him in one way or another. He expects to be hurt, cheated on, manipulated, or humiliated. Naturally, as a reaction, he becomes suspicious in relationships. Thus, the initial abuse is managed by mistrust.

3. *Emotional deprivation:* The person believes that her primary needs will either not be satisfied or will be inadequately met by others. This includes physical needs and needs for empathy, affection, protection, companionship, and emotional care.

4. *Defectiveness-shame:* The person feels incomplete and bad. As others get to know him better, he believes his defects will be discovered, and then they will want nothing to do with him. There is overconcern with the judgment of others. A sense of shame resulting from feeling defective is always present.

5. *Social isolation (alienation):* The person has the feeling that she is isolated from the rest of the world, is different from others, and does not fit in anywhere.

Second Domain: Impaired Autonomy and Performance

The person feels incapable of functioning and performing independently. The family of origin may have been clingy, overly protective, and not supportive of any autonomy in the child.

6. *Dependence-incompetence:* The person is not capable of taking on normal responsibilities and cannot function independently. He may lack confidence to make decisions about simple problems or to attempt anything new. He feels helpless.

7. *Vulnerability to harm or illness:* The person is convinced that, at any moment, something terrible might happen and there is no protection. Both medical and psychological catastrophes are feared. She takes extraordinary precautions.

8. *Enmeshment (undeveloped self)*: The person is overinvolved with one or more of his caregivers. Because of this fused relationship, he is unable to develop his own identity. At times, he feels he cannot exist without the other person. He may feel empty and without goals.

9. *Failure (to achieve)*: The person believes that she is not capable of performing at the same level as her peers with regard to career, education, sports, or whatever is valued. She feels stupid, foolish, ignorant, and without talent. She does not even attempt to succeed because of an abiding conviction that the attempt will lead to nothing.

Third Domain: Impaired Limits

The person may have inadequate boundaries, lack of a sense of responsibility, and have poor tolerance for frustration. The person struggles to set realistic long-term goals and to cooperate with others. The family of origin may have offered little direction or given the individual the sense of being superior.

10. *Entitlement-grandiosity*: The person thinks that he is superior to others and has special rights. He thinks he can get away with what he wants without taking others into consideration. The main theme here is power and control over situations and individuals. Rarely does the person have empathy.

11. *Insufficient self-control (or self-discipline)*: The person cannot tolerate any frustration in achieving her goals. She has little capacity to suppress feelings or impulses. It is possible that she is attempting to avoid being uncomfortable in any way.

Fourth Domain: Other Directedness

The person is overly responsible, always having to take into account the needs of others at the expense of meeting personal needs. The individual tries to receive love and approval. The family background may have been one of conditional love. The needs and status of the parents took priority over what was important to the child.

12. *Subjugation*: The person gives himself over to the will of others to avoid negative consequences (that is, being rejected). Sacrificing his own needs can lead to pent-up rage, which is eventually expressed in an inadequate manner (by being passive-aggressive or by developing psychosomatic symptoms).

13. *Self-sacrifice*: The person voluntarily and regularly sacrifices her needs for others whom she views as weaker. If she does act to meet personal needs, she is likely to feel guilty. In the long-term, she may feel some resentment toward those for whom she has sacrificially cared.

14. *Approval seeking (recognition seeking):* The person searches for approval, appreciation, acknowledgment, or admiration at the expense of his personal needs. Sometimes this results in an excessive desire for status, beauty, and social approval.

Fifth Domain: Overvigilance and Inhibition

The person suppresses spontaneous feelings and needs to follow rules and have common values. It is likely that the family stressed achievement, perfectionism, and the repression of emotions. Caregivers were critical, pessimistic, and moralistic, while at the same time they expected an unreasonably high standard of achievement.

15. *Negativity-pessimism:* The person always sees the negative side of things while ignoring the positive. Eventually, everything will go wrong even if it is currently going well. She may be constantly worried and hyperalert. She often complains and does not dare to make decisions.

16. *Emotional inhibition:* The person holds tight control over his emotions and impulses, as he thinks that expressing them will damage others and lead to feelings of shame, abandonment, or loss of self-worth. This leads to him avoiding spontaneous expressions of emotions such as anger, sadness, and joy, and also avoiding conflict. Often, he will present as very detached and overly rational.

17. *Unrelenting standards (hypercriticalness):* The person believes that she will never be good enough and must try harder to avoid criticism. This results in perfectionism, rigid rules, and sometimes a preoccupation with time and efficiency. She does this at the cost of enjoying herself, relaxing, and maintaining social contacts. According to Young and colleagues (2003), this schema can be directed toward oneself or others.

18. *Punitiveness:* The person feels that individuals must be severely punished for their mistakes. He is aggressive, intolerant, and impatient. There is no forgiveness for mistakes. Individual circumstances or feelings are not taken into account. According to Young and colleagues (2003), this schema can be directed toward oneself or others.

The five domains can be linked to childhood needs. Schemas can result from the frustration of a need for attachment (domain 1), autonomy and assertiveness (domain 2), or adequate limit setting in order to develop an adequate sense of self-control (domain 3). The schemas of the fourth domain tend to result if the child sacrifices his need for self-expression in order to maintain attachment (domain 1). The schemas of the fifth domain result from sacrificing the need for spontaneity and play in order to avoid appearing incompetent or flawed (domain 2).

Recognizing Schemas

It is important to learn to identify schemas. Test yourself with the following examples:

Nardi was abused in childhood. She has profound difficulties with trust. She has met someone whom she is strongly attracted to but is very jealous, thinking he will leave her for a "more attractive option."

Mike is very self-important. He was recruited for a merchant bank straight out of college, and it has gone to his head. He looks down on his less successful friends.

Betty is too anxious to leave home, even though she is in her late thirties. She says, "I have to look after my mother. She needs me. Oh, I know she's in good health, but I'm a good daughter and need to be about the place."

Brad is excessively hard on his teenage sons. They complain about his put-downs and how he embarrasses them in front of their friends. Brad's oldest son has recently started talking to a counselor at school, who thought that this treatment was "abusive."

Can you use the domain and schema list to identify any schemas that might be operating for Nardi, Mike, Betty, and Brad? We see the following schemas in the examples:

Nardi has a mistrust-abuse schema. She is not able to trust in her new relationship because of previous experiences.

Mike has an entitlement-grandiosity schema. He has to be important and constantly recognized for his achievements. He has an entitled way of looking at his new job as proof of his superiority as a person.

Betty has enmeshment and self-sacrifice schemas operating in her relationship with her mother.

Brad has punitiveness and possibly unrelenting standards schemas.

Consider playing a game of "spot the schema" when you watch a TV show or movie to familiarize yourself with the schemas. Persist and make learning them fun!

Reflect: Think about the list of schemas and try to identify any that seem familiar to you. Are you beginning to be able to recognize schemas in your clients? Consider one of your more complex clients, and think about which three or four schemas you see.

Core and Compensatory Schemas

While we hesitate to add another layer to an already complex model, distinguishing between core and compensatory schemas is also important, allowing for a greater sense of development in the schema model. Young and colleagues (2003) call the core schemas "unconditional." They reflect the pure experience of the child when his or her needs were not met. The schemas of the fourth and fifth domains are "compensatory" or "conditional" schemas. They are conditional because they include input from the environment, and they are compensatory because they can be seen as automatic coping behaviors a person employs to avoid activating schemas from the first two domains. Consider these examples:

Claire is a successful corporate lawyer, but she is very submissive to her partner. This helps Claire to remain connected and to avoid the activation of her emotional deprivation and abandonment schemas.

Ralph has an obvious approval seeking schema that he developed to avoid activating his underlying defectiveness-shame schema.

Matilda is highly ambitious. Her unrelenting standards schema helps her avoid activating her dependence-incompetence and failure schemas.

Zac is highly negative toward his wife. This helps him to avoid activating his vulnerability to harm or illness schema.

Compensatory schemas often drive clinical symptoms such as depression, avoidance resulting from fears, overly suspicious thoughts, or compulsions. Unfortunately, the frustrated needs leading to the underlying unconditional schemas remain unmet, and so, perversely, the original schemas end up being reinforced.

Principle: Unconditional schemas mirror the direct experience of the child. Conditional schemas are coping reactions to the wounds at the schema level.

The mistrust-abuse schema in the first domain is a special case. This term describes a combination of the unconditional schema of being abused and the conditional reaction, which is the development of mistrust to prevent being abused again. In this book, we focus on the unconditional part of the experienced abuse. Another interesting example is the entitlement-grandiosity schema in the third domain. It can be an unconditional schema if no limits were set for the child, leading primarily to narcissistic behavior. Entitlement can also be a compensatory conditional reaction to the defectiveness-shame schema in terms of a "secondary" narcissist (see the therapeutic implications of this distinction in "Integrating Schemas and Modes," in chapter 3; in the text about primary and secondary emotions in "Child Modes," in chapter 6; and in "The Narcissistic Client," in chapter 13).

Responses to Schemas: The Coping Styles

Young and colleagues (2003) also described three schema-coping styles that serve as responses to schema activation.

Schema surrender. A person gives in to the schema and acts accordingly. He finds himself in the hurtful childhood situation, not trying to change it. This schema-coping style relates to the psychodynamic concept of repetition-compulsion or the idea of a self-fulfilling prophecy (Merton, 1948). People simply stay in an old attractor state because it feels familiar, and they do not feel empowered to try something different. This tends to reinforce or confirm the underlying schema and blocks opportunities for meeting needs in the long run.

Vetta was in a violent relationship with her partner, Thomas. Even though neighbors would call the police when she and Thomas fought, she would defend him: "We were just having an argument." Later, in therapy, she explored her feelings of defectiveness and the belief "I am unlovable," which she managed by putting up with Thomas's assaults, surrendering to the subjugation schema.

Schema avoidance. An individual avoids engaging in activities that potentially trigger the schema and related negative emotions. The restrictions resulting from avoidant coping reduce participation in life, block needs satisfaction, and can contribute to clinical symptoms such as depression, substance abuse, or an avoidant lifestyle.

Matt had PTSD after serving in Afghanistan. He was unable to work and remained on disability. He rarely left the house, he said, because "any sudden noise tends to freak me out."

Schema compensation. A person goes in the opposite direction of the schema and counteracts it. Examples of this coping style are counterphobic behavior compensating for vulnerability, the exaggerated assertiveness of a secondary narcissist compensating for a defectiveness-shame schema, or the aggression of an antisocial client physically abused as a child.

Brent became a gym junkie. He built up his body with relentless exercise and steroids. He was pleased when he started to win bodybuilding competitions and was featured on the front pages of magazines. This was an exaggerated compensation for a lifetime of feelings related to the defectiveness-shame schema.

At any one time, there is only one kind of coping for each schema. However, individuals might use different schema-coping styles for different schemas and may change the way they cope with a single schema over time. Thus, detecting a schema behind a visible behavior requires some understanding of the biography of your client. Imagery work as described in chapter 9 is a very helpful approach to accessing schema-inducing childhood scenes.

You now have what you need for building a basic case formulation using schemas. Think about a client you are currently treating. Can you identify three or four main schemas and characteristic coping styles? Can you distinguish core from compensating schemas?

On labeling schema coping. We have already noted that "schema coping" describes internal reactions to an individual's schemas over the course of time. In contrast, a coping mode is a way to describe someone's behavior in relation to another person (in terms of being submissive/self-sacrificing, avoidant/withdrawing, or dominant/overcompensatory; see chapter 3). Young and other authors frequently use the term "overcompensation" for both activities: as a label for compensatory schema coping in the schema model as well as to describe an interpersonal coping mode in the mode model. This double use of the same term for two different kinds of behavior frequently leads to irritations in our trainings. Thus we suggest the term "compensatory schema coping" to clarify when we are talking about schema coping. We follow this distinction throughout this book, and things will get clearer as you continue reading.

Limitations of the Schema Model

When working with a low-functioning individual, for example, someone with borderline personality disorder, it may be difficult to choose just three or four schemas. With such a case, working with the schema model quickly becomes too complex. Remember that eighteen schemas combined with three schema-coping styles makes fifty-four possible combinations of observable behavior. We recommend that you just try to identify the most common schemas you encounter in sessions with clients (see chapter 4).

For less complex cases, the schema model is still very helpful because it goes beyond the surface and connects the presented behavior with the underlying childhood experience (the schema) and reveals how the client dealt with it (schema-coping style).

Consider trying the Young Schema Questionnaire (YSQ; more on this later in chapter 4), preferably the revised short-form 3, to assess the most relevant schemas for treatment. (See http://www.schematherapy.com. You may have to buy the YSQ, as it is not freely available.) Note the three or four schemas that you score most highly on, as you do if you administer the YSQ to your clients. Alternatively, for a rough overview of a client's common schemas, you can assign a score of 1 to 6 to the schemas listed above or fill out the eleven schema listings in Young and Klosko's *Reinventing Your Life* (1993).

Why Is the Schema Model Still Relevant?

Observing schemas is like looking at the bottom of a pond. The ripples on the surface are activated modes, but the modes (activated schemas) are largely driven by past experience (dynamics beneath the surface), which we can understand only in terms of schemas.

Oscar had difficulties with romantic relationships. While he could attract women, he was unable to remain in a stable relationship. The therapist identified the entitlement-grandiosity schema as part of the problem; however, she considered it to be a secondary schema to the underlying one of defectiveness-shame.

As this case example illustrates, what's at the surface may not always be the core of the problem, since an underlying unconditional schema can be covered by a secondary conditional schema or be turned into the opposite by compensatory schema coping. The result is a presented mode. We cannot judge the book by its cover but instead have to dig deeper for a sound understanding of the case and the history of its onset. It is easy to see that our emotional reaction to a present situation may be the result of a trigger. The schema model (along with its neurobiological underpinnings described in chapter 1) helps us to understand that in a schema-triggered state we are not emotionally in the present, but that schemas based on past experiences are driving our experience, which will distort experience beyond conscious awareness.

Perhaps a metaphor might help explain this. Imagine a doorbell. It rings if someone outside pushes the button. At first glance, this is the cause of the ringing. However, the ringing requires a preinstalled, well-working bell system. If there is no functional connection between the button and the bell, there will be no ringing, so the cause of the ringing is actually the bell system. The person ringing the bell is only the trigger. If we disconnect the bell, the ringing stops, and this will influence whether the person keeps pushing the button.

This illustration has an important implication for therapy. Cognitive behavioral approaches with a here-and-now focus tend to remove the trigger (or symptom), but not necessarily the cause. If we think about clinical symptoms, a client with obsessive-compulsive disorder (OCD) will avoid germs, a depressed client might try to escape negative feelings through social withdrawal, and a phobic client will avoid environmental triggers to a particular fear. From a schema perspective, the cause of the OCD is not germs, withdrawal is not the only factor in depression, nor are environmental triggers the cause of a phobia. As we outlined in chapter 1, it is the activation of latent schemas that sets off a chain of events that lead to distress and eventual dysfunction. Once your client can distance (or defuse) from (often automatic) thoughts and the resulting feelings, the symptoms become less threatening and more irrelevant (like the person pushing the doorbell).

Now we can appreciate how understanding schema vulnerability gives depth to our case conceptualization. If we remain with what is seen—the modes—then case conceptualization remains ahistorical, decontextualized, and just another model describing "parts of the self." Only when we can appreciate that a schema has been derived from not having a childhood need met, *and* a corresponding schema-coping behavior, can we see the mode in a biographical context.

It will be helpful for your clients to realize that there is an old schema operating unseen behind their current mode presentation. It will then be easier for them to distance from intrusive thoughts and emotional reactions. Consider this case example:

Ella realized that her jealousy with Bill came from a mistrust-abuse schema, which was related to the repeated affairs of her father. It was easy for a harmless behavior to trigger her: "Just yesterday Bill brought home flowers. That's exactly what my dad did when he came back from seeing a girlfriend." By understanding the schema, she could see that she had chosen Bill for his faithfulness "and need not remain haunted by old ghosts."

> *Principle:* Schema theory is a unified theory based on both past patterns (schemas) and present reactions (modes).

The doorbell metaphor illustrates something else. We cannot remove the electrical wires, because they are hardwired into the building. So too are schemas hardwired *in* our brain structures. As outlined in chapter 1, healing in schema therapy occurs through two main processes:

- Promoting adaptive schemas and reducing the old maladaptive schemas in a change-oriented way

- Promoting a healthier style of self-processing, including acceptance

Together these processes comprise *schema* or *mode awareness* and encompass learning to identify triggers, perceive schema activations, identify and label them as "old," emotionally distance, abstain from spontaneous maladaptive reactions, and regain behavioral flexibility.

Thus we make use of the idea of *disactualization* (Teasdale et al., 2002), which is the process of consciously choosing to emotionally distance oneself from a thought, feeling, or impulse. Indeed, schema therapy combines the depth of developmental and attachment theories of longer-term treatments; the active change-oriented approach of short-term therapies, such as cognitive behavioral therapy; and the acceptance stance of third wave therapies, such as acceptance and commitment therapy.

Attunement: The Glue of Schema Therapy

One of the most important skills of any therapist is the ability to listen and empathize. Schema therapy goes beyond the basic level of reflecting emotions to provide a higher level of understanding called *schema attunement*, which is attuning to the experience of schema activation.

Fran had an emotional deprivation schema. In a therapy session, she said, "I feel completely empty. Nothing is ever enough." Her therapist attuned to her experience, saying, "Your needs don't get met. It's like you're always emotionally hungry."

Through this attunement, the therapist conveys a deep understanding of the client's internal reality. The focus on attunement was initially developed in the psychoanalytic and attachment literature. The purpose of attunement is for client and therapist to share an experience of an inner state in order to give the client a sense of "feeling felt" (Siegel, 1999).

Creating resonance. Back to therapy. Your client's developing self requires a deep sense of understanding from you that may in some (limited) way mirror the relationship between mother and infant. Erskine (1998) built on the work of Stern (1985) and argued that attunement in psychotherapy is a two-part process that starts with, first, empathy (being sensitive to and identifying with another person's sensations, needs, and/or feelings) and moves on to, second, communicating that understanding to the other person to create a feeling of resonance.

This process has clear implications for schema therapy. Schema attunement assists the therapist in implementing limited reparenting strategies. First, the communication of attunement validates the client's needs, feelings, and experiences, laying a foundation for healing the failures of previous interpersonal experiences (Erskine, 1998). Second, making the client aware of her emotional needs provides the groundwork for effective interventions, as it communicates the importance of emotional experiencing for the therapeutic process. It also helps the client to share, experience, and, ultimately, tolerate smaller, more manageable amounts of emotional pain.

In our experience, we can trace problems in the application of experiential techniques back to a poor capacity for attunement on the part of the therapist, or to the client being unable to tolerate negative emotions, or to both. Thus, the level of felt attunement between the therapist and client can be a good predictor of responses to more experiential interventions. As described, a high level of attunement sets so much of the groundwork for schema therapy that it can be thought of as the "glue" of schema therapy—a necessary skill that underpins all the schema therapy intervention strategies. The therapy room becomes a laboratory to detect interactional patterns in terms of schema chemistry.

In brief, to achieve schema attunement:

- *Recount.* The client recalls a recent event when difficult emotions were triggered.

- *Attune* to the triggers, underlying schemas, emotions, body sensations, behavioral urges, and needs in that moment.

- *Tune in to current feelings,* both for you and your client.

- *Slow down.* Do not allow your client to gloss over and move on to another narrative or trigger.

- *Intensify* attunement. The client closes their eyes to increase the level of emotional experiencing, including any body sensations and emotional reverberations.

- *Provide historical links* to expand the broad narrative.

- *Move into experiential techniques* such as imagery rescripting or chair dialogues once your client is in touch with his or her emotional activation and can tolerate it.

Therapist Tip: Schema attunement is a very effective way to be empathic with clients and to detect their underlying schema-driven "scripts."

Summary

This chapter explored the eighteen schemas and showed how identifying schemas provides depth to clinical work. Schemas carry the memories of the past and may be distinguished as either core or compensatory. In addition, we explained how schema activation leads to three schema-coping styles: surrender, avoidance, or compensation. And we explained the important skill of schema attunement. While some schema therapists focus almost exclusively on modes, we believe that schema therapy should remain schema focused. In the next chapter, we take a look at modes.

CHAPTER 3

Modes—In the Present Tense

As we noted in the previous chapter, modes are what we see clinically. In this chapter, we outline why there has been a shift in focus from schemas to modes in schema therapy; introduce the various types of modes, including inner critic, child, and coping modes; and describe a developmental understanding of modes and introduce infant modes. Finally, we open the door to understanding how modes drive clinical symptoms. In this way, we present a dynamic model describing the ways in which modes interact.

From Schemas to Modes

When Jeff Young treated severely disturbed borderline clients, he found that the schema model was too complicated (Young et al., 2003). Clients "flipped" between different schemas, schema-coping styles, and mood states. This resulted in a different conceptualization of what he saw in the here and now—the currently activated states that he called modes (initially called modus or schema states)—and led him to develop the mode model.

Marty was enraged in his therapy session. He reacted badly to his therapist's announcement of a two-week holiday, during which she would not be available for regular sessions. Marty had an abandonment schema, and in a compensatory coping style he verbally attacked his needed attachment figure. What his therapist saw was intense rage pushing her away, not the hurt little boy who needed soothing and reassurance that there would be continuing support. After Marty got in touch with his underlying schema, he then flipped to crying and begging to be able to call his therapist while she was away.

> **Reflect:** Was it obvious to you at first glance that Marty had abandonment issues? What language would you use to describe this situation? How would you respond clinically?

Modes are the ways schemas appear after being modified by schema-coping styles, as we see in the case example above. A single mode can be the expression of multiple schemas and incorporate different coping styles. If Marty had also activated a mistrust-abuse schema, he may have been withdrawn and suspicious. He may have wanted to end therapy. Thus, a mode is a transient expression of a schema vulnerability. While you *have* a schema, you are *in* a mode. To understand this, it may help to remember the difference between a trait and a state that you learned in undergraduate psychology; schema and mode are similarly different.

Modes are user-friendly. They condense the complexity of the underlying schema procedures into a workable number of states. The gain is a manageable case conceptualization, but this comes at the cost of disconnecting modes from their historical origins. Working with a mode map, which we will soon introduce, allows for a limited focus on four or five modes in individual treatment. However, the number of potential modes is unlimited (hence the increasing number of modes described in the schema therapy literature).

There are other benefits to thinking in terms of modes. A focus on schemas can emphasize the pathological aspects or "deficits" of a person. Modes basically represent the normal spectrum of human behavioral reactions in a condensed and simplified form. Two of the modes, healthy adult and happy child, draw attention to your client's resources. The mode model gives a framework or a road map of normal or "healthy" behavior. As in traditional cognitive behavioral therapy (CBT), we can describe behavioral deficits, excesses, or distortions while already knowing the direction to take to rebalance the behavior in a healthy way. Introducing modes such as the healthy adult mode also includes healthy problem solving, which is closer to the positive psychology approach. Finally, the healthy adult mode provides the missing link that makes schema therapy a third wave therapy. This book has such a strong focus on describing healthy adult functioning because we want to make this connection. Now we'll return to a more detailed description of the mode model.

Types of Modes

Modes can be grouped into four broad categories (see figure 3–1):

- *Child modes*, in our understanding, express basic emotions if the needs for attachment or self-assertiveness are not met. Thus, they have a signal character. However, in happy child mode, all needs are adequately met.

- *Inner critic modes* (formerly called parent modes) preserve the internalized core messages, beliefs, and judgments of significant others heard by the child since infancy.

- *Maladaptive coping modes* show behavior resulting from the interaction of child and inner critic modes, including current thoughts and social emotions. They represent the best solutions developed by a person over the course of his or her life.

- *Healthy adult mode* is an executive function to integrate other modes and display functional coping behavior in a needs-based, value-driven, flexible manner.

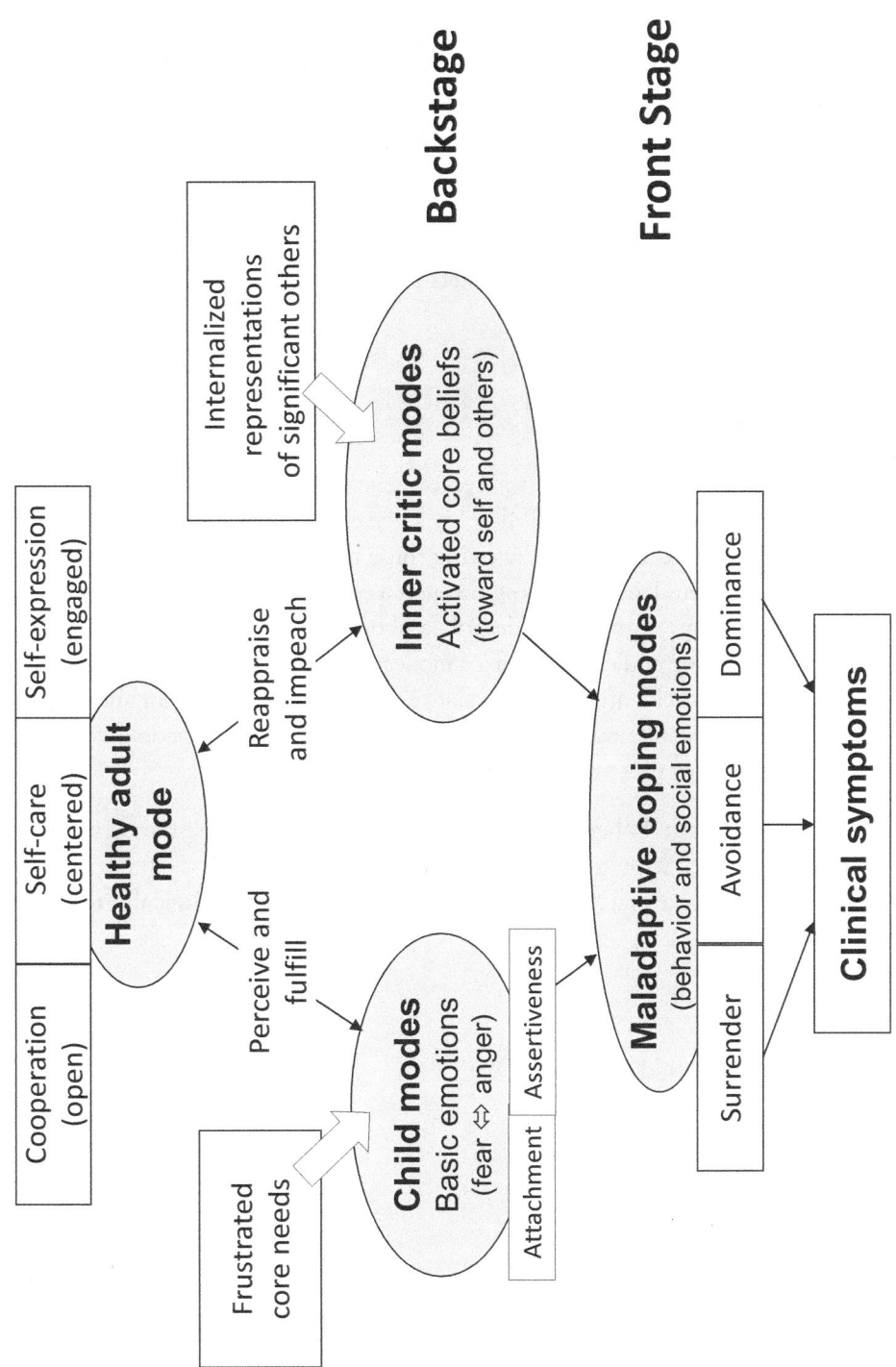

Figure 3–1. The mode model

The theater metaphor. The modes in figure 3–1 not only represent the major mode groups, but their organization also conveys a subtle dimensional order based on global workspace theory (Baars, 1997). On the "front stage" (seen from the outside), we see the coping modes as consciously displayed behavior. On the "backstage," we find the mostly hidden (and primarily unconscious) internal motivational drivers from needs-based emotions (child modes) and internalized display rules (inner critic modes). They serve as context operators, unconsciously shaping the visible "event" onstage. The overarching healthy adult mode, assumed to be located in our working memory, is able to access the backstage motives and rebalance the system in order to develop functional behavior. In this way, the healthy adult acts as the "director" of the theater, deciding what is in the spotlight of consciousness.

The Modes in Detail

We now describe the fourteen most accepted schema modes as they are presented in the Schema Mode Inventory (SMI–1.1r; Lobbestael, van Vreeswijk, Spinhoven, Schouten, & Arntz, 2010). When reviewing these modes, it can be helpful to imagine using different camera lenses. Looking through a wide-angle lens, there are only three (or four) major groups of modes, as described above. If we use a close-up lens, we can distinguish an almost endless number of modes. It makes sense, for therapeutic and scientific reasons, to identify modes related to the different personality disorders (Bamelis, Renner, Heidkamp, & Arntz, 2011). Listing them in a mode inventory and recognizing what they present clinically can assist us in treatment.

> **Therapist Tip:** When working with your client, it is best to choose a moderate scope, with a manageable number of modes represented in the dimensional mode map, and to relate the modes you see clinically to your client's difficulties.

Child Modes

1. Vulnerable child
2. Angry child
3. Enraged child
4. Impulsive child
5. Undisciplined child
6. Happy child

Maladaptive Coping Modes

7. Compliant surrender

8. Detached protector

9. Detached self-soother

10. Self-aggrandizer

11. Bully and attack

Inner Critic Modes

12. Punitive critic

13. Demanding critic

Integrative Mode

14. Healthy adult

The Child Modes

When a schema is triggered, the person feels like he's stepping into a time machine and returning to a similar situation in childhood. The adult becomes the child again. Hence this state is called a *child mode*.

- The *vulnerable child* usually feels empty, alone, socially unacceptable, undeserving of love, unloved, and unlovable based on childhood experiences and because his most important emotional needs have generally not been met.

- The *angry child* feels infuriated, frustrated, needy, or impatient because her core emotional (or physical) needs have not been met. She vents her anger in inappropriate ways. Be aware that an angry child mode can cover an underlying vulnerable child mode. Especially when one is highly energized, falling into anger feels better than getting in touch with underlying sadness. So, once more: Dig deeper!

- The *enraged child* experiences intense feelings of anger that result in him hurting or damaging people or objects. This displayed anger is out of control mostly when his assertiveness need or his autonomy is threatened.

- The *impulsive child* acts on her desires or impulses from moment to moment in a selfish or uncontrolled manner to get her own way, without regard to possible consequences for herself or others. She often has difficulty delaying her gratification, cannot tolerate limits, and may appear spoiled.

- The *undisciplined child* cannot force himself to finish routine or boring tasks, gets frustrated quickly, and gives up.

- The *happy child* feels at peace because her core emotional needs have been met in a well-balanced way. She feels loved, safe, and competent.

Child modes are early survival-based responses. These modes represent the basic emotions described by Ekman (1993) and are closely related to body sensations. We can understand a lot about the basic emotions behind these modes by looking at Edward Tronick's "still face" experiment video (Tronick, 2009), which helps relate the basic emotions to the mode model.

"Still face" experiment. Tronick's video features infants and their caregivers. After an initial phase of responsive interaction, the mother is instructed to make a still face. The child responds to this threat to attachment in the relationship with a sequence of reactions. Initially, the child shows anxious surprise, then tries to reconnect by being nice in a submissive way. This is what Tronick calls "the good way," because the alarm system of the child is not yet activated. In the next step, when the mother does not respond, the child's alarm system gets activated and is connected with a secondary anger. The anger drives an overcompensatory coping mode, what Tronick calls "the bad way." Both strategies try to repair the rupture, but they take different roads: submission uses the attachment system and builds on trust and devotion, whereas overcompensation builds on assertiveness skills and control. After both reconnection strategies fail, the child looks for help outside the dyad in a self-soothing way. The alarm system remains activated. Finally, the child remains trapped in a painful detachment, which Tronick calls "the ugly way." We will see later how these mode states are related to clinical symptoms.

This description of the experiment reflects how the concept of basic emotions relates to Greenberg's understanding of emotions in emotion-focused therapy (EFT). He distinguishes between the initial primary and later secondary emotions (Greenberg, 2015). The EFT model has a focus on the course of emotions over time, while we emphasize the separation of basic from social emotions (Leary, 2009). We regard basic emotions as indicators of what is missing, the determination of which leads to a road map to meet unfulfilled needs:

- *Basic emotions* are the person's most fundamental and original reactions to a situation. They are precognitive, hardwired, embodied physiological expressions of survival patterns. Basic emotions indicate that a person's core needs are not being met. They include sadness in relation to loss, anger in response to violation of autonomy, and fear in response to threat or abandonment. These emotions cover the whole spectrum between the attachment and assertiveness orientations, and they enhance the self and intimate bonds.

- *Social emotions* are secondary, postcognitive emotional reactions, including internalized appraisals and beliefs induced by significant others. They are part of the resulting coping behavior (Leary, 2009). Examples include embarrassment in response to being hurt, envy after being set back, hopelessness following several fruitless attempts to fight for one's rights, guilt after being punished, and shame following embarrassing criticism. Basic emotions are precognitive, whereas social emotions are postcognitive, influenced by thoughts and beliefs.

Principle: Basic emotions are universal and inborn (child modes). No one is born with social emotions. These have to be learned by identification with an internalized belief (inner critic modes).

Therapist Tip: All over the world, in Finland as well as Korea (Nummenmaa, Glerean, Hari, & Hietanen, 2014), people feel the basic emotions of the child modes in their bodies, while they perceive social emotions in the head. Sometimes it is difficult to put basic emotions into words. However, they frequently result in nonverbal expressions or subtle physical movements. Pointing this out can help clients to get in touch with their underlying basic emotions hidden behind social emotions.

Poles in the spectrum of emotions. It is important to appreciate the two tendencies of assertiveness and attachment illustrated in figure 3–1. They are not categories but a spectrum of emotional activation—two poles between which we constantly move back and forth. If you take a pacifier out of a baby's mouth, the baby will probably react in an angry child mode. After some minutes of helpless crying, the sound may change to moaning, indicating sadness, and end with an expression of fear. There is no jump between the emotions, but more of a smooth shift, as demonstrated in the "still face" video. Sometimes both tendencies are activated at the same time and we might feel a mixture of anger and sadness (or a quick flipping between them). The mode inventory cannot fully represent the subtlety of such emotional movements. Research may need categorizing models for collecting data, but our clinical understanding is more nuanced. A dimensional use of the mode model is helpful because you can place each existing mode somewhere in the given dimensions while keeping the model simple.

Maladaptive Coping Modes

Maladaptive coping modes are interpersonal coping reactions based on early childhood experiences in an environment that lacked an appropriate child focus. The child's experiences often included social emotions such as shame, guilt, or feeling superior. They are linked to behavioral reactions on a spectrum including submission, withdrawal, and dominance, as seen in the "still face" video. These modes reflect both basic emotions (child modes) and appraisals (inner critic modes). However, there is also a biologically entrenched influence from temperament and the character of the person. Some people are overregulated or shut down in their emotional expression, whereas others are underregulated and overexpressive, easily giving vent to negative emotions. Naturally, this also influences options for coping.

Submission

- *Compliant surrender:* The person acts in a submissive, reassurance-seeking, or self-deprecating way toward others out of fear of conflict or rejection. He anticipates or gives in to the perceived expectations of others, especially those he sees as more powerful, in order to remain accepted.

Avoidance

- *Detached protector:* The person withdraws from the pain of schema activations by emotionally detaching. She shuts off all emotions, disconnects from others, rejects their help, and functions in an almost robotic manner. She feels "nothing," appears emotionally distant, and avoids getting close to people. Signs and symptoms include depersonalization, emptiness, boredom, and psychosomatic complaints. She shuts off from her inner needs, emotions, and thoughts, and usually feels empty.

- *Detached self-soother:* The person tunes down negative emotions by engaging in activities or taking substances that will somehow soothe, stimulate, or distract him. His activities are generally pleasurable or exciting, but he does them in an addictive or compulsive way. They can include workaholism, excessive exercise, gambling, dangerous sports, promiscuous sex, Internet addiction, compulsion, or drug abuse, but also self-mutilating behavior. Others will compulsively engage in solitary interests that are more self-soothing than self-stimulating, such as playing computer games, overeating, watching television, or excessive fantasizing.

Dominance/Overcompensation

- *Self-aggrandizer:* The person feels superior, special, and powerful and behaves in an entitled, competitive, grandiose, abusive, or status-seeking way in order to have whatever she wants. She sees the world in terms of "top dogs" and "underdogs." What is most obvious may be a drive for dominance or control, so all kinds of overcontrolling modes are related to overcompensatory modes. She's concerned about appearances rather than feelings, is almost completely self-absorbed, and shows little compassion for the needs or feelings of others. She demonstrates superiority and expects to be treated as special, and she does not believe she should have to follow the rules that apply to everyone else.

- *Bully and attack:* The person uses threats, intimidation, aggression, and coercion to get what he wants, including retaliation, and directly harms other people in a controlled and strategic way, be it emotionally, physically, sexually, verbally, or through antisocial or criminal acts. He wants to assert a dominant position but has the edge of threat. The motivation may be to compensate for or prevent abuse or humiliation. There may be an element of sadism.

In childhood, these coping modes were the "best" solution. Unconsciously, they "define" our interpersonal relationship with another person based on the innate biological interactional patterns of surrender, freeze, flight, or fight. Coping modes reflect the biological options described by Cannon (1915; see chapter 1). Thus we can differentiate avoidant coping into a more passive and a more active form, ending up with four major coping styles represented by the maladaptive coping modes in a dimensional spectrum between the compliant surrender (surrender), detached protector (freeze/passive avoidant), detached self-soother (flight/active avoidant), and overcompensation modes (fight).

A note on freezing. We relate submissive behavior with surrender, not with freezing. A "frozen" rabbit (or a dissociative person) is trying to avoid harm through withdrawal. The message of the frozen rabbit to the fox is "I'm not interesting for you, so don't take notice of me" (detachment). Freezing is thus an example of coping through passive flight, and not surrendering. The dog's message as it offers its throat is "I accept your superiority and my lower social status, but in return I want to remain in the group" (submission). Thus, submission is prosocial and keeps groups together. The triad of freeze, flight, and fight does not represent the full spectrum of coping options.

Inner Critic Modes (Formerly Parent Modes)

Our legacy from childhood includes parental messages experienced as nonpsychotic "voices in the head." Like Joan Farrell and Ida Shaw (2018), we prefer the term "inner critic modes" over "parent modes." Clients tend to connect the "parent" label with images of their real parents, and that can lead to loyalty conflicts. The term "inner critic" is also used more widely in other therapeutic approaches. Using this term indicates that in therapy we talk about internalized dysfunctional beliefs and not about memories of real parents (which are usually much more complex and bring forth ambivalence). The beliefs that a client internalized may not have been explicitly said, rather they might be the result of the child's mentalization activities. Consider this case example:

In therapy, Bart recalled coming home and going into his depressed mother's room. She lay stiff in her bed with the curtains closed. There was no response when he entered. Although his mother did not say a word, Bart's internalized inner critic messages were "Don't bother her. Care for yourself. You're too much for her. It would be better if you'd never been born!"

There are two main inner critic modes to watch for in therapy, because they can point in contradictory directions and thus should be separated and approached differently in therapy:

- *Punitive critic:* This is usually the internalized voice of caretakers criticizing and punishing the person. She'll become angry at herself and feel that she deserves punishment for having or showing normal needs that her environment didn't allow her to express. The tone of this mode is harsh, critical, and unforgiving. Signs and symptoms include self-loathing, self-criticism, self-denial, self-mutilation, suicidal ideation, and other self-destructive behavior. In our interpretation of the mode model, these expectations can be directed at others, too, just like the underlying punitiveness schema (see chapter 2).

- *Demanding critic:* This critic continually pushes and puts pressure on the child (or other people) to meet excessively high standards. He feels that the "right" way to be is to be perfect or to achieve at a very high level, to keep everything in order, to strive for high status, or to be efficient and avoid wasting time. Like the underlying unrelenting standards schema, this mode can be directed at the self and others.

About internalization. The process of building up the inner critic modes is comparable to the idea of internalization or introjection described by Freud (1915). In psychoanalytic thinking, internalization leads to the formation of a superego (Freud, 1923) as a parental introject. Picture a child in a dysfunctional environment trying to express his needs to a stonewalling or neglectful mother. Those needs will not be met either by submission or by getting angry and trying to fight. The child tries to reduce the resulting emotional tension by building up an internal representation of the caregiver in order to survive. The inner critic modes help the child avoid conflict with the powerful parent, but at the price of sacrificing assertiveness. People show similar behavior when helpless under torture, in isolation cells, or in relationships involving ongoing traumatic abuse. They even start to sympathize with their abusers.

We internalize significant others in two ways:

- *Self-directed:* We have an internal representation that continues to speak in the self-directed voice of the demanding or punitive critic modes.

- *Directed at others:* We also internalize significant others as relational models. Beliefs are then directed at others: "You should do…" This is why parents often treat their children just the way they were treated as children. There is a natural shift from victim to offender as the parent unconsciously "trains" the child. Only the actors change, not the patterns!

Consider the following case example. Kathy internalized the beliefs her mother had about her and then, many years later, expressed the same beliefs to her own kids:

Kathy had a volatile single mother. Though her mother died ten years ago, Kathy can still hear her voice speaking to her: "I hear the words condemning me. And the harsh tone." She finds herself using the same harsh words with her own kids.

Though CBT describes internalized thoughts as negative core beliefs and automatic thoughts, schema therapy emphasizes their origins in childhood experience as well as their internalized nature. Unlike the psychoanalytic superego, the inner critic by definition represents only toxic and dysfunctional core beliefs. Despite Farrell, Reiss, and Shaw (2014) suggesting using a "Good Parent mode" as a representation of functional parental behavior, we assign functional beliefs to the healthy adult mode and sort out the toxic beliefs as inner critic voices. The goal of therapy is to identify and label them as internal toxic voices.

> **Reflect:** Think about a time when you were critical of others. What were your thoughts? Did you send them as negative messages, as you do to yourself? Note that the blaming words may be the same, but the direction can be internal or external—to the self or to others.

> **Therapist Tip:** The mode model helps us to attribute dysfunctional beliefs to the critical modes. Inner critic modes drive social emotions and drag our clients into their accustomed maladaptive coping modes. Once we have identified the backstage motivational drivers behind front-stage ego-syntonic coping (that is, perceived as part of the self), it is much easier to distance ourselves from uncritically following those beliefs, reappraise them, regain flexibility, and develop more realistic choices to change automatic behavior patterns.

The Healthy Adult Mode

The *healthy adult mode* is the adaptive self-regulating aspect of a person. Naturally, in this mode, the person integrates reasonable thoughts and self-insight, leading to functional problem solving. This mode nurtures, validates, and affirms the vulnerable child mode and regulates the angry and impulsive child modes. In healthy adult mode, the person reappraises the beliefs of the inner critic modes and chooses her own functional values. She modifies the maladaptive coping modes, moving them toward functional coping behavior. She performs appropriate behaviors such as working, parenting, taking responsibility, and committing. She pursues pleasurable adult activities, such as "good" sex; intellectual, aesthetic, and cultural interests; health maintenance; and athletic activities. There's a good balance of her own and others' needs.

The healthy adult mode is the "therapist inside" that is strengthened in therapy. The therapist, as a kind of coach or a good parent, can assist the client's healthy adult mode and help the individual grow stronger. Through therapy, a client will normally internalize the therapist as a role model, just as significant others were internalized in the past. This enables the client to regain autonomy and end therapy without feeling abandoned. One can think about the therapy continuing, but being conducted by the internalized therapist through the healthy adult mode.

When a child's needs are met, the vulnerable child becomes an open and sensitive child again, willing to socialize with others. The angry child calms down and becomes a contented and empowered child ready for exploration and creativity with adequate assertiveness. It is the job of the healthy adult to reappraise the old beliefs and balance the needs for attachment and assertiveness, resulting in functional coping behavior.

In schema therapy literature, the term *healthy adult mode* is used with a dual meaning:

- An invisible regulating *mental function* that induces functional coping behavior
- The visible functional *coping behavior* itself

Throughout the book, we focus on the healthy adult function and call the resulting behavior "functional coping that replaces maladaptive coping modes." In the attractor model, shown in figure 1–4 (in chapter 1), the energetic low on one side represents the accustomed maladaptive coping. The new, functional behavior is represented by the energetic valley on the other side. The healthy adult mode is the control parameter (or catalyzer) inducing the change across the energetic hill, from one side to the other.

The healthy adult cannot invent new coping tendencies beyond the described polarity, because the spectrum is naturally defined. The small boxes above "Healthy Adult Mode" in figure 3–1 show how the healthy adult modulates the extreme reaction tendencies of the coping modes. He balances and adapts them to the situation and the needs of others, including by using a long-term, value-based perspective. Instead of mode flipping, the healthy adult can flexibly change from one pole to another.

Principle: The healthy adult mode is the director of our successful life drama. This mode continues the work of therapy over the whole lifetime in a flexible and balanced way.

A Developmental Perspective

A developmental understanding of modes is inherent in schema therapy: we look at the maturation of modes in terms of developmental trajectories. We propose a further elaboration using the concept of infant modes (Simeone-DiFrancesco, Roediger, & Stevens, 2015).

Schemas are built up or developed from birth. The earlier the imprint, the rougher, more isolated, or more extreme the schema will probably be—it will be comparable with schemas formed during experiences of trauma. The later the onset, the more the schema will be embedded in an instrumental way of thinking and behaving. Early and intense schemas will probably lead to a more infant-like appearance on the mode level, such as in the following case example.

Vanessa has a strong abandonment schema. Every time her husband tries to leave home she falls into a panicky state clinging to him (vulnerable child mode). She forces him to text her ten times a day (overcontrolling coping mode).

More complex and embedded schemas might appear in a more instrumental mode:

Sergio lost his girlfriend to Ron. One night he picked Ron up on the street, saying, "I know where your little sister lives." His voice was cold and ruthless. There was no anger visible, but his bully and attack mode was driven by a cold and instrumental anger.

This distinction has an impact on our interventions, since we try to match them with the state of maturation the mode is in. For example, when an infant mode appears, we talk to the client as we would to a very small child, sitting very close to the person and even offering to cover him with a blanket (Farrell & Shaw, 2012). We address adolescent modes with relaxed or casual speech, respecting the individual's growing sense of autonomy.

Integrating Schemas and Modes

Visible behavior in terms of modes always results from the applied coping style. Table 3–1 shows how surrendering to one schema or compensating for another one can drive the same coping mode. We cannot judge the book by its cover: we have to dig deeper in therapy by understanding that the behavior is a coping style used to deal with an underlying schema.

Table 3–1. The relations between schemas, schema-coping styles, and presented coping modes

Underlying Schema	Primary Feeling	Schema-Coping Style	Resulting Behavior	Coping Mode
1. Defectiveness-shame	Worthless	Surrender	Act humble	Submission
2. Defectiveness-shame	Worthless	Compensation	Act entitled	Overcompensation
3. Entitlement-grandiosity	Entitled	Surrender	Act entitled	Overcompensation
4. Entitlement-grandiosity	Entitled	Compensation	Act humble	Submission

In the second and third rows in table 3–1, different underlying schemas lead to the same overcompensatory, narcissistic behavior, but the background is different. The second row describes the history of a secondary narcissist. The following example demonstrates this type of coping:

Mal is a successful property developer. His wife insisted that he come to therapy. It soon became evident that behind his grandiose overcompensatory facade was a vulnerable child. This child learned to compensate for a defectiveness-shame schema to become less vulnerable and gain approval.

Therapist Tip: It is crucial that we do not react to the overcompensatory front-stage coping mode but do label and acknowledge it in order to bypass it and access the vulnerable child mode backstage (for practical details, see chapters 6 and 13).

The third row describes a primary narcissist suffering from an entitlement-grandiosity schema. The schema is so integrated into the personality that it is never questioned. This client needs empathic limit setting that provides exactly what the client's parents failed to do. In this way, reparenting becomes *secondary* parenting.

Looking behind the presented scene. When we connect these ideas with the mode model in figure 3–1, schema compensations make the client change between the coping-mode poles (characterized as internalization or externalization). On the one hand, when we compensate for the Vulnerability to Harm schema we no longer surrender but might become externalizing overcompensators: a secondary narcissist turns from victim to offender. On the other hand, when compensating for entitlement-grandiosity, the wolf hides in sheep's clothing: the client shows superficially submissive behavior. Understanding this is crucial to be able to differentiate schema surrendering from schema compensating. If you are dealing with a schema-surrenderer, you get what you see. The schema-compensator, however, hides his core in a shell. This is why we work with the backstage and front-stage model.

It is important in therapy to get in touch with the underlying schema and the emotional dimension associated with it. A client with an underlying insufficient self-control schema might develop a heavy dieting lifestyle or even become anorexic and thus appear very controlled, but backstage, there is still the schema ready to be activated in episodes of impulsive eating. When working with a secondary narcissist, for therapy to be successful, it is essential to bypass the schema-compensating behavior and get in touch with the hidden vulnerable child mode derived from the unconditional defectiveness-shame schema, which, at first glance, is concealed behind the overcompensatory presentation. We make this point because some books about schema therapy do not always make the distinction between schema-coping and coping modes. The inconsistencies become obvious when one digs deeper into the modes and the relations between them. There is no inconsistency between the schema and mode models if you approach them in the way we have outlined.

Principle: To understand current behavior in terms of coping modes, you have to understand the underlying schemas and schema-coping styles and separate schema-coping from coping modes (see figure 3–2).

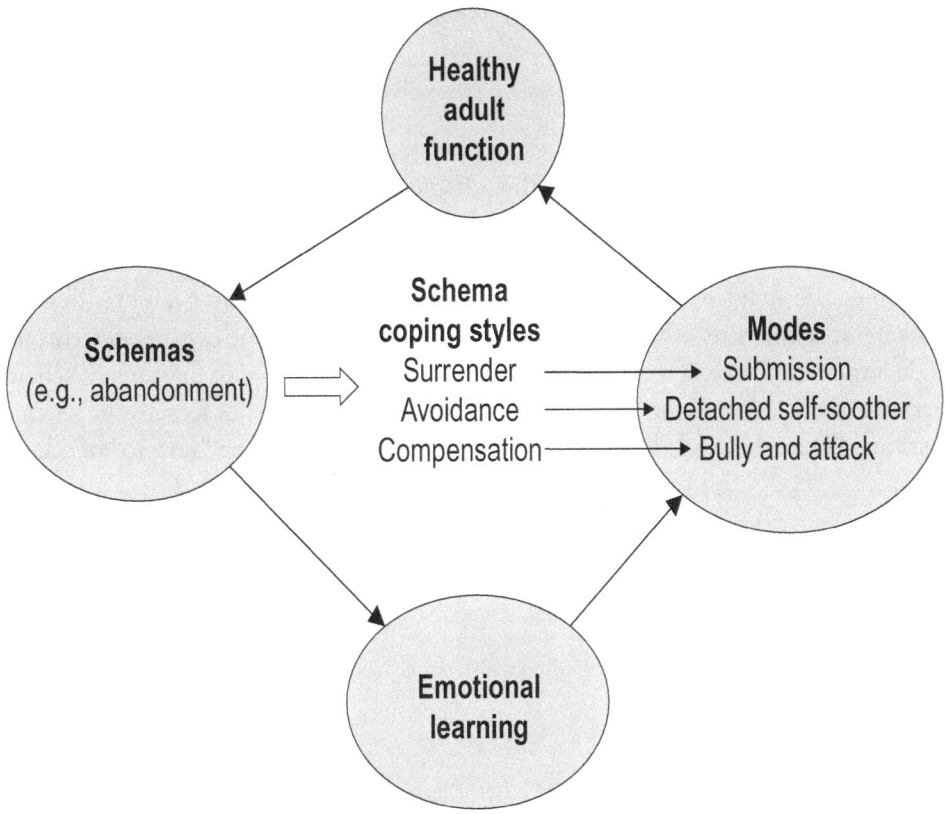

Figure 3–2. Connecting schemas, schema-coping styles, and coping modes in terms of learning processes

Modes and Clinical Symptoms

The dynamic mode model is also helpful for understanding a range of clinical disorders. Figure 3–3 relates clusters of clinical symptoms with the assumed underlying coping modes. Interestingly, most of the symptoms derive from ongoing active or passive detached coping. This is exactly what we described in our analysis of the video of the "still face" experiment: submission and overcompensation are ("good" or "bad") ways of getting in touch with other people and satisfying our need for connection. Detaching violates this need, leading to the ("ugly") feeling of isolation and paving the way for psychological disorders.

The results of this experiment are in line with research findings showing that early emotional deprivation leads to an increase of psychopathology (Heim et al., 2010).

Unfortunately, modifying maladaptive coping does not necessarily make these symptoms disappear. Like all attractors (or schemas) they fight for themselves and have to be addressed in therapy with specific strategies (as described in chapter 12). Thus, the more that isolated clinical symptoms prevail, the more we have to make use of specific CBT strategies as part of an overarching treatment plan.

Summary

We introduced the mode model in this chapter. Modes are activated schemas and coping styles—basically what we see in the therapeutic session with our clients. The list of modes is not fixed and is open for additions. The challenge of using this model is developing the ability to become aware of the modes you see in therapy. It may be easier to recognize modes in others, but don't stop there. Seeing your own modes through mode awareness is one of the most important skills you will need to master as a schema therapist (see chapter 15 for details). Also, challenge yourself to not forget your schemas operating below the mode level. In the next chapter, we begin the "how to" of schema therapy.

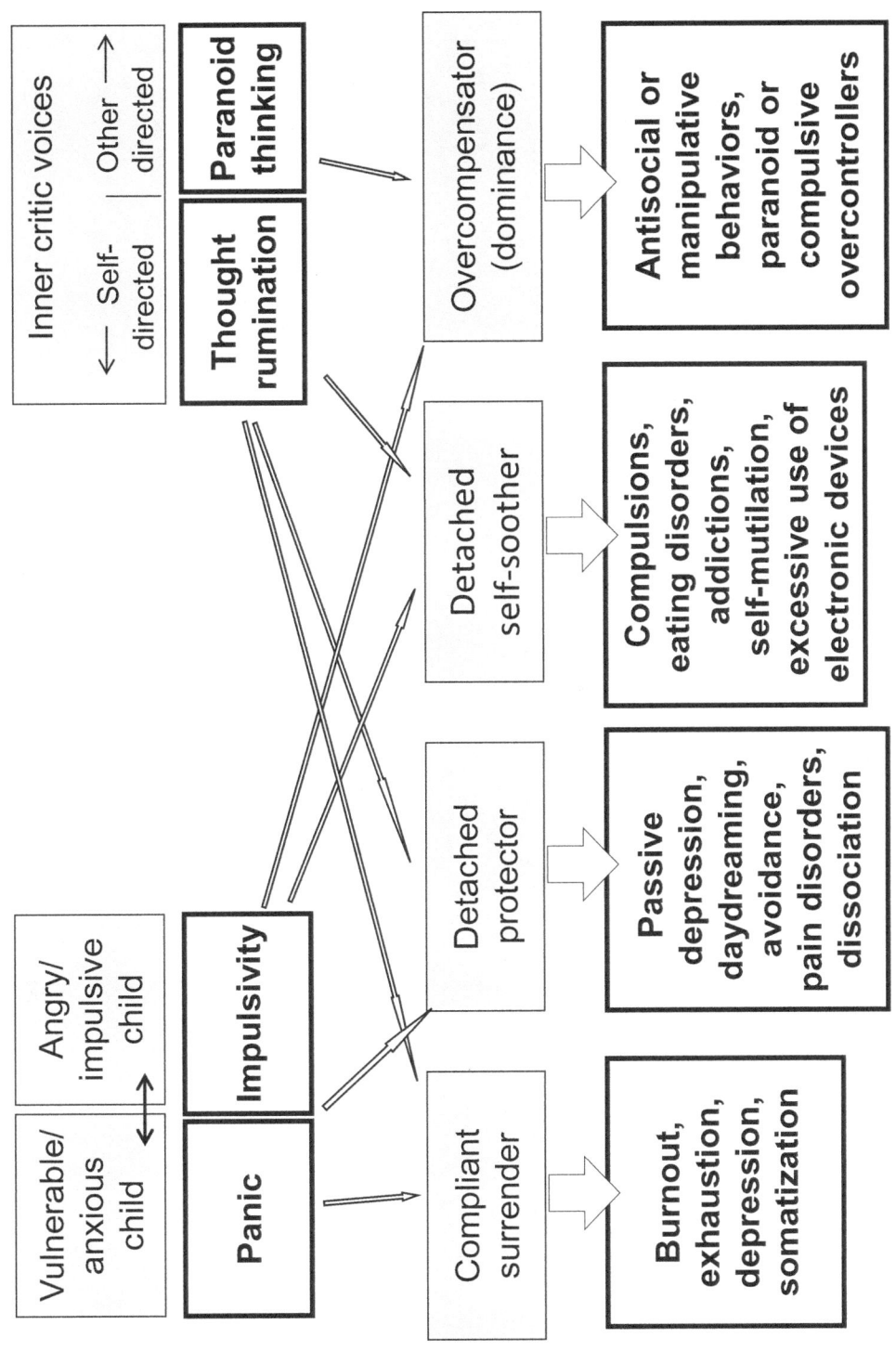

Figure 3–3. Maladaptive coping modes and clinical symptoms

CHAPTER 4

From Past Tense to Present Tense—The Case Conceptualization

In this chapter, we look at the role that case conceptualization plays in the therapeutic process. It is a matter of *seeing*. The therapist sees through the lens of assessment and forms an understanding of what is needed. In the next step, we teach our clients to look at themselves from a healthy adult perspective. A good case conceptualization provides something broader and maybe more objective than your client's personal view. This working formulation of therapy can be like a life raft in rough seas, providing a safe place for client and therapist, especially when problems emerge in the therapeutic relationship. We also introduce an extended case study of Joanne to illustrate aspects of schema therapy.

The Role of Case Conceptualization in Schema Therapy

When working with personality disordered clients, their maladaptive behavior will soon affect the therapeutic relationship. By quickly implementing a case conceptualization, we can introduce a "third party" to the treatment. Both the client and the therapist are thus provided with a conjoint reference point outside any turbulence in their dyadic relationship. The following example is a case in point.

Martina was highly reactive. She would explode with anger over trivial things. One day her therapist had to cancel a session. In the next session, Martina said, "You think I am worthless, not worthy of your respect, so you canceled our regular session." Sarah, her treating psychologist, responded, "I can see that I've upset you. I'm sorry to have let you down, but this gives us an opportunity to look at our case conceptualization. We've already thought together about your fighting mode and the sources of your anger, so…"

Many of our clients experience a flooding of negative emotions. The case conceptualization enables both therapist and client to reorient themselves toward a mutual understanding of what is happening.

Principle: The case conceptualization as a joint reference point reinforces the therapy relationship and helps therapist and client find common ground again when there has been a rupture in the relationship.

We usually base the case conceptualization on:

- Client self-reporting (biographical narrative, conceptual self)
- Schema and mode questionnaires and inventories
- Within-session observations of client behavior
- Our own schema-based reactions
- Third-party narratives (from spouses, parents, or others)
- Diagnostic imagery work

The initial narrative of clients at the beginning of therapy is often more of an indication of what they want their life to be. In acceptance and commitment therapy (ACT) terms, this is called the *conceptual self*. However, in schema therapy, we are interested in what is developmentally relevant, as the following example alludes to.

Thomas, when first asked about his childhood, said, "It was wonderful." Later in imagery work, it emerged that both he and his mother lived in fear of his father's explosive rage.

We have found vivid and reliable access to relevant childhood scenes using diagnostic imagery work. Indeed, you will find that most of the significant scenes you encounter visually were never reported in the initial narrative. So, when a new client comes in, we suggest you take the lead and ask what you need to know for therapy. You can limit the amount of biographical information to what you put into a genogram (as follows) and gather only a brief historical narrative. Schema therapy is based on a normative model of healthy versus maladaptive human functioning. Like tourists following an informed guide familiar with the territory, most clients feel safe and comfortable with such a structured process.

Therapist Tip: After listening to your client's current problems, in the second or third session, start with some education about the mode model, integrating the information you already have to illustrate it. Perhaps first give some practical advice to enable the client to function better and to provide emotional support to lay a good foundation for your work.

We recommend watching the video of the "still face" experiment (Tronick, 2009) with your client. After watching the video, most clients will come to understand what a child mode is, what everybody's needs are, and where their coping modes come from, as Gina did.

Gina was shocked to realize that her single mother completely failed as a parent: "I know my friend's mothers were more available, but I never realized that Mom's drinking let me down so much." This helped Gina to feel like less of a failure: "I suppose I actually coped rather well, and I shouldn't be so hard on myself."

Here's the most essential information about the schema therapy model:

- *Frustrations of the two emotional core needs* of attachment and assertiveness lead to schemas.

- *Early maladaptive schemas* drive our current experience and automatic coping, even if we are not aware of them.

- *The four negative basic emotions* (fear, sadness, disgust, and anger) are red lights on the dashboard, indicating that our needs are not met and leading to child mode activations.

- *Inner critic mode voices* in our head result from the internalized beliefs of significant others.

- *The coping modes*, according to Cannon's (1915) animal model, were previously our best way of dealing with our past, but they have become maladaptive.

- *Healthy adult mode*, learned in therapy, can help one find more adaptive solutions by reappraising inner critic mode voices and fulfilling child mode needs.

Therapist Tip: It is helpful to give your client an easy-to-read book on schema therapy to support psychoeducation. *Breaking Negative Thinking Patterns* (Jacob, van Genderen, & Seebauer, 2015) explains the mode model nicely. *Reinventing Your Life* (Young & Klosko, 1993) describes in detail the eleven most-common schemas. If you prefer a more personal style, you might prepare handouts for your clients.

Understanding Family Patterns: The Genogram

The genogram is a visual way of organizing information about families over three generations, using symbols in a kind of family tree. Derived from family therapy, it provides an overview in assessment. You can keep track of family members and maintain an intergenerational systems perspective.

The following can be included in the diagram:

- *Significant people (parents, siblings, other relatives)*: Name, age, highest level of education, occupation, and any significant problems.

- *Times:* Significant dates, such as births, deaths, marriages, divorces, separations (anniversaries tend to raise anxiety or cause sadness). Note any other significant stressors or transitions (accidents, illness, change of job, moving) and whether any occurred just before a relevant event, such as work-related stress, a separation, or an injury.

- *Locations:* Geographical locations of parents and other family members; any patterns of migration.

- *Ethnic and religious affiliations.*

Then add indications of intergenerational psychopathology, including alcohol abuse, genetic defects, suicide, violence, accidents, job instability, problems with gambling, criminal behavior, sexual abuse, drug addiction, other addictions, and mental illness. It is easy to use shorthand symbols, such as $ for financial problems, but make up your own for any theme that you find significant.

If all this provides the bones, then the flesh is emotional patterns. Who is considered successful in the family? By what criteria (business, academic, sports, number of children, or financial success)? Are there gender roles? What is expected of sibling positions? Who are the black sheep? Are there family rules, hot issues, secrets, family scripts, and taboos? Note anything that interests you.

Think about the wider context. What are the historical forces that shaped each generation? What wars, economic conditions, birth-rate changes, and cultural and political changes were influential? If there was a migration, what did the change in culture introduce? What changed in the family? Has the meaning of work changed through the generations?

Therapist Tip: While a genogram might become very comprehensive, it is possible to sketch it out and include enough relevant details to inform your assessment in about ten minutes. Aim for being brief and add additional information later. The genogram presents the most clinically relevant data on one page. It is flexible in use and guides your exploration to access the information you need for the schema case conceptualization.

Extended Case Study of Joanne

Consider the following extended case example of Joanne, which we will use throughout this book.

Background. Joanne (name) is a thirty-six-year-old woman (age and gender) who has been married for the past ten years to Brandon (relationship status). She has two children from this relationship: Angel (eight) and Joseph (six). Joanne has an

Anglo-Australian background (ethnicity, country of origin) and completed high school (highest education). She is currently a full-time mother and homemaker (occupation).

Joanne suffers from chronic worry (diagnosis: generalized anxiety disorder) but, with time, characteristics of borderline personality disorder have become obvious, including difficulties regulating emotions (extreme anxiety, loneliness, anger outbursts), impulsivity (binge alcohol use, spending money, Internet addiction), chronic emptiness (feeling detached and numb), self-harm (superficial cutting), and chronic relationship problems due to what she describes as her "controlling behavior."

When Joanne was a child, her father was frequently absent on work trips overseas. While she felt close to him when he was at home, she felt abandoned when he was away (abandonment schema). Joanne's main caregiver was her mother, who was emotionally cold (emotional deprivation schema) and also overly critical (defectiveness-shame schema) and perfectionistic—in Joanne's words, "like a drill sergeant" (unrelenting standards schema). Joanne could see that many demands were placed on her mother, who had four children to look after and little support from her absent husband.

Joanne came to therapy with fears that her husband might finally give up on her and leave because of her "erratic and demanding behavior." She wanted to be "a better mother" to her own kids. She felt she "was too much like" her mother, who didn't know how to "relate" to her. "She could only be a drill sergeant herself" (unrelenting standards again). In Joanne's first therapy session, her therapist prepared the genogram shown in figure 4–1.

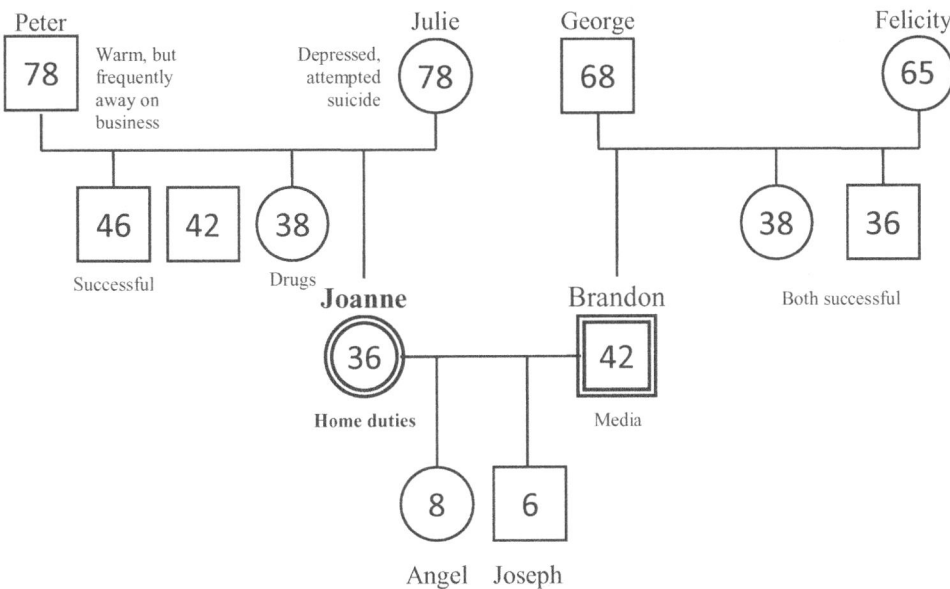

Figure 4–1. Genogram for Joanne

The ISST Case Conceptualization Form

An International Society of Schema Therapy (ISST) workgroup has developed a comprehensive case conceptualization form for training and certification purposes. Here, we show how to use this format with Joanne's case.

Background Information

Axis I Symptoms or Diagnoses

1. Generalized anxiety disorder

Current Major Problems and Life Patterns

Problem 1: Chronic loneliness

Life pattern: Client often feels overwhelmed and lonely, has not managed to make social connections outside of her immediate family, and is overly reliant on her partner for emotional support. As he is frequently away on work trips, this often leaves her in an angry or vulnerable mood. This is a repeat of her childhood experience, as her father was warm and caring but often away on work trips.

Problem 2: Perfectionism and control

Life pattern: This is very similar to her experiences of her own mother as a role model, and perfectionism and control are core ways that Joanne copes with her chronic overwhelming feelings. She becomes overly focused on cleaning and starts to relate to others in the house as a kind of drill sergeant. While there is a kind of functionality to this (her house and children are always spotless), the husband feels that this is "too much" and is worried about the children's welfare when he is away and they are left with her coping this way.

Problem 3: Relationship problems

Life pattern: Joanne's extreme demandingness and control are becoming problems in her relationship. Her husband, Brandon, is becoming less supportive as he moves more toward protecting the children from her perfectionism and control. This often leads to erratic "anger outbursts" in the home as Joanne protests the lack of support.

Developmental Origins
(Mother, Father, Siblings, Peers)

1. Joanne's father was warm but often away on work duties for extended periods.

2. She was mostly left in the care of her mother, the "drill sergeant," who Joanne experienced as cold, critical, and overly demanding.

3. Everything in the house had to be perfect or else Mom would "explode," particularly when Dad was away (frequently).

4. Mother would discourage fun in the household by imposing excessive chores and rules.

5. She was getting bullied at school, feeling "different" and ostracized, particularly in high school.

Core Childhood Memories or Images

1. When she was five years old and her father was leaving for a trip, she recalled "hammering on the door" as he left. Her mother did not offer comfort but scolded her for making such a fuss.

2. At seven years old, she spilled some spaghetti and was made to eat it off the floor.

3. She remembered getting in trouble for playing in the backyard and was made to do hours of chores for punishment.

4. In junior high school, she was all alone in the schoolyard. She had no one to share lunch with, even though she was surrounded by so many children. She felt completely alone.

Core Unmet Needs

1. Stability and quality of attachment
2. Acceptance and validation
3. Fun and play

Most Relevant Schemas, with Origins
(Link with Developmental Origins Above)

1. Abandonment
2. Defectiveness-shame
3. Emotional deprivation
4. Unrelenting standards
5. Social isolation

Current Schema Triggers
(Specify M or F if Limited to Men or Women)

1. After a buildup of tension prior to her husband going away on a trip, she often exploded just before he left or verbally abused her children soon afterward.
2. Husband rebuking her about her overcontrolling and demanding behavior.
3. Children making a mess or breaking "the rules."
4. Being alone in the house (partner away, children in school).

Schema-Coping Behaviors

Schema-Surrender Behaviors

1. Her own self-criticism

Schema-Avoidance Behaviors

1. Alcohol dependence
2. Emotionally detaching

Schema-Compensatory Behaviors

1. Perfectionism and overcontrol
2. Excessive worry

Relevant Schema Modes
(in Addition to the Healthy Adult)

1. Vulnerable child
2. Angry child
3. Punitive critic
4. Detached protector
5. Detached self-soother
6. Perfectionist overcontroller

Possible Temperamental or Biological Factors

1. "Sensitive" temperament; needed more attention than older children, who seemed more self-sufficient

Core Cognitions and Distortions

1. "No one cares about me."
2. "No one sticks around... People are always leaving me alone."
3. "I'm not good enough."
4. "I must be perfect or else I'll be worthless."

This format may seem complex, at least initially, but it has the advantage of being systematic and comprehensive. Once filling it out becomes routine, and you can easily keep in mind the dynamics it illustrates, you can shift to more simplified forms that we will introduce later in this chapter. A modified case conceptualization form, currently under development by an ISST workgroup, had not been finalized at the time of writing.

Schema and Mode Questionnaires

Young and colleagues developed a set of schema questionnaires for clients to fill out to explore the full range of schemas and coping behaviors. (You can purchase these schema questionnaires on Jeff Young's website, http://www.schematherapy.com.)

- The Young Schema Questionnaire (YSQ) asks for schemas that can still be activated today. The YSQ has been revised several times. Currently, a long form with 203 items (YSQ–L3) and a short form with 90 questions (YSQ–S3r) are in use.

- The Young Parenting Inventory includes seventy-two questions about the client's memories of parental behavior, including the mother and father or significant others.

- The Young Compensation Inventory assesses the client's compensatory behavior with forty-eight questions.

- The Young-Rygh Avoidance Inventory asks forty questions about avoidant schema coping.

The first three questionnaires all refer to the eighteen (formerly nineteen) schemas. If you compare the scores for each schema, you can see which ones have probably been caused by the caregivers, which ones are still active, and which ones are no longer visible due to a client's compensatory attempts. The Young-Rygh Avoidance Inventory offers typical avoidant schema-coping behaviors but does not relate them to specific schemas.

Therapist Tip: Be aware that the YSQ only indicates schemas that are coped with by surrendering to the schema. Schema avoidance and schema compensation make the schema "disappear."

When using these questionnaires, you should know that only the YSQ has good validity (Lee et al., 1999). Nevertheless, the other inventories are helpful clinical tools to investigate a broad range of schema-related activities. Do not take the results too seriously. If your client does not agree with the results, do not insist that they do so; instead, just consider the results additional information. Maybe later the results might make sense to the client. However, discussing questionnaires to build a joint reference point seems to increase the effectiveness of therapy by up to 12 percent (Lambert, 1992). In practice, many clients accept the results of the questionnaires much more easily than they accept personal feedback from the therapist. Perhaps using questionnaires appears more professional!

Besides the schema questionnaires, Young and Atkinson developed the Young Atkinson Mode Inventory (YAMI) that a Dutch group modified into the Schema Mode Inventory (SMI). The first revision, with 118 questions related to 14 modes, shows good validity (Lobbestael et al., 2010) and is widely used (like the YSQ). A second version with about 21 modes is currently under development. The SMI, which is quite sensitive to changes and can track the progress of therapy, is freely accessible.

Mode Monitoring for Assessment

Self-awareness is important to schema therapy. Mode monitoring forms provide tools to help the client become more "mode aware" in the diagnostic and working phase. In chapter 7, we describe how we use mode monitoring to build and reinforce the healthy adult mode. In the present context of assessment, mode monitoring helps us understand what modes and schemas may be operating for a client. We triangulate the results with the other assessment information to strengthen our attunement with the client. This links well with other discovery techniques, such as downward arrowing and sentence completion.

Using the forms, clients learn to identify and label their own mode activations, at first during sessions and later between sessions. Gradually, clients assume responsibility for keeping records of their own mode activations with significant others and the resulting interactional mode cycles with their partner, family members, or work colleagues. This is the first step in developing the healthy adult mode. It is nonjudgmental self-awareness!

Figure 4–2 is an example of a mode monitoring form used in Joanne's case formulation. Notice that the four STEPs of monitoring information are the same as in any other cognitive behavioral formulation, setting up the links between triggering situations and associated thoughts, feelings, and behaviors. Once you are able to train your clients to notice these four aspects, they can use this information with their case conceptualization in mind and guess what modes may have been active in different situations.

In the first sequence, Joanne was feeling angry after noticing that her son's room was a mess, and she self-identified a pattern in which her angry child mode was activated, resulting in the eventual activation of coping through her perfectionist overcontroller mode (urging her to scream at her son to clean his room). Once she was able to identify her own modes, the formulation became easier each day! Depending on the strength of the healthy adult mode, the client can try to get a healthy adult perspective of the situation. (You can download an empty mode monitoring form, along with this book's other online accessories, at http://www.newharbinger.com/40958.)

Situation: Describe the physical situation as it was.	Thought: Notice what your mind was telling you.	Emotion: Rate your feeling using a scale from 0 to 10 (0 = nothing at all, and 10 = an extreme feeling).	Preferred reaction: What did you feel like doing following this thought and feeling? What modes are involved?
(S) I notice that my son's room is a mess.	(T) He just doesn't care about his room—or me.	(E) Anger 9/10	(P) Scream at him to go and clean his room, then check on him until it's perfect. Mode: Angry child → then perfectionist overcontroller
(S) I see my husband wheeling his luggage toward the garage. I know he will leave soon.	(T) I don't care.	(E) Detached/numb 10/10	(P) Stop talking to him. Go and distract by cleaning up. Mode: Vulnerable child (?), definitely detached protector
(S) I'm alone at home and there's nothing left to clean.	(T) I'm so alone!!	(E) Sad/lonely 9/10	(P) Drink wine to ease the pain. Mode: Vulnerable child → detached self-soother

Figure 4–2. Mode monitoring form for Joanne

Descriptive Mode Diagram

Modes are what we *see* in a session. Usually, we notice chains of mode activations. In your notes, you can record any mode that occurs using abbreviations such as *VC* for vulnerable child, *DC* for demanding critic, *DSS* for detached self-soother, and so on. Observe your client's mode sequences, perhaps initially on the genogram or as activated in a session. As a second step, we now suggest some other ways to map the interaction of modes. Figure 4–3 shows a descriptive mode diagram for Joanne. (You can download a blank version of this form, along with this book's other online accessories, at http://www.newharbinger.com/40958.)

> **Therapist Tip:** The descriptive mode diagram enables both you and your client to see repetitive interactional patterns in a more systematic way.

Six Steps to Sharing a Descriptive Mode Diagram

In practice, we use a descriptive mode diagram to convey a six-step story, starting on the right-hand side of the form and moving left.

1. Introduce the need for mode mapping. For Joanne, we might say something like:

Therapist: Okay, Joanne, now that I've taken the time to get to know you, let me try to convey to you what I've learned so far in this form. This will help us determine what to do next.

2. Summarize what you have learned about the client's history in terms of needs satisfaction and thwarting. This is usually an easy step for the client, as you are merely summarizing what she or he already told you but through a developmental-needs lens and by connecting it with schema or mode terms:

Therapist: First, from what you've told me, Joanne, it was really hard for you to get your needs met while you were growing up. Even though you loved your dad, he was often away, leaving you to your mother, who you experienced as quite cold, critical, and demanding. This meant that you often felt very alone and abandoned, resulting in abandonment and emotional deprivation schemas. At the same time, there were so many demands and criticisms that you also got the message that you weren't good enough. This led to a defectiveness-shame schema and an unrelenting standards schema.

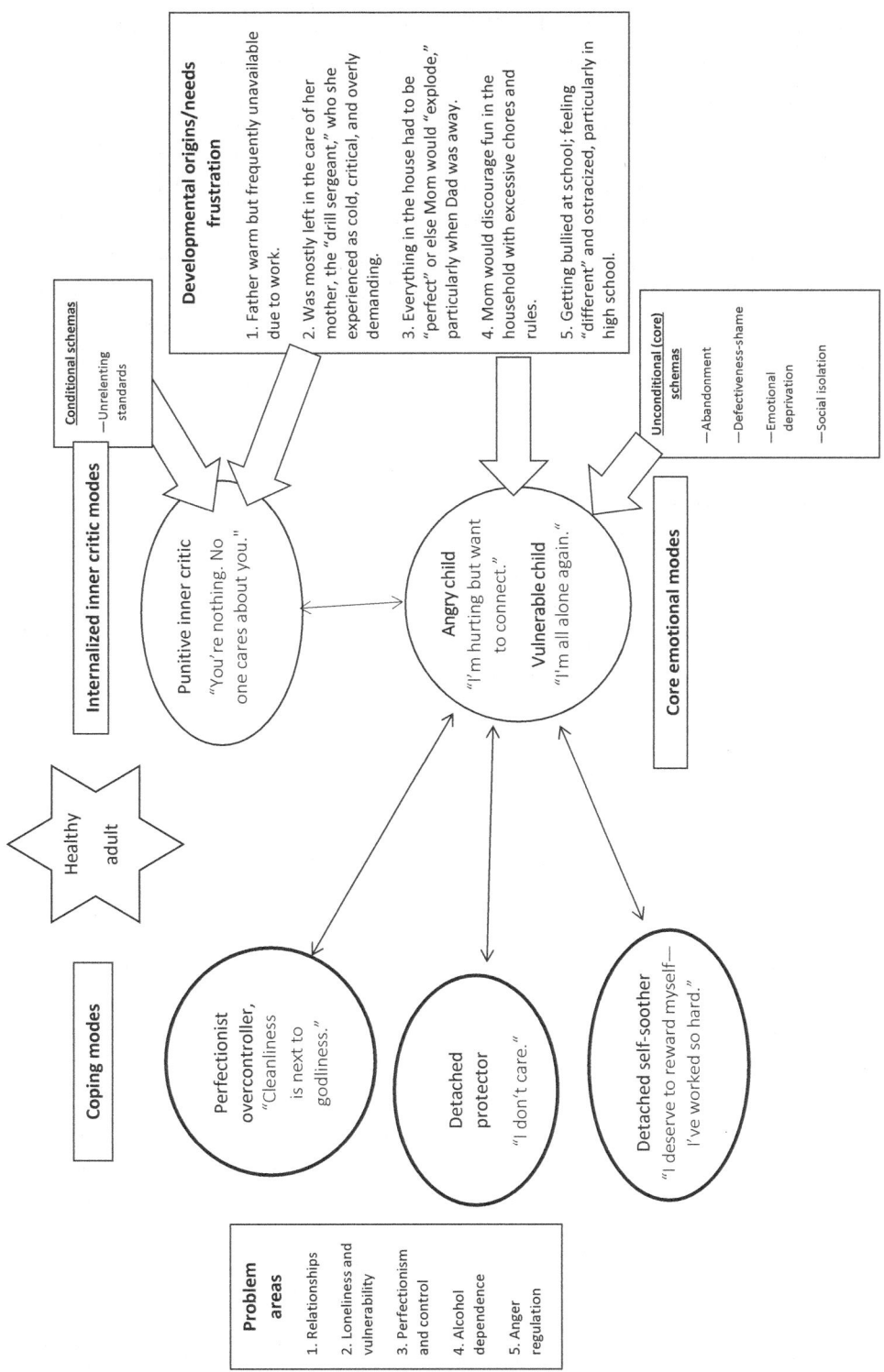

Figure 4–3. Descriptive mode diagram for Joanne

3. Communicate to the client that this left him or her with some core emotional modes. For Joanne, we might say something like this:

Therapist: As a consequence of not getting your needs for stable connection and validation met, a part of you felt vulnerable about the way things were, while another part felt angry. It's normal for children to feel vulnerable and angry when their needs aren't met. We call these parts of you—the vulnerable child and the angry child—core feelings. These modes can be quickly triggered if something from today's context activates your schemas. For example, when you notice that your husband is getting ready to go away, that can trigger the abandonment schema, inducing your vulnerable child mode feelings.

Next, you can educate the client about a particular inner critic mode:

Therapist: So, Joanne, another part of this is that you have internalized a lot of the critical messages about yourself that you used to hear from your mother, and to some degree from your peers in high school. This all induces your unrelenting standards schema. This shows up as a part of you that is harsh and critical of yourself, particularly when you make mistakes. We call this the punitive critic mode. Do you recognize this harsh and self-critical part of you?

4. Describe the coping modes and their function. For Joanne, we might say something like this:

Therapist: And so little Joanne had a rough time of things, and she had to adapt. She developed some ways of coping. First and foremost, I think she coped by trying to be perfect. She learned that if she was in control of things in her environment, and followed her mother's perfectionistic rules, then she was in a lot less trouble and she could avoid feeling overwhelmed [Note: Submission in childhood]. This makes a lot of sense even these days [Note: Short-term negative reinforcement function], but it can also put you under a lot of pressure to keep everything perfect, and it affects your relationship with your husband and children today if you force them to be perfect too [Note: Longer-term negative consequences linked to presenting problem]. We call this the perfectionist overcontroller. Can you recognize this mode?

Do this for all of the coping modes in the formulation. In Joanne's case, we would do it for the detached protector and Self-Soother modes, too.

5. Educate the client about the healthy adult mode. It is very helpful to complete this story with a positive conclusion, so we suggest that you provide a description of the healthy adult mode and your task of building it up:

Therapist: And so, while all of this is happening, there's another healthy part of you that can sit back and notice all of it going on. That part wants help. It wants to get unstuck from this… Perhaps it's that part that has brought you into therapy?

And so, yes, there's a healthy part of you there but sometimes there's so much going on [Note: Point to the other modes] that it's hard for that side to be in charge.

6. Gain informed consent to move into the experiential phase of schema therapy. Once you have had significant "buy in" to the formulation, it is helpful to ask your client to start monitoring his modes so that he can take this new awareness or perspective into his daily life and start applying it. You can revise the form when any new information emerges, making it more complex and differentiated over the course of therapy.

> **Therapist Tip:** Try to allow your clients to have as much control as possible about designating names for their modes. Often they will connect strongly with an idiosyncratic label such as "the wall" (detached protector) or "the tough guy" (bully and attack). This approach is in line with our understanding of shared decision making (Beauchamp & Childress, 2001).

If you use schema questionnaires, we suggest focusing on just a few schemas and immediately linking them to relevant modes and the profile from the Schema Mode Inventory. Linking presented modes with some representative underlying schemas helps your clients to become more sensitive to the childhood origins of their present experience. But, to avoid getting bogged down, do not try to be too much of a perfectionist. You can always bring in details later. The form in figure 4–3 has two separate boxes to add conditional schemas that are "feeding" inner critic modes and unconditional (core) schemas that are activating child modes.

You can also indicate how to deal with each mode to achieve a better outcome: bypass the detached protector, soothe the vulnerable child, direct the angry child, let the inner critics go, and set limits on the overcompensators. This work is bidirectional, linking an activated mode and the healthy adult mode dealing with it (or, initially, the therapist), and quite similar to the way cognitive therapy deals with irrational beliefs. It is a matter of extending skills that most therapists already possess. Applied this way, schema therapy basically remains a second wave therapy.

The Mode Map: A Contextual Perspective

Schema therapy has a number of ways to map modes. In this book, we add an additional case conceptualization (to distinguish it, we call it the dynamic and dimensional perspective) that has been slightly modified from the one described above. This brings the mode model, with a contextual perspective, a step closer to psychodynamic, transactional analysis, and emotion-focused therapy models. We want to help you to gain a dynamic overview of your client's mode presentation and to conduct therapy in an efficient, goal-oriented way. This is a more medical top-down approach to helping the client get into healthy adult mode and find flexible balance in life. (You can download a blank version of the mode map, along with this book's other online accessories, at http://www.newharbinger.com/40958.)

The mode map serves several purposes:

- It describes and tracks interactions over time (or flipping between modes) to provide your client with a comprehensive internal working model.

- It puts a dimensional framework around the modes to place each in a normal spectrum of behavioral tendencies. This leads us into a transdiagnostic framework in line with the alternative model in the DSM-5.

- It allows your client to understand maladaptive coping as normal behavior tendencies that are exaggerated. This is helpful because behavior only has to be rebalanced in order to become functional again.

- It gives your client guidance for actions to become more balanced and effective (functional contextualism).

Working with the Dimensional Mode Map

Here's an example of how you might introduce your client to working with the mode map:

Therapist: We've started to work with a description of your modes and put them into a descriptive diagram. In the next step, to deepen our understanding of what is going on inside of you, I want to show you how these modes relate and interact with each other. What we see first on the front stage are the coping modes. Can you see that the box on the left side for submissive coping is empty? You're tending more to the dominant and avoidant side of coping.

But the coping modes aren't coming out of the blue. They're resulting from inner emotions and beliefs on the backstage level. Understanding the origins of our coping modes on the backstage level is like analyzing a color. Think in terms of the three primary colors, blue, red, and yellow. Basic emotions such as fear or sadness belong to the vulnerable child mode, or blue. Disgust or anger belong to the angry child mode, or red. We found you more in touch with your angry child pole than with the vulnerable side. Do you remember?

In the boxes on the right side, we find internalized beliefs. For the purposes of this illustration, let's call them yellow. What we do on the coping mode level is composed of or mixed from the basic emotions

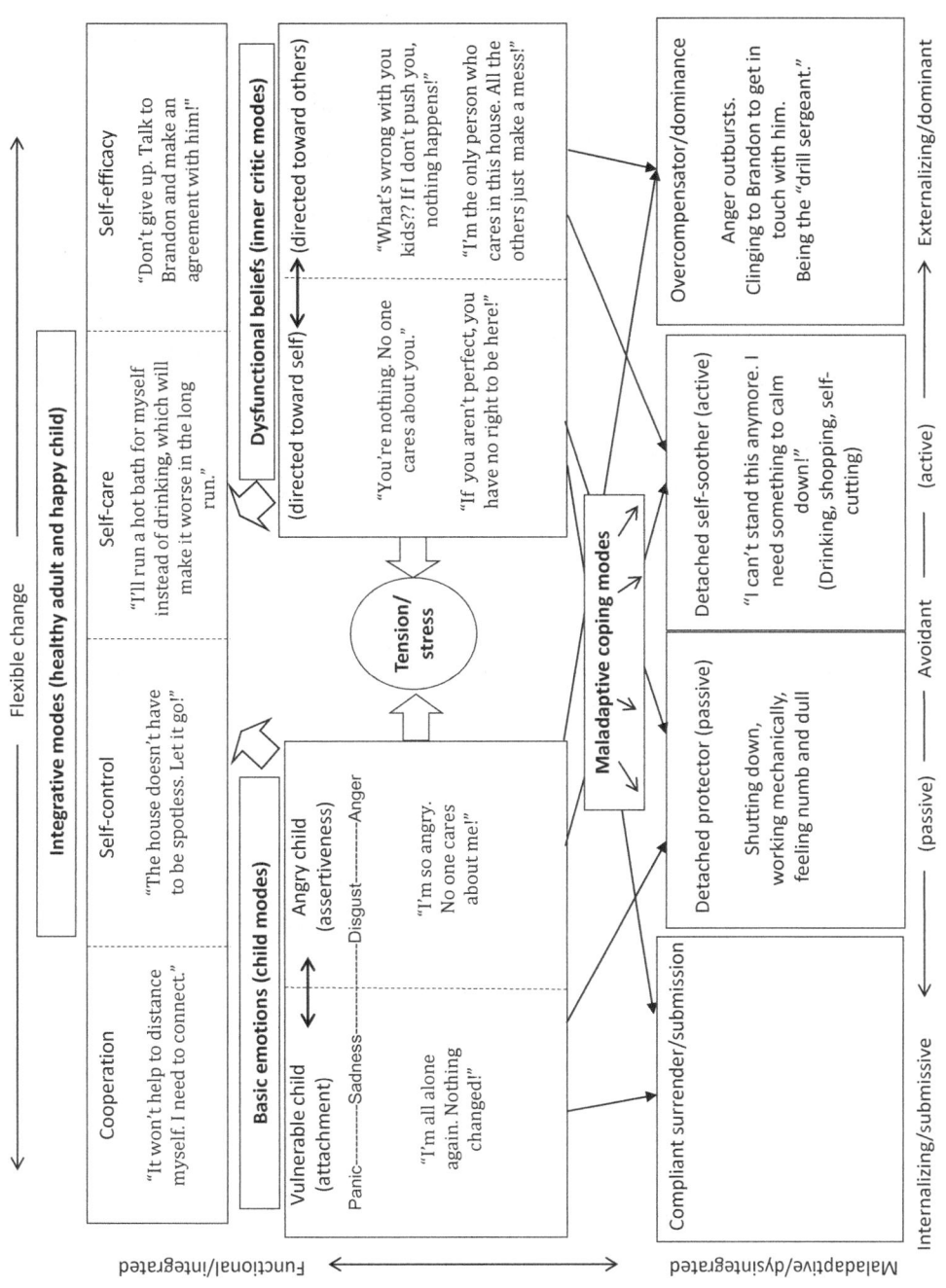

Figure 4–4. Mode map for Joanne

(between the poles of blue and red) and simultaneously activated core beliefs (yellow). You have strong beliefs about yourself, and they push you to clean up or escape into your self-soothing coping modes. Sometimes, the beliefs are about the others, and your anger breaks through in an overcompensating outburst.

In therapy, we'll work toward strengthening your healthy adult mode. This will help you to react more flexibly between the poles of cooperation and showing assertive behavior.

Separating emotions and beliefs strictly is, of course, somewhat artificial, because even in a child mode we express our feelings with words (cognitions). After introducing the mode map, we try to access the client's precognitive emotions, which are not tainted by beliefs. We want to compare experiencing the child modes to showing one's "true colors." Additionally, inner critic mode voices have an aura of negative affect, but they convey toxic beliefs that are uncritically entrenched in our appraisal system and maintain suffering. It is an important goal in schema therapy to dismantle those toxic beliefs and reduce their power by impeaching them. Therefore, we have to bypass the coping modes that our clients bring into therapy, thereby reaching the backstage as soon as possible. The beliefs of a coping mode frequently sound rational. Once we identify and sort them out on the backstage level, they reveal their toxic essence. The mode map guides the way.

Joanne suffered from her anger outbursts that hid her underlying loneliness. Her inner critic voices blamed others, and she felt entitled to boss them around. Once they withdrew, the inner critic voices turned back on her and she either detached or started self-soothing. However, she was too stubborn to submit. When she became familiar with her mode map, she realized that she was avoiding feeling overwhelmed in her vulnerable child mode and was weak when it came to cooperating or giving in.

She said to her therapist, referring to her husband, "Brandon said he wouldn't be home this weekend. I felt desperate, but then I shut down and started drinking. I know you're going to say I need to get in touch with my feeling so my needs can be met."

The therapist asked Joanne to see herself as a child feeling alone. Gradually, she was able to become present enough with her emotional vulnerability to develop more willingness to cooperate with Brandon.

The mode map is designed to reveal the backstage dynamic, as illustrated in the example above. It is dimensional rather than categorical. Despite its complexity at first glance, it keeps the model clear and manageable—once you understand the underlying ideas. You can place all the basic emotions on the spectrum between vulnerable child (blue) and angry child (red). Inner critic voices (dysfunctional beliefs) are either directed toward the self or others, and the resulting behavior is somewhere between internalizing/submissive, passive or active avoidant, or externalizing/dominant. No more modes are needed. Like a lens, this approach reduces the complexity of our experiencing and places it neatly on the therapy work stage.

Think about moving from the narrowed perspective of being in a coping mode to a broader healthy adult perspective. It is then possible to move from a hypothesis to a solution. This perspective provides you with a comprehensive internal working model, not only of the self, but of others, too. The mode map continually provides orientation and guidance toward more flexible and balanced ways of need- and value-based acting. The map can also be used in therapy supervision (Roediger & Laireiter, 2013). Consider how Joanne reacted to the introduction of the mode map:

By the end of the session, Joanne was not only able to feel sad but could think about how her vulnerable child might be comforted. She said, "I know Brandon will be away, but I could invite my sister to stay for the weekend. We can really share, and I know she'll understand how I feel. She really has her life together."

Therapist Tip: You may find that a client with a personality disorder will nominate a goal that is unhealthy, such as a narcissistic or avoidant goal. Avoid talking back to these intentions and instead go back to the map and label the behavior. Examine the backstage motivational modes, such as the inner critic modes, to detect the subtle influence of not yet discovered and reappraised beliefs. Add them to the appropriate boxes on the mode map. Thus the map becomes more and more comprehensive. Finally, you might also try another strategy, such as suggesting, tentatively, "Let's try this out and see how it works, then you can reevaluate it. This is what healthy adult mode is about: it's flexible, learns from experience, and is open to reevaluation." This method works like tai chi, gently guiding the energy of your enemy in another direction instead of going against it. We describe in detail how to work with overcompensating clients in chapters 6 and 13.

Fine-Tuning Mode Recognition

Practice doing a mode map with your family members or colleagues. You will become familiar with detecting modes (that is, separating coping modes from the underlying child and inner critic mode activations). Also, be aware of your own feelings and include them in your understanding of the client's mode map (for example, a child mode might be present). This awareness will help you to identify subtle manipulative messages of coping modes that might appear "innocent" at first glance. Or you may recognize protective anger. Consider this example of a hostile client:

Tracy, a young client suffering from borderline personality disorder, came to a session swearing: "This stupid therapy doesn't help me at all. Let's stop!" Initially, her therapist thought it might be an overcompensating mode, such as bully and attack, but he did not feel threatened. By including his own emotional resonance he was able to identify a mode that could be idiosyncratically labeled as "angry protector," which was keeping any perceived risk of therapy from Tracy's vulnerable child.

This angry protector mode can be placed somewhere between the Self-Soother and an overcompensatory mode. Another person might come in asserting, "You're wasting your time with me. I'm a hopeless case. Better spend your time treating more promising people!" This might look submissive, but is this person trying to connect with you? No—he's keeping his distance. So this is another self-defeating protector that can be placed between the detached protector and the compliant surrender box.

> **Therapist Tip:** The mode map works like the zoom lens of a camera to allow a closer look at the four basic mode groups in order to help you understand the interpersonal meaning of a behavior.

Other examples come to mind. A person may seem completely calm (as many antisocial personalities will present), but you may then have a sense of threat when he says, "I know where you park your car." Although there is no anger in the statement, you realize that this is an overcompensatory response, because the person is trying to frighten and control you. Sometimes behavior can incorporate aspects of two coping modes. Obsessive handwashing to "wash away" guilt feelings is evidence of detached self-soother, but requiring others not to touch anything in a room becomes overcompensatory. Giving a gift may appear submissive, but getting angry when it is not acknowledged reveals a manipulative (and, by that, overcompensatory) foundation.

Finally, remember that from a dynamic viewpoint, displayed behavior always has an interactional meaning: it is a means of defining an interpersonal relationship. This is why including your inner reverberations in the diagnostic process adds value. Somebody might present as highly perfectionistic, and because of that appear overcompensatory, but as long as the person is driven by the will to please you, this is submission. Take time to explore the layers driving the behavior.

> **Therapist Tip:** When uncertain, be like Columbo, the TV detective. Play ignorant and ask seemingly foolish questions until your client reveals her real needs or the implicit beliefs of the motivational level backstage. Use questions that induce mentalization (as described later) to understand more about your client's inner world. Then insert the behavior, and the underlying intentions, in the box that fits best (but remember that the client's behavior may be somewhere in between boxes or may have to be placed in two boxes).

This model is dynamic, with an interactive perspective. In it, every coping behavior is *fueled* by underlying emotions and *directed* by inner critic mode appraisals. In this way, an anxious vulnerable child combined with a self-directed inner critic mode will lead to surrender. An angry child and an outward-directed inner critic mode leads to overcompensation. If the punitive critic mode blocks an angry child's tendency to fight, this leads to an increased inner tension, resulting in avoidant coping modes such as detached protector or detached self-soother (for example, self-mutilating behavior). Following the arrows on the mode map will reveal the dynamics.

Tracy was an emotionally unstable client. Her therapist tried to convey the message that Tracy's insurance company would not continue to pay for her inpatient treatment, and that she had to leave the clinic by the end of the week. Tracy was flooded by anger (angry child mode) and started yelling and swearing at the therapist (bully and attack mode). When he remained firm, she ran out of his office, slamming the door (angry protector mode). Later, when she sat in her room alone, her unresolved tension brought up sadness (vulnerable child mode). Then, to manage her emotional pain, she cut herself (detached self-soother) and silently approached a nurse, leaving a trace of blood on the floor behind her (submission).

This example shows *mode flipping*, rapid changes in modes in an emotionally unstable client.

The Six ACT Processes: Describing Healthy Adult Functioning

Healthy adult behavior is no mystery. And it is not just what the therapist engages in. In most schema therapy books, you will find only a brief description of how the healthy adult mode works. However, if we look at the six core processes from acceptance and commitment therapy (ACT), described in chapter 1, we find the important characteristics of the healthy adult mode. In chapter 7, we show how to strengthen them. In this chapter, we add the therapist's rating of the six functional processes of Joanne to the case conceptualization using a 0 to 10 scale.

Defusion (2/10): A clear target for Joanne. When her vulnerable and angry child modes are triggered, she is dominated by thoughts of defectiveness and unlovability, and she finds it difficult to distance from these thoughts. In particular, when her punitive critic is at the fore, she seems to become completely fused with it, even experiencing it as ego-syntonic.

Acceptance (3/10): Joanne is generally low in acceptance, as evidenced by her strong urge to go into avoidant or overcompensatory coping modes (detached protector, detached self-soother, and overcontroller). However, the strong presence of vulnerable and angry child modes, which often show up in therapy, means that there are times when Joanne can stay with, tolerate, and accept feelings.

Present-moment contact/mindfulness (2/10): This is a definite target for Joanne. One facet of her overcontroller mode is the degree to which she adopts an overanalyzing style of interaction in the therapy room. There is a great deal of rumination and cognitive analysis in the room, such that keeping a clear focus and accessing emotions is difficult. This issue is also prominent in Joanne's daily life, as she often engages in many hours of rumination while avoiding or cleaning. Mindfulness skills are implicated.

Self-as-context (3/10): Joanne's capacity to see herself as the context of her experiences is relatively poor. Any exercises that build the observer stance will help develop and reinforce her healthy adult mode.

Personal values clarity (9/10): This is a clear strength of Joanne's healthy adult mode. While she struggles to engage in value-consistent behavior, she is mostly clear about what is most important in life for her (companionship, motherhood, friendship, social bonds, competence, achievement).

Committed action (2/10): This is another definite target for Joanne. Despite her relative clarity about values, she chronically struggles to get her needs met and is thwarted by both her strong coping modes and a current context that triggers her abandonment schema (for example, when her partner is away on business trips).

Use your client's strengths, such as Joanne's strongly held values, as leverage for change and to work on less-developed processes.

Joanne strongly values being a good mother. Driven by the overcontroller mode (cognitive fusion), she puts pressure on her children (self-as-process) to avoid feelings of discomfort at not meeting her inner critic demands (experiential avoidance). Connecting her with her values makes her more willing to "change sides" and defuse from her demanding inner critic modes and face her forthcoming fear (acceptance) while mindfully watching the tension rise and later fall again (self-as-context).

You can also use the ACT core processes and scale them over the course of therapy for monitoring progress.

Bringing It All Together: Integrating the Schema Mode Model into a Comprehensive CBT Conceptualization

Figure 4–5 provides an overview of what we described in this chapter. It is not meant to be shared with your client, rather its purpose is to give you a comprehensive view of your conceptualization embedded in a CBT case formulation. It merges schemas, schema coping, and visible modes, as well as the six ACT processes describing healthy adult mode functioning with a behavioral analysis system, including stimuli and consequences (Kanfer & Schefft, 1988). You can use the figure as a blueprint for your individual case conceptualization and use the tools demonstrated above to assess schemas, modes, and healthy adult functioning.

Figure 4–5 brings together in one big picture everything we described in this chapter. The figure is not designed only for schema therapists, as it also embeds our model into the broad stream of evolving behavior therapy. We hope this visual presentation makes it easier for mainstream CBT practitioners to understand the purpose and the conceptual framework of our work.

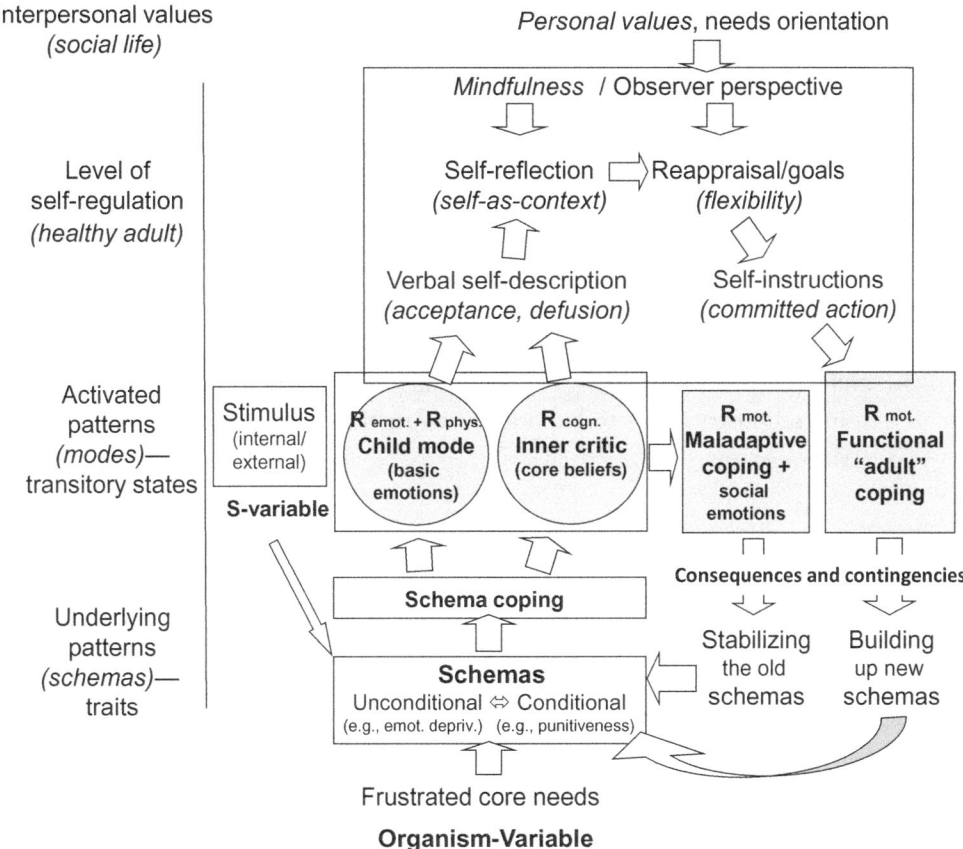

Figure 4–5. Schemas, schema coping, coping modes, and ACT processes integrated into the behavioral analysis system

To make this complex figure more accessible, we'll go through it step-by-step. Four functional levels are described on the left side:

- Underlying patterns working as traits (the schemas)

- Activated patterns in terms of transitory states (the modes)

- The level of functional self-regulation (healthy adult mode)

- Our connection with the social life around us, resulting in our personal values

An external or internal stimulus (S-variable) activates the underlying schemas in our organism-variable that result from frustrated core needs. Depending on the kind of schema coping used, they appear in terms of activated basic emotions (R emot.) and body activation (R phys.). This is what we call a child mode. On a parallel track, the conditional schemas induce inner critic mode beliefs (R cogn.). Both result in expressed behavior (R mot.) accompanied by social emotions reinforced by consequences and contingencies. This chain leads to a loop of automatic processing (Kanfer & Schefft, 1988), reinforcing the old schemas. To step out of this loop of schema-reinforcing patterns, we have to shift into healthy adult mode by taking three steps (see box in the upper part of the figure):

1. *Shift out* into a self-reflective stance by mindfully accepting and nonjudgmentally describing the activated emotions and beliefs in a defused way, leading to a self-as-context perspective (open response style).

2. *Shift gears* by reappraising the situation based on one's needs and values in a flexible way (centered response style).

3. *Shift into* functional coping behavior and guide oneself into committed action using self-instructions to build up new functional schemas (engaged response style).

Summary

Schema therapy treatment involves working with modes. While schemas are the bedrock, modes are the targets of treatment interventions, so it is essential that we accurately assess their presence. In this chapter, we introduced various tools to induce mode awareness and create case conceptualizations, such as mode mapping, and we added ACT processes to the conceptualization. The case conceptualization helps us to better appreciate the dynamic interplay of modes in clinical sessions and, more broadly, in the lives of clients. Understanding such an interplay can help us fine-tune the way we approach modes. Thus the case conceptualization is the heart of therapy, serving as a joint reference point and guiding us through therapy.

CHAPTER 5

Harnessing the Therapy Relationship

Clients with a personality disorder come to therapy with relationship problems, and they will naturally display these problems in the therapeutic relationship. Schema therapists deal with more than symptoms and try to work on wider dysfunctional patterns. Hence, we need a clear strategy for analyzing and improving relational processes, making cooperation easier for our clients and less stressful for us as therapists. In this chapter, we identify the main underlying patterns in schema therapy before going into detail about how to balance and guide the process.

Micro to Macro: Interactional Patterns in the Therapy Relationship

Goal setting is central to cognitive behavioral therapy (CBT) treatment (Kanfer & Schefft, 1988). It is also important in schema therapy, but we go beyond presented symptoms or concerns to assess the underlying interactional patterns of our clients. This digging deeper is what a schema therapy case conceptualization will add to the treatment plan.

When we explore the client's interactional patterns, behind a multitude of everyday struggles (on the microlevel) we find a small number of underlying dynamic patterns (on the macrolevel). We base the analysis of these interactional patterns, or scenes, on three sources (see figure 5–1; based on Menninger, 1958):

- *Biographical scenes:* Information from childhood scenes recalled by the client (from narrative or imagery work)

- *Current scenes:* Reports of interactional problems in the client's current life (nominated by the client or determined from other relevant sources)

- *Therapy scenes:* Observations of the interaction in therapy between client and therapist

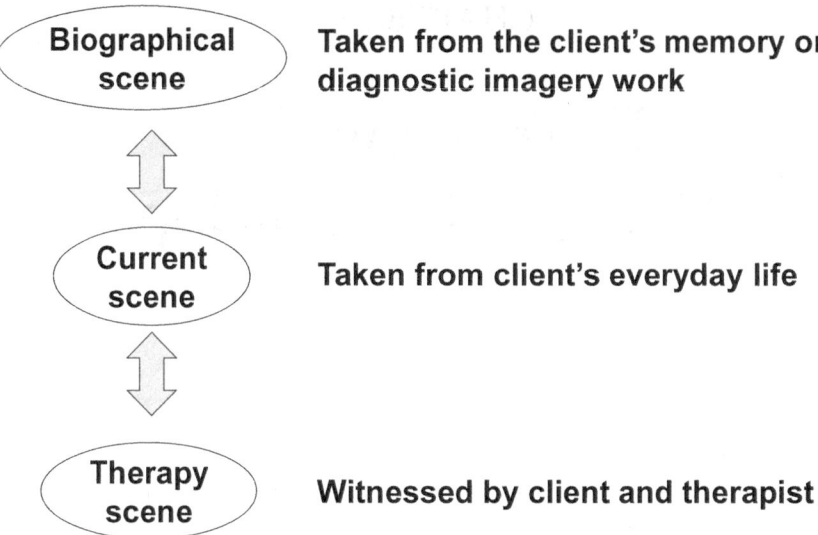

Figure 5–1. Connecting the biographical, current life, and therapy scenes

These three sources are all important to understanding the progress of therapy. Water is the same whether it's a drop or a large lake, and so we can assume that an incident recalled in therapy reveals underlying interactional patterns common to those in the client's life outside therapy.

Daniel was in therapy for relationship difficulties. He had separated from his third wife and wanted more insight into what was leading to "Why did she leave me?" In sessions, there were long monologues about perceived insults. Eventually, his therapist gently challenged him: "I notice you often talk at me, hardly waiting for me to respond. Was this how you talked to your wife when you got home from work?" When they explored Daniel's family background, he revealed that he received approval from his parents when he showed precocious knowledge and was called a "little professor."

Connecting the micro with the macro, seen in this example, is roughly comparable to transference-focused approaches. The client brings earlier experiences of significant others, which provide a blueprint of what to expect in a relationship. Similarities between the scenes affect perception, judgment, and reactions. This means that we often fail to see the other person, instead seeing our interpretation. In psychodynamic therapy, this has been called projection. We cannot escape this cycle of expectation and interpretation. However, identifying the sources in life experience and the dynamics in underlying schemas (the macrolevel) can help the client to escape from endlessly repeating old patterns, or "life traps," in today's interactions (on the microlevel).

Kosslyn, Thompson, Kim, and Alpert (1995) provided an appropriate analogy for this blind spot, arguing that about 90 percent of what we perceive from a picture in an art gallery derives from inner information processing, and only 10 percent derives from the picture itself. At the macrolevel, we can see that our entrenched schema-based patterns drive our personal reaction tendencies. It is almost impossible to escape precognitive emotions that tend to emotionally hijack us (Goleman, 1995). This leads us to conclude that there is a need to distance from the current microsituation and identify the underlying patterns on the macrolevel. Doing so requires shifting to an observer's perspective, for which we need the healthy adult mode.

Margie found that her emotional reactivity was linked to fear of abandonment (her schema). She came to understand that being left for long periods as a young child set her up to react to anything that might indicate that she was being left—no matter how briefly. Her therapist confirmed this: "It was dangerous; you were right to react. But now you may be misreading a situation." Margie recalled the previous weekend, when her husband wanted to take their son fishing for a few hours. She said, "It felt like they were both leaving me and would never come back!" This feeling was triggered when she saw them getting into the car and driving down the road (microlevel). "I can now see that the feeling was familiar, from my childhood (macrolevel), but they weren't really leaving—so my fear wasn't reality based."

Once we are familiar with the schemas on the macrolevel, we can understand and accept reaction tendencies but manage and downregulate the impulses toward a more considered and functional action (see "The Emotional Tolerance Window," in chapter 1) in a kind of "cortical override" (Siegel, 1999).

Balancing the Therapy Relationship in General

So far, we have described the overall goal that we try to achieve within the therapy relationship. The relationship works as a laboratory in which we activate patterns on the microlevel (in session) and relate them to patterns discovered on the macrolevel. The therapy relationship is the object as well as the means that we base our process on.

Therapy is a balancing act. Therapists walk on a tightrope, with two fundamental dimensions we have to balance (figure 5–2). We need to balance the level of emotional activation (the vertical axis); we've labeled the poles of this axis "self-actualization" (Millon, 1990) and "self-reflection," and the axis represents a balancing of emotional engagement and mentalization, along with helping to put feelings into words and connect them with the case conceptualization. In acceptance and commitment therapy (ACT) terms, the poles are "self-as-process" versus "self-as-context." We also balance support, acceptance, and validation with confrontation and challenging our clients to induce further development or change (the horizontal axis). In schema terms, the poles are "reparenting" and "empathic confrontation." Like a map, figure 5–2 gives you direction for which way you can direct the therapy relationship to get the best therapeutic results.

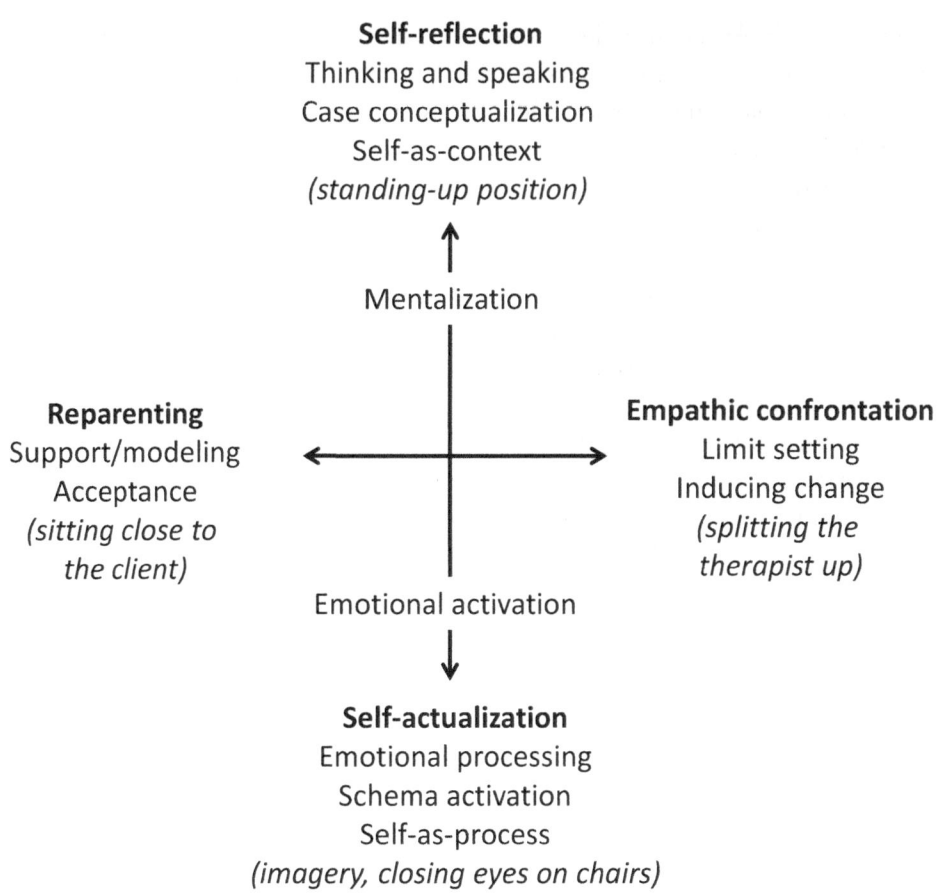

Figure 5–2. The dimensions of the therapy relationship

If a client remains entangled in ruminating and fused thoughts, "take the emotional elevator down" to the pole of emotional activation by using experiential techniques. If your client is flooded by emotions, stop the process and "take the emotional elevator up" to the standing-up observer position, connecting the microsituation with your case conceptualization for an orientation and overview. When your client feels lost and helpless (for example, in the vulnerable child mode), be supportive in tangible ways, such as by sitting close to her and talking to her as you would to a real child. But when the process is stuck, use empathic confrontation to give therapy a push. The schema therapist needs to be flexible to balance these poles.

Balancing the Level of Emotional Activation

Schema therapy relies on emotional activation, which the therapist must first induce and then balance.

Inducing Emotional Activation

We begin with emotional activation, or the pole of self-actualization. This emotional intensity provides the energy required for change. Emotional activation in schema therapy brings a focus to the basic emotions of the child modes. In schema therapy we use several chairs to represent different parts of the self (or states of activation) and work with them (for details, see chapter 10). Thus, you can make internal dialogues visible in the therapy room. For example, ask the client to move to an additional chair labeled as "child mode chair" to indicate that you do not want to talk to the coping mode anymore. To increase your client's access to his child mode feelings, we suggest leaving the face-to-face position and sitting close to the client, talking with a very soft and warm voice (see figure 5–3). If your client still tries to turn his head to look at your face, you haven't found the perfect position yet. Move a little bit farther backward, and also encourage the client to close his eyes, because this will enable him to connect more deeply with the emotional world behind his everyday coping modes. The therapist in this position starts to shed the presence and intrusion of an "other" person, becoming something more like a good parental voice more easily integrated into the client's mind. Talking this way (as well as imagery work) creates a kind of "transference free space" (Zindel, 2009).

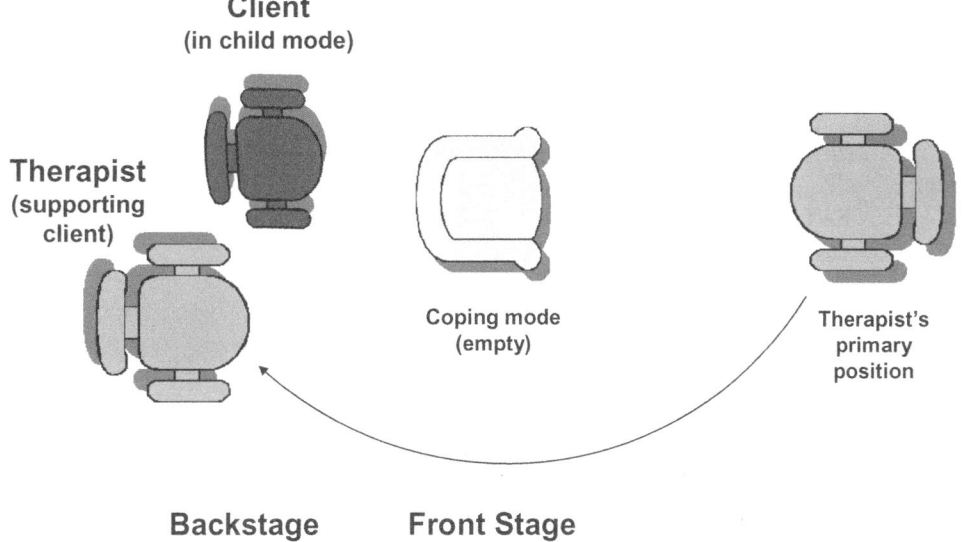

Figure 5–3. Sitting positions to support emotional activation

Having a focus on body sensations and feelings (especially in the chest and the stomach) helps the client to get in touch with the somatic representations of basic emotions, because basic emotions are closely connected with body sensations (Damasio, 1999). This complex pattern of activation is part of the macroscene. Floating back in imagery from this state usually brings up a vivid picture of an initial schema-inducing scene. You can both now agree on taking this scene (for example, "the abandoned child") as a symbol for the macroscene (or schema).

Improving Access to Soft Emotions

To improve your clients' access to soft emotions:

- Encourage them to close their eyes.

- Sit close to them.

- Talk in a very soft voice, using simple words, as you would talk to a child.

- Do not talk too much.

- Give your clients time to get in touch with their underlying emotions.

- Let clients take an open body position (no crossed arms or legs) and lean forward.

- Watch for physical indications of emerging emotions (eyes getting wet, changes in voice, deeper breathing, breaks in the flow of speech, changes in body posture).

- Amplify the small movements that your clients make unconsciously.

- Bring up an image of a painful situation.

- Focus clients' attention on the inside, especially on the chest and the stomach area.

- Offer the four basic emotions, and connect them with body sensations.

- Use imagery techniques, including a "float back" into childhood scenes in which maladaptive schemas formed, to access the patterns on the macrolevel.

Once you become more skilled at increasing the level of emotional activation, you can combine several techniques in order to gain maximum effect.

Making Use of Gestures and Bodily Changes in the Therapy Relationship

Schema therapy incorporates the nonverbal dimension of amplifying small movements. Attuning ourselves to signals, small movements, or body language in general can be a useful way of detecting hidden emotions or reactive tendencies (for example, those of the child modes). Consider the following brief case examples:

Mary, while talking about her mother, makes a dismissive movement with her hand, as if pushing someone away. Her therapist notices this and asks her to intentionally increase this movement. This helps Mary to get in touch with her anger and the hidden intention "to put the mother out of the way," drawing a clear boundary with her.

Tom squeezes his fingers while talking about his boss. The therapist asks him to focus on his fingers to amplify his fear.

Roger speaks fast and with a strong voice about his argument with his wife. Nevertheless, he always tries to remain "objective." Pointing this out helps Roger become aware of his hidden disgust and anger.

Susan pretends that everything is fine, but she bows her head and looks at the floor. Her therapist encourages her to intensify her posture. Then she starts to cry.

In these examples, we see clearly how small body movements can indicate underlying schemas, and how drawing attention to the movements can be therapeutically beneficial.

Changing postures. Besides reacting to clients' spontaneous expressions, we can also induce movements actively. We can, for example, encourage body changes that bring feelings from the bottom up. We can also guide their attention and thoughts and, in that way, influence their emotions from the top down. Schema therapy uses both channels in a systematic way, and this method has become an essential part of the extended schema therapy application described in this book.

Try it for yourself. Stand up and stretch, as if trying to keep your head above water. Take a powerful body posture (power posing). This can help you to connect to your resources and shift from an emotional to a self-reflective state. Or, even more simply, force a smile and try to feel depressed at the same time. It just doesn't work!

Using Perspective Changes to Cool Emotions Down

There is a close link between personal meaning and lasting change. Such change requires us to embed what we experience emotionally in a consistent self-concept (Lieberman et al., 2007). This thinking is in line with the results of the Boston Change Process Study Group, suggesting that "the gestalt of implicit experience, emergent reflective verbalization, and the relation between these two…together…make up meaning" (2008, p. 144). It is important to combine the level of implicit emotional activation and explicit meaning making in a compassionate, supportive relationship. The schema therapy case formulation guides the therapy process on a reflective level, serving as a framework for the corrective emotional experiences in the therapy relationship.

Therapist Tip: Drawing a mode map on a whiteboard or a sheet of paper, or using a prepared form like the mode map, creates a joint perspective and establishes the working alliance. Once you have mapped out the various active modes, you can add chairs for the relevant modes. This will make the case formulation concrete in the therapy room. After making the modes visible in the therapy room by putting them on a number of chairs, you can try taking another stance. Try standing up, side by side, with your client and watching the "game" unfolding on the chairs below (see figure 5–4). You are both "floating" above the problem, looking in the same direction in a joint perspective with the problem before you, forming a "reflecting (or consulting) team" (Anderson, 1987).

Joint perspective. We adopt a joint perspective to encourage the client to talk about herself as if she was a different person. *Changing our language* supports this perspective shift. The first- and second-person perspectives "send the emotional elevator down" (figure 5–2) and increase emotions, while the third-person perspective "lifts it up" and helps the client to distance from the emotions.

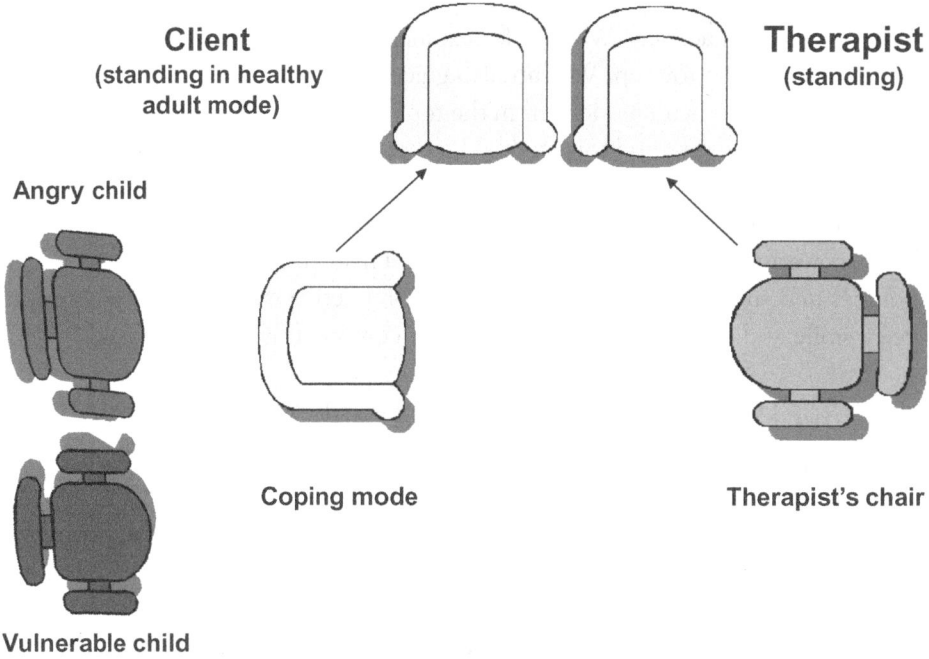

Figure 5–4. Therapist and client positions while reflecting on the process in a working alliance

Disactualization. Consider your stance. The goal of the standing position is to avoid being drowned in the emotional flood. Teasdale and colleagues (2002) call this disactualization. It is achieved by being mindfully aware of our thoughts and feelings ("being" mode while standing up) but abstaining from taking action ("doing" mode, seated on chairs). Establishing an internal observer is essential to getting out of schema activation and shifting into healthy adult mode. Standing up and looking down on the scene on the chairs below supports this kind of emotional distancing. This is the client's starting point to defuse her thinking and regain cognitive flexibility, identify the activated microscene, and relate it to the mode map framework. Once the microscene is contextualized, the client can connect it with the macroscene behind it.

A case vignette. Here is an extended example showing in detail how to guide the disactualization process. Tom comes into the session very depressed and paralyzed.

Tom: I can't go on like this…

Therapist: Okay, but could you please tell me what has happened? [The microscene]

Tom: We had a meeting yesterday, and my boss put down my business plan in front of the whole team.

Therapist: Well, this is really hard. If you close your eyes now and let the image come up in your mind again, how do you feel?

Tom: I feel devastated, like a piece of sh—!

Therapist: I see. Although it might be hard for you to stay in this terrible scene, how does it make you feel in your body?

Tom: I feel like a concrete wall's coming tumbling down on me. No air to breathe. Totally trapped!

Therapist: Stay in touch with those feelings and allow yourself to float back to a much earlier time in your life…maybe all the way back to your childhood…and let an image of yourself as a child come into your mind. What do you see?

Tom: *(After a few seconds)* I see myself in the classroom. The teacher tears the paper with my first words into pieces, saying I'd better leave school and go back to kindergarten. [Dependence-incompetence schema on the macrolevel]

Therapist: Well done. This is a macroscene behind the scene today. Now let's stand up and look at the scene together. *(Both stand up, side by side.)* Let's put the modes that we've found on the chairs. You came here today in a paralyzed coping mode. In the image, we got in touch with the vulnerable side and

	your underlying dependence-incompetence schema. Now we know the background scene, too. But what to do? If you look down on the scene now, how do you feel?
Tom:	I can feel some anger, too. But I can see now that the anger is basically directed to the teacher, not to the boss. This helps me to cool down a bit.
Therapist:	So now you see what's really going on here, and you start to understand that Tom's actually reacting to a very old memory rather than to his boss. This is the main reason he feels so devastated. If you could give him a piece of advice as a good friend, what would you suggest he could do to make the best out of the situation?

Dealing with ruptures in therapy. While being connected with your client on the healthy adult level, you can talk about conflicts or ruptures on the mode level while "floating above" the chairs as well. This also works if there is any break in the working alliance. Stand up together, shift into the third person, create a joint perspective, look down on the activated modes on the chairs below, and try to repair the rupture from the conjoint healthy adult level by saying something like this: "It looks as if the therapist moved too fast and lost the client. What does the client need now to reconnect again?" Talking in third-person language and looking down on the chairs together makes reconnection much easier. Give it a try!

Furthermore, perspective changes in the "therapy lab" support behavioral changes outside the sessions because they involve not only mental processes but body movements, too. Hence, we support clients to stand up, take a break, and walk a few paces when they feel trapped in a conversation in their everyday life.

Resource Activation Using Extension and Substitution Techniques

Once the client regains some cognitive flexibility—for example, by standing up—try to encourage cognitive reappraisal. Traditional cognitive therapy primarily uses purely cognitive strategies, such as identifying information biases, identifying formal errors in thought operations and logical inconsistencies, and probability checks (Beck, 1967). When we achieve perspective changes using therapeutic actions that might be considered "impact techniques" (Beaulieu, 2006), change is embodied. This is probably more effective than using purely cognitive maneuvers.

It is always easier to shift into an already existing thinking pattern than to create a new way of thinking. Clients usually bring some helpful resources to therapy but can remain in an emotional gridlock, in which they cannot access those resources. Impact techniques help to unblock the resources.

We now introduce two ways to achieve a perspective change: extension and substitution.

EXTENSION TECHNIQUE

In the extension technique, the therapist asks the client to take on the perspective of another person (for example, a friend), while both therapist and client stand above the client's chair.

1. You both stand side by side, looking down on the chairs.

2. Ask for the name of your client's best friend, and address the best friend directly (make the scene as real as possible):

    Therapist: Welcome, Sue. I'm happy that you're here to help us out. You know Mary quite well. What's she feeling right now? Why is she reacting like that? Does that happen in other situations, too? What do you think she really needs?

3. Ensure that your client actually shifts into the perspective of the best friend and talks about "the client on the chair" in the third person. This encourages the client to be fully present on the observer level:

    Therapist: Sue, now that we understand a bit better what Mary feels and what she actually needs, do you have any idea how she could deal with the situation better?

4. Once your client develops a promising strategy, ask her to convey the strategy to the "client on the chair":

    Therapist: I think this is actually a good idea. Can you suggest this to Mary sitting down there on the chair?

5. If your client feels fine with her proposal in the Sue position, ask her to take a seat on the Mary chair again to implement the solution you found on the process level. Sit close by her:

    Therapist: Mary, you heard what Sue said. How does that make you feel? Do you trust her? Do you want to give it a try?

    Now you can shift into a role-play, trying to solve the initial situation in a realistic way.

You will be surprised by how well this technique works! Usually, your client will activate inner images of the friend and then make a serious effort to step into the friend's shoes. If you cannot identify a close friend (some borderline clients lack good friends), you can introduce a friendly observer, a personal hero, or a well-known wise person, such as Gandalf from *The Lord of the Rings*. If that does not work, then you can make some suggestions in your role as therapist.

SUBSTITUTION TECHNIQUE

In the substitution technique, the therapist replaces the client on the child mode chair with a "real" child, such as one of the client's offspring, to activate the client's hardwired caretaking circuits.

1. Start by standing side by side with your client, looking down on the chairs.

2. If your client has children, ask him to nominate one of them. If not, let him name a child he knows well and likes.

3. Replace the client's child mode on the chair level with the image of the real child. Then ask him to look at this child "from the outside":

    Therapist: Ron, if you see this child, Brian, treated so badly, what do you feel toward the person treating him this way?

    This will usually bring up vicarious anger and an urge to protect the child.

4. Validate your client's emotions:

    Therapist: Looking at your anger, is it justified?

    This helps the client to accept that his anger is justified (especially for submissive or avoidant clients having difficulty unblocking healthy and constructive anger).

5. After connecting your client with his assertiveness need and powering through his anger, try to activate a sense of compassion for the child in front of him:

    Therapist: If you look at Brian right now, what do you feel toward him? Is there anything you would like to say to him or maybe do for him?

6. Once the full spectrum of caring emotions is active, try to shift the feelings from the substituted child to the child mode of your client by adding a chair for the child mode:

    Therapist: If you look at little Ron, being the same age as Brian, having the same feelings and needs, what do you feel toward him now?

7. If your client hesitates to show the same feelings, be persistent:

    Therapist: What makes little Ron different from little Brian?

    Inner critic thoughts will probably show up. They can be identified, labeled, and sorted out on an inner critic mode chair on the chair level below. Now you can continue with a chair dialogue between the inner critic mode chair and the vulnerable child mode of Ron, as described in detail in chapter 10.

8. If your client can now overcome his emotional distance from his child mode (on the chair below) and be sympathetic, you can train him in self-compassion. It can be helpful to record this in an audio "flash card."

9. In a final step, to strengthen the new behavioral pattern, ask your client to sit down on the client chair, placing yourself close by, and ask how it feels hearing this healthy adult mode voice now. When your client feels weary outside therapy sessions, he can listen to the audio flash card again.

Distancing from Emotional Activation

To help your client distance from emotional activation, try one or more of the following:

- Actively stop the process.

- Change to the standing-up observer's perspective.

- Put modes on several chairs, making them visible in the room.

- Connect the emotional process to the case conceptualization.

- Move to the standing position and get closer to your client, or take some steps back together (body movements induce mental movements).

- Use third-person language while talking about the chairs below.

- Use the extension technique to broaden the perspective and access blocked resources.

- Use the substitution technique to induce self-compassion and supportive behavior.

- Do not allow your client to remain stuck. Give him or her support while looking for possible solutions, offering your own experience.

- Strengthen the client's mentalization skills.

Improving Mentalization

Mentalization (Fonagy et al., 2004) is a key for therapy and healthy adult functioning. It enables us to connect feelings with words as a prerequisite for self-understanding and stepping into another person's shoes. However, doing so requires us to step back from the problem-solving or doing mode and to shift into a more not-knowing stance (Fonagy et al., 2004) or into "creative helplessness" (Hayes et al., 2012) while remaining emotionally connected with our client.

Mentalization-inducing questions include the following:

- What triggered your feelings?
- What did you feel in your body?
- What thoughts were running through your head?
- What was your intention at that point?
- What did actually happen?
- What do you really need?
- What do you think the other person felt while you did that?
- How did you expect this person to react?
- How would you have felt, standing in this person's shoes?
- How would you have probably reacted yourself?
- I have the impression you might feel a bit sad. How does that resonate with you?

Mentalization creates bridges between people's minds. It encourages the development of language to synchronize our mental processes, merging them into one shared perspective (Siegel, 1999). Through mentalization, the interpersonal perspective comes into play. In conflicts, for example, this perspective provides a good starting point for finding solutions.

Balancing Reparenting and Empathic Confrontation

In this section, we examine how to balance reparenting techniques with empathic confrontation.

The Principle of Limited Reparenting

Schema therapy likens the process of therapy to raising children. Thus, one key concept is reparenting (the left pole in figure 5–2). We believe that this concept may prove to be an important milestone in the development of psychotherapy generally. Nevertheless, there are precedents: Ferenczi (1932/1988) observed that some clients appeared to be so needy that it seemed as though they needed to be adopted by their therapists.

However, emphasizing reparenting is provocative and against the trend in therapeutic circles. Freud developed the notion of abstinence in psychoanalysis, comparing the therapist with a surgeon who tries to keep the operating theater sterile (see Ivey, 2010). Freud's ideal was to keep the therapy setting free from "contamination," which he conceived as input from the therapist. Because the founders of cognitive therapy (Beck, 1967; Ellis, 1969) were originally trained in psychoanalysis, they probably favored Socratic approaches over more directive forms of intervention.

Indeed, the idea of limited reparenting differs significantly from the working alliance in CBT to include a much deeper emotional involvement of the therapist as a real person. In a sense, we must give a little bit of ourselves to our clients, relating to them in a very personal way. Without this, their core emotional needs will not be met through the therapy relationship. Our clients need to *feel* warmth and authenticity from us as therapists. In this way, the schema therapist espouses many of the essential therapist qualities described by Rogers (1951). However, perhaps in contradiction to Rogers, schema therapists must balance these "warm" tasks with also being far more active and goal directed. Schema therapists will use the full spectrum of tools available, from supportive attunement to powerful limit setting. The breadth of their interventions and their flexibility in using them makes schema therapy a very dynamic and effective therapy.

The quality of the therapy relationship has proven to have a strong influence on outcomes (see, for example, Lambert, 2013). Evidence suggests that schema therapy has comparatively low dropout rates (Jacob & Arntz, 2013). In a comparison of major borderline personality disorder treatments, schema therapy demonstrated less than half the dropout rate of other treatments (table 5–1). Something clearly keeps clients engaged in schema therapy, and we think it is the intensity of therapeutic involvement.

Table 5–1. Dropout rates in borderline personality disorder treatments

Type of Therapy	Dropout Rate	Confidence Interval
Schema therapy (Jacob & Arntz, 2013)	10.1%	95% CI 3.7–24.7
Dialectical behavior therapy (Kliem, Kröger, & Kosfelder, 2010)	23%	95% CI 16.6–30.8
Transference-focused therapy (Clarkin, Levy, Lenzenweger, & Kernberg, 2007; Doering et al., 2010)	34.9%	95% CI 26.6–44.3
Mentalization-based treatment (Bateman & Fonagy, 1999, 2009)	24.8%	95% CI 16.9–34

The Need for Reparenting

New learning experiences work best when our client's emotional activation remains within the window of emotional tolerance (for details, see chapter 1). One way to limit the amount of emotional activation is by standing together and looking down on the scene from a distanced perspective. The cost is that the client emotionally disengages and steps away from the process level. This is safe, but can lead to experiential avoidance. A second option to cool down overshooting emotional activation is to keep clients emotionally activated while supporting them through reparenting. This helps clients overcome experiential avoidance and provides them with a corrective experience on an emotional level.

The two pathways work by using different channels of information processing: the observer stance through contextualization and explicit processing on a metacognitive level, and reparenting by mentalizing the emotional processing in a more implicit way. Since both approaches create a connection with the complementary system, they build the bridge from both ends by linking emotional experiencing with cognitive processes. We now examine how reparenting works in detail.

Reparenting means maintaining an emotional connection by giving your client the feeling of being "seen" and unconditionally accepted. Clients matter, and we want to help them. Open questions invite clients to engage in the process and induce mentalization. Paradoxically, slowing down the therapy process may result in faster progress. Reparenting requires that the therapist balances validating where the client is at ("Change is hard") with encouraging incremental change ("Let's give it a try").

Indeed, Miller (2000) related therapeutic feelings to one kind of nonsexual love (in Greek, *agape*), which is comparable to the loving emotions parents have for their children. Parents see in their children what they can become and not (only) what they already are. Children grow up better under loving eyes. The schema therapy relationship is devoted to this ideal, too. A schema therapy relationship is a real relationship—within the boundaries of therapy, of course. This relating includes making mistakes. How we deal with our mistakes and how we try to repair ruptures in therapy will serve as a model for our clients.

Therapist Self-Disclosure and Involvement

Acting as a real person includes at least partly revealing true personal emotions. Jim McCullough (2000) proposed "disciplined personal involvement" in his cognitive behavioral analysis system of psychotherapy (CBASP). This overlaps with our idea of self-disclosure. We believe it is important to judiciously share personal feelings and some personal experiences related to our clients' experiences. This has the potential to normalize their experiences, reducing guilt and shame, and to provide a sense of shared suffering that can promote safety, connection, and compassion.

Roy was struggling with panic attacks. His therapist shared that she had an experience of overwhelming panic while presenting at an international conference: "I felt very exposed and wanted to hide."

Showing vulnerability provides a link to the attachment system, to connect our pain to the pain of others, which can result in an improved sense of validation and connection. Thus, self-disclosure is another source of modeling that gives our client insight into our mental processes as far as they concern the client. If done well, it increases respect and trust. In inpatient, day-clinic, or other group settings, other clients can contribute tremendously to a sense of the universality of suffering, and the group thus can become a source of limited reparenting (Farrell & Shaw, 2012; Yalom, 1983).

Naturally, it is important that we ground the feelings and experiences that we share in truth and that they are not phony. Be honest! A client might start the session with something like "Oh, you're looking a bit tired today. Are you okay?" Don't deny it if there is some truth in the client's concern. Don't give your life story, but an appropriate reaction might be to say, "Well observed! You're right. I'm struggling with some personal problems. This has nothing to do with you or our therapy, and I'll still try to do my best in our session today. Thanks for asking." Self-disclosure reveals that everybody struggles to some extent, because we are human. This is reassuring. We journey through life, starting from different points but often dealing with similar issues. We don't need to be perfect to provide a model of the healthy adult dealing with stress. The act of self-disclosure might include taking some deep breaths to get out of a current schema activation, standing up to get a new perspective, taking a short time-out if overwhelmed, or just committing: "I'm irritated right now. Give me a minute. What just happened here between us? Where are we now in terms of modes?".

There are, of course, important limits to self-disclosure. It must be brief, not take the focus off your client, and respect the ethical boundaries of the therapeutic setting. Our goal is not to be an actual parent but to give clients a consistent yet small dose of what has been missing in their life, kick-starting a sense of needs satisfaction and their emotional development. It is not easy for us to keep the balance, so intensive video-based supervision is essential in schema therapy training (Roediger & Laireiter, 2013). This process also helps us recognize that we have schemas ourselves (Leahy, 2001), which can distort therapy. This understanding is familiar from psychodynamic therapies, which recognize transference and countertransference dynamics.

Fine-Tuning Reparenting and Empathic Confrontation

Should dependence on the therapist be avoided? This is a crucial question, because many therapists are afraid of encouraging any degree of dependence, but it is natural in the reparenting model of schema therapy. No good parent would abstain from offering support and help to a young child. Clients in a child mode are in an equally helpless emotional state. Indeed, it is only when the infant's needs for attachment and safety are consistently met that healthy emotion regulation can develop.

There is a natural developmental process that occurs in schema therapy over time. First, the therapist offers reparenting, and then, second, clients' own healthy adult mode will lead them to naturally develop their own autonomy. The therapist as "parental figure" must be attuned to this shift, because later in therapy, empathic confrontation, limit setting, and challenging the client become important, and their use in therapy parallels the course of personality development, from infancy through adolescence and eventually to adulthood.

Amanda was severely traumatized as a young child. Her mother was a heroin addict who had a succession of partners. Amanda first entered therapy when she started cutting herself at age fifteen. She needed weekly therapy for a number of years, but gradually her suicidal crises became less frequent and she was better able to manage her impulsivity and low moods. But, as her therapist reflected, "Amanda needed years of therapy to meet safety and attachment needs. She learned to trust, but that was only the beginning."

During the reparenting phase, it is important that we balance being directive with giving space to our clients (for example, by asking open questions to induce mentalization processes). We encourage you to ask your clients how they experience therapy. Usually, they feel deeply understood and well guided, not dominated or subjugated (De Klerk, Abma, Bamelis, & Arntz, 2017). However, it's important to be aware of the risks. A schema therapist can become too dominant in the relationship, hindering the developing autonomy of the client. The developmental needs of each client need to be tracked over time on a case-by-case basis. Effective reparenting balances the more caring maternal parenting mode with a parental mode that challenges the client (Lockwood & Perris, 2012).

> *Principle:* Do not do anything for your clients that they can do for themselves, but do not let them remain swamped, and step in immediately if they need support.

Joanne's Micro- to Macropattern and Therapist Balance

After about six months of schema therapy, the therapeutic bond between Joanne and her therapist was growing. Joanne rarely went into her coping modes during sessions, and the therapy seemed to be progressing well. However, as the therapeutic bond became stronger, Joanne became increasingly anxious about the consistency and frequency of the sessions. She started demanding more and more contact (emails, extra sessions, longer sessions). An obvious pattern was unfolding in therapy, compensating for the abandonment she had experienced when her father or husband would go away for work.

This led to a dilemma. While the therapist wanted to give Joanne more time and consistency through reparenting, the more he gave, and the more she would take, because she found it difficult to find consistency in her level of care (abandonment schema). There was no point in giving more and more. Clearly, she needed empathic confrontation. The following dialogue illustrates how the therapist applied empathic confrontation to set a limit on the client's increasing demands for more reparenting, thus rebalancing the left-to-right axis of the therapy relationship (see figure 5–2).

Therapist: Joanne, there's something I wish to talk about today that I think is very important to us and to our therapy together.

Joanne: Okay, this sounds bad…

Therapist: Nothing bad, or scary… You know that sometimes it's important for me to be more direct about what happens in the room, because it can help provide an opportunity to link what happens in therapy to real-life stuff.

Joanne: Sure…

Therapist: Okay. I've noticed something happening between us as therapy has progressed, and it has progressed well. You've really started opening up, and you have become more comfortable here. You've been able to bring issues to discuss in therapy and talk about your needs and feelings. And you've become better and better at showing me what you need. And that's really great! And I really try to help you get your needs met, 'cause that's a really important experience I want you to have in our therapy. I know that you've not always had a space like this in your life, where you can share your needs and feelings and someone actually listens to you and takes you seriously. On the other hand, I sometimes get the feeling that you get quite anxious in terms of maybe not getting enough time or even attention. You know? As if you wanted to get more and more time in therapy, either by planning extra sessions or by making our sessions last longer or even by contacting me via email. Do you know what I'm talking about?

Joanne: Yes. I like coming to therapy. I find that it has really helped, but I feel like there is too much time between sessions and I need you to be there to help me at other times, when you aren't available, and it makes me feel panicked sometimes. But the more time I spend with you, the more it helps, you know?

Therapist: I know it does help soothe little Joanne when she feels lonely or even insecure about my availability, so it helps to settle her down when she reaches out, right?

Joanne: Right.

Therapist: And there's a very nice side to that, and I can also understand why it feels like that's what you need to do. But there's another side of it too… I think I start to get a sense of why your friends often pull away. Perhaps they start to feel a little burned out if you start to rely on them too much to support you. What do you think?

Joanne: That always happens in the end. Everyone leaves me.

Therapist: That's right. I think sometimes it feels like you want more and more to settle down the painful feelings [Note: Behavior points to the vulnerable child mode on the case conceptualization], but it can be too much for people, you know? And in the end they pull away.

Joanne: Yes, then I'm alone again.

Therapist: And I get the feeling that this is happening now in some way between us. And although I'm a little afraid of hurting your feelings or being too harsh on you, I really want to be honest with you and show you how I'm feeling. I think it's very important for us to work on getting your needs met here in therapy, but that it's just like out there in the real world: there's a limit to what people can do. And I want you to be able to recognize when you push too hard to get your needs met, even though I can understand it.

Joanne: Sure. I'm such an idiot. I'm just too needy. [Note: Punitive critic mode]

Therapist: I don't think you deserve to beat yourself up over this. I think it's only natural that little Joanne wants to connect, because it has been really hard for her to connect and have stability in this. But I do wonder if we can negotiate about my availability and what might be a healthy level of contact between sessions…a level that's sustainable?

It is important to go beyond the cognitive level when reparenting. Applying empathic confrontation is sometimes the only way to help clients become "unstuck" in therapy. The therapist must emphasize emotional activation and then look for a workable solution. Doing so involves a delicate balance. As previously indicated, face-to-face therapy can activate prior negative experiences. Thus, we have to look for ways to bring critical and confronting messages into the therapy room without pushing our client into automatic maladaptive coping modes.

Fine-Tuning the Therapist's Balance Using Motivational Interviewing

Motivational interviewing, as proposed by Miller and Rollnick (2002), demonstrates a good balance in the therapy relationship that we can use in schema therapy. In the first edition of their book, they outlined their balancing strategies with the acronym FRAMES:

- *Feedback:* Give your client clear feedback about your observations, concerns, feelings, or impulses (self-disclosure); neglected aspects of the situation; or possible consequences, as a good friend would. This means taking a step to the left in figure 5–2 by offering something to the client.

- *Responsibility:* Point out that this feedback comprises just *your* perspective and concerns (and that you might distance from the client as parents distance from their children if they show unwanted behavior), and that the client, as an adult, is responsible for personal actions. This means movement to the right in figure 5–2.

- *Advice:* Like a parent (or a friend), do not wait on the sidelines for the client to develop a solution. Picture yourself at a new workplace, learning to drive a car, or at a piano lesson: Would you not expect some advice from a teacher or trainer? In the same way, therapists make use of their expertise by offering ideas on how to deal with a situation. This is essential if your client is having difficulties coping. Being supportive means a movement to the left in figure 5–2.

- *Menu of techniques:* We never tell clients what to do; instead, the choice is left to them. Giving space this way means another movement to the right in figure 5–2. People like having choices, which meets their autonomy needs. Maybe this is why supermarkets offer forty different kinds of toothpaste! In the therapy sequence, we might start giving them feedback about the potential outcome and consequences of their choice.

- *Express empathy:* This might sound self-evident. However, many therapists do not use the full power of expressing empathy. Think about how parents respond to the first steps of an infant: for them, it is like watching the first footstep on the moon! But this reaction is natural, and children respond well and continue learning to walk as a result. Therefore, we encourage you to praise your client, even extravagantly, especially at the beginning of therapy. Doing so also soothes their attachment needs, strengthens the therapeutic bond, and increases self-efficacy.

- *Support self-efficacy:* The experienced level of self-efficacy is the strongest predictor of a good outcome in therapy (Bandura, 1977). Even if we start being directive at the beginning of therapy, on the left pole of the spectrum (see figure 5–2), the ultimate goal of therapy is to increase successful self-regulation and autonomy in our client. Thus, we have to strengthen their assertiveness step-by-step. This works best in the healthy adult "laboratory" that is therapy. From making suggestions and proposals early in therapy, we gradually shift to asking clients about their own ideas and help them to practice new skills between sessions. Initially, we motivate through praise, but over time it is the experience of success and efficacy in real life that will provide longer-term intrinsic motivation.

Therapist Tip: What could go wrong when you express empathy in a more enthusiastic way? The worst case is that the client regards your praise as exaggerated or phony. Then you can cut back, saying something like "Okay, I might have chosen words that were too strong when saying that it was great you did your homework this week. But I actually know how difficult it is to remember what we agreed to in the session and then to do it during the week. So I really appreciate your efforts to change things and just want to convey this to you."

Making Progress by Bringing Perspective Change

When working with low-functioning clients, it makes a lot of sense that the therapist would take a more active role, serving as a role model for the healthy adult. In these cases, therapy needs to be less Socratic (Brockman & Calvert, 2016), at least in the early stages of treatment (Arntz & Jacob, 2013). However, more functional clients are able shift into healthy adult mode, finding solutions themselves. We suggest a sequence of interventional steps that are dependent on the strength of the client's resources or healthy adult mode:

1. Change to the observer's perspective

2. Use the extension technique (best friend, wise mind)

3. Use the substitution technique (replace the child mode with the client's child)

4. Embody the therapist as a role model

In these steps, the locus of control (Rotter, 1966) moves from the client to the therapist. Less-functional clients, at least at the beginning of therapy, need us to perform the healthy adult mode functions first in an imagery or role-play exercise. An important goal of any schema therapy work is to bring the session to a good end, providing a corrective emotional experience, and to achieve this it is sometimes necessary for us to adopt a more active role, as is shown in the following case example:

In an imagery exercise, Joanne found herself as a small child waking up in her bed after vomiting. She went to her mother's bed, asking for help. Her mother refused to help, staying in bed and giving the excuse of a headache. The therapist entered the scene and told the mother that she acted irresponsibly by leaving her daughter alone in the dirty bed and that a good mother would not do that. After the exercise, she asked the client how she felt, and she answered, "Terrible!" The client said that her mother was sick and not able to help her, and that she should not make a fuss about it. She felt an urge to quit therapy.

This case vignette reveals two mistakes:

1. The therapist moved too quickly and ignored the inner critic modes of the client. Remember that the beliefs of the inner critic modes are often completely ego-syntonic, and that clients trust those voices more than their own feelings and needs, especially if they were "parentified" children trained to play a caring role for a parent. Having a strong inner critic mode helps, as we have noted, to reduce the inconsistency between the child and the expectations of the environment. In this way, there is an adaptive value. So it makes sense that many clients cannot easily change sides. Slow down the pace and explore the critical beliefs in some detail, put them on chairs, and take an observer's stance again to carefully reappraise them. Later in therapy, when the inner critic modes have been softened, you might impeach the caretakers successfully.

2. There was no caring for the child. It is always safer to begin imagery with the therapist actively reparenting the child, rather than confronting an inner critic (no matter how abusive the critic). Also, this strengthens the therapeutic bond.

Therapist Tip: There is a pitfall to consider. If you move too quickly, you might push your clients into a loyalty conflict with their deep convictions (in chair dialogues) or with their significant others (in imagery work). Your client might react badly and leave therapy.

Indeed, it is often easier to develop needed dissonance by looking at the long-term *effects* rather than the *content* of the inner critic mode voices. Sometimes the content is at least partly true, but the way it is applied to the child reveals its toxic potential. We recommend that you take an active role but do not exaggerate the emotional intensity of the impeachment. Instead, focus on the toxic effects of the inner critic modes. To prevent a rupture, you could ask for your client's beliefs, label them as inner critics, and put them on an extra chair to work with through a chair dialogue in the same or a future session. (We go into the details of how to apply chair dialogues and imagery in chapters 9 and 10.) If that had been done, the above case vignette might have taken a different turn.

Therapist: You can enter the scene as the adult person you are now. What do you feel?

Joanne: I feel sorry for my mother.

Therapist: Oh, this surprises me. I actually feel sorry for the child. What does the voice in your head say?

Joanne:	The voice says that the mother is sick herself and that the child should not make a fuss and should go back to bed.
Therapist:	This sounds like an inner critic voice taking more care for the mother than for the child. How does that voice make the child feel?
Joanne:	The child feels ashamed and guilty.
Therapist:	Oh, yes, I can feel that too! Let's keep these inner critic mode voices on our mind and work with them later. What I see is that they keep you from acknowledging the child's needs. Would it be okay if I took care of the child now?
Joanne:	If you feel the urge to do so.
Therapist:	Yes, I actually do! I don't want to judge the mother right now. Maybe you're right and she's too sick to care for the child. But then I would expect her to go and get some help. However, what I see is that the child is anxious and needs some soothing. Now I'm talking to you, little Joanne. You're a small child. You don't understand what happened in your body. This is nothing dangerous. You just ate something your body doesn't like. This is why your body is throwing it back out. You know? Just to protect you. It's not your fault. You've done nothing wrong. It just happens. Let me put a fresh blanket on your bed, give you some clean pajamas, and then invite you to come into my bed. How would you like that?
Joanne:	Oh, this feels good!
Therapist:	Right. This is just what every child needs. And you need it, too. That's totally normal! Now let me ask grown-up Joanne a question: If you look at little Joanne now, what do you feel?
Joanne:	You're right! She is a cute little girl. *(After a moment of hesitation)* You are a nice girl. It's not your fault. Come into my arms.
Therapist:	How does the child react?
Joanne:	She likes it. She leans her head on my shoulder.
Therapist:	How does that feel?
Joanne:	A bit strange, but not bad.
Therapist:	How does it make you feel in your body?
Joanne:	I get a warm feeling in my belly, and my chest feels wide.
Therapist:	That's great. This is how you can feel when your healthy adult mode cares for your needs. You get into a contented happy child mode.

Summary

In this chapter, we detailed how important it is for the schema therapist to be active, flexible, and highly involved. We offered a balance of theory and practical advice about how to do interventions in schema therapy. We also discussed the role of reparenting; the benefits of physically changing positions in the therapy room (such as standing up together or sitting beside or behind the client); and the need for perspective changes that encourage mentalization, resource activation, empathic confrontation, and therapeutic balance, as we illustrated with motivational interviewing.

CHAPTER 6

Dealing with Child, Inner Critic, and Coping Modes

In this chapter, we address the basic strategies for addressing maladaptive patterns resulting from client schemas. The focus is on the "theater" played out by child, inner critic, and coping modes. The therapist as stage director must learn to change the script and direct the mode actors. Changing the script involves gaining access to the child modes, where emotions and "hot" memories are found. These modes are mostly backstage but seriously affect what happens on the front stage. The coping modes are what we see on stage, but we have to bypass them to gain access to the client's unmet needs. We describe how to strengthen the healthy adult mode in the next chapter and go into detail about how to change the patterns using experiential techniques from chapter 8 onward.

> *Principle:* "A session spent solely on coping modes is a wasted session" is a mantra in schema therapy. We must bypass the coping modes.

Dealing with Coping Modes

To deal with coping modes, we must first identify and label them.

Identify and Label Coping Modes

We described the many aspects of coping modes in chapter 3. Now we offer some strategies for dealing with them. Some are basic, others more advanced. The suggested strategies listed below are not sequential steps, so try them in any order. They are part of a toolkit. Think about your therapeutic goals with each client and thoughtfully apply what you need to balance reparenting and empathic confrontation.

- *Label* the coping modes once you identify them: "Oh, the way you're sitting makes me wonder if you're in a detached protector mode."

- *Validate* the coping mode initially to strengthen the connection with the client before you say something critical: "I can fully understand your need for safety and protection. I assume you've found it by retreating into detached protector. Can you help me understand why you find it safer to stay there?"

- *Emotionally engage* by expressing your own feelings about how your schemas activate in response to your client: "If you talk to me in this sharp way, I feel intimidated. I think this is a sign that you're in one of the overcompensator modes, putting pressure on me!"

- *Remain connected* if your client threatens to leave therapy: "I realize you're not feeling good. Please help me to understand you better. Tell me what you're feeling."

- *Discriminate*: "Okay, you said you don't feel understood. But what do you see me doing right *now*?"

- *Look at the effects*, both intended and induced: "If you're so friendly to me, I might be reluctant to say something critical. To risk being direct might hurt our connection, but being too submissive will keep you stuck."

- *Note nonverbal signals*, which express emotional reactions. Note voice tone, body posture, tears, and small movements. Bring them to your client's attention and amplify them, if possible. They signal what the child modes are trying to say.

- *Regard psychosomatic symptoms as ambassadors of hidden child modes*: "What would your headache say if it was a person? What would it take to make you feel better? What would you do without it? What would you have to do if it wasn't there?"

- *Access core beliefs*: "What's the voice in your head saying?" Such talk is usually in the grammatical first person, such as "I feel under pressure"; "I have to perform"; "If I show feelings, I'll lose control."

- *Look closely at the pros and cons:* Spend a session really evaluating both sides of the coping mode, considering its adaptive value, both past and the present, and its negative impacts. Offer your client a chair for both aspects. It is important to acknowledge how the coping mode leads to problems or blocks your client from getting needs met. The goal is to activate and then to "do a deal" with the client's healthy adult mode. Though the client may often express ambivalence about the coping mode, there is always a part of the client that wants to get better and regain flexibility. You will need to get permission from the client to address the coping mode in this way, but, unfortunately, therapy will stagnate if you do not get that permission.

A "Visible" Case Formulation

We recommend using chairs in the therapy room to lay out your case formulation (for example, for the mode map from chapter 4, see figure 6–1). You might start with one chair representing a coping mode, such as detached protector. Then, identify the client's underlying core beliefs (inner critic modes) within the automatic thoughts that seem so natural, as well as the basic emotions (child modes) within the superficial social emotions. Once you have tracked them, sort out the inner critic mode beliefs and the child mode basic emotions and place them on two separate chairs behind the coping mode chair, as if each grouping of beliefs represented a different person. Representing the mode map with chairs conveys to the client that there is something "behind" superficial thoughts and emotions. After sorting out these internal representations on the chairs, you can start working with them on a kind of inner stage, taking different perspectives and letting them interact.

Creating a physical representation for hidden modes brings the formulation to life and symbolizes what we intend to explore with clients (through chair work and imagery). Standing together with a client behind several chairs can bring to life the dynamic interactions between mode states without the process being emotionally overwhelming for the client.

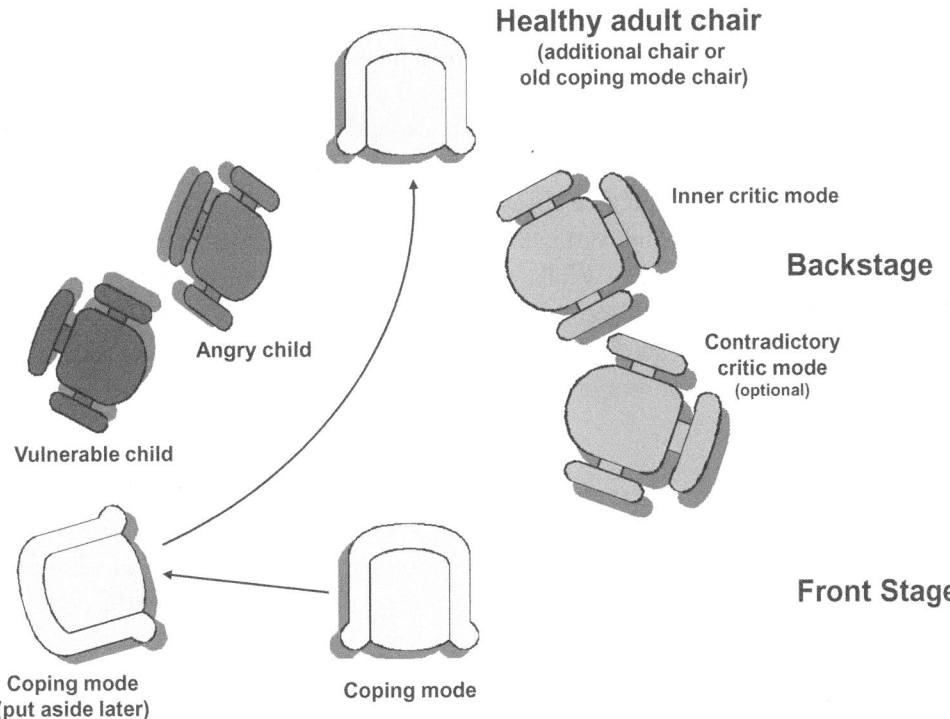

Figure 6–1. Chair positions according to the mode map

Consider how you might use the chairs to express common concerns that your client will bring to therapy. You can put the messages from the client's "voices in the head" on the inner critic chair, perhaps distinguishing punitive critic from demanding critic, and let them speak out to the child chair to see the child's emotional reactions. In this way, we can see the interaction and why the coping modes need to protect the child modes. We suggest placing the chairs according to the mode map so their positions in the room are consistent with those of the map.

Addressing Coping Modes

Accept that the coping modes have provided the best solution your client has found so far. Start by acknowledging that in the past, the coping modes functioned in important ways. However, when a coping mode gets rigid and fixed, it becomes maladaptive. Sometimes the way coping modes provide protection can be quite subtle. The hardest part of therapy may be helping the client to see that what appears to be rational and normal is actually avoidance.

Suzie was an academic suffering from feelings of emptiness and depression. Based on her standards, she sought out a cognitive therapist with a strong research profile. They had great talks and both shared the illusion of making good progress. But when it came time to end therapy, Suzie nevertheless felt left alone by the therapist. Unfortunately, both had the same coping mode of intellectualizing, which they failed to get beyond. Suzie's lonely child behind the detached protector did not become a target during the course of therapy.

Clients usually pretend or believe that maladaptive coping is their healthy adult mode. They will resist any therapeutic attempts to challenge the coping method. Don't talk with a coping mode, because this only reinforces it. Moving slowly while persistently trying to access the motivational backstage level is the most promising approach to dealing with coping modes. While remaining present and empathically supportive, you "pay into the relationship account." When the client feels connected, he or she will "pay you back" by opening up. This reciprocation develops as a result of mutual attachment systems, creating connection.

Bypassing Avoidant or Detached Coping Modes

Detached or avoidant coping modes are true chameleons in therapy. They are disguised in many different and sometimes subtle ways. Here are some expressions of the detached protector:

- Denying feelings, rationalizing, going too deeply into details
- Lack of concentration, answering "No idea," stopping talking altogether, dissociating
- Talking too much or in a rough or joking manner
- Bringing up new issues every session
- Coming late, not showing up, forgetting homework assignments

- Talking about psychosomatic symptoms or presenting pain
- Showing up drunk or on drugs
- Falling in love with the therapist

We recommend that you focus on the *here-and-now interaction*. You can name the detached protector while remaining emotionally supportive. You might try some of the following:

- If your client continues with surface *chattering* to avoid deeper emotions: "I know it isn't polite to interrupt you, but I want to draw your attention to our conversation over the past few minutes. If you try to summarize it, what's the core message?"
- If the client *remains detached* from emotions and gets lost in details: "I can appreciate that you think I have to know all the details about what's been going on, but I would like to feel what it meant to you."
- If your client is hiding behind a shell of *sarcastic humor*: "I see that you try to cope with your feelings by being strong, but I wonder if there's something behind this shell."
- If your client is sitting in a *withdrawn* way: "When I notice the way you're sitting, I ask myself if you are trying to protect yourself. Is it from me? This is okay, because you don't know me yet. And it makes a lot of sense, especially if you've been hurt before."

Reflect: How would you deal with a client seemingly stuck in detached protector mode?

Therapist Tip: In order to strengthen your connection with your clients, always validate them and their coping before saying something critical! Using empathy in response to a coping mode almost always softens what you say.

Now that we can appreciate the role of the coping modes in protecting the child modes, we can describe in detail how to bypass them. In chapter 13, we suggest additional strategies for dealing with more difficult cases, but many coping modes are not rigid and are surprisingly easy to bypass once you have identified and validated them. Here's a core strategy for interviewing a coping mode:

1. *Identify*, *label*, and *validate* the mode, as described above.
2. Ask how *long* the mode has *existed*. Add some additional validation: "If you can't remember when this mode came up, he must be very important for you. This means that we have to give him respect and really understand how he has helped you!"

3. Ask about the *purpose* of the mode (functional analysis):

    "What is the mode taking care of?"

    "What could happen if he wasn't here?"

    "What's the worst thing that could happen?"

    "What does the 'voice in your head' say now?"

    "What do we have to do in order to allow the avoiding or protecting mode ('the wall') to step aside for a few minutes so we can try something new that might work better?"

4. Based on the information from step 3, *summarize* the job description of the mode's coping style: "Okay, I understand that you have to carry on. You can't let [person's name] down. You risk getting hurt when you show feelings. Maybe nobody understands you anyway, and life is disappointing. Is that right so far?"

5. Ask for an *experiment* and invite the protector to return: "Can you please give me ten minutes to try something different? Maybe it will work and you'll discover something new. This gives you a choice—like two roads you can take. If it doesn't work, you can consider it useless. After the session, I'm happy if your coping mode comes back to keep you safe over the week. You can keep that coping style for as long as you need, until the new strategy works. But for now, I'll ask him to step aside, just for a moment."

Therapist Tip: Many clients fear losing their coping mode. Once let go, they worry it will be lost forever. Reassure them that the coping mode is welcome to return after the session. In fact, we feel safer knowing that our clients can return to their well-trained coping modes in order to make it to the next appointment.

There are various points of entry for bypassing a coping mode. You can choose to access the backstage through the voices of the inner critic or the emotions of the child modes. Use your clinical judgment as to which ones feel most relevant or most activated at the time in therapy.

Empathic Confrontation with the Submissive Client

We do not usually consider submissive clients to be difficult. The role of "nice client" comes easy, but such individuals can be very good at avoiding difficult emotional work. Therapy is not "rent a friend." As therapists, we need to know when therapy is stuck, to bring the energy needed to overcome experiential avoidance, and to encourage emotional engagement in the therapy process. According to our model, too much submission results in a dominance of the attachment need and a lack of assertiveness. Thus, the goal of the intervention is to put the client in touch with underlying blocked anger to make him or her capable of rebalancing again.

We do this by encouraging the client to take the "elevator" down toward self-actualization (see figure 5–2). Consider taking the initiative with the following intervention, in which we outline the typical sequential steps:

1. *Introduce your intention:* If your client does not present with something urgent, then you can take the lead and start the intervention: "Today, I'd like to talk with you about our therapy. You know that our work is a goal-directed and time-limited process. I want to reassess our progress together. If you look back over the last two months, what significant progress did you make to change behavior?"

    If your client is quickly activated, you reached your goal. You may consider a perspective change, such as standing up or asking the "best friend" a question, to soften the procedure and avoid being too confrontational. If the client remains stuck, continue confronting with slightly increasing intensity.

2. *Split yourself up:* "If you agree, I want to give you some insight into what I think. To make this safer for you and me, I'll put this 'bad therapist' on an extra chair beside me." Add an additional chair.

Therapist Tip: Avoid saying anything critical from your normal chair, which should remain clear for the "good therapist."

3. *The "bad therapist" confronts:* Be sure to sit on the other chair. "Okay, there's a part in me that's unhappy with how therapy is going. I feel paralyzed by the process so far, and we need to change things. My impression is that you try to avoid getting into deeper emotions and keep playing it safe. But this means we get nowhere. If we want to make progress, you'll need to become more active."

4. *The "good therapist" empathically supports:* Confrontation may distress your client, so move your normal "good therapist" chair quickly and sit down close behind the client in a supportive way (see figure 6–2). The "bad therapist" chair remains empty in front of the client in order to induce a reminder of this persona. "Okay, how do you feel when that impatient therapist over there talks that way to you? How does that resonate in your body? Please tell him how he makes you feel!"

    To try your best to support the client in releasing his blocked anger, you can push him by feeding him a line (Perls, 1973): "You're right! Don't be shy! He can stand that. Let it out; let your anger vent! What do you feel in your body now?" The idea is to unblock hidden anger within your client in order to work with the blocked basic emotion. This will trigger your client's anger. Constructive anger is the driver of assertiveness. It's like gas in a tank: no gas, no driving!

5. *Shift into solution-directed imagery work:* Once the constructive anger is unblocked, ask the client to close her eyes and picture a scene in which she can make her dreams come true. "Imagine everything is possible, like in a fantasy movie. What would you like to do with this energy you feel?" This helps to loosen cognitive fusion and indicate the next steps for therapy.

6. *Look for the first steps to take:* Once your client has an idea about what she would like to do, you can both stand up side by side as the "consultation team." Consider what concrete first steps the client might take in the next week to achieve value-based goals. End the session with some small but clearly outlined homework assignments to overcome stuckness through some breaking of behavioral patterns.

It is important to make at least some progress to strengthen the client's sense of self-efficacy. This is especially important for demoralized clients. Remember to give praise for every step taken! As long as clients rely on us rather than developing and trusting their own strength, dependency will remain their major coping strategy.

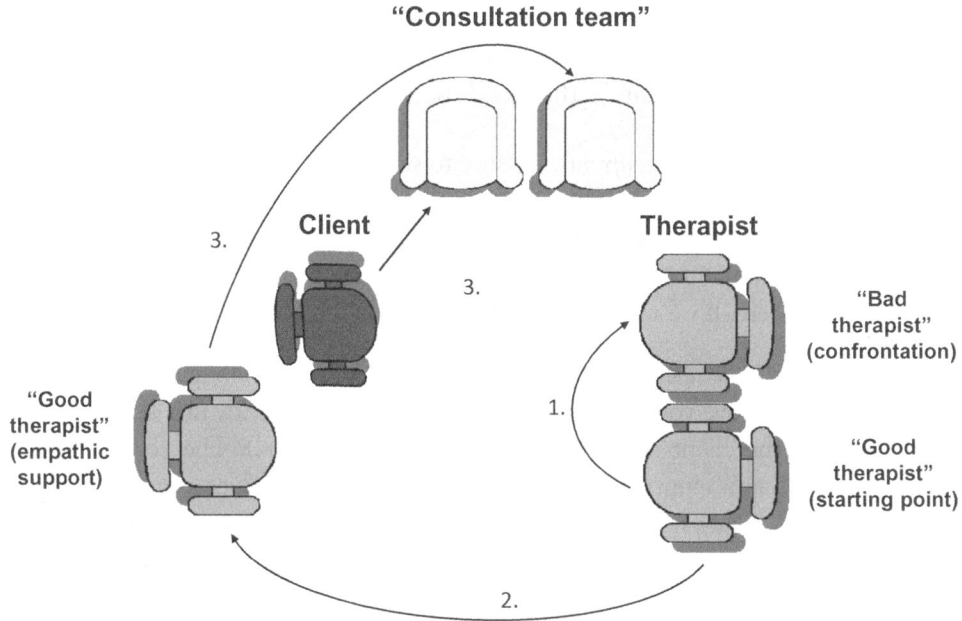

Figure 6–2. Chair positions for empathic confrontation

Dealing Gently with Overcompensatory Modes

Why do people go into protective coping modes? Usually there is an inner conflict between inner critic voices and the assertiveness need of the child modes. Going into a nonfeeling coping mode was once the best way for the individual to avoid such conflicts. But people in an overcompensatory coping mode don't have this problem: their beliefs and emotions are in line and directed toward other people, as illustrated in this case example:

Bradley spends much of his life in self-aggrandizer mode. He genuinely believes that he is vastly superior to almost everyone. This is ego-syntonic because he never doubts his superiority. There is no internal conflict or pressure to avoid feelings.

Our role as therapists is to create some inconsistency, first through empathic listening and then by highlighting the client's blocked attachment need. We can illustrate this with Bradley, whose therapist changed the therapeutic focus to an interpersonal perspective by adding a chair for the other person, in this case Bradley's wife (see figure 6–3). You can also add a therapist's chair if you are having difficulties in the therapy relationship.

Bradley's therapist gently confronted him after first encouraging Bradley to act out his bully side: "Bradley, your third wife is now threatening to leave you. You came into therapy because you want some relationship stability in your life. So let's try to understand what 'script' you are following."

Clients will offer no resistance to therapy if you initially let them express their overcompensatory impulses, but doing this will not help them in the long run. One effective intervention for dealing with overcompensation follows these sequential steps:

1. *Stop the flow of conversation and label the behavior you want to work with:* "Okay, Bradley. Sorry for interrupting you, but I'd like to focus on exactly what just happened in order to understand you better. Could we please both stand up to take a look at the scene together from a little distance?" This is usually acceptable if you have a good relationship. With more difficult cases, such as when your client has explosive rage, you may need to take some intermediate steps (described in chapter 13) to strengthen the connection.

2. *Stand side by side, forming an observer and consultation team:* "Okay, let's consider the therapist's chair as the chair of your wife now." Then connect the modes with the mode model in third-person language: "What kind of coping mode is the client below in?" You may need to explain, based on the model: "Okay, if it is not submission or withdrawal, it must be some kind of dominant or control-oriented mode that we call an overcompensator. What's the basic emotion driving this coping mode?" It is important not to allow your client to distract you into giving reasons or justifications.

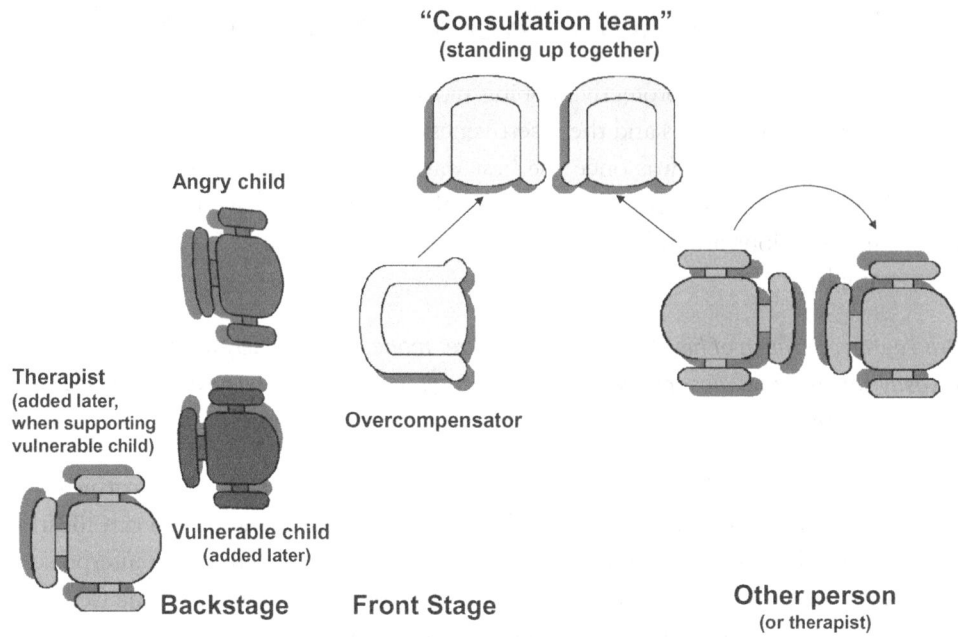

Figure 6-3. How to place the chairs when working with overcompensators

3. *Go to the backstage level* (add a chair behind the coping mode chair): "Right, when angry, he is standing on the assertiveness leg."

4. *Look at the consequences:* "Okay, how does he expect the other person to react?" Usually the answer is to be submissive or to give in. "Right. But how does the other person finally react to the overcompensatory mode?" Sooner or later, the other person usually withdraws.

5. *Turn the other person's chair away* in order to make the withdrawal visible.

6. *Generalize:* "Now if we look at the desired outcome and compare it with the actual outcome, may I ask you a question? Does it happen more often in Bradley's life that people sooner or later disconnect and turn away?" Eventually, use the extension technique from chapter 5 and ask the "best friend" the same question.

7. *Add the vulnerable child mode chair* (for reflection, shift back to first- and second-person language again): "Okay, we found that you were on the assertiveness side. Everybody was born with the need for attachment too. Do you remember the child in the 'still face' video? So let's add a chair for this need!" Add an additional chair beside the angry child mode or the chair for the assertiveness leg. Ask the client to sit in this chair, adding an additional chair for you close to but slightly behind the client.

8. *Access vulnerable child and attachment needs:* "Thank you. Now look at the turned-away chair representing the people who have left you. How does that make you feel in your body?" This hopefully awakens the client's attachment need. If the client resists this awareness, you might challenge him in this way: "Okay, I got the message! You don't need anybody and can do it all by yourself. You're still driven by your assertiveness need seated beside you. I want to talk to the vulnerable part inside of you that everybody was born with and that's still there. Please close your eyes. Picture yourself alone at night in your bed. What do you desire? Or, if you're eighty years old in a nursing home, what do you need now?" Let the client rest for a few minutes to get familiar with the vulnerable part inside of him and to validate it. "Yes, loneliness feels bad. But this is the sad part inside of you that you're always running away from. I am happy that we are in touch with you now. You are who the therapy is for!"

9. *Look for a balanced solution:* Once your client can acknowledge his attachment need, stand up together and face the opposing chairs. Put the overcompensator chair aside and turn the turned-away chair back so he is facing it again: "Now you're 'standing on both legs.' What could you say to this chair to express your needs in a balanced way?" It is best that you guide this process.

10. *Start the scene again:* After both of you are sitting in your accustomed chairs again, ask your client to start the session again by talking to you (or his wife).

11. *Induce discrimination and a take-home message:* Finally, ask the client how he feels now compared to the beginning of the session. What is the principle that he can take home after this session?

(The worksheet "Empathic Confrontation with Externalizing Clients" contains these therapist instructions and is available for download, along with this book's other online accessories, at http://www.newharbinger.com/40958.)

Child Modes

The basic emotions of the child modes indicate that needs are not being met. We try to access the needs of the client, knowing that this is the only way forward. Here we look at how to enlist the child modes to make progress in therapy.

Accessing the Child Modes

To access child modes, you can look for signs of emotional activation (wet eyes, body postures, gestures, voice tone, and so on) and then point them out to the client: "When I look at your eyes, I can see your deeper emotions coming to the surface. Sit on this chair, please." The client takes a seat on the child mode chair behind the protective coping mode chair, and you sit beside her, as shown on the left side of figure 6–3.

"What feelings are coming up? What do you feel in your body? What do you need or want to do now?" Then place a chair representing the inner critic modes in front of the child mode chair on the backstage level according to figure 6–1, and ask the client to express what her needs are toward this empty chair. Now, you both change to the inner critic mode side. Ask the client, while sitting beside her, "What do you think about this?" You can switch to a devil's advocate role and use dismissive words; for example, "What do you think about this little *creep* over there?" If you sit slightly behind the client to avoid being seen, it is surprisingly easy to stimulate the client's toxic beliefs. Both underlying motivational modes and their internal conflict of interest are now present, and the stage is set for deeper chair dialogues (described in detail in chapter 10).

Here are some additional tips for how to access the child modes using chair dialogues.

Offer an additional chair for the child mode. Put this chair behind the coping mode chair where your client will usually begin a session. This will remind the client that there is another part inside of her you want to talk to. Tell her that this chair represents the child mode feeling you want to get in touch with when you ask her to sit in it and close her eyes. Remember, closing our eyes helps us to disconnect from the external world and makes focusing on internal processes much easier.

Make use of your sitting position, speech, and voice tone. Move your chair close to the client. Breaking up the conventional sitting position makes shifting into child mode easier because sitting face-to-face tends to fix us in our socially adapted coping modes. If the client still turns her face toward you, move a little bit more behind her or ask her to close her eyes. With eyes closed, the client will not see you anyway. Your voice now goes directly into the client's head, like the voice of a good parent. This works best if you close your eyes and speak as if talking to a small child you really care about, as mentioned in chapter 3.

> **Therapist Tip:** Be aware of the effect of sitting close to your client. Sitting close is usually fine if you have built up some trust. If any explanation is needed, you might say, "I see that you might feel a bit uncomfortable when I move so close to you. My intention is to address the emotional part inside of you that we call the child mode. When we talk to children, we talk differently from the way we speak to adults. Is this okay for you? Shall we give it a try?"

Let the client decide on the distance. It is natural for sexually abused clients to feel threatened by the closeness of the therapist. If that is the case, find a way for the client to stay in control. Let him choose a comfortable distance. Then say something like "Thank you for showing your irritation to me. It's important to me that you feel safe and comfortable here in therapy. So, what's the distance that works best for you?"

Address the child mode directly. Ask, "What do you feel in your body, in your chest or belly?" Usually this helps the client to access basic emotions when sitting on the child mode chair. If the client is having difficulties identifying basic emotions, suggest the four relevant basic emotions and ask which of them fits best. Men might be grateful to receive some options, because they tend to easily feel "tested."

Meet the needs of the vulnerable child mode. Ask the vulnerable child mode, "What do you *need* now?" Usually the need will be for attachment. You can meet this need using imagery or chair dialogues:

Henry was shaking when he recalled getting lost as a child in a theme park. He identified his fear...well, more like terror. His therapist asked him what he needed, and he said, "My mom to be there and to give me a hug." The therapist continued, "Can you see the joy in your mother's face when she sees you? She's relieved and rushes over to hug you."

Meet the needs of the angry child mode. Ask the angry child mode, "What would you like to *do* now, if anything is possible?" This question allows clients the opportunity to meet the need for assertiveness and autonomy, as illustrated in this case example:

Vella recalled a time in school when a bigger child snatched a toy from her. She was flooded with frustration and a sense of being helpless. Her therapist asked her what she would do to this child if she were ten feet tall. "I would slap her in the face and get my toy back!" The therapist asked her to feel the power of being that strong in her body and being able to keep the other child away forever: "Nobody will take away something that's yours ever again!"

On primary and secondary emotions. When we access the child modes, we try to develop the energetic resources the healthy adult mode requires to employ self-compassionate and assertive behavior in a balanced and flexible way. Frequently, the challenge is accessing the full range of the client's emotional spectrum. Greenberg (2015) uses the concept of primary and secondary emotions, which differs from the concept of basic and social emotions. The primary emotion (for example, fear) can be concealed by a secondary emotion (for example, anger). For example, narcissistic clients show anger first as a secondary emotion, and the therapist must dig deeper to get in touch with the primary fear. In schema terms, the anger is related to the compensatory schema coping of, for example, a defectiveness-shame schema, while fear indicates the activation of the schema itself.

In our approach, we connect basic emotions with the child modes and social emotions with the coping modes. In the model, basic emotions can be primary or secondary, depending on chronology or their onset. Both concepts contribute to a deeper understanding, but for our approach, the time sequence is less relevant than accessing the full spectrum of needs. Therefore, what matters most is the distinction between social emotions (induced by significant others) and basic emotions (spontaneous expressions of a child's needs). We show clients how to separate basic emotions from social emotions so that they will not remain stuck with only social emotions.

Principle: Basic emotions guide us to unmet needs. A secondary basic emotion (such as anger or disgust) can hide a blocked primary basic emotion (generally fear or sadness). In schema therapy, we try to get in touch with both emotion poles.

Inner Critic Modes

Think about one of your clients who enters therapy completely identified with the values of his internalized belief system. He might have said something like "I have to fulfill the wishes of my partner or she'll leave me," or "I have to be perfect or my boss will fire me." How do we deal with such ingrained beliefs? A helpful question to make the belief more ego-dystonic is "Were you born with these beliefs?" Obviously not, so social influence must be at work! You can help to make implicit values explicit, which makes them accessible for conscious reappraisal. Recognizing beliefs as having originally come from others helps clients with cognitive defusion, giving them room to move and to regain flexibility.

You can also use chair work to access underlying beliefs by detecting the self-directed "message" within the coping mode voice, and then translating it from the ego-syntonic "I form" into the ego-dystonic "you form" (as we described above in the section on detached coping modes). In this way, "*I* have to fulfill these wishes" becomes "*You* have to fulfill these wishes," or "*I* have to be perfect" turns into "*You* have to be perfect." These ego-dystonic sentences reveal their origin because they sound like the voices of significant others. This shift from first- to second-person grammatical form reexternalizes the internalized message. In this way, an *intra*personal conflict can once again become an *inter*personal conflict, which is much easier to deal with. You can then put this reexternalized voice on a separate chair and let it talk to the child mode chair in front of it like in an interpersonal setting:

Sally had a demanding critic voice in her head. She came to therapy because she felt constantly guilty that she was not meeting her father's expectations at university. She said, "I'm such a failure. I managed to get on the dean's list but I didn't get all A grades." Her therapist said, "If I hear you right, you're saying 'I have to make an A for every test, every assignment, and every grade'?" She said, "Yes, of course. Or I'll be a failure."

Her therapist challenged her: "But you weren't born with such a belief. It has come from outside you, from your parents or teachers." She agreed. So he said, "Can you change the demanding voice to 'You must get only As'?" She tried this, saying it to herself. Then her therapist said, "Imagine that the voice is coming from that inner critic chair in front of you. Does it feel more distant? Can you argue back?"

In dealing with inner critic modes, our approach is influenced by third wave ideas and differs a bit from the conventional schema therapy approach that teaches the client to "battle the Punitive Parent" (Young et al., 2003, p. 342). The inner critic modes will come back anyway, so trying to get rid of them will lead to endless struggle and disappointment, as we see in the following clinical example:

Mary went to a Catholic school. She developed the idea of burning her inner critic modes at the stake. In her next session, she stumbled into therapy with disappointment on her face: "I can't believe it! They actually came back, stronger than ever!"

Instead of ghostbusting—that is, trying to destroy inner critic voices—we suggest the following steps for clients:

1. Identify a thought as critical or demanding.

2. Label the thought as an inner critic mode voice in your head.

3. Put the voice outside of your mind, beside you on a (real or imaginary) chair.

4. Look at the effect the thought has on you. Does it make you feel or perform better?

5. If not, label it as dysfunctional and let it go. This is especially important if the voice is punishing or condemning.

6. Focus your attention on what you are busy with in the here and now.

7. Whenever the inner critic voice comes back, remain patient and humble, but let it go, again and again.

8. Accept that thoughts come and go but you have the choice to *think* them or not. To illustrate this point, a metaphor might help:

Picture a cow. What does she do when flies continue to buzz around her back, bothering her? She gently waves her tail without getting angry or "fighting" the flies. When the flies come back again (and they surely will), she waves her tail again without getting impatient. The cow accepts that flies are a part of her life. Nevertheless, she reacts to them in a patient way. She maintains her energy and keeps her mind calm.

Reflect: Think about how you might use the acceptance principle with your clients to manage the voices of inner critic modes. What words would you use? Can you think of a metaphor other than the cow accepting the flies to capture this approach?

Therapist Tip: Your client might try some ACT techniques, such as repeating "It's just a thought" or speaking the sentence out in a squeaky mouse voice.

The goal of this step-by-step procedure is to detect the dysfunctional thoughts in the client's mind and the underlying values represented by them, to distance from them, to let them go, and to replace them with values that the client chooses. It is much easier to get emotional distance when your client looks at the *effects* of an inner critic mode message rather than at its *content*. A sentence such as "If you don't learn enough, you won't pass the exam" is definitely true. Looking at *how* it is displayed reveals its devastating and paralyzing effects. And the effects count!

Summary

In this chapter, we looked at how to approach and deal with different modes. Each mode of the larger groupings of coping modes—child modes and inner critic modes—requires a different approach. We described three basic strategies for dealing with coping modes: bypassing avoidant or detached coping modes to reveal and work with the conflict between inner critic and child modes, empathic confrontation to induce anger in overly submissive clients or those with blocked anger, and focusing on the consequences with the overcompensator mode in order to access vulnerable emotions. We also showed how child and inner critic modes can be accessed directly by changing physical and psychological positions. When client and therapist stand together in therapy, they work on an explicit cognitive level toward contextualizing the situation from a metacognitive perspective. When sitting close to the client on the chair level, they work on integrating the activated emotions on a more implicit level. The therapist decides which approach is more promising or relevant at each moment in the therapy process.

CHAPTER 7

Building the Healthy Adult Mode

In this chapter, we explore the healthy part of the self. We define the healthy adult mode and outline how you can build on your clients' strengths. There is a strong practical focus on using some techniques from other therapeutic approaches. It is essential that you, as a schema therapist learning these skills, first try what we suggest on yourself.

What Is the Healthy Adult Mode?

The *healthy adult mode* is the state of mind that embodies maturity and psychological health. It equates with sound judgment in making decisions, responsibility in relationships, and good self-care. The healthy person has more independence and is less reactive. In this adaptive mental space, a person is able to balance personal needs with the needs of others.

Jeff Young and colleagues (2003) defined the healthy adult mode as the healthy, adultlike part of the self that performs an "executive" function relative to the other modes. If the inner critic modes are like a toxic parent, the healthy adult mode can be thought of as a kind of healthy inner parental voice. This mode helps people to meet their own emotional needs. In this way, it tends to relate to a longer-term view of emotional well-being, connecting needs with values.

More recent schema therapy understandings of the healthy adult mode have added to this definition. The healthy adult mode can be thought of as a state made up of mindful here-and-now perceptions; an interruption of spontaneous, maladaptive coping behavior; an emotionally detached reappraisal of internalized parent mode cognitions; and at least supportive self-instructions to induce and maintain functional coping. This definition encompasses a more distanced, defused, and mindful style of self-processing that has become characteristic of contextual behavioral approaches (for example, Hayes et al., 2012).

This focus on the healthy adult mode as being mindfully aware is supported by a series of cross-sectional studies conducted by Brockman and others, which found the healthy adult mode to correlate with mindfulness, psychological flexibility, self-compassion, and valued living (Lazarevic et al., 2013; Remond, Hough, & Brockman, 2013; Wieczorek & Brockman, 2016). Furthermore, decades of research on core emotional needs using a self-determination theory approach supports the centrality of mindful awareness to healthy emotional functioning and regulation (Ryan & Deci, 2017).

We added techniques derived from more traditional schema therapy methods aimed at modifying negative self-content (such as cognitive techniques) to our conceptualization of the healthy adult mode; we did this because we believe that many of the techniques promoting awareness, flexibility, and valued living, developed by the third wave of behavioral therapies, including acceptance and commitment therapy (ACT), compassion-focused therapy, and dialectical behavior therapy, have much to offer in terms of explicitly building the healthy adult mode. This extension is wholly consistent with the integrative philosophy of schema therapy and makes use of other treatment techniques grounded in research evidence showing their clinical effectiveness. Furthermore, from this position, schema therapy techniques should be practiced in a way that balances the need to develop *both* healthy self-content and a healthier style of self-processing and self-awareness (for example, in chair dialogues). Perhaps most importantly, we see the healthy adult mode as being related to needs satisfaction *and* the fulfillment of values. The implication is that the healthy adult mode affords a great deal of psychological flexibility. It is not primarily driven by avoidant (detached protector mode) or hedonic (impulsive child mode) motives but can put those motives aside for value-based, long-term needs fulfillment. Maladaptive coping modes are often driven by short-term contingencies.

Everyone has *some* capacity for healthy adult functioning—sometimes more for the sake of others than for oneself. Often, this includes functioning for one's own children. Therefore, developing the healthy adult mode is more a case of identifying and building on what is already present, though problematic modes may overshadow such abilities.

What follows in this chapter is a set of schema therapy techniques (related to the functional ACT processes) designed to build key aspects of the healthy adult mode. While these skills are directed toward your clients, we believe the best way for practitioners to learn them is through experiential learning. Audio recordings for several of these exercises are available for download at http://www.newharbinger.com/40958.

Identifying Strengths in the Healthy Adult Mode

Think for a moment about a client who is having great difficulty coping with the demands of life. It is easy to see her limitations, but try to identify five strengths that she has and uses on a daily basis. This might be difficult, but doing it will help you to think about your client's strengths.

The healthy adult mode:

- Nurtures, validates, and affirms the vulnerable child mode

- Sets limits for the angry and impulsive child modes

- Promotes and supports the happy child mode

- Abstains from acting out maladaptive coping modes and eventually replaces them with functional coping behavior

- Identifies and lets the inner critic modes go
- Performs appropriate healthy adult functions, such as working, parenting, taking responsibility, and committing
- Pursues pleasurable adult activities, such as sex and intellectual, aesthetic, and cultural interests
- Pursues health maintenance and athletic activities

Now think and write about the following:

- What is one of my areas of strength from the above list?
- In which area am I weakest?
- What would be different in my life if I operated in the healthy adult mode way more often?
- What would be different in my relationships, work, and leisure time?
- Would there be people in my life who would resent me operating in a healthy way?

Some clients are fearful of their emotions. They will benefit from some initial skills-based sessions to build their healthy adult mode and prepare them for more intense emotive work. In chapter 11, we present a list of techniques to moderate emotional activation. Later, in the behavior change phase, we extend these techniques into homework assignments to build the healthy adult mode up gradually as therapy progresses.

The Healthy Adult Is Self-Aware

Building an awareness of modes is essential in schema therapy. The healthy adult mode can act to overcome the influence of unhelpful modes only if it is able to *notice them* when they are active. When a person is aware of a mode, she or he has a chance to shift gears.

Mandy found herself crying for seemingly no reason. She thought, I'm really sad and I'm feeling alone. Unprotected, as if no one cares for me. She had been reading about schema therapy and realized, I feel very young, maybe five or six years old. I'm in a child mode. She looked at the mode list and saw that she was in vulnerable child mode.

Through mode awareness, Mandy was able to move forward in therapy. One of the best ways to build mode awareness is through the use of the mode monitoring form we already introduced in chapter 4 (see figure 4–2).

Using the Mode Monitoring Form

Once you have helped your clients to be familiar with their case conceptualization, encourage them to leave it somewhere prominent, such as in the front of a diary or pinned to their computer screen. Then they can start connecting the modes on their mode map with the *experience* of the modes in daily life.

Encourage your client to follow these STEPs, making notes in a diary:

1. *Situation:* Start by identifying the triggering situation.

2. *Thoughts:* Note the comments of the "voices in your head" at the time.

3. *Emotions:* Now label and then rate the intensity of the emotional response.

4. *Preferred reaction:* Finally, consider what you feel like doing in this situation in response to these thoughts and feelings (your spontaneous coping impulse). Later you can add your activated mode.

When your clients have successfully identified the triggers, thoughts, feelings, and reaction tendencies, encourage them to take a guess about what mode or modes they might have been in. Essentially, as the first step of healthy adult functioning, they train in self-reflection in order to step out of their automatic coping impulses. If a client has trouble with self-reflection, encourage him to try thinking about how you, as therapist, or another trusted person would respond in the given situation.

The Healthy Adult Is Mindful

Mindfulness is awareness. Increasingly, mindfulness theory is having an impact on schema therapy—a valuable contribution, which we acknowledge here. We draw on mindfulness and its evidence base in this section to strengthen our description of the healthy adult mode. We like to equate the role of the healthy adult in the process of behavior change to shifting gears (Schore, 1994), which has three steps:

1. *Self-reflection:* Become aware that the current gear is not working and shift out (disidentification, defusion) of it. This process matches with the "open" response style from ACT.

2. *Reappraisal:* Assess the situation from a more distant perspective and choose a different gear (take a mindful perspective and connect with your values). This relates to the "centered" response style from ACT.

3. *Taking action:* Decide whether to shift into a new gear based on your needs and values in this situation (breaking behavioral patterns). This is comparable to the "engaged" response style from ACT.

Mindfulness has been adapted from Buddhist and Christian spiritual practices and is now widely encouraged in third wave therapies, but it is practiced in these therapies in a more secular way. It may prove to be highly relevant in schema therapy, where it can act as a counterbalance to the powerful impact of schema activations (Roediger, 2012). Indeed, mindfulness can help people to switch to a more distanced, self-reflective level of functioning when they need to balance intense emotional activation (see chapter 5).

William learned mindful breathing. He used it to center himself when he felt stressed at work. Previously, he would go into angry protector mode, and his irritation would affect his employees. A workplace coach suggested using mindfulness techniques to avoid being a negative influence. William was gradually able to better manage his reactions: "I find that my staff members are more open to talking with me and don't avoid me at coffee breaks."

In mindfulness practice, we observe rather than actively dispute negative beliefs associated with schemas or modes. Van Vreeswijk and colleagues (2014) noted that this process can strengthen the healthy adult mode. They described the function of the healthy adult mode as allowing the presence of intense observations without behaving in an automatic fashion. This can lead to the realization that schemas and modes come and go, but that desperately trying to control or avoid them will lead only to tunnel vision instead of having several options at hand. If mindfulness practice is adopted more widely in schema therapy, then schema therapy will become like dialectical behavior therapy in attempting to combine Eastern acceptance strategies with Western change strategies in a balanced way.

The Attention Time Line Exercise

Consider the place of your conscious attention on the time line in figure 7–1. On one end of the spectrum, your mind is paying attention to past events. Reexperiencing "past" thoughts can therefore be placed anywhere on the left side of the time line.

To get a sense of what we mean, close your eyes and form an image of what it was like having breakfast this morning. What can you see in this image? What are you eating? What does it taste like? What are you thinking? How do you feel? Notice what it is like to be in this image.

Now come back into the room, in the present moment, and notice your immediate surroundings. Direct your attention back toward the figure and the star representing the present moment in the middle of the time line. Notice what it is like now to experience this moment—just you with your current surroundings and this page of the book—and let all other content related to the past go. Notice that these are somewhat different (mental) behaviors: one is what we might call "dwelling on the past" and the other is what we might call "attending to the present moment." (An audio recording of this exercise, along with this book's other online accessories, is available for download at http://www.newharbinger.com/40958.)

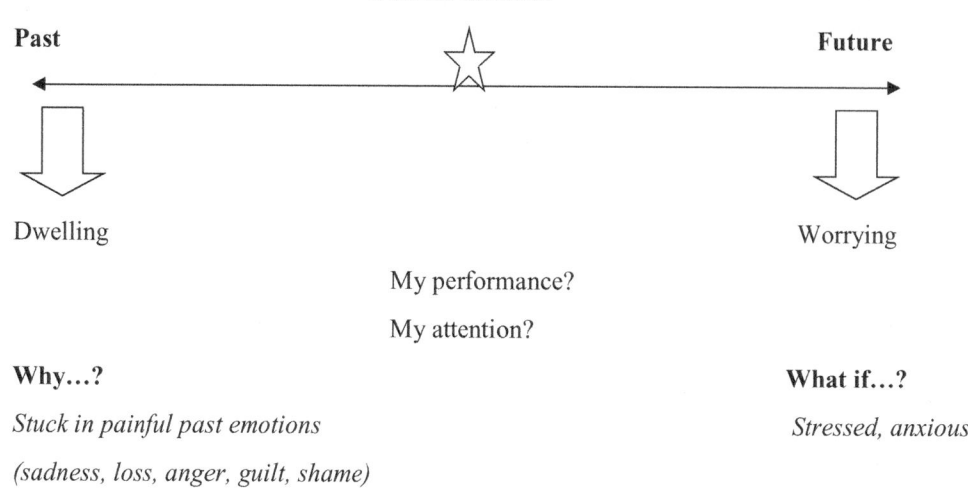

Figure 7–1. The attention time line

While dwelling on the past is completely normal and, in many instances, adaptive (for example, briefly analyzing a mistake so that you can learn from it and move on), many people get stuck in this process, ruminate, and feel worse. This is often characterized by a rash of "why" questions. Why did this happen? Why me? Why didn't anyone help? Hearing yourself ask too many of these questions is often a clue that you may be spending too much time dwelling, which is often associated with feelings of sadness, loss, guilt, shame, and anger.

Now, direct your attention to the right side of the time line. To experience the difference between future-oriented thinking (worry) and attending to the present moment, close your eyes and picture all of the things that you have to do tomorrow to get through the day. Notice what this is like. Do you notice any anxiety or excitement about what is in store for tomorrow? Now come back into the room, to the present moment, and notice your immediate surroundings again. Again, notice that these are somewhat different (mental) behaviors. Now, consider what the impact will be on your attention and performance in the present moment if you spend much of your time processing past memories or future problems.

Reflect: Not surprisingly, excessively dwelling on something negative is closely associated with clinical depression, as well as many other clinical problems. You might ask your clients what proportion of their time they spend worrying. How much time does that leave for being in the present? What is the impact of this process on their life?

Now consider how being mindful of the present moment might improve your life, as it did for the following client:

Ned decided that he needed to have a daily "oasis" of mindfulness in his routine. He began the day by walking his dog. He determined that he would discipline himself to make this a mindfulness experience. After a few days, he found that he was more aware of the sun shining on him, the coolness of the breeze, and the sounds of birds and wildlife. He began to "smell the flowers." He wryly noted, "That is what Fido does. I suppose I'm trying to be more like my dog, living in the moment, and I feel less caught up in my thoughts. I feel more alive."

Building Mindfulness Skills

Mindfulness is a behavioral skill just like any other. When we try mode awareness as the first step of healthy adult functioning, this is an everyday application of mindfulness. Just like any other skill, the more you practice mindfulness, the better you will become at using the skill. Before trying to use mindfulness in times of distress, it is best to start learning it when you are feeling relatively calm. You can use the following exercises with your clients to develop present-moment awareness, but you can also try them for yourself.

The 5–4–3 Mindful Grounding Exercise

Mindful grounding can be particularly helpful if you tend to spend a lot of time inside your head rather than in the present moment. This exercise helps you to be mindful of the difference, and to flexibly choose to focus your attention on both internal and external stimuli, depending on the demands of your situation. (An audio recording of this exercise, along with this book's other online accessories, is available for download at http://www.newharbinger.com/40958.)

> Take some time out from your normal routine to go for a walk. Before you start, try to remind yourself of all the current problems that you have been thinking about recently about which you feel stuck. Notice what it feels like to be in this state of being in your head. Now that you have induced the experience of being in your head a little, begin your mindful walk.
>
> As you walk, take a moment to broaden your awareness of what is happening around you with your sense of sight. Now notice and label, just in your mind, five things you can see around you: for example, *I notice the cracks in the sidewalk, I notice the stop sign across the road*, and *I notice the brown bark on the tree ahead*. Keep going until you have noticed five things that you see.
>
> Once you have noticed those five things, focus your attention on your sense of hearing. Focus on four things you can hear now: *I notice the sound of the car as it drives past me, I notice the sound of my footsteps*, and *I notice the sound of the wind rustling the tree's leaves*. Keep going until you have noticed four things that you hear.
>
> Then switch your attention to your sense of touch. Focus your attention on three things you can feel right now: *I notice the warmth of the sun on my face, I notice the feel of my hand in my pocket*, and *I notice the feel of my toes pressing down on the bottom of my shoes*.

Now that you have taken some time to practice broadening your externally focused attention using these three senses, notice what has happened to whatever it was you were "stuck" with at the beginning of the walk. What happened to that stuff when you broadened your attention to notice the present moment? How did you feel, focusing on the present moment? How was your concentration? Notice how this mode of processing is different from the mode that usually gets you stuck. Consider whether this technique might have some value in building your healthy adult mode.

Therapist Tip: Once your clients become skilled at the 5–4–3 mindful grounding exercise, encourage them to use their senses to anchor themselves in the present moment, such as when they are taking a shower, washing dishes, or even doing yoga. Mindfulness can be combined with virtually any activity, and getting some mindfulness practice in this way can lessen the need to set aside dedicated time.

Mindfulness of Breath Meditation

There are various mindfulness of breath exercises available to practice. We present the following one for the purpose of building the healthy adult mode. (An audio recording of this exercise, along with this book's other online accessories, is available for download at http://www.newharbinger.com/40958.)

Find a comfortable position in which to sit and practice. Start by directing your attention toward your breathing in this very moment. Notice the air as it comes in through your nostrils and moves down to the bottom of your lungs. Now, follow it as it goes back out again through your mouth. Follow the air as if you are riding the waves of your breathing, in and out, in and out. Take, say, ten seconds to notice how the air feels slightly warmer as it comes out, and somewhat cooler on the way in. Then notice the gentle rise and fall of your chest with every breath, in and out. Travel down now to your belly and notice the rise and fall of your belly with every breath you take in this moment.

Now that you have anchored yourself to different aspects of the experience of breathing in this moment, harness your attention and fix it on any one of these areas. The task is to hold your attention there, just noticing the movement of your breath as it moves in and out of your body.

As you attempt to do this, you may notice that thoughts and feelings try to come in and distract you from staying with your breath. This is completely normal and is, in fact, the point of the exercise. The mind does not like to be out of work, and so it is common for it to generate a stream of thoughts and feelings for you to notice. Whatever thoughts, images, feelings, sensations, or urges arise, whether pleasant or unpleasant, gently acknowledge their presence and allow them to be, coming and going as they please, all the while attempting to just stay with the experience of your breath. Each time you get distracted, the task is just to notice what it is that distracted you, and then gently bring your attention back to your breathing. Silently connecting breathing in with "in," breathing out with "out," and the break in between with "break" helps to focus your attention. In addition, you may try counting off each breath cycle, from one up to ten and then from ten to one again. Practice mindfulness of breath for ten to fifteen minutes. This is sufficient time for a maximum effect. Then gently bring yourself back into the room and open your eyes.

Practicing this formal meditation may be difficult at first, or it may simply be difficult to set aside the time for it. If the latter is problematic for you, try to approach the practice in smaller time increments. However, we suggest making it part of your daily routine, at least until you get some practice (for example, at least a month). Determine what time of the day works best for you. Is it in the morning, during lunch break, while coming home from work, or before going to bed? For what amount of time can you practice daily? Start with that and then see if you can slowly increase the time. Later, you can apply an ultrabrief version of this exercise, which we call the thirty-second breathing space, to your daily life. If you are feeling overwhelmed by things or distracted, take just thirty seconds to anchor yourself using this method. Once you are a bit more grounded, ask yourself, *How do I want to proceed in this moment?*

Reflect: Think about some of your clients who might benefit from such exercises. How would you suggest that they give them a try? Think about how you would use the exercises in sessions, and then ask your clients to practice them as homework.

Maintaining Mindfulness During the Day

We chose these two exercises because they provide a good foundation for building mindfulness skills. It is normal to be constantly falling out of mindfulness over the course of the day, but you can encourage your clients to develop landmarks to remind them to become mindful again. For example, every time they touch the door of their house or office they could shift back into mindfulness for a moment. When they feel body tension, they might slow down their walking pace and take a few deeper breaths. Or they could take a mindful time-out while waiting in an elevator, for the subway, or at a traffic light. Help them to choose and to shift gears!

The Healthy Adult Is Accepting

Clients usually start therapy because they want to change something. However, changes in the outside world are sometimes hard to achieve. When a particular change cannot be made, what is a client left to do?

A Theoretical Note on Acceptance

In this section, we outline the philosophical background for acceptance. Acceptance derives from Buddhism and Christianity. The Buddhist view seems to carry less moral baggage, so we prefer it. To bring "acceptance" into a scientific context, we connect it with the so-called contingency theory of Klaus Grawe (2004). While he is a very famous researcher in Germany, he is not well known in the English-speaking world. (Maybe he had to *accept* that!) If we think in terms of his theory, people feel contented when their expectations match their achievements (figure 7–2).

After people attain a goal, they will feel good for a short time, but then they may face the next challenge. It is like going for a walk in an area with many hills: as soon as you climb one hill, the next one shows up on the horizon. Having a strong demanding critic mode makes us feel like we're performing the task of Sisyphus, forever rolling a large rock up a hill only to have it roll back down again.

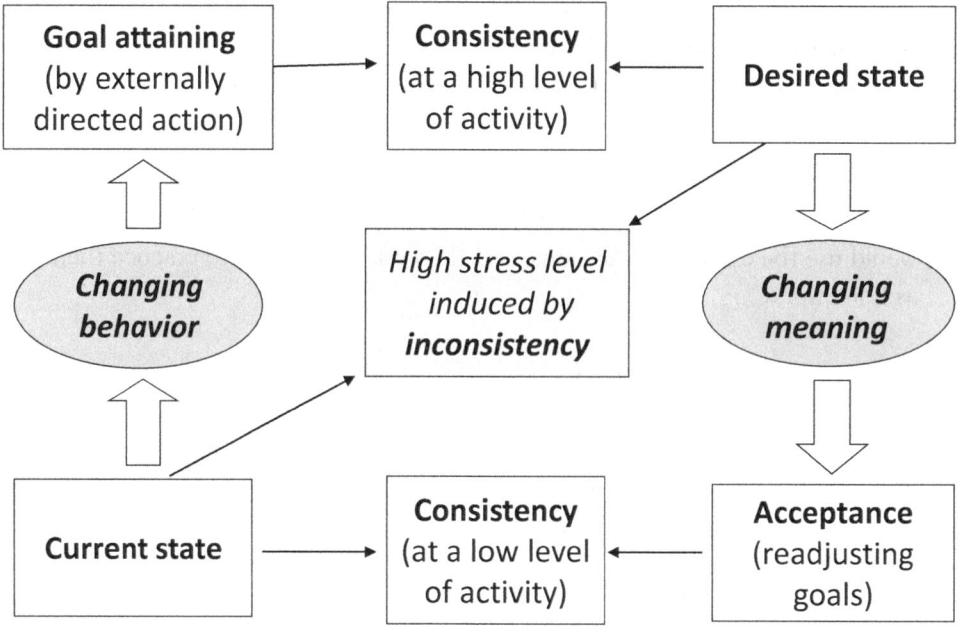

Figure 7–2. Two ways to consistency

Buddhist philosophy advises us to achieve consistency between our desired state and our actual state through another approach: accept things as they already are and let desires go. Pain comes from having desires. This may sound like stating the obvious, but the sentiment contains deep wisdom. Without acceptance, there is a risk of falling into automatic coping responses that may become increasingly maladaptive, especially if things turn out to be hard to change. Think about one of your clients with a difficult set of life circumstances. Could that person learn to be more accepting? After all, it is easier to change a thinking style than a life situation.

Uno and Vella

Think about the following and perhaps discuss it with someone over fifty years old. In the first half of your life span, striving for change might be a promising strategy. But in the second half, this strategy turns out to become increasingly difficult. Perhaps it is wise to make acceptance the goal in the second half of life and regard goals as something relative. There can be benefits to trying to live more in the present than in the future.

Uno found himself dissatisfied working for minimum wage. He was frustrated that some of his friends, who were better educated, had greater incomes. He thought about this and realized that he had enjoyed a better income while they were still full-time students. Also, he found that he was pleased to have a stable job when a number of his well-educated friends lost their management positions during an economic downturn.

Vella had chronic pain, which gradually led to a "shrinking" of her world as she became more and more housebound. In desperation, she saw an ACT therapist. He encouraged her to experience and accept her pain. He led her in a series of mindfulness-of-pain meditations in which she focused on her pain, sensing its parameters and "texture" and eventually assigning it a color. She was able to visualize changing the color of her pain, which she found helpful. Vella identified what was most important to her, what reflected her values, and that was to spend more time with her two grandchildren. She wanted to go to a local park and watch them play. She knew that walking a few hundred yards would cause her additional pain, but she said, "Yes, it will hurt, but it's worth it. I can accept this as a cost of living more fully."

Emotion Surfing

The term "emotion surfing" derives from the approach of Allan Marlatt and Ruth Gordon (1985) for dealing with the craving to drink alcohol. However, you can use the technique with every intense emotion. To fight the feeling you may be having, picture yourself on a surfboard, allowing the wave to lift you up; focus on keeping your balance and riding the wave until it rolls on. People relate to their emotions and body sensations on a spectrum that ranges from fighting them to avoidance to tolerance to acceptance.

Most people with chronic life problems tend to avoid their emotions and body sensations. It is natural to try to run away from painful emotions using avoidant coping. The healthy adult mode has a relationship with emotions and body sensations that directs clients toward the acceptance end of the spectrum.

> **Reflect:** A useful word to substitute for acceptance is "willingness." This is not the same as wanting or liking painful experiences, rather just being willing to have them, as long as they are there, using a compassionate stance instead of desperately trying to get rid of them.

You can compare emotions to a cork in water: it takes energy to keep the cork below the surface—that is, to drown your emotions. Though not easy, accepting emotions requires less energy, and it is a fundamental shift many people need to make in order to experience improved mental health.

Claire spent many years of her life repressing negative feelings. She came to this realization at a meditation retreat. She said to her best friend, "I know I had a troubled childhood, but there's nothing I can do about that now. Recently, I've been more accepting of my anger toward my mother and her problem with alcohol. Well, I suppose I have had to grieve about not having a 'normal' childhood. It's sad, and I wish it had been better, but I don't have to fight it now, twenty years later."

Acceptance Meditation (Practicing Full Acceptance of Emotions and Sensations)

An audio recording of this exercise, along with this book's other online accessories, is available for download at http://www.newharbinger.com/40958.

Find a comfortable position in which to sit and practice an acceptance meditation. Close your eyes and direct your attention toward your breathing in this very moment. Pause for ten seconds, and then focus your attention inward to recognize what you are feeling in your body right now. Slowly scan your body, up and down, to recognize any feelings in it, such as your heart beating, your hands sweating, your stomach churning, or a lump in your throat. Whatever sensations you feel, take some time to notice and acknowledge each of them, one by one. Pause again for ten seconds.

Now become aware of your emotion, as you experience it in the body. Consider how you would label such a feeling. Is it sadness, anxiety, or anger? Is it loneliness or loss? Is it excitement or some other positive feeling? Is there a mix of emotions? Whatever it is that you are feeling, select a label (or labels) that fits best for you in this moment.

Now that you recognize a particular set of sensations and emotions, actively welcome and allow them to be present in this moment. Make space for the sensations and emotions to be there. Expand yourself through your breath to accommodate them, as if you are large enough to have them there. Imagine breathing into the sensations and emotions, breathing in and around them. Imagine giving permission for them to be there even though they may be uncomfortable. Rate (for example, on a scale from 1 to 10) how willing you are to have these sensations and emotions at this moment. Whatever they are, continue allowing them to be present. Try to drop any struggle with the sensations and emotions, increasing your willingness to have them there. Continue this new, accepting stance toward these sensations and emotions for a few more minutes. Practice allowing them to be there, breathing into them.

Reflect: How did it feel, dropping your struggle with a sensation or emotion? What happened when you tried to accept it and allow it to be present? Did that make it worse or improve it? Did it stay the same over time? How could relating to your sensations or emotions in this accepting, willing way improve things in your life? Would you be able to use this stance to manage sensations or emotions in a way that would allow you to engage in more valued living?

The Healthy Adult Is Self-Compassionate

Self-compassion can counter messages from the punitive critic mode and, to a lesser extent, a demanding critic. Compassion involves being empathic to suffering. Kristen Neff is a leading researcher in this area (see her website, http://www.self-compassion.org). Also, read *The Compassionate Mind: A New Approach to Life's Challenges* by Paul Gilbert (2010), who has useful suggestions for becoming more self-compassionate.

Reflect: Think about a client who has a strong inner critic mode voice. How would he or she respond to the suggestion to write a letter to the vulnerable child from the nurturing side of the healthy adult mode?

Being Kind to Yourself Exercise

As we noted when we introduced mindfulness, it is important to remain practical in therapy. It is better to take a small step safely than to take a big jump only to fall. Make self-compassion and treating yourself kindly a part of everyday life—at least for a few minutes each day. To accomplish this, you need to schedule time to look after yourself, such as going to see a movie, getting a massage, or playing sports. Intentionally schedule activities that give you a sense of fun and pleasure. As with scheduling behavioral commitments, you may need to break this practice down into small steps using hierarchies; nonetheless, it is important to start somewhere small and then slowly build up your practice. Remember, the healthy adult mode is kind to itself. If you don't look after yourself, eventually you will burn out and be of no help to others.

Creating a Self-Symbol

For some clients with very low self-esteem and very toxic inner critic modes, it is easier to care for another person than for themselves. In therapy, they can choose a doll or a soft toy to represent their vulnerable child, which they can adopt, talk to, and care for. Later, they can apply this caring function to themselves in an internal dialogue. Such dialogues work better if clients continue talking to themselves in second-person language: *You worked hard today. You deserve a break now.* This process is how symbolization develops.

The Healthy Adult Is Connected to Personal Values

Coping modes function on some level as a form of experiential avoidance. ACT practitioners have emphasized the central role of values in guiding our life choices in contrast to experiential avoidance, which narrows our repertoire and disconnects us from what matters. We believe that this model of values-based goal setting and behavioral activation, which is core to ACT, is also a central part of healthy adult mode functioning.

The healthy adult mode is, therefore, aware of both needs and core personal values. Values are landmarks guiding us toward long-term needs fulfillment. Values-clarification exercises are a good way to open up autonomy and start connecting with the world by taking time to reflect on which values are most important. In this way, clients can voluntarily *choose* their valued directions in life. Consider this example, which highlights how an individual can make life choices based on the values of others:

John has been a criminal lawyer for the past ten years. On the surface, he appears to have everything one could possibly want to be happy: a well-paying job, a seven-year marriage, and three beautiful children. Despite this, John has suffered from chronic depression characterized by a profound lack of meaning and the feeling of being stuck and rudderless. To cope, he has abused alcohol and cocaine. After completing several values-clarification exercises, he realized that the life he is living is the life that society (and his parents) values, not him. He married someone from his parents' cultural background to make them happy, and, as a result, his value of companionship has been poorly met. Furthermore, he chose to be a lawyer defending criminals to make money, which was consistent with society's values, even though it moved him away from his core value of helping others.

Russ Harris (2009) likened values to one's taste in pizza (see https://www.thehappinesstrap.com). He has come up with sixty values, including acceptance, adventure, assertiveness, authenticity, beauty, caring, challenge, contribution, conformity, connection, cooperation, courage, creativity, curiosity, encouragement, equality, excitement, fairness, fitness, flexibility, freedom, friendliness, forgiveness, fun, generosity, gratitude, honesty, humor, humility, industry, independence, intimacy, justice, kindness, love, mindfulness, order, open-mindedness, patience, persistence, pleasure, power, reciprocity, respect, responsibility, romance, safety, self-awareness, self-care, self-development, self-control, sensuality, sexuality, spirituality, skillfulness, supportiveness, and trust.

Try adding your own values to the list. You can also share it with clients and help them to identify ten values that are very important to them. You might also try developing a personal mission statement reflecting your most deeply held values, and then encouraging your clients to do the same. It is best to develop your statement first, because schema therapists try to practice what they preach. You will appear much more convincing and trustworthy when clients realize you are talking from personal experience.

The point of values clarification is to guide committed action. ACT practitioners encourage clients to engage in activities informed by values, and we believe that this endeavor is wholly consistent with the notion of building the healthy adult in schema therapy.

Stacey has a strong ideological commitment to living in an environmentally sensitive way. The local government was planning a new road that would cut through a natural forest. She organized a petition to protest this action and led a community group that made presentations against the road to a state agency.

Positive Affect Imagery Exercise

Imagery can also be used to help clients draw upon and experience (or reexperience) positive affect by placing their attention on times in life when they experienced high levels of emotional strength and positive affect. For example, if your client is feeling strong and happy by recalling a memory from school, what needs are being met in this moment that are giving her a feeling of strength and positivity? Is it a feeling of being connected to peers, or of accomplishment in school work, or both? Processing such a scenario early in therapy can be a useful assessment tool the therapist can use to ascertain the likely needs and values that have connected the client to positive schemas in the past, *and* to experientially connect the client to the importance of satisfying these needs and values. In addition, this exercise can help strengthen the healthy adult in preparation for experiential work (read more about future-directed imagery in chapter 9). Remember, the healthy adult is the trustee of a person's healthy adaptive schemas. Processing these experiences in memory primes the positive schemas for activation and prepares the client to intervene more autonomously in experiential tasks using the healthy adult mode. (An audio recording of this exercise, along with this book's other online accessories, is available for download at http://www.newharbinger.com/40958.)

> Start by closing your eyes and getting comfortable in your chair. Focus on your breath in this moment. Pause for ten seconds, and then try to become aware of a time in your life when you felt most strong, happy, and vital. Scan your memory for experiences, for moments, when you felt really alive, when whatever struggles you might have had just seemed to fall away without any effort, a moment when you may have experienced a sense of knowing who you were and where you belonged in this life. It could be something that occurred recently or it could be a moment now long past. Pause again for ten seconds.
>
> Now allow yourself to drift back into that moment of vitality. What do you see? What do you hear? What do you feel? Who are the main characters in the scene and how do they contribute to the feelings of vitality that you have? Notice this moment with all of your senses. Pause for ten seconds, and then notice what your mind is telling you about this moment. How would you describe your feelings? Really take in what is most vital in this moment right now. What might this moment say about who you are, and what you care about most? After a fifteen-second pause, open your eyes slowly, and reorient yourself to the room in this moment. Reflect on your experience in a personal diary.

Eightieth Birthday Imagery Exercise

The eightieth birthday imagery exercise can connect you to your values and needs. (An audio recording of this exercise, along with this book's other online accessories, is available for download at http://www.newharbinger.com/40958.)

> Find a quiet place to sit or lie down to reflect. Now close your eyes and imagine that you are about to celebrate your eightieth birthday. Who will host this occasion? Now, paint the full picture of the gathering. What do you see in the image? Is it a large event or a small, intimate gathering? Who would you like to attend? Remember, this is a hypothetical exercise, so you can have anyone attend who you would like to be there. Do you want your parents in attendance? Your grandparents? Do you have children there? A spouse? Your siblings? Friends? How do they all look? How do you look in the image? Take a few moments to fully flesh out the image and reflect on what it feels like to be here in this moment.
>
> Now imagine that three people are preparing to step forward to say a few things about you on your eightieth birthday. Carefully choose the three people whom you would like to speak. Imagine each person. Who are they? How do they look? What would you like them to say about you in their commemorative toast? What kind of person you have been, and what you have stood for so far? How do you feel in response to their toasts? After a few minutes, open your eyes and reorient yourself to the room.

Reflect: Who was at your eightieth birthday party, and what might this say about the kinds of relationships you value? Were you the person you want to become? Do you have a sense that you are currently on track to becoming that person, or are you off track in some way? See whether you can extract five important values from this exercise that you want to work on to get more on track. Write them down and assess how consistent you have been in living according to those values in the past month. Finally, take a moment to imagine how your life might be different if you were able to live it more consistently with those values. How does it make you feel to imagine this?

Therapist Tip: Prepare your clients for the possibility that doing eightieth birthday imagery exercise may activate one or more of their problematic modes, such as vulnerable child, punitive critic, or demanding critic. If they find such modes activated, ask them to pause for a moment and eventually stand up and move around a bit to shift into healthy adult mode. This is an opportunity to increase their awareness of which modes tend to move them away from their values.

Toward Committed Action

Once your clients have become aware of their personal values, you can help them to use those values as a compass to increase motivation for breaking behavioral patterns and moving toward needs satisfaction. Start with value domains from the values-clarification exercises above (such as companionship, work, achievement, family, social, friendship, fun, play) to generate manageable and graded goals. We call these "behavior change hierarchies."

Behavior Change Hierarchies

Examine figure 7–3. One of the authors (Rob Brockman) shared his own behavior change hierarchies based upon his own values. (You can download a blank version of the values road map, along with this book's other online accessories, at http://www.newharbinger.com/40958.)

Therapist Tip: If you are feeling overwhelmed by a goal, consider how you might break it down further. If you cannot do that, at least fill out a mode monitoring form (figure 4–2) so that you gain awareness of the modes that stop you from moving toward your goals or values. Sometimes being aware may be enough to help you push through your block to behavior change. After you have identified one or more modes as blocks, you may want to work on them using the mode-specific techniques discussed in this book. Remember, even very small changes can be significant, so be kind to yourself.

Summary

In this chapter, we looked at how important it is to strengthen the healthy adult mode. This mode provides an important positive psychology counterpoint to just addressing dysfunctional modes in schema therapy. What are the qualities of the healthy adult? We outlined characteristics such as being mindful, accepting, self-compassionate, and committed to valued living. We also provided a number of resources to use with clients to strengthen their healthy adult mode.

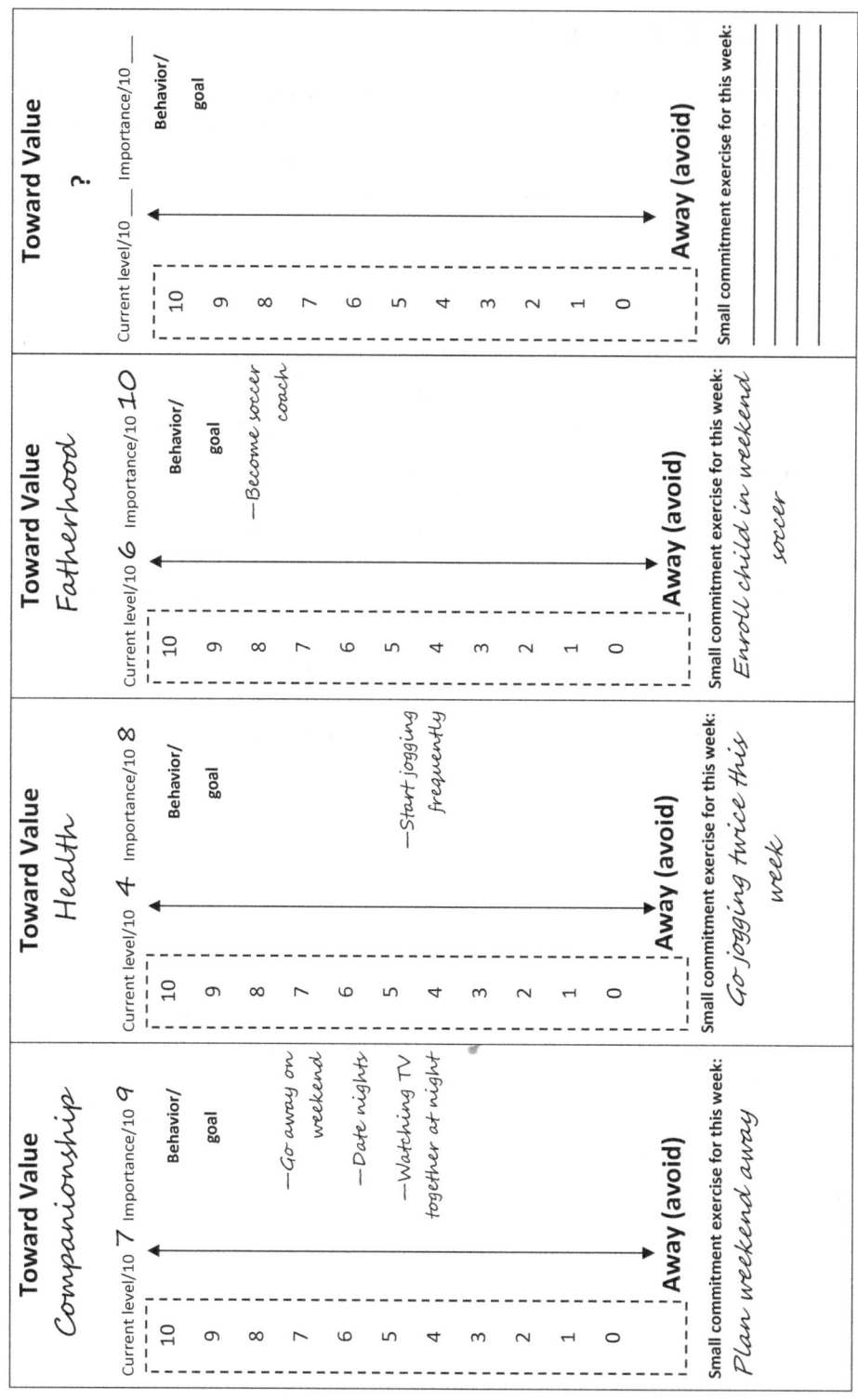

Figure 7–3. Values road map

CHAPTER 8

How to Bring Change

The brain is remarkably plastic, and experiential techniques can be powerful methods for promoting rapid change to the brain. We've also found that emotionally reprocessing past events can substantially weaken the impact of formerly overwhelming memories. In this chapter, we introduce the principles of experiential work as a way to implement behavior change in the daily life of our clients.

Emotional Processing Involves Connecting Two Levels of Cognition

Some clients will initially resist experiential techniques. You might hear a client say something like "Emotions are the problem. I can't see how dragging them up can help," or "I can't change the past. I only want to look to the future." You need to present a clear rationale for how reexperiencing works. You can explain that emotional processing will ultimately help to heal the past, and that you must activate emotional memories in order to affect them.

Figure 8-1 shows a model for emotional processing. The two minds reflect at least two levels of cognition relevant to psychotherapy: one consisting of emotional memory and the other consisting of rational processing. See Siegel (1999) and Schore (2014) for in-depth reviews of dual-process models of cognition.

In this model, we start on the left side with emotional memory. Schemas are encoded in emotional memory not through rational means but through early life events, often traumatic ones. The person reflected in the figure developed a defectiveness-shame schema in childhood because of too much criticism, coldness, and anger, and too little acceptance and validation. In this context, the child encoded in his emotional memory a schema that he is "defective" as a person, concluding, "There's something inherently wrong with me." The child missed the opportunity to learn the adaptive schema that he is inherently okay and worthwhile as a person. He remains trapped by the maladaptive schema.

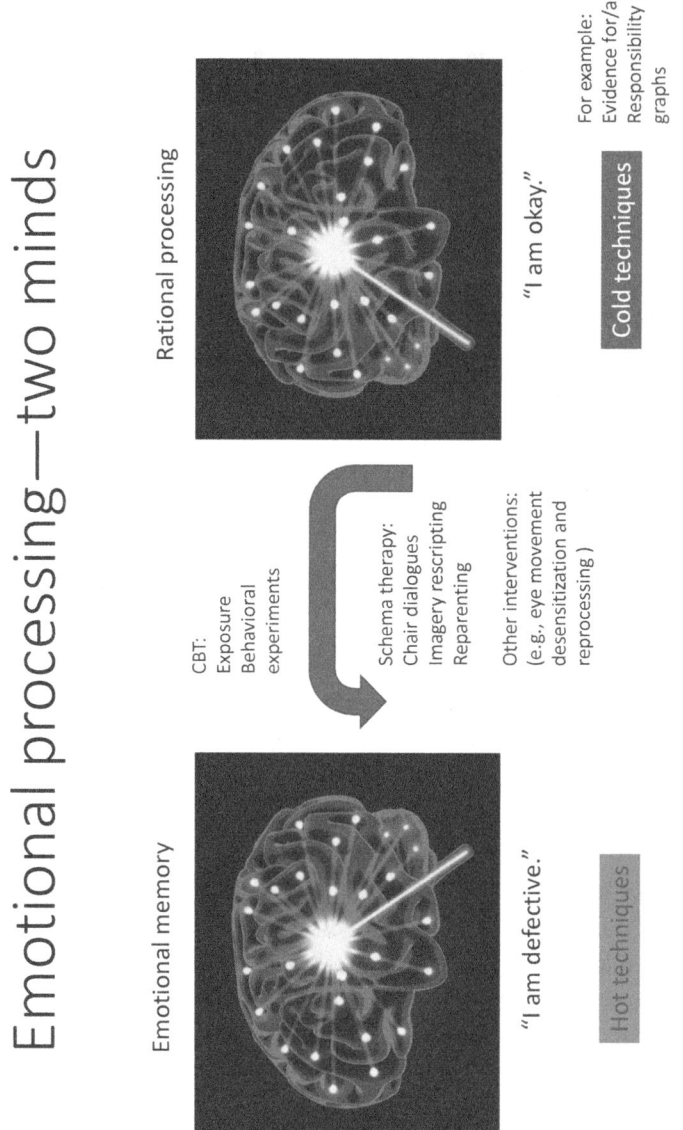

Figure 8–1. Emotional processing using the two-minds metaphor

When the maladaptive schema is "hot" (that is, activated in emotional memory), so too are all four aspects of the schema: associated feelings (such as shame), body sensations (for example, a lump in the throat), memories (for example, the mother screaming), and cognitions (*I am worthless*). There is evidence that the activation of this emotional memory is associated with distinct brain regions, including the amygdala (LeDoux, 1996).

The story does not end there. Figure 8–1 depicts rational processing on the right-hand side. As the child developed, his capacity for a more rational, cold, and reflective form of processing emerged. This form of rational processing is associated with specific brain regions, too, but ones that developed later in human evolution, including the prefrontal cortex (LeDoux, 1996). Later, as an adolescent, the child developed a capacity to reflect on his negative childhood experiences and create a superposed narrative of being "okay" as a person, rather than "defective."

This rational perspective is not necessarily permanent and may be overwhelmed by emotional reasoning. This can often lead to the well-known experience of clients feeling of two minds about something: "I know *rationally* that it's true I'm not worthless, but I still *feel* worthless!" This two-minds experience is also characteristic of some clinical problems, such as obsessive-compulsive disorder ("I know it's silly, but I feel that if I don't ritualize, someone will die").

After cognitive work, sometimes a client will be in a state of two minds during sessions. While the healthy adult mode disputes feelings of defectiveness, the unaffected emotional memory maintains the feelings. This brings us to a key point of the schema therapy model. Therapy in this case must go further than cold cognitive techniques. It is important to achieve change in the early maladaptive schemas through hot interventions, accessing the schema by activating the emotional memory. Schemas cannot be modified via rational processing alone; if there is no activation of the schema in emotional memory, the schema will remain largely in place.

The most promising techniques for schema change *activate* and *integrate* the two perspectives:

1. Intervention first activates the schema in emotional memory,

2. creating the opportunity for new and adaptive information to connect to the activated schema and

3. to integrate with the emotional memory.

Some techniques from traditional cognitive behavioral therapy (CBT) are good candidates for this kind of therapeutic experience (such as exposure techniques and behavioral experiments), but schema therapy builds on them to offer an array of techniques that can perform this function (for example, dealing with schema activations within the therapy relationship, chair techniques, imagery rescripting). Other psychotherapy techniques not traditionally associated with schema therapy also hold promise for schema change (for example, eye movement desensitization and reprocessing).

The General Process of Schema Activation and Modification

In our approach to schema therapy, the same principles underlie both imagery rescripting and chair dialogues. While imagery usually deals with an interpersonal situation, chair (or mode) dialogues play out the inner world of clients as an interpersonal drama.

Imagery rescripting can help clients to escape the original external scene in which they once felt trapped. However, it can be more challenging to escape from their "internal prison." Imagery rescripting alone will not accomplish this, so mode dialogues on multiple chairs then come into play. The steps for imagery rescripting described below largely parallel those for the putting the mode map on chairs dialogue. This process enables us to transfer interpersonal skills learned in imagery rescripting to the client's inner world and makes further learning much easier. Here are the steps of this general road map:

1. *Start with a schema-activating situation* (from the present, the past, or the therapy relationship).

2. *Label the activated coping mode* and use response prevention.

3. *Focus on the activated emotions and body sensations.* Then either float back (in imagery) or access backstage basic emotions. In imagery, you end up with an *inter*personal situation, in chair dialogues, *intra*personal states.

4. *Get in touch with the needs of the activated child mode.*

5. *Now aim for a perspective change and create a joint perspective.* In imagery, the healthy adult mode and the therapist enter the scene side by side; in chair dialogues, both stand up side by side.

6. *Reappraise the situation* based on the perceived needs and chosen values of the client.

7. *Try to activate the blocked or inactive child mode and need* ("standing on both legs"). With anxiously detached or submissive clients, try to unblock constructive anger. Angry protectors and overcompensators need to get in touch with their attachment need again.

8. *If necessary, use the extension or substitution technique* (chapter 5), or act as a role model yourself.

9. *Impeach negative influences,* such as significant others (in imagery) or inner critic modes (in chair dialogues), using constructive anger.

10. *Develop compassion for the child mode* and either soothe the attachment need of the vulnerable child or support the blocked angry child mode so it can become more assertive.

11. *Look for a realistic and sustainable solution* for the initial situation.

12. *Shape your clients' behavior* in order to access their full resources (using impact techniques, body posture, voice, gestures), and fix the change in role-play.

13. *Use discrimination* to increase your client's awareness of the induced change and to support self-efficacy.

14. *Agree on a behavior experiment* for the client to carry out over the following week and on how to track the outcome (for example, with a diary card).

It is your client's behavior in daily life that counts. It is possible that gestalt therapy had limited effectiveness because it focused more on in-session processing, rather than on transferring skills to daily life. Schema therapy connects emotional experience with the overarching case conceptualization. The insight gained in therapy sessions leads to new principles and values guiding healthy adult behavior outside the sessions. Usually, the behavior change phase is the longest in treatment. When your client's healthy adult mode emerges, guide her in applying her new understanding to behavior experiments outside of sessions.

Making Things Real: About Motivation

Setbacks and falling back into old patterns are fairly normal occurrences. (We discussed the underlying neurobiological factors in chapter 1.)

Larry wanted to quit smoking. He thought about it a lot, but there was no change. His thoughts were just transient activations in his neural networks, like small ripples on the surface of the sea. He needed a more visible motivation. He decided to put the money he saved by not smoking every day into a jar and then spend it on a weekend at the beach. The visualization of his progress helped him to access his habits on a deeper level and to change them.

Unfortunately, there are no neurological shortcuts between thinking and doing (Siegel, 1999), as Larry's story indicates (see figure 8–2). To implement change in our lives, we have to take the long way around through the associative implicit and episodic memory structures that are better connected with deeper neural networks. Thus, using emotional engagement to work with solution-directed imagery is more powerful for the reward system. Actions dig deeper than even transient emotions, leading to more complex and intense activations in our neural networks. Only repetitive (or very intense) activation can lead to lasting changes. As therapists, we need to insist that our clients engage in behavior change between therapy sessions. This phase of treatment in schema therapy has a lot in common with conventional behavior therapy, thus you can use well-evaluated, traditional behavioral techniques to enhance self-efficacy, such as skills for relaxation or emotional stabilization, assertiveness training, anger management, self-control strategies (self-monitoring, goal setting, self-reinforcement), and graduated exposure to feared situations (Kellogg & Young, 2006).

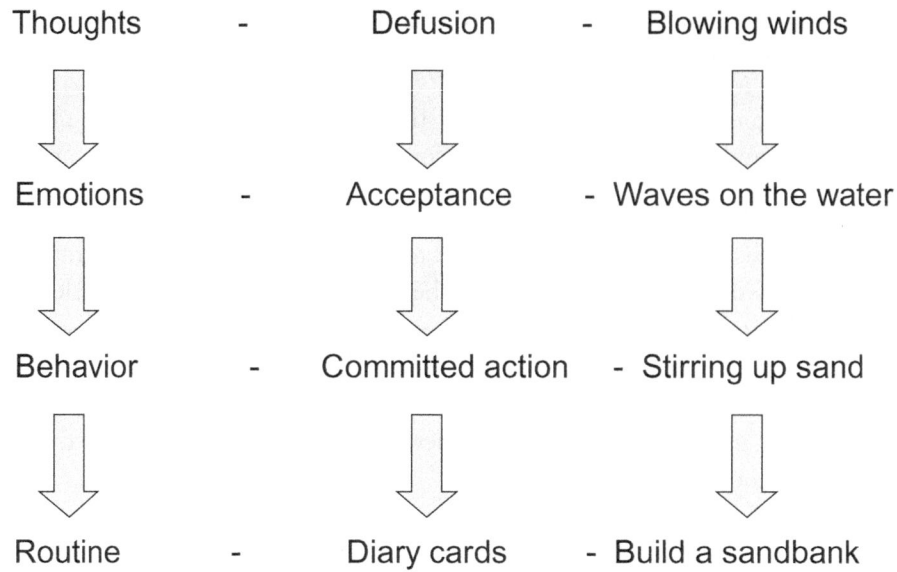

Figure 8–2. Steps for lasting change

Summary

In this chapter, we highlighted some of the underpinnings of the change processes used in schema therapy, including the two-minds model and the need for emotional activation. This knowledge will help you to understand the details of our approach to schema therapy (connecting the implicit and the explicit level of processing), which we outline in the next chapters, starting with imagery work (chapter 9) and then moving to chair dialogues (chapter 10). We describe how to use behavior change techniques in schema therapy in chapter 11.

CHAPTER 9

Imagery Techniques to Induce Mode Change

We now look at specific therapy techniques to help clients manage dysfunctional schema activations. We can also describe this as shifting out of a maladaptive mode. We emphasize the practical in this chapter.

Introducing Imagery Exercises

The past is not past in schema therapy. Imagery exercises lead us back to childhood events to understand the true origin of current schema activations. When clients close their eyes and focus on a remembered scene, that action disconnects them from the surrounding environment and increases their emotional activation.

In this way, "hot," emotion-driven, episodic information processing comes to the fore. "Cold," language-related, semantic information processing steps back. Rather than remaining in semantic memory, imagery takes us across an "affect bridge" to work with associative processes in the episodic memory. This opens up vivid images of scenes that created schemas in childhood. Your clients will eventually realize that behind their current schema activation lies an incident in childhood. This helps them to distance from the urge to act out (see figure 9–1).

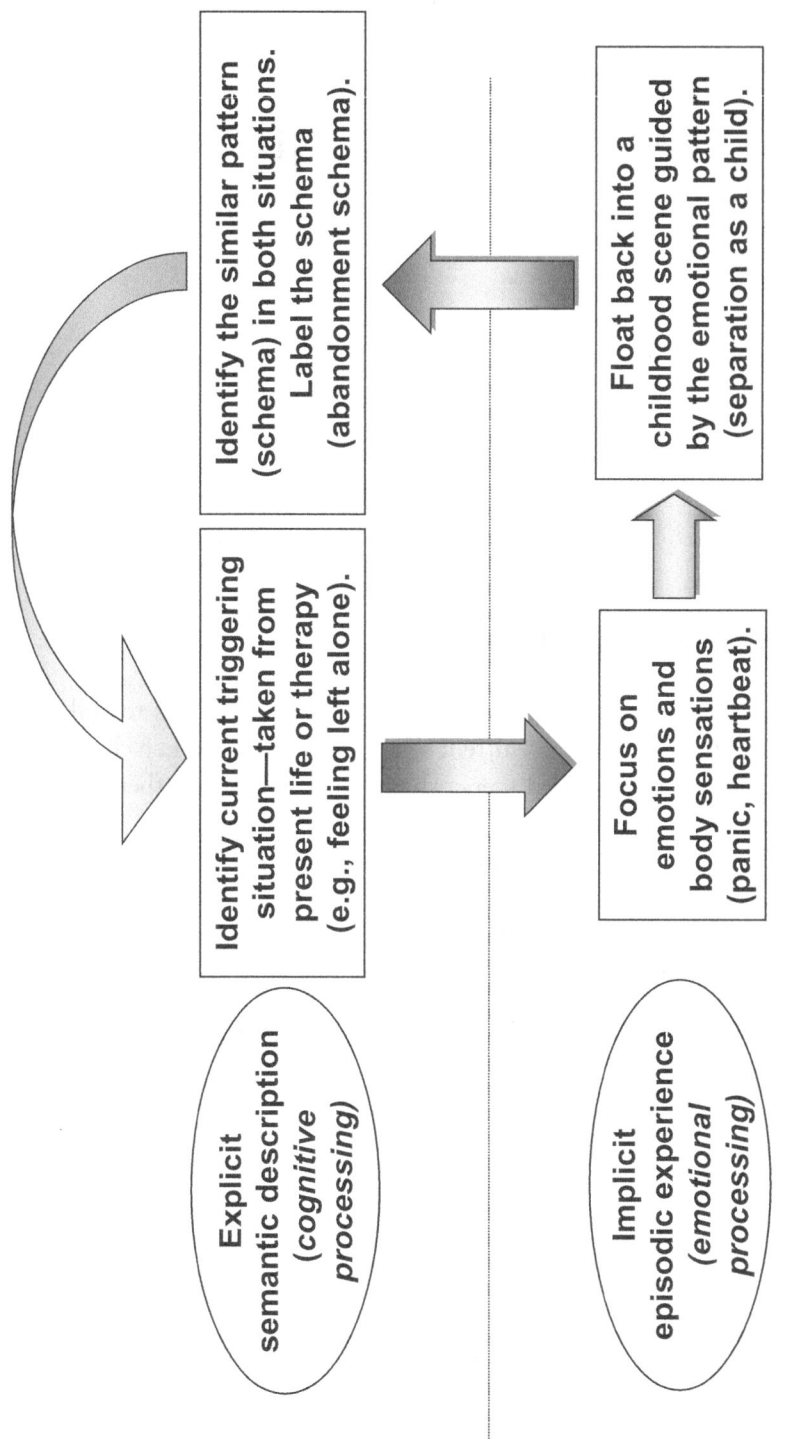

Figure 9–1. Working with the two systems of information processing in imagery (based on Schacter, 1992)

Preparing Clients for Imagery Exercises

When you suggest that clients do imagery exercises, they may initially be reluctant. The following guidelines can help increase their appetite for the work.

Instruction. Assure your clients that imagery has nothing to do with hypnosis. They will remain in full control and can stop the process at any time if they feel uncomfortable.

Closed eyes. Closed eyes can help clients disconnect from the present situation and get in touch with their inner world. Close your eyes at the beginning of the exercise, too. If your clients still feel uncomfortable, give them the option to focus on a spot on the floor or on an empty wall. It is not essential that their eyes be closed.

Open body position. An open body position supports being in touch with softer emotions. Crossed legs or arms fix your client in detached protector mode.

Announcing the length. The length of an imagery exercise varies from about ten to fifteen minutes (for resource- and future-directed imagery) to twenty-five to thirty minutes (for imagery rescripting), and sometimes more than forty minutes (when rescripting traumatic events). Announcing the expected length can prevent clients from becoming impatient.

Different Kinds of Imagery Exercises

Imagery exercises serve several purposes in a variety of ways:

- *Short diagnostic imagery* for a few minutes (as described in the first three steps of "Imagery Rescripting," below) deepens the client experience during sessions.

- *Resource imagery* strengthens self-compassion, well-being, and self-care, bringing clients into a happy child mode.

- *Imagery rescripting* creates a corrective emotional experience of change and strengthens the healthy adult mode.

- *Rescripting traumatic events* deals with traumatic experiences in a gentle way.

- *Imagery dealing with loss, grief, and guilt* helps clients to overcome prolonged grief and resolve unfinished business.

- *Future-directed imagery* prepares clients to carry out behavior experiments.

Resource Imagery

Resource imagery will strengthen client self-efficacy. Through these types of exercises, clients will realize that they have the power to create positive feelings and that there is no need to remain a victim of circumstances. They can take off the "child glasses." Finally, with this type of imagery, the healthy adult mode cares for the vulnerable child mode, just as a caregiver does for a real child.

Principle: Soothing ourselves means creating an internal interpersonal relationship between the healthy adult and child parts by splitting the client into two interacting parts of the self.

There are many resource imagery exercises, including the following three effective options that are frequently used in schema therapy:

- *Safe place imagery* is a rather simple exercise to help clients to relax and feel safe. Through it, the healthy adult mode can learn to create a safe space when needed. This imagery is especially useful for clients who have suffered abuse.

- *Body scan and light ball meditation* is a more challenging and intensive technique to create a deeper sense of peace and a healthy sense of spiritual connection.

- *Caring for the vulnerable child in imagery* builds up the ability for self-compassion and self-care in clients who have a disturbed relationship with themselves (such as feeling worthless, or feeling dirty and guilty after having been abused).

Safe Place Imagery

Safe place imagery is an important skill. The goal is to create a safe place for clients that is always accessible and fully under their control. This is especially important for survivors of childhood trauma. Emphasize, especially for lower-functioning and trauma clients, that they will need to do their emotion regulation exercises as homework. This is the only way for them to develop competence with the practice.

Therapist Tip: Using safe place imagery also provides you, as the therapist, with an indication of whether your clients are willing and able to contribute to their own progress. Once they overcome any initial reluctance and get used to doing safe place imagery, they will feel better.

Willa thought about a beach, the place her family always went on vacation. This was her warmest memory from childhood. She said, "Strangely, my family tended to be nice to each other on vacation. We would get along. It was better without all the stresses of our normal city life."

To support a good result with this exercise, you can suggest something like the following to your client (an audio recording of this exercise, along with this book's other online accessories, is available for download at http://www.newharbinger.com/40958):

1. *Choose a comfortable position.* Loosen constricting clothing. Close your eyes. Try to breathe deeply into your stomach. If it helps, put one hand across your stomach and gently push the hand aside when breathing in. Take some slow, deep breaths, and, as much as possible, let all muscle tension go.

2. *Create a completely safe place.* Choose any place you like. There are no limitations, and anything is possible. Let yourself dream. Everybody dreams! Make sure that the place is completely safe and nobody can enter against your will. Avoid having anyone else present in your safe place. It is a place just for you.

3. *Add more details.* Use all of your senses. What do you see? What do you hear? What do you feel? Any smells? You can provide yourself a house to give you everything you need to feel comfortable. Animals and fantasy figures are welcome.

4. *Relax physically.* Enjoy how your breathing is easy and your heart beats calmly. Feel the warmth of your body. You don't have to do anything, just be there.

5. *Stay awhile.* Start with five minutes. If the exercise works well, you can stay for up to ten minutes. Don't stay too long, though; it's better to practice more frequently. If you want to come back, start counting back from ten to one. Open your eyes when you reach three, and bend your arms when you reach one.

6. *Reflect.* Do you recognize any emotional or physical changes as a result of the exercise? It is *you* who brought those changes about! You can go back to your safe place whenever you want.

There are many ways to create a safe place. If your client is unstable, choose a simple image, such as a "safety bubble" (Farrell & Shaw, 2012). The bubble is flexible, unbreakable, light, warm, and absolutely safe. More stable clients have the ability to develop more complex images, including those of their own individual paradise. For them, going to their safe place will feel like a short vacation.

Body Scan and Light Ball Meditation

Light ball imagery is perhaps closer to a meditation technique, hence our decision to call it a "meditation." You can lead into this exercise with a short body scan, a relaxation technique that is also used in mindfulness-based stress reduction (Kabat-Zinn, 1990) to ground and center clients (audio instructions are available online). You can also use the body scan independently. The light ball meditation can provide some emotional nurturing by creating a sense of light streaming down onto the client. It touches deep places and can bring a sense of connection with a source of light and power outside. This transcendence is especially helpful for clients with a sense of spirituality.

BODY SCAN

The following guidelines are for the body scan. Try this first yourself before introducing it to clients in session. Start with five minutes and extend the time up to fifteen minutes, if you like. (An audio recording of this exercise, along with this book's other online accessories, is available for download at http://www.newharbinger.com/40958.)

1. *Close your eyes.* Take a comfortable seat in an almost upright position, with as little tension as possible. Feel free to correct your position to be more relaxed. Loosen restrictive clothing.

2. *Start with your feet.* Focus your attention on the soles of your feet. Feel how they touch the ground. Relax your feet and each toe. Feel how your bottom rests on the chair. The earth carries all your weight. Let go of the tension from your legs as much as you can.

3. *Feel your back in the chair.* Try to balance your spinal cord. Let your head balance. Try to move your head a bit forward, backward, and to the left and the right, finding the best position. Try to relax the muscles of your neck. Let your arms hang down and relax both hands and all your fingers. Everything hangs down like the rags on a scarecrow.

4. *Breathe into your stomach,* trying not to move your chest. As you breathe out, release a bit of the tension from your body. Try to breathe into your pelvis and relax all muscles there as much as you can. Initially, this might feel artificial—just try to let go!

5. *Relax all the muscles of your forehead.* Also, relax the region around your eyes and cheeks. Open your mouth, if you like. Let your attention wander through your body and let all tension go when breathing out.

6. *Focus on your chest.* Finally, for about five minutes, focus your attention on the space behind your breastbone. Make it the center of yourself. Let all thoughts and feelings pass by, and remain centered as much as you can.

The body scan can stand alone as a relaxation technique, but you might have the client continue with a mindfulness of breath meditation, as described in chapter 7, or any other kind of meditation, depending on your experience in that field. The following is a nice option.

LIGHT BALL MEDITATION

You can do this exercise for ten to fifteen minutes. (An audio recording of this exercise, along with this book's other online accessories, is available for download at http://www.newharbinger.com/40958.)

1. *Focus on your head:* Keep your eyes closed. Don't focus on a specific part. Try to imagine your whole head as a sphere. Make it a clear ball. Take your time. Let all thoughts and feelings go. If you wish, you can think, **My mind is open**.

2. *The light stream:* Try to feel a constant beam of light gently streaming down from above into your clear ball, turning it into a light ball. You may think to yourself, *I'm living in the light*. You might feel that the center of your mind moves a bit upward toward the light. This is okay, but don't let it leave your body.

3. *The light ball:* Let your light ball slowly grow in all directions, up and down as well as to the sides. Don't push yourself, just try to let it grow by itself. The ball should grow around your shoulders and chest and above your head but not below your chest. Your forehead can feel the light, and it's tinted yellow; the region around your heart becomes warm and orange. The thought **Light and warmth are within me** matches well with these sensations.

4. *Nurture the body:* You can let golden light shine from your chest down into your body. The light nurtures your body. Be aware that your body carries you through life like a humble servant. Develop a sense of thankfulness toward your body while the center of your awareness remains within the light ball. Take some time to enjoy the peace you feel now.

5. *Release energy:* You might feel energy streaming through your body from the bottom of your pelvis. Acknowledge it and let it flow while remaining centered in your chest, peacefully observing what is going on.

6. *Awareness:* How do you feel now, compared to the beginning of the exercise? If there is a change, your mind made it. You can do this whenever you want. The light ball is available to you whenever you feel like you need a break. You can find your way to this source of inner peace, to the safe place within yourself.

Caring for the Vulnerable Child in Imagery

This exercise is useful for clients who have difficulty caring for themselves. It is key in schema therapy to support clients in developing self-compassion and the capacity to care for themselves when in vulnerable child mode.

Abuse has many consequences. It is natural for survivors of sexual abuse and domestic violence to think bad thoughts and feel badly about themselves as a result of internalized toxic beliefs. It is hard to approach this challenge in a purely cognitive way. Interestingly, many abused clients are nevertheless able to care competently for their own children. Why the contrast? We find that their inner critic modes keep them from applying this resource to themselves. Through imagery, we try to redirect and help them link this resource to themselves using their innate attachment system. This connection goes deeper than cognition. Try this exercise with a client who shows a lack of self-compassion and self-care. (An audio recording of this exercise, along with this book's other online accessories, is available for download at http://www.newharbinger.com/40958.)

1. Picture yourself returning home from work. It's late and the daylight is fading. You're walking along the street. In front of you appears the silhouette of a child. The child is about six years old. [Note: Match the gender of the child to the client's sex.] Can you see the child?

2. When you get closer, you realize that the child is weeping. Can you see the tears on his cheek? How do you feel? What is your impulse for reaction?

   [Note: If your client shows a healthy, caring reaction, you can continue as described below. If he shows a lack of compassion, you will need to care for the child in the imagery and model an appropriate response for the client.]

3. Can you ask the child what has happened to him?

   [Note: Now you, the therapist, respond as the child by telling a story you know from the life history of the client or from prior diagnostic imagery work.]

4. How does it make you feel when you listen to the story of the child?

   [Note: Once the client realizes that it is his own story, stop and support him to remain in or shift into a healthy caregiving mode.]

5. What does this child need now? What can you say or do for him? How do you see the child reacting? What else can you do for him? How do you feel, taking care of the child?

When the exercise is complete, ask your client to remain with this feeling for some minutes, and then come back into the therapy room. This will help the client to develop self-soothing skills as part of the healthy adult mode.

You might assign this imagery as homework, eventually basing it on an audio recording from the session. Ask the client to go into this picture of self-soothing for a few minutes every evening before going to bed. This could become part of a good-night ritual, such as the one we describe in chapter 11.

Imagery Rescripting

The schema-inducing scenes our clients carry with them were often painful for them, leading them to experiential avoidance. We cannot undo the past, and we cannot delete memory that has been imprinted, but new neural circuits that inhibit the old ones can be established (Hayes et al., 2012). How do we do this? Imagery rescripting builds on an emotional activation and leads us to the original childhood scenes. Rescripting is what brings healing in imagery work. This is where schema therapy becomes *deep*, going back to the origins of schemas. Then we rescript the event based on a reappraisal, bringing a better outcome for clients.

Principle: Rescripting does not change the memory itself, but rather the meaning for the client (Arntz, 2012).

When "floating back" into the client's childhood, you will usually find yourself in a scene that the client did not report during initial history-taking. The client might not remember the incident because, seen through the eyes of an adult, it didn't appear to be significant. However, with a child's view, the relevance changes, and "floating back" reveals that scenes other than those from the client's narrative of the conceptual self contributed to the building up of schemas and thus led to intense emotional activation. So, if your client comes into the session distressed, you will want to access the underlying schemas by immediately going into a diagnostic imagery exercise by using the first three steps described below, presuming the client is stable enough. Here's an overview of the steps for imagery rescripting (these instructions, along with this book's other online accessories, are available for download at http://www.newharbinger.com/40958):

1. *Enter the current scene:* Step out of the ongoing narrative and have the client close her eyes. Let her describe the current scene in the present tense (if not otherwise indicated), with sufficient detail and using a range of senses. Focus on the activated basic *emotions* and *body sensations* while letting the image fade.

2. *Float back:* Avoid long breaks. Keep the client activated by focusing on the emotions and body sensations induced in the scene.

3. *Let a childhood scene appear in the client's mind, guided by emotions:* Encourage the client to use the words of a child to describe the childhood scene she ends up in. Keep her in the emotional tolerance window. Try to get a clear picture of the child's situation for yourself. Ask the client to report feelings and body sensations. When the client is readily activated, "stop the video" and ask for the child's *needs*.

4. *Change perspective:* Enter the scene, together with the client, in the adult state she is in today, standing side by side. Ask for spontaneous feelings. Try to release constructive anger toward any neglectful or abusive people. Determine the degree of released anger that might be helpful in the moment, and decide how to proceed. You might ask for interfering critical thoughts from backstage, use the extension or substitution technique, or act as a role model.

5. *Reappraise the scene:* Look at the effects of the caregiver's behavior on the child. Do not judge the caregiver. However, do disregard the caregiver's intentions and reveal this person's self-centeredness. Let your client choose sides.

6. *Impeach the significant others:* Let your client do as much as she can, but do not leave her on her own. Support her if necessary. Leave the significant others in the care of somebody else. Then try to find some feelings of assertiveness in your client.

7. *Care for the child:* Focus on the child's needs. Ask your client for any soft feelings felt toward the child. Those feelings should be self-compassionate. If not, check inner critic mode voices and use the extension or substitution technique, or act as a role model. Eventually, let your client take the child's role. Ask about any shift in her feelings. You can stop here or continue.

8. *Return to the current scene:* Retain any positive feelings while slowly letting the image of the original scene return.

9. *Find an adaptive solution:* Encourage the client, in healthy adult mode, to find a realistic solution for the original problem. Ask about any feelings that remain.

10. *Discriminate and extract a take-home message:* Encourage your client to compare her feelings now with her feelings at the beginning of the exercise. There should be a significant difference. Then encourage the client to say in one sentence anything she learned from the experience. This will be a principle to apply in other situations.

Rescripting in More Detail

Below, we add details to our description of the ten steps above that may help you to deal with typical problems that occur during imagery rescripting. We offer sample dialogue you might use, too.

For a client's first time with rescripting, we typically use a recent event that the client brought to therapy. Strong emotional reactions indicate the activation of maladaptive schemas.

1. Enter the current scene with an emotional focus.

Nikki started therapy after a negative work evaluation. She saw her supervisor giving her the feedback and felt considerable distress.

Therapist: Instead of talking over the situation, I suggest doing an imagery exercise to understand more about your underlying schemas. So, close your eyes. I'll do the same. Bring up an image of the situation you want to work with. What do you see? What do you hear? Is there anything you smell or taste? How does your body feel? What are your feelings now? [Note: If there are other people in the image, ask] What do the people around you do? Now let the image start to move. Do your feelings get more intense? Go over the most intense part in slow motion again. What do you feel in your chest and your stomach?

Therapist Tip: Letting the client talk in present tense increases emotional activation.

2. Float back.

Therapist: Let the image fade and stay in touch with these feelings, and then drift back in time to your adolescence or childhood. What pictures come to mind? Our mind always has images, which is why we dream in images while sleeping. What picture comes up right now? Tell me without trying to analyze anything!

Nikki thought about bringing her report card home to her father. She was frightened about what his reaction might be.

Therapist Tip: It is helpful to continue talking when you go back to the childhood scene. Do this in a trance-inducing way to keep the client focused and to avoid distracting thoughts. Your words can act like handrails, guiding the client back to the scene. If you stop talking, the silence might encourage intruding thoughts.

3. Picture a childhood scene in detail.

Once your client has gone back in imagery, ask her to describe the scene using a number of sensory channels. This will support emotional activation. Ask for details until you can also see what the child in your client is seeing. Be persistent. Fonagy uses the term "inquisitive stance" to describe the persistence this requires (Fonagy et al., 2004). Research has demonstrated that activating the core scene as vividly as possible for one to three minutes matters (Dibbets & Arntz, 2016). Once the client is sufficiently activated, you can ask her to "stop the video."

Therapist: Everything is on hold right now. You have the remote control in your hand. Nothing happens! You have full control. What do you feel? What do you need right now?

Nikki felt frightened of her father's disapproval. Asking her to identify what she felt in her body intensified the feeling. "I feel tight in my chest. It's intense." Her therapist said, "If it gets to be too much, just raise your hand. I can help you get back a sense of control." Nikki was able to manage and keep doing the imagery work.

Therapist Tip: Don't stay long with the details once the client is readily activated. The purpose is emotional activation, not investigating the scene in detail.

4. Change perspective—the adult enters the scene.

Therapist: Can you picture yourself entering the scene as the adult person you are now?

Note that the situation becomes safer if you also enter the scene, standing side by side with the client. This creates an opportunity for you to intervene immediately if your client is not able to adequately rescript the scene.

Therapist: What do you feel now, as an adult, coming in and watching the scene?

Eventually, your client's anger will grow as she describes the scene.

Therapist: What do you feel now, seeing how the child suffered? How does that resonate in your body?

Your client needs to feel the power of her anger. This will help her to oppose any abusers in the imagery.

Identify whether any anger is blocked. If anger remains blocked, say something like "I feel that you're still blocked. Maybe you're trapped in vulnerable child mode feelings (or detached protector mode). This is okay, but it means that we have to do something different." There are two approaches you can take, depending on the time left in the session and the state of the therapy:

- Take the initiative and use the extension technique or substitution technique described in chapter 5. Alternatively, carry out an impeachment as therapist. This is probably most appropriate early in therapy or when a session is close to ending. It is best not to be overly dramatic when using this technique.

- Go backstage into the client's inner world to reveal blocking demanding or punitive critic mode voices that do not allow the client to feel anger. (This should be done later in therapy, in order to strengthen healthy adult mode and encourage assertiveness.)

Consider how the therapist handled the client's blocked anger in this case example:

Nathan was not able to feel any anger at the scene in which he was bullied by a group of older students. He said, "I feel helpless. It isn't right to feel anger; it's not a safe emotion." His therapist asked who had given him such a message. He said, "Mom. She was a religious person and thought the Bible said it was wrong to be angry." His therapist reminded Nathan that "even God was angry at times in the Bible, and Jesus was angry with the money changers. When you're angry, you are protesting unfair treatment. It wasn't right for those bullies to treat you that way. I want you to turn down the volume of that demanding critic voice. Now can you feel some anger about how the child in the picture was treated?" Nathan was silent for a moment and then said, "Yes, I can feel some anger. It wasn't right!"

Therapist Tip: Your client may be strongly identified with the originator of such messages, as Nathan was with his mother. Often, such a significant other has turned into the inner critic through internalization (see "Mentalization and the Theory of Mind," in chapter 1) and thus feels ego-syntonic.

5. Reappraise the scene and choose sides.

This is a critical step for many clients. You may invoke a loyalty conflict if your client identifies too strongly with an inner critic mode. In order to avoid loyalty conflicts, be careful about being too confrontational or harsh.

Chloe had a powerful demanding critic mode, which she recognized to be "the voice of my mother." Her therapist recognized that if he tried to oppose this voice he would lose. The mother's influence was too strong. He went slowly and was careful to bring his client with him step-by-step by doing some chair dialogues first (see chapter 10).

Focus on the effects. Again, choose your words carefully. Your client may need time to accept them from a healthy adult point of view. You can focus more on the *negative effects* rather than on *judging* significant others. This will help to demonstrate understanding.

Therapist: (*To a punitive critic mode*) Okay, we have to acknowledge that Tom is still loyal to you. However, from an outside perspective, I must state that the effect of your words on Tom is not helpful for him. You have paralyzed him, pulverized his self-esteem, and been delighted when he has failed. Whatever your intention was, it didn't work and he is now in therapy. So we recognize that you're not helpful. Now we ask you to stand aside. We'll take over.

Ask for the resonance. Once you have made such a statement, ask your client how it resonated with him. Make sure you include both the emotional impact (in the body, say) and whether he thought that your words sounded reasonable. Both elements are required to be able to impeach the influence of a significant other. The combination of constructive anger felt in the body and the permission from the client's healthy self is powerful.

Let clients use their own words. Ask your client to convey the message using his own words, speaking directly to the significant other. If he hesitates, be direct: "What irritates you in what I was saying?" Generally, if you have been moderate, your client will come to agree with you.

Be aware of loyalty conflicts. Nevertheless, sometimes your client will feel bad. In that case, try something like this: "Okay, so we have a conflict between your healthy adult mode seeing the truth and the inner critic mode still defeating it. What are they saying to you?" The response might be something like "Don't be so hard. It's your father. He was mistreated as a child. He only wanted what was best for me…"

Once you gather the statements of the demanding or punitive critic voices, either shift into a chair dialogue or ask the client to put the voices aside for a moment. Then affirm that the caregivers did the best they could but nevertheless violated the child's needs.

Therapist: (*To the inner critic modes*) I know you wanted what was best for Tom, and that this seemed the best way to encourage him. However, the result shows that it didn't work. So we're taking over now and letting you go.

Then ask your client how it felt to hear the words. Repeat this process. Slowly try to lead him into a healthy adult perspective. It does not matter if you become stuck. What is most important is to remain connected with your client and to start a process of disidentification from the significant other through the inner critic voices. This might take several attempts over a long time frame. Remain patient but persistent!

Remember to keep in mind the following goals when doing imagery rescripting:

- *Help* your client to become familiar with constructive anger and to make effective use of it.

- *Insist* that your client choose sides. It is imperative that the client takes a stance for the child, sorts out internalized and toxic beliefs, replaces them with expressions of personal values, and then meets the child's needs.

This combination of goals encourages the client to distance from the harmful legacy of negative relationships.

6. Impeach the significant others.

Therapist: What do you want to say or do now, making use of the power of your constructive anger?

Your client will not make much progress without being in touch with underlying anger. The anger the client feels in the healthy adult mode is coming from the angry child mode (and the activated assertiveness need behind it). This is the way the healthy adult experiences emotions (through being connected with the child modes). Remember to do the following.

Take a slow pace. It is important not to rush to rescripting before your client feels his anger. This is what empowers the healthy adult in imagery work. Without anger, the confrontation with the abusive person can fail.

Access constructive anger. Unless constructive anger (Greenberg, 2015) is unblocked, your client will not be able to escape the "dungeon of submission." It is crucial that the client accesses adaptive anger in order to empower self-assertiveness under the control of the healthy adult. You may find that a passive client starts to have outbursts of anger on other occasions. This is a sign of progress, so it makes sense to unblock the client's anger and show him how he can use it in a constructive way.

Strengthen your client in the imagery. If the client feels powerless, use imagery to increase her size and strength.

Chloe's therapist found that she was intimidated by her father. She was looking up to him in the imagery. So the therapist made her ten feet tall, enabling her to look down on her father. In this way, she felt confident enough to tell him how she felt about him being so authoritarian.

Avoid involving people from the past. Some schema therapists use a good grandmother or a favorite teacher to assist in imagery work, but this has the drawback of being part of the "old story." Our goal is not to undo what actually happened in the past, since this is carved into the client's memory. Imagery rescripting is not about changing history, but changing the meaning.

Check the facts. The intention is to separate intrusive memory from current perception, and in this way to help our client escape flashbacks and being trapped in old reaction patterns. The reason we help clients to check the facts in the *present* is to help them realize that in imagery they can enter the *past* and rescript it.

Avoid parentification. Many of our clients were parentified children, so we emphasize that they are not responsible for taking care of significant others in imagery. While rescripting, we prefer to leave a parent in the care of professionals (for example, psychiatric care for a depressed mother, inpatient treatment for a drug-addicted father, or jail for an abusive person). Affirm that there is no longer any risk of harm and that the child is safe now.

Chloe stood up to her father in imagery work. Her anger empowered her, and by entering healthy adult mode she was able to protect her child self. She felt less responsible for her father when her therapist suggested that her father could see a therapist to help him deal with his anger.

> *Principle:* The role of the healthy adult is not to care for the others but to care for the child!

Check back about the client's feelings. When you have impeached offenders in imagery, ask about what is happening for your client's healthy adult. If the work goes well, we expect a feeling of assertiveness (emotion) and the thought that the action was justified (adjusted beliefs). Also ask about any feelings in the body (look for some sense of strength). Then care for the child. This requires some self-compassion.

7. Care for the child.

Activate self-compassion. Make sure that the client really feels compassion for the child. If she doesn't, ask for interfering "voices in the head" from inner critic modes and work with them in chair dialogues, using the extension or substitution technique, or acting as a role model. Caring requires unblocking or building up self-compassionate feelings.

Therapist: Be aware of feeling some compassion for the child. What do you want to say or do now to care for him? How does the child react? What do you see in his eyes? What else does the child need?

Shifting into the child perspective increases emotional activation (Holmes & Mathews, 2010) and, in our experience, the impact of the intervention.

Therapist: So take the place of the child now. How do you feel? What do you notice in your body? What else do you need from the adult?

Frequently, the child asks that the adult never leave again. This is a good point at which to suggest the good-night ritual, explored in chapter 11.

And finally, check in with the client and ask him to shift back into the adult perspective:

Therapist: How do you feel now, at the end of this exercise? How about your feelings? Can you feel any difference?

There are four options for continuing now:

a. *Terminate* the exercise here by counting backward from ten to one. This is appropriate when the session is close to ending.

b. *Exit* the exercise with a safe place imagery to strengthen self-compassion.

c. *Return* to the situation from which you started the exercise to support the client's problem-solving skills.

d. *Change* to a chair dialogue to continue working with the inner critic modes, if they appear very powerful, and to counteract the rescripting.

Exit via safe place imagery. If you exit via safe place imagery, we suggest that you, as the therapist, go with your client in both the adult and child states to make sure they both arrive safely and feel comfortable. Then you can say good-bye to both, assigning the adult the responsibility to care for the child. You can leave a cell phone (in the imagery) in case the client needs your support. This builds a bridge to reality, because in our practice we allow clients to call us if they are at risk (or send a text message). Having such an option in the imagery helps clients feel calm, and they can then let you go.

8. Return to the current scene you started from.

Therapist: Can you now become aware of your emotions and what you sense in your body? What do you feel? Now, very slowly bring up the image of what you first talked about. Bring it up slowly enough that you can stay in touch with your current emotions.

9. Find an adaptive solution.

Therapist: Now that you're again in the scene we started with, what would you like to say or do now to bring about a better result? Can you see yourself doing that? How do the other people react? Can you try something else?

10. Discriminate and offer a take-home message.

Therapist: Once the scene comes to an end, tell me how you feel? If you compare your feelings now with your initial feelings, is there a difference? If you were to try to say, in one sentence, what you have learned from this experience, what would be the take-home message?

Exit by asking the client to come back into the therapy room slowly while you count backward from ten to one, asking her to open her eyes at four and to have a stretch at one. Usually, the atmosphere in the therapy room changes dramatically.

It is helpful to repeat this imagery exercise a few times early in the therapeutic process to put the client in touch with the schemas inducing child mode feelings (diagnostic part) and to foster the therapy relationship by being supportive during the rescripting. You can work with either the same or a different scene. If the client acted passively in the first session, it especially makes sense to bring him into a more active role in the second attempt. Early in therapy you will be a role model, showing the steps for confronting significant others and caring for the child. For many clients, especially those with significant trauma, this might be the first time they experience anyone caring for them. Gradually, over the course of therapy, the goal is to strengthen clients' healthy adult mode by letting them take a more active role. Complex schema therapy techniques such as imagery rescripting and mode dialogues on chairs (see chapter 10) always include a behavior change part. Thus, the therapist gently lets the client take over.

> *Principle:* Over the course of therapy, it is essential for the locus of control to shift from the therapist to the client in order to encourage self-efficacy and prevent possible overdependence on the therapist.

If your client has difficulties taking an active role in the rescripting process, it makes sense to repeat the exercise. Once she has coped with a particular situation, you can go on to other (eventually more painful) episodes from her current life. After working through two or three typical situations, your client will begin to realize how similar the situations are. You can try to link each to a specific schema from your case conceptualization. In this way, the microlevel of the current episode is linked to the underlying schemas on the macrolevel.

Additional Ways to Access Childhood Images

Sometimes the invitation to float back in imagery does not work. There are other options using various starting points.

Start from an emotionally activated state arising in session. If a client becomes angry or sad in a session (for example, when moving to a child mode chair in a chair dialogue), do not "talk it down," rather, start imagery work immediately: "Oh, I see you're feeling some strong emotions right now. Let's shift into an imagery exercise to get in touch with your underlying schemas. This is an opportunity to achieve something important. Close your eyes, please, and look at the image you are reacting to."

Pick up on a conflict with the therapist. Be watching for an incident that involves you as a therapist: "When I informed you about being away for four weeks over the summer holidays, I saw something in your eyes. You seemed tense. Could you please close your eyes and get in touch with your feelings when I first told you of my vacation?"

Use critical past scenes. Start with an incident from the client's history: "You told me in your life history about the scene when your brother burned your puppet in the fireplace. Do feel strong enough to work with this image?"

Everyday life in childhood. Start with a typical day in the client's childhood and then approach a seemingly difficult situation. Begin with something relatively safe. For example, if the problem was in the childhood home, start with coming home from school. If the problem was being bullied in school, start with leaving home in the morning. Look for details that trigger emotional activation.

Therapist: You said there are no troublesome memories from your past. That's fine. However, I would like to know more about your life as a child. How about school? Can you picture the school building? Can you see your friends at school? What are their names? [Note: Use present tense for more intensity!] Do you know the name of your favorite teacher? What do you eat during the breaks? What do you play? How do you feel? How does that resonate in your body? Now let's go back home. Can you see the street? What details do you remember? Now you see your home. How does that feel? Any changes? Can you see the door? How many steps do you take to get in? Can you see the staircase? You're standing in front of the door to your apartment. How does that feel in your body? What's waiting for you behind the door? Who is there? Okay, you're alone. Nobody's at home. There's something for you to eat in the fridge. What are you going to do? How does that feel? What do you need now?

This strategy is helpful if your client has difficulties retrieving images from the past.

Special events in childhood. Enter typical domestic situations, such as Christmas or vacations, and explore the atmosphere in general and what used to happen.

Ask for an image of the parents. In a video Jeffrey Young shows in his workshops, he asked this of one of his clients who pretended not to have any childhood memories. He asked him to bring up an image of his mother from when he was four years old. The client said, "I see a marble statue." This provided a good starting point for therapy.

Photographs of the child. Ask clients to bring to therapy some photographs from their childhood. Many clients appreciate looking at the photographs from a joint perspective. You might notice one showing a sad child. Ask the client how the child feels and what it needs. Once some emotions emerge, ask your client to close his eyes and start the imagery exercise.

Rescripting Traumatic Events

You can also work through upsetting or traumatic scenes from childhood using a direct approach (without floating back through the associative memory processes). List the client's memories in a hierarchy rated by level of distress (from 1 to 10). Start with a less challenging one.

Safety First: Keeping the Client in the Emotional Tolerance Window

When you work with traumatic incidents, it is important to check the client's levels on the subjective units of distress scale (SUDS) and try to keep her in a therapeutic window (other than in the few minutes of vivid imagination in the beginning) of about 6 to 8. What follows are some techniques for keeping clients in the emotional tolerance window.

Increase intensity. Ask clients to keep their eyes closed, look through the child's eyes, describe details in a multisensory way, focus on body sensations, and speak in first-person language and in present tense.

Reduce intensity. Ask clients to describe the scene from a distant observer's perspective, as if watching a video or a movie, in a general manner and avoiding details. Remind clients that they can slow down or stop the video. Ask them to talk in the past tense and the third person. If these methods fail to reduce their activation level, ask them to open their eyes.

The observer's perspective reduces emotional activation compared to the immersive experience of being part of the scene (Holmes & Mathews, 2010). Rather than leaving the image altogether, try to stabilize the client in the "frozen" picture.

Therapist Tip: Leaving the image can be a sign of avoidance on the part of both client and therapist! It is the job of the therapist to support the healthy adult mode of the client, not the experientially avoidant side!

You can also help your clients to regain control by using the following techniques:

- Keep reminding them that they are in healthy adult mode, the picture is frozen, and they have full control. Sometimes this requires being persistent. Insist that your client is capable of switching into healthy adult mode and of using an observer's perspective.

- Make them ten feet tall. Give them supernatural powers and, if necessary, weapons!

- Make the child safe behind a thick, unbreakable glass wall, or use a safety bubble.

- Bring police officers into the picture.

The idea is to make clients feel stronger than the offender. This will help them to regain control in the situation. Sometimes this requires our persistence.

Dealing with Dissociation

The therapist must respond when faced with dissociation. Take the initiative if your client is having difficulty, which can include a felt sense of losing control in the imagery or of shutting down emotionally. Gently lead the client without giving any sense that he or she has failed. Your task is to bring the exercise to a good end. We recommend the following three basic steps: change the content, change the position, change the room.

Dissociation does not usually mean that your client is in a helpless or victim-like state. Think about dissociation as a shift in the quality of perception. The ability to perceive is itself not generally diminished. Also, in a dissociative state your client will still maintain some control and not be in danger. (Even if she drives home in her car!) To manage dissociation, we have a few recommendations.

Consider the interpersonal meaning of the displayed behavior. Dissociating in an imagery exercise is usually a sign of a self-protecting mode, but it can also be part of a manipulative overcontroller mode. If your client starts dissociating close to the end of a session, consider the possibility that this might be a manipulative strategy. It may express the wish of a needy child mode trying to get attention or extend time with you. As for all coping modes, you should address, label, and validate them—but don't reinforce them!

The following guidelines can be followed step-by-step. If a step does not work, do not remain stuck there. If you face dissociation, do not be daunted but demonstrate strength and self-confidence. Your clients will hear you even if they don't react:

1. Maintain the verbal connection in the imagery. Avoid silence, because you will not have any indication about what your client is experiencing.

2. Maintain contact by having you and your client each hold the end of a scarf or fleece (Farrell et al., 2014). You can maintain contact with your client by gently pulling the article of clothing.

3. Ask the client to open his eyes and describe the room in which you are both sitting. Changing sensory input will bring attractor changes.

4. Give up a visual task and return to grounding: "What do you see now in my office? What sound can you hear right now? What can you physically perceive?" Start with one perception in each modality and note up to five things seen, heard, or felt at a good pace, keeping the client busy.

5. Ask your client what she had for breakfast, or to remember the names of the streets she took to reach your office.

6. Throw a pencil, a soft ball, or a little pillow toward your client so he will try to catch it in a reflexive way. You might offer a damp cloth for his face.

7. With an appropriate warning, grab one of your client's wrists with one hand and, putting your other hand on her shoulder, move them gently in the opposite direction.

8. Tell the client that you will assist him up out of his chair to walk around your office. Go to a window and look outside. If it is safe, perhaps open it to let fresh air into the room.

9. If possible, walk down some steps in a staircase.

10. If nothing else works, place the client in your waiting room and tell her she can leave whenever she wants. Calling an ambulance only makes sense in a genuine emergency.

11. Try to remain in touch with an email or a phone call during the day. This will help you to reconnect.

Therapist Tip: Helping a client come back from dissociation requires delicate balance. Try to stop dissociative behavior quickly, while not reinforcing it by offering too much attention.

Steps of the Imagery Exercise with Traumatized Clients

For imagery exercises with traumatic scenes, you can start with a scene reported in the client's history or use something from the hierarchical list. Ask the client to write an outline of the scene he or she wants work with. This will provide you with an overview. The rescripting follows three steps:

1. Go through the whole scene at a moderate pace and assess the client's level of activation and distress using SUDS ratings. Remember to identify the hot spots (there might be more than one). Just scan; don't go deeper into the client's feelings.

2. Start working with one of the hot spots. Activate the client for about two minutes on the upper edge of the emotional tolerance window, and then "stop the video," asking for the child's experience and needs.

3. Enter the scene with both you and the client in the healthy adult mode under safe conditions, and then impeach the offender and care for the needs of the child. We recommend that *both* you and the client enter the image in healthy adult mode (eventually supported by some powerful others) because it helps to balance the locus of control.

SUDS ratings. Keep asking your client for SUDS ratings to monitor his level of activation. When he gets close to dissociation, he might appear distanced while internally suffering from unhealthy stress. However, do not be overly concerned if the SUDS score is elevated during the visual exercise, especially once you enter the hot spots. This is just the body's alarm system. After impeaching offenders, your client will remain in an activated state but usually perceive this activation as less distressing, feeling better afterward. Generally, SUDS scores will not drop much further until you meet the needs of the child.

Remain patient. Do not expect too much from the first exercise. Any reduction in SUDS levels is significant, indicating that your client has regained a level of control over the situation and developed some self-efficacy. Repeat the exercise to increase the effect. Then gradually use it to manage more challenging situations.

Audio recordings. We recommend that you tape an imagery session, using the client's smartphone, or whatever is convenient for her, and ask her to listen to it between sessions at least once or twice (as recommended by Smucker & Dancu, 1999). It is not so much that habituation is effective (Craske et al., 2008), but listening to the recording again seems to strengthen the adaptive message of a successful imagery session and connect it with everyday experience. Imagery rescripting and reprocessing is a powerful tool, so do not hesitate to spend several therapeutic sessions making use of it. The recording has greater effect than just talking about a situation. Many of our clients have regarded such recordings as the most important and helpful element of their therapy.

Limitations. With severely traumatized or low-functioning clients, it can help if you let them watch the rescripting from behind a thick glass wall (Smucker & Dancu, 1999). Some colleagues recommend taking the child out of the picture, but we consider this helpful only in extreme cases, such as with clients with dissociative identity disorders. Although Arnoud Arntz is currently using the schema therapy approach with such clients (personal communication at the Attachment and Trauma Conference in Rome on September 25, 2015), for now we suggest using more specific approaches, such as the structural dissociation model (Van der Hart, Nijenhuis, & Steele, 2006). Our approach requires the client to contribute a minimum amount of healthy adult mode. Once aligned with a growing healthy adult mode, the client can loosen the emotional connection with abusers.

Dealing with excessive anger. Sometimes a client will unleash extreme anger against abusers. This is a natural reaction, but it can feel excessive. At one level, it is healthy assertiveness and an important rebalancing of power, but the expression can appear frightening.

Harry was in a rage when he felt the violation of sexual abuse as a young teenager. He said, "I keep thinking about killing him. All the ways I could do it, with a knife, a gun, or, my favorite...strangle him with my hands."

Reflect: How do you respond when a client is very angry and speaks in a violent way?

What do we do if a client wants to be violent toward an abuser in imagery? Schema therapists have mixed views about this. One option is to go with the flow and initially allow the client to fully vent anger in imagery. But some research suggests that the amount of expressed anger is not related to the outcome (Seebauer, Froß, Dubaschny, Schönberger, & Jacob, 2014). To support self-assertiveness, we consider it best to allow the client to fully express anger within the imagery exercise.

The reprocessing of sexual abuse usually follows three steps:

1. Revengeful outbursts of aggression toward the abuser

2. Revealing the secret and making the abuse public

3. Getting rid of the abuser and "throwing the person away"

These three steps follow a natural process of overcoming feelings of helplessness and dependence on the abuser. Remember that with sexual abuse, the offender is not only the source of pain but very often was also the only source of some emotional attention. The responsible caregivers (usually the mother) were primarily absent or neglectful, and the abuser filled the gap. It is common for the abuser to first gain the trust of the child, through what is called grooming, possibly inducing emotional dependency. Hence, stepping out of the abuse also means giving up the emotional attachment.

Additionally, attempts to make the abuse public may have failed if detached caregivers did not believe the child. Therefore, helping clients abused in childhood means both dealing with the trauma and supporting them in their individuation from the abuser. The three steps above do this along a path leading to autonomy. Usually the emotional connection with the therapist provides a lifeline for clients crossing their valley of despair (see figure 9–2).

> **Therapist Tip:** You might encourage clients to write down traumatic experiences that they are ashamed to speak openly about in session. Some victims of severe abuse were prohibited from saying anything about their abuse to strangers. However, drawing pictures or using modeling clay might be "allowed." Once you have a clear picture of the abuse, shift to processing the material and bringing in clients' healthy adult mode to restabilize their everyday life.

The healing process includes integrating prior isolated traumatic events into the clients' self-narrative and making those events part of their life history. This can help them emotionally disconnect from such an event and "forget it"—that is, let it go. It is then possible for them to avoid triggering situations and getting caught in flashbacks. This lays a foundation for revising the internal working model and impeaching inner critic modes through chair dialogues as part of the working phase of therapy.

Imagery Dealing with Loss, Grief, and Guilt

You can use imagery with many different clinical presentations. It will deepen any kind of emotional experience, so it's a natural fit for working with grief or loss of any kind. Imagery work is more effective than thinking about the loss or talking about it, because ruminating thoughts tend to reinforce current thinking. As a result, maladaptive schemas remain. Change needs a strong push, and imagery work can provide it. You will find that your case formulation will guide your work with complicated grief reactions, too.

Jenny's father committed suicide two years before she entered therapy. She could not get over her grief and associated symptoms, which included overwhelming sadness (vulnerable child), anger toward her father and others (angry child), guilt (inner critic), alcohol binges (detached self-soother), and distancing herself from her loved ones (detached protector). From this perspective, her ongoing grief reaction could be understood as a collection of maladaptive coping modes (self-soothing and detachment) serving to block the "normal" processing of underlying emotional states, thus keeping her stuck.

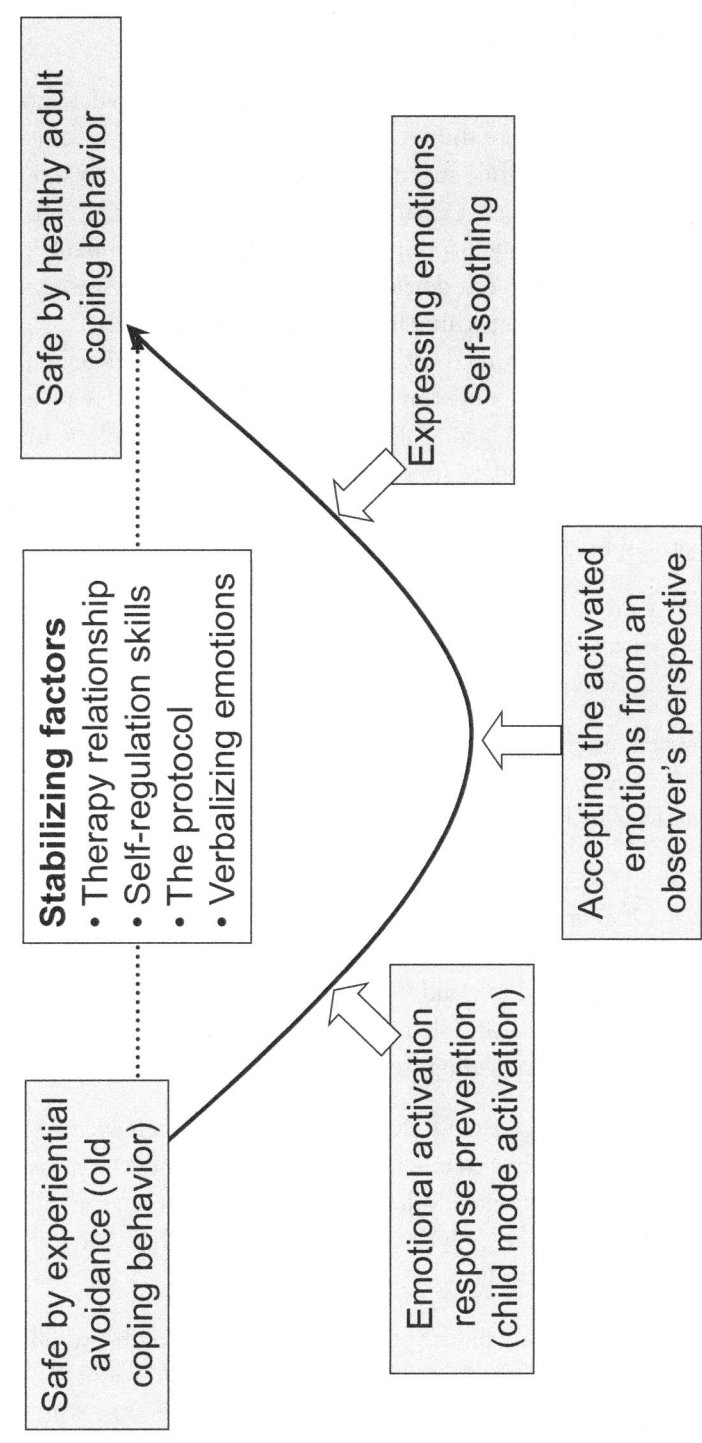

Figure 9–2. The healing process in experiential work

Farewell Imagery

Consider a challenging case of grief following the loss of a daughter who committed suicide. Clearly, this is more than a "simple" loss, as it also involves issues of guilt about possible mistakes made while raising the child. It is not easy to sort this out emotionally. It is understandable that one would dwell on any possible mistakes made while raising the child, so simply disputing negative thoughts is unlikely to be helpful. The client may well respond, "You don't understand my feelings, since you didn't lose your child." We recommend something like the following approach.

A schema therapist worked with Mary, who had lost her daughter, Sally. The therapist asked Mary to close her eyes and asked her permission to create a special encounter with Sally in an imagery space. Calling the daughter by her name instead of talking of "your daughter" increased Mary's emotional engagement. The therapist placed an empty chair in front of Mary. Then he dimmed the light in the therapy room to create a special atmosphere and encouraged Mary to bring up a vivid image of Sally.

Therapist: Can you see Sally clearly? What is she wearing? She's sitting right in front of you. You can see and talk to her. How does she look? What can you see in her eyes? How do you feel? What do you want to say to her?

He moved his chair close to Mary, speaking in a soft voice, and encouraged her to go deeper into her pain, disappointment, and guilt feelings. He guided her from general statements to a more emotional expression of her deeper and evidently ambivalent feelings.

Therapist: Of course you felt abandoned when she decided to kill herself instead of trying to get in touch with you. Tell her how you feel. It's normal that you feel guilty. How did you feel then and how do you feel now? You are disappointed, and there are some kind of angry feelings, too. You can now convey those feelings to Sally. She can take it. She's on the other side!

He gave Mary enough time—five minutes or so—to remove herself from her cognitive state and be in touch with her emotions. At this point, Mary was in tears. He knew she had reached an emotional level. Once Mary had explored the full range of her emotions, he asked her to take Sally's position in the other chair. He moved his chair close to hers in order to support her.

Therapist: Hello, Sally. Thank you for coming here. You heard all that your mother said. How does that make you feel? What do you want to say to her from the place you're in now? What do you want her to do?

Then Mary, sitting on Sally's chair, answered toward the empty chair that she had been sitting on.

The outcome of this exercise may depend on the assumed reaction of the person who died. Surprisingly, your client's reaction may be mild and not resentful. It is natural for us to try to move hurtful or difficult situations toward some kind of resolution, because anything else would mean remaining in a state of unresolved grief. When the response comes to a natural end, ask your client to return to her original chair. Give her a moment to arrive back. Usually, your client will accept messages from the deceased. This may give some relief and peace, as it did Mary.

Therapist: How does it make you feel, hearing these messages from Sally? Do you believe her? Does this change anything? Now that you've been in touch with Sally and you know that she's well and safe, is there something more you want to convey to her? You mentioned in an earlier session that you feel guilty about all the mistakes you made. Now we have the chance to tell this to Sally. Go ahead! How does Sally react? And you told me that you felt kicked out of her life when she left without a word. Tell this to her face now. She can now face your feelings from her side!

Encouraging such underlying, and sometimes not socially acceptable, feelings requires some sensitivity from the therapist. Usually, we take the lead when the client becomes stuck. Sometimes it is safer to take a Socratic stance by asking more or less open questions. You can softly bring in your own feelings by saying something like this: "Sitting beside you now, I feel some disappointment that Sally didn't give you the chance to talk to her before she decided to leave."

The word "disappointment" is helpful for getting in touch with the angry child mode because it combines sadness with some anger. Once you have reached a deeper and more complex (or honest) level of emotional activation, ask the client to move to the daughter's chair once more. Again, as Mary's therapist did, you should change sides and sit beside the client.

Therapist: Sally, you heard what your mother said. I'm happy that she opened up to you even more. How does this make you feel? Do you understand her? What do you want to say to her? Knowing this, what's your message to her now? Can you forgive her?

These last questions are intended to break the chain of mutual disappointment and fatal enmeshment. We cannot change history, but when the underlying feelings have not been expressed, they continue blocking and undermining everyday life. This is the toxic effect of the "forbidden" and thus unspoken messages. Once we set the stage by creating an interpersonal encounter in imagery, we then encourage our client to speak out the blocked feelings. Only then can reconnection and social healing happen.

Therapist: You heard that Sally understands your feelings and can forgive you. What do you see in her eyes now? How does this make you feel? Can you accept what you did in the past? What do you want to say to her now? Can you forgive her, too? Do you want to follow her advice for you? Is there something else to say before we let Sally go?

Do not avoid using powerful words such as "forgiving." They carry emotional weight. Eventually, these words help to reconnect the threads that have been severed. It is now time to bring your client back to the present by asking her to return to her accustomed chair.

The effect of this exercise is often surprising. Repeating it a few times in sessions deepens the experience and makes it lasting. If you have an emotional connection with a client who is an offender, this exercise can also help the individual reconcile guilt. This makes imagery work even more valuable, because recovery from human-related trauma is more difficult than recovery after fatal events, such as accidents or natural disasters. You can put God or fate on the other chair, if you need to work through catastrophic events in nature in which loved ones were hurt or killed. (Instructions for imagery dealing with loss, grief, and guilt, along with this book's other online accessories, are available for download at http://www.newharbinger.com/40958.)

Future-Directed Imagery

Imagery is not only for dealing with the past. We can use it to prepare for future changes, too. The mental steps in preparing to do something can be complex. Think of what happens when we go from intention to an executed action: the move can be long and difficult. Images are the interface between what we think we want to do and the emotion-driven processes in our limbic system. Enriching a desired goal with a vivid picture through imagery is beneficial. It gives salience (Berridge & Robinson, 1998) and energizes the client.

Some of our clients need additional help, perhaps to deal with cognitive fusion or to overcome experiential avoidance, in order to develop an image they can approach. It helps to access empowering energy, because some depressed clients find it difficult to make a wish or name a goal. They just feel blunted, blocked, or dead inside. We discuss how to deal with such clients in chapter 13. One potentially helpful tool is the "best day" video.

The "Best Day" Video

Based on the crystal ball technique (De Shazer, 1985), the "best day" video technique tries to bypass a fused cognitive state by jumping into the future. Imaginatively, this brings clients into a new setting different from their current blocked state. It is like pushing the reset button to reboot a computer.

> Okay, I get the message that there is nothing for you. You're not hoping for anything good. Nothing interests you. So let's do an imagery exercise instead of talking things through. Please close your eyes and relax as much as you can right now. Tomorrow, a camera team will show up and record a video of your best day. You're the director of this movie. Anything's possible and your budget is unlimited. Everybody dreams at night, and now it's time for your dream to come true. Just let your thoughts flow

and answer as spontaneously as you can. What bed are you waking up in? Is there somebody lying in the bed beside you? Describe the place where the bed is. What breakfast do you have? Where are you going to work? What job are you doing? What else are you going to do today? Who will you meet? How does it feel, being the main actor in this video? How does that feel in your body?

The purpose of this exercise is to bring clients into a kind of dream reality and entangle them on an emotional level. Then you stand with them, forming a consultant team and deciding which features of the video could become part of "real" life. The images clients bring forth may include a lot of unrealistic features, but they will also include some needs-based elements, such as meeting other people or starting some activities. We take those elements that are connected with the induced feeling of empowerment and then consider what first small steps clients might take to move toward them. (An audio recording of this exercise, along with this book's other online accessories, is available for download at http://www.newharbinger.com/40958.)

Imagery Rehearsal and Behavioral Activation Imagery

Another use of imagery is for clients to rehearse for upcoming attempts at breaking behavioral patterns. First, have the client choose the concrete situation he wants to work with. What are the relevant details? Find out the goal or best outcome. Then let your client rate (from 0 to 10) his level of confidence in being able to complete the new behavior.

Therapist: Okay, Gary, you want to date Christine. Where do you want to meet her? When will that happen? What do you want to do with her? Where can you initiate a conversation with her? Where could you invite her to go that would appeal to her? What will you wear? What else could you do as preparation? *(Pause.)*

Now let's go forward in time. Can you see her standing in front of you? How does that feel? What happens in your body? What are you saying to yourself for motivation? What are you saying to her? What are you doing? Can you see yourself saying and doing that? How does she react? What can you say or do to cope with this reaction? What's a realistic but modest goal you can try to achieve to stay somehow connected with her? How do you end up seeing her if you are successful? What about if you feel you failed?

Now Christine is gone. What thoughts are running through your head? Can you identify which mode is talking? How do you feel? What child mode is present? What is a healthy adult response to the inner critic voices and to your child mode?

After ending the imagery exercise, stand up with your client as part of the consultant team looking down on Gary and Christine seated on the chairs. Together you can decide how to transfer the experience to real life. Finally, let the client rerate (0 to 10) his level of confidence for being able to complete the task. A good ending would be to assign homework, such as a behavior experiment, to be completed before the next session.

Summary

In this chapter, we looked more closely at therapeutic interventions in schema therapy, with a specific focus on imagery and imagery rescripting. We described the overall process of using imagery and imagery rescripting, provided details about using specific types of imagery (for trauma, loss, grief, and guilt and rehearsal for future events) for particular client cases, and explained how to remove obstacles in various applications. For illustration, we provided extended therapist-client dialogues to give a clear idea of how to engage with clients in imagery practices.

CHAPTER 10

Mode Dialogues on Chairs

The mode dialogue, one of the main schema therapy techniques, is an important method for bringing the case conceptualization into sessions. It is derived from gestalt therapy, but in schema therapy we apply it in a very specific way. We externalize psychological entities, or modes, in a concrete way by placing them on different chairs. Thus we can treat them as if they were different people. This follows the inclination of our mental process to symbolize abstract entities (see the section on relational frame theory in chapter 1). Naturally, the entities interact, and modes/chairs can display inner dynamics, especially when we encourage an intense conversation between them.

Principle: Whereas imagery usually deals with real interpersonal situations, mode dialogues play out the inner world of clients as if they were different people interacting.

The mode dialogue comes into play where imagery rescripting reaches its limits. Just because you and a client successfully rescript a childhood scene does not mean the client escapes from the internal prison set up by inner critic modes. In the previous chapter, we discussed the imagery rescripting process and putting the mode map on chairs in tandem. However, there are many ways to work with chairs, and the following represents a selection of dialogues you can use to facilitate therapy:

- *Diagnostic chair dialogues* give you an overview of a client's modes and link what is experienced to the case conceptualization. It makes the results of mode awareness visible and lasting in the therapy room.

- *Historical role-play* broadens the client's understanding of what happened in childhood and supports perspective changes.

- *Working with two chairs* strengthens the healthy adult mode.

- *Putting the mode map on chairs* helps you to work backstage in the client's inner world, impeaching the inner critic and caring for the vulnerable child.

- *Integration on one chair* deals with experiential avoidance and supports acceptance.

Diagnostic Chair Dialogues

Chairs can represent anything you want to work with in therapy. In schema therapy, we usually use them to represent the modes from our case conceptualization. However, a chair can also represent a symptom such as pain, a compulsion, or a craving, giving it an anthropomorphic representation to work with. Chairs can also represent another person, or even an affair.

The first step in a diagnostic chair dialogue is to label any mode or behavior that is occurring and then use a separate chair to represent it. Naturally, this can add up to a large number of chairs. However, to show you are interested in all aspects of your client's inner world, add a chair for every mode that shows up in the clinical session. In this way, you should get a more complete picture. You can ask your client to draw a map with all the modes or put the modes in the descriptive case conceptualization (described in chapter 4). Then you can both work to link the map with chairs. Eventually, you will be able to reduce the initial complexity through a conjoint refining process by forming groups of modes. For example, for a traumatized client with several child states, assemble them in a vulnerable child group and an angry or impulsive child group. Try to reduce the number of inner critic modes as well. Nevertheless, it might be necessary to separate the demanding critic from the punitive critic chair because the two modes lead the client in opposite directions. By denoting all of the modes in play and then grouping them as necessary, you can build a conceptual and later experiential road map for therapeutic work.

Historical Role-Play

Historical role-play combines some elements of imagery, the mode dialogue, and role-play to represent a troubling childhood scene and support the client in finding a healthy adult perspective beyond the activated child mode. You will find this technique especially helpful, more so than just talking through the scene, if your client feels ambivalent about an incident. This technique can help the client develop a more subtle understanding of what happened and begin to change perspective.

Start by identifying the scene with which you want to work. You can take it from the client's life history or from a previous imagery exercise. The technique works best when the caregivers are present in the scene. In the following example, Sally was the last child picked up by her mother from kindergarten. The therapist has her begin the session seated in the child mode chair:

Therapist: Close your eyes now, float back in time, and bring up a vivid picture from the scene when you were four years old and waiting for your mother in kindergarten. Be aware that you were smaller than today and objects appeared bigger. What do you see (*pause*), hear (*pause*), smell (*pause*), or feel in your body? What do you need now?

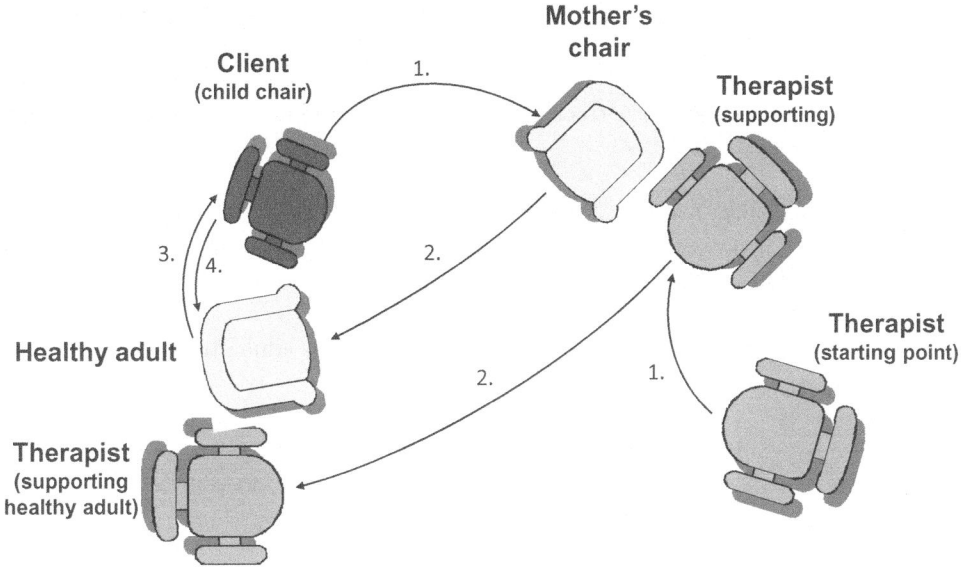

Figure 10–1. Chair positions in historical role-play

You start in the conventional face-to-face position, but once you have a clear picture of the scene, including the experience of your client, ask her to move to an additional chair you place in front of her (see figure 10–1). This chair represents the caregiver or any other person in the scene. If the caregiver was absent during the incident, bring the person into the picture in order to talk to the child. Give the client a few moments to adapt.

The therapist asked Sally to sit in her "mother's" chair:

Therapist: (*Sitting beside the mother's chair*) Okay, Sally, you're now sitting in the chair of your mother. Thank you for making that change. Can you please give me your view of the scene? What made you act that way? Can you tell this to Sally directly, to help her understand you better? Can you look at little Sally? What can you see in her eyes? How does that make you feel? What do you want to say to her or do now?

Once the client has answered, place a third chair for the healthy adult mode close beside the child mode chair and ask the client to move to it. Put your own chair beside the healthy adult chair.

The therapist then asked Sally to sit in the healthy adult chair:

Therapist: You are big Sally now. You heard what your mother said. What do you think about that? How does that feel now? If you look at little Sally and what she needed in this situation, what do you want to say to your mother now? How does she react? Is this okay for you, or do you want to add something? What can you say to little Sally, explaining the situation to her? What can you say or do to take care of little Sally as the adult you are now?

After the previous step, ask the client to sit on the child mode chair again, as Sally's therapist did:

Therapist: Hi, Sally. You heard and saw everything. How does that make you feel? What do you think about what happened now? Is there something you want to say to your mother? Or to big Sally?

To close the session, ask the client to sit in the healthy adult chair again, as Sally's therapist instructed:

Therapist: Can you please come back into the therapy room now and open your eyes again? Now, looking back on the exercise, how do you feel? What's the message describing your experience? What does that mean for future encounters with your mother?

The goal is not to change history but to broaden clients' understanding of what happened. In this way, clients learn to change perspective, which can help them to gain empathy for their caregivers. Sometimes a parent is something of a dry well, so clients have better outcomes if they can reduce their expectations and take responsibility for caring for the child mode feelings themselves in their present life. Eventually, this can help them to emotionally disconnect from the caretakers, better care for themselves, and improve their current relationships.

Working with Two Chairs: Strengthening the Healthy Adult

The chair dialogue described here is appropriate at the beginning of therapy or with more emotionally fragile clients. It is quite easy to learn, and you can apply it to all modes. The therapist takes an active role, something like that of a trainer coaching the client's healthy adult mode. Sit next to the client and put the mode you want to work with in an empty chair in front of your client. Then have the client convey the messages of the targeted mode:

Therapist: (*Sitting beside the client and pointing at the chair in front of both of them*) We understand that the voice in your head always putting you down is the demanding critic mode. We put this mode in this chair in front of us now. Can you tell me what the voice is saying to you?

Nancy: She says, "You'll never learn how to deal with your problems. You're a hopeless case. You'll spoil this therapy, too. The therapist will soon find out that you're just plain nuts!"

Therapist: How do these messages make you feel?

Nancy: I just feel like a piece of sh—. Not good for anything, just something to be thrown away.

Therapist: It's understandable that you feel this way. Anyone would if treated that way. What do you need now? What could make you feel better?

Nancy: Two or three beers would help.

Therapist: I see, but that would be the old escape into detached self-soother mode. But if you feel like the child addressed this way, what do you need?

Nancy: Somebody to stop these voices!

Therapist: Yes, of course! Nobody deserves being put down that way. It's humiliating and not at all helpful. Is there a part inside of you that can see this and wants to stand up against these voices, with my support?

Nancy: Well, if we look at the inner critics as if they were a person talking to me, that makes me angry.

Therapist: I'm very happy that there's a part of you beside the helpless child. This strong part feels justified in standing up against these voices. I'm on your side, so let's fight them together! What do you want to say to the voices? Maybe tell me first and then talk to them directly. [Note: Offer the emotional support necessary. Encourage and praise each step.]

In the next step, you and your client can form a consultation team. Once you find the right words, speak them to the inner critic mode. You can also give the client a start with some suggested words. The symbolic "speaker's baton" can move back and forth between the client and you as long as necessary. Initially, you will take a more active role and make suggestions. Later, you can return to Socratic questions and be encouraging.

Therapist: How do you feel after our dispute with your inner critic mode?

Nancy: Surprisingly good. But I would have never been able to do that without your help!

Therapist: But you're learning quickly and you gradually got stronger. What else do you need to strengthen this healthy adult side within yourself?

Nancy: You at my side when the voices come back when I'm at home!

Therapist: This is a good idea, which is why I suggested recording this intervention with your smartphone. So every time the voices get strong again you can put your earphones on and replay this sequence we recorded. Hearing this will help you regain what you feel today. As a homework assignment, you could write down one of these toxic messages a day in your diary and bring it into our next session so we can continue dealing with them. It's a long road to walk down, but every step in this direction makes us stronger.

Nancy: But will this ever have an end? Will I ever get rid of these bastards?

Be careful at this point: it is a potential trap to promise something that is unrealistic. These voices are carved deeply into your client's brain circuits and behavior patterns. They may be ego-syntonic, so the client may identify with what the voices say. Work at this cutting edge of therapy, retaining a realistic and modest outlook that is compatible with the healthy adult mode. Promises might soothe the vulnerable child mode for now, but that comfort will not last.

Therapist: I want to be honest with you. I know that the child mode inside of you longs for this to end one day, but these thoughts are planted deeply in your brain. What we're doing is developing the strength to resist. And you'll become an expert in this. Resisting won't resolve all pain, but it will help you to function better in your everyday life.

In a further step, your client can take the place of the targeted mode and talk face-to-face with you. This will lead to intense interactions. It is accepted practice among schema therapists to not seat a client in a chair representing the punitive critic mode, so as not to reinforce that destructive influence. However, you can stand side by side with your client behind the punitive critic chair, while the client speaks the toxic messages toward the child mode chair, but in the third person. This technique will limit the level of the client's emotional activation.

Finally, it is in the hands of the therapist to fine-tune the level of activation. Once there is a stronger healthy adult mode available, you can shift to a more comprehensive kind of chair dialogue, putting the client in touch with her full spectrum of modes.

Putting the Mode Map on Chairs

Putting the mode map on chairs for a dialogue provides clients with an overview of their internal mode world. We suggest using the modes from the mode map and placing the chairs in a consistent way (see figure 10–2). This helps to create a stable internal map for your clients. The chairs in the room align with the written mode map you provide. Keep the dialogue simple. There is no need to have too many chairs or to label them in idiosyncratic ways. You can use personalized names, but they should match the modes on the map. The number of the modes on the map is basically constant, but keep in mind that the working memory can only cope simultaneously with a maximum of seven distinct bits of information. Thus keep the number of chairs you use below this number.

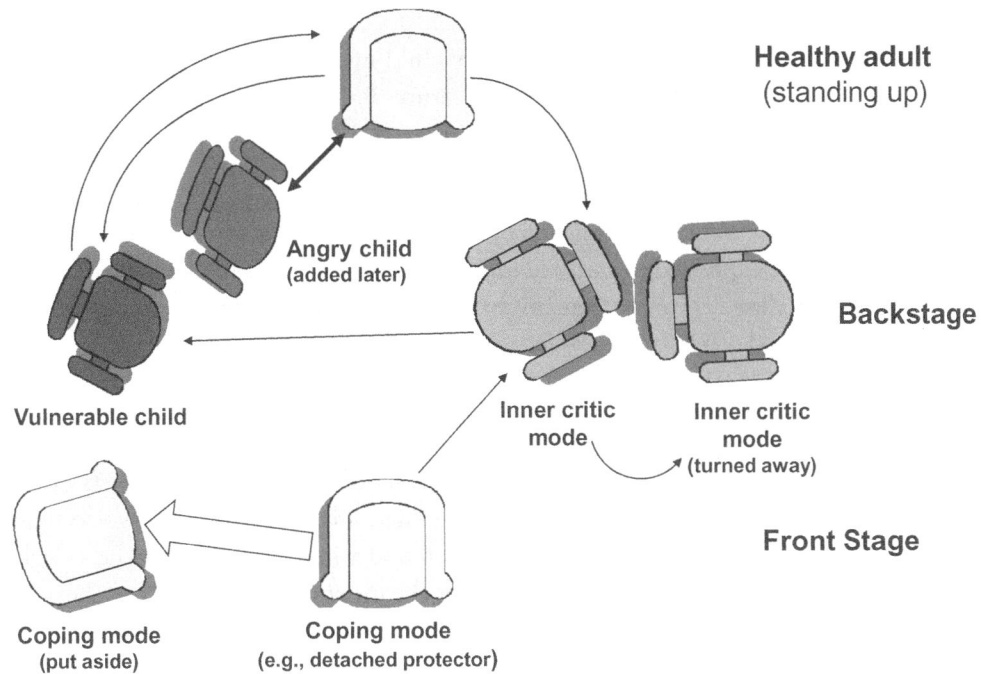

Figure 10–2. Chair dialogue based on the mode map

In most cases, start the dialogue with a schema-activating situation that the client has brought to therapy. This can be either a current event or something from the past. The dialogue we describe here starts after the initial steps of labeling the coping mode, identifying the inner critic mode voices, and changing them to second-person language, as described in chapter 6. After bypassing the initial coping mode and dealing with the backstage inner critic and child modes, you end up working with three chairs. We recommend that you place the chairs according to the positions on the mode map.

Overview

Here is an overview of the steps for putting the mode map on chairs:

1. *Put the inner critic mode voices on a separate chair.* Seat the client on this chair, sit beside him, and let the modes speak out their beliefs and appraisals to an empty child mode chair in front of the client. You can play the devil's advocate to increase the client's involvement.

2. *Both client and therapist change to the child mode side* and look for any activated basic emotions, including body sensations. Label upcoming coping impulses, and sort them out on the coping mode chair. Stick to feelings in the body. Eventually, offer the four negative basic emotions (fear, sadness, anger, or feeling annoyed) for choice.

3. *Access the needs and wishes of the child modes.* What does the vulnerable child mode need, and what does the angry child mode want to do? Perhaps make your client bigger in imagery or use a future-directed image. If only the vulnerable child mode is involved, you only need one chair. If both child mode poles are active, offer two chairs.

4. *Both client and therapist stand up to "float" above the chairs.* Seek any constructive anger expressed toward the inner critic modes and self-compassion for the child modes. If the client remains blocked, this can indicate detached protector coping mode. Ask the client for remaining "voices in the head," and put them on the inner critic mode chair. You might also consider using the extension or substitution technique or acting as a role model.

5. *Impeach the inner critic mode voices.* Focus more on the negative effects of the modes than on the content. Shape the client's body posture and voice tone. Ask how your client feels after this step and whether he believes he is right (reappraisal). Encourage the client to let the inner critic thoughts go. They can remain unchanged. Warn the client that they will probably come back.

6. *Care for the child modes.* Use any self-compassionate feelings identified by the client to encourage him to care for the child mode. Eventually, let the client sit down on the different child mode chairs, and ask him about his feelings or remaining needs.

7. *Look for a functional solution.* Now you can look for a realistic solution to the issue brought to the session. Do this together from a standing position. Try to integrate both child poles into the solution.

8. *Strengthen the healthy adult mode.* Add a healthy adult mode chair and sit beside it. If the situation the client brought into therapy involves another person, add a chair in front of the client for this other person. Ask the client to convey his solution to this empty chair in front of him. If the situation was an internal conflict, let the client speak to the inner critic mode chair. Shape and model how to act until your client feels confident.

9. *Check back with the child modes.* Let the client have a seat on both child mode chairs, and ask how both modes feel. Is the vulnerable side contented, and is the angry side willing to comply?

10. *Discrimination and take-home message.* Encourage your client to compare present feelings with those from the beginning of the exercise. As a principle, it is good to have the client say one sentence that expresses the essence of his experience.

Below we describe these steps in more detail, offering what you, as the therapist, might say at each step. (Instructions for putting the mode map on chairs, along with this book's other online accessories, are available for download at http://www.newharbinger.com/40958.)

1. Put the inner critic mode voices on an extra chair.

Sort out the toxic voices of your client and place them on the inner critic mode chair, seat your client on the chair, and let the client speak to the empty child mode chair in front of her. Sit close by to support the client, and eventually fuel the fire:

Therapist: *You* have to do better. *You* are a failure. *You* don't deserve any love. *You* are a burden. Better that *you* were dead! Isn't there anything else you want to tell this loser? Is this really everything you want to say? What would you like to do with her? Express what's deep in your heart!

Consider the following when you carry out this part of the dialogue.

Pitch the level of emotional activation. Try to keep the client at a moderate to high level of emotional activation within the emotional tolerance window. Your action will depend on the client's emotional response. Use your judgment about when to take the next step, and then change to the child mode side.

Deal with the coping modes. Interrupt immediately when the client starts to shift back into a detached or submissive coping mode. Watch out for any intellectual explanations or rationalizing. Discourage the client from looking at you. Redirect her to address herself by speaking to the child mode chair.

Notice identification with inner critic modes. Surprisingly (Or not!), many clients like speaking for the inner critic chair and dive easily into this role (which is usually very strong inside their head anyway, and very ego-syntonic). How easily they identify with the inner critic modes will demonstrate how familiar they are with these voices.

Separate contradictory inner critic modes. Be aware that sometimes there are two contradictory inner critic modes at work, particularly demanding and punitive critic modes. They create what Bateson (1972) called a double bind: whatever your client does is wrong. Use two inner critic mode chairs to distinguish the contradictory messages to the client.

2. Both client and therapist change to the child mode side.

Therapist: Close your eyes, please. How do you feel, hearing these voices and their messages? How does that make you feel in your body—your chest, your belly?

Label and interrupt coping modes. Very often, clients surrender to the toxic voices, saying things like "I feel guilty. They're right. I'm a failure!" Immediately interrupt the client:

Therapist: Are any children born with guilt feelings? This isn't your child mode answering with a basic emotion. This is already your self-defeating coping mode, sitting on the chair on the front stage. I want to talk to the innate and innocent child mode deep inside you. What do you feel, hearing these voices? Is it more fear, or sadness, or do you feel annoyed or angry? What do you feel in your body?

Offer basic emotions. Gently offering the basic emotions in a "take your choice" manner guides your client away from superficial social emotions to underlying basic emotions. Surprisingly, we think that your client will not feel bossed around but rather well guided. We offer all four basic emotions (fear, sadness, anger, or feeling annoyed) to avoid being preselective.

Offer two child mode chairs. If your client experiences conflicting emotions, such as sadness and anger, offer two child mode chairs to express both modes separately. This will make the ambivalence visible.

Identify the type of coping mode. You will probably find that most of your clients who show detached or submissive coping are driven by underlying fear or sadness. Some detached coping modes will also be a response to feeling annoyed or angry. Being able to judge the kind of client you are dealing with will help you to set the focus of your work: Is it a blocked angry or annoyed protector, or a fearful or sad protector? (See chapters 3 and 6.) Understanding your client in this way will guide you to the already involved child mode and core need and which child mode and core need the client needs to activate.

3. Access the needs and wishes of the child modes.

Address the two basic child modes in different ways, since their underlying needs are different. When the vulnerable child mode is active, we tend to look for attachment, support, and help in a cooperative and internalized way. When we find ourselves in an angry child mode, our assertiveness need seeks dominance, control, and externalization. If we are somewhere in the middle or ambivalent, avoidance seems to be the best choice, but avoidance is the "ugly way" (see the section on the "still face" experiment in chapter 3). This is why we try to distinguish the two child modes. If the client expresses ambivalence about needs, talk to both child modes separately on their own chairs to access all the unmet needs.

Vulnerable child mode. We ask the vulnerable child mode, "What do you need now? What are you longing for? What would make you feel a little bit better?"

Angry child mode. We ask the angry child mode, "What do you want to say or do? Anything is possible. You have all the power you need. You are ten feet tall. What do you want to do if nobody is watching?"

4. Both client and therapist stand up to "float" above the chairs.

Once the client's emotions, needs, and wishes are unlocked, you and the client stand up together, side by side, looking down on the chairs. Taking this "standing above" position is similar to the way that the therapist and client enter the image during imagery rescripting.

Therapist: How do you feel, watching the inner critic modes beating up the vulnerable child?

Also consider the following.

Talk to the mode as to a person. Especially when working with chairs, the scene becomes more vivid if we talk to the modes as if they are different people (for example, the vulnerable child or little Suzie). Externalizing parts of the self in such a personalized form intensively activates memory traces and resource networks.

Add an angry child mode chair. Even if your client feels sad or fearful, standing up can unblock constructive anger. You can validate this anger and place an additional chair to represent the angry child close to the vulnerable child chair, so both sides of the child's emotional spectrum on the mode map are represented by separate chairs. This helps your client get a mental representation of all parts of the emotional spectrum. Remember, the anger the healthy adult mode feels is always provided by the angry child mode (as well as the anger in a bullying coping mode). There aren't different kinds of anger—it's like condensed energy. The question is how it is expressed.

Additional perspective-change techniques. If standing up fails to bring a perspective change, you have two options (as in imagery work): either try the extension or substitution technique or act as a role model (for details, see chapter 5).

5. Impeach the inner critic mode voices.

If your client feels anger, the road is clear to impeach the inner critic modes. Doing so requires both the power of the angry child mode (energy) and a value-based justification (reappraisal). We base reappraisal on what is most important to us (for example, fairness rather than the inner critic values). Therefore, we encourage clients to become aware of their functional values.

Therapist: Based on what you feel now in your body and your new insights, what do you want to say to the inner critic modes?

Ask the client where she wants to place the inner critic mode chairs (for example, turning them away or putting them out of the room). Ask the client how this feels, emotionally and in her body. Does she believe she did the right thing? If doubts remain, inquire further about remaining inner critic mode thoughts. They will occur again and again!

Identify remaining inner critic mode voices. If your client cannot release constructive anger, then it is likely that remaining inner critic mode voices are blocking her. Point this out to the client and continue assessing the voices: "What does the voice in your head say now, when you look down on the inner critic modes beating up little Suzie?" Identifying such remaining roadblocks and placing them on the inner critic mode chair can give your client a clear view of life traps.

Distance, do not fight. As in imagery, the goal is not to change the inner critic modes or defeat them, but to get some distance from them and to let them go. They will come back anyway!

Warn your client that the inner critic modes will return. There is often considerable relief at the symbolic banishment of inner critic mode voices, but it is equally common for doubts or guilt feelings to return through the back door when the voices return. It is better to work on such pull-back messages in session, instead of leaving your client alone with them after the session.

6. Care for the child modes.

Once your client has managed to gain some distance from the inner critic modes, the way is clear to develop healthy, self-compassionate feelings. This is why we recommend impeaching first and self-soothing later.

Therapist: If you look at the child now in a compassionate way, what do you want to say to or do with the child?

Note whether the client's speech to the child modes is adequately warm and caring. If not, look for interference from leftover inner critic mode voices.

7. Look for a functional solution.

Now that there is some clarity about the client's emotional dynamics, you can look for the best possible healthy adult solution for the situation you started with. You can use the extension or substitution technique for this, or you can make suggestions based on your own judgment. Once you have found a way to act (or not act!), you and your client can enter the next phase.

8. Strengthen the healthy adult mode.

Now we seek to integrate the emerging healthy adult function in the processes of everyday life, so we represent the healthy adult mode with an additional chair (see figure 10–2). There are two options:

a. Place an additional healthy adult chair beside the child mode chairs. The old coping mode chair remains set aside as a warning to not fall into the old life trap again.

b. Pull the old coping mode chair back beside the child mode chairs to symbolize that the new functional behavior is replacing the old maladaptive coping.

If there is another person involved in the critical scene that the client brought to therapy, place an empty chair in front of the client to represent that person. The full process of implementation can be done in three steps:

a. *Standing position:* The client talks to the empty chair while standing. You may make suggestions about what to say or do. Ask the client how this part of the exercise resonates. Continue until the client feels satisfied and well balanced.

b. *Empty chair dialogue:* The client sits down in the healthy adult chair while trying to experience her feelings, with your support (sitting alongside). The client tries to direct toward the empty chair in front of her the same sentences she spoke while standing. Assist her when required. Talking from a standing position feels very different, which your client will experience.

c. *Role-play:* In a role-play, sit down in front of the client and have her speak the same sentences to you, face-to-face.

Consider the following.

Balance the locus of control. The overall goal is to bring the exercise to a good and satisfying end for the client. If you were very active early in therapy, then make sure that the client has adopted a more active role as therapy has progressed.

Face the fear of being responsible. Some clients will become irritated by the "empty space" after removing the inner critic mode chair. It is frightening to have the responsibility of the healthy adult chair all alone. Abused clients trying to get rid of their abusers have a similar response, which is a form of attachment. Gradually loosening these bonds is an important step of individualization. Do it carefully.

Deal with reoccurring critic mode voices. The punitive critic mode will not accept being removed from the scene. It will protest and predict your client's failure without the inner critic's assistance. Do not argue with this inner critic mode voice. Encourage your client to recognize and make a record of what the voice says over the week. Make it a homework exercise, and work on how to talk back to those statements in the next session.

Defusion techniques. You might also consider trying specific thought defusion techniques used by acceptance and commitment (ACT) practitioners (briefly mentioned in chapter 7).

Bill was in treatment for chronic depression. His therapist encouraged him to identify the harsh inner critic voice that constantly spoke in his head. Later, the therapist encouraged him to say back to the inner critic's comments, "You're just a thought. You have no substance." He also played with the tone of the voice, trying to soften the tone and to subvert the message by speaking the words using a pirate voice.

Note that chair dialogues work toward defusion by establishing a physical distance from the inner critic mode voices. This process of externalization indicates that the demanding or punitive critics are not a genuine part of the client. They do not belong to the client!

9. Check back with the child modes.

To stabilize the effect of the intervention, you can ask your client to sit on both child mode chairs. Ask the vulnerable child mode, "How do you feel about what the healthy adult said and did? What else do you need from the healthy adult?" If the child mode still feels frightened, hidden inner critic modes remain an influence. Then we ask what the child is afraid of and what it needs to feel safer. Typically, the child modes ask the adult to never leave them again. This is another opportunity to implement the good-night ritual (see chapter 11).

Say to the angry or impulsive child mode, or both, "Do you accept the proposed solution, and do you support it? Are you willing to contribute from your end? What could eventually interfere with the plans of healthy adult mode? What can we do in order to make you part of the team?"

Make the impulsive or undisciplined child modes part of the team. Carefully investigating and anticipating possible obstacles and pitfalls contributes a lot to the success of behavior experiments, as described in the next chapter. You might want to return to the healthy adult chair and see whether your client is willing and able to manage emotional activations. Sometimes you may have to move back and forth until the needs of both the impulsive and undisciplined child mode chairs have become clear and the client commits to the chosen solution. Whether the solution works in a sustainable way depends on the level of integration. Behavior experiments will reveal the truth.

10. Discrimination and take-home message.

The dialogue terminates with your client making a contrast between how she felt at the beginning and end of the session. This is usually reinforcing and helps the client to place the experience in her mode map. Remember to reinforce helpful key messages to help the healthy adult cope with recurring accusations from the inner critic modes: for example, "You can stand up for your rights now! You deserve to be treated fairly!" Or, "If you ask for support, chances are good that you'll get some! You give a lot to other people, so you can ask for some help in return!" You can write these messages on sticky notes that the client can place around her home as an aid to memory. We suggest writing the messages in second-person language, as if they are coming from a good parent. Our assumption is that the second person antagonizes the inner critic mode voices more effectively than other linguistic forms and is easier for clients to internalize.

Putting the mode map on chairs has many steps, especially if you want to be comprehensive. We encourage you to be active and try to accomplish the entire dialogue in a fifty-minute session. This is possible if you start the exercise early in the session (see "Session Planning" in chapter 12). It is a worthwhile exercise to repeat. Doing it again and again offers clients the opportunity to practice problem-solving skills, and they will find it easier to get into a healthy adult observer stance in relation to their thoughts and emotions over time.

Integration on One Chair: Working in the Emotional Resonance Sphere

Lukas Nissen and Michael Sturm, two leading Swiss schema therapists, coined the term "emotional resonance sphere" when developing an approach to dealing with difficult clients, including those who remain entangled, resistant, complaining, and passive in the detached protector mode (Nissen & Sturm, 2014). While in the previous sections we split clients up on separate chairs, this exercise works again toward integration. Their approach combines emotional exposure and response prevention with an ongoing mindful, self-compassionate, and accepting attitude. They embed their approach in a physiological model, too. Hence, it makes sense to include elements of their approach in this third wave–oriented book.

In chapter 1, we introduced the role of the alarm system, which in some clients fails to turn off because they continue coping through experiential avoidance, and remain trapped in their coping modes in a vicious cycle. You will see many clients for whom this is an issue! Figure 10–3 illustrates the core elements of the cycle and indicates some escape routes based on mindful self-reflective behavior directed by the healthy adult mode.

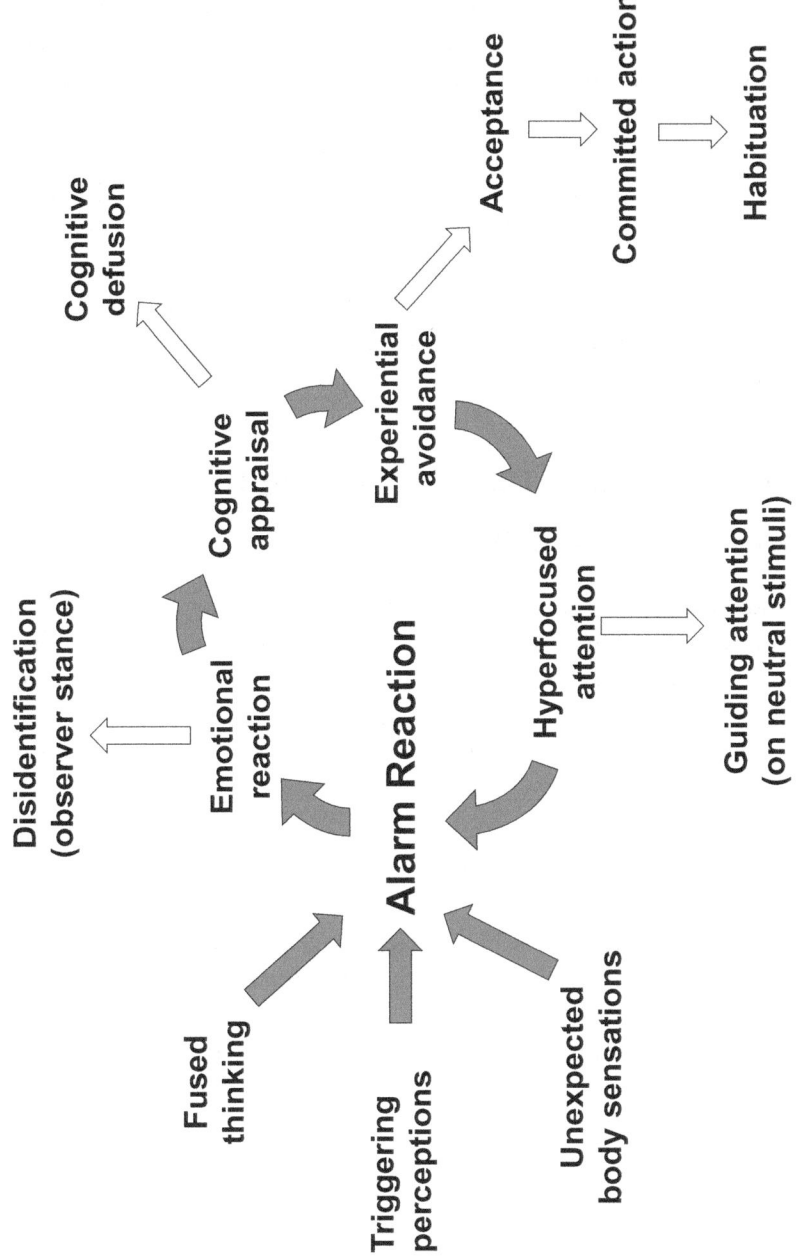

Figure 10–3. The vicious cycle of an alarm reaction, and how to escape

When working with such clients, the focus should be on overcoming experiential avoidance behavior. The idea is to help clients get into a mindful observer stance while oscillating between emotional activation and calming down, a process assisted by response prevention. You can do this using the emotional resonance sphere technique, described here:

1. *Label the triggering situation.* The client describes the situation with open eyes, as we outlined for rescripting traumatic events (see the section "Steps of the Imagery Exercise with Traumatized Clients," in chapter 9). Identify and rate the most stressful incidents. Eventually, make use of the subjective units of distress scale (SUDS) to find the hot spot.

2. *Activate a self-compassionate state* (Gilbert, 2010).

    Therapist: Now that we've found a scene to work with, please sit in a comfortable but upright position. Close your eyes. Be aware of your feet, how they touch the ground. Sense your breath and notice the movement in your stomach. Relax your neck, shoulders, and hands as much as you can. Return your attention to your breathing. Recognize how a stream of calm, warm light tints everything appearing in your mind with a warm and friendly color. Welcome every thought that comes to mind, whatever it is, in an accepting and peaceful manner. Let everything remain. There is no need to do anything. Just stay in the state that you're in.

3. *Evoke the schema activation.*

    Therapist: Now please bring up the scene again that you described at the beginning of our session today. What do you observe?

    Brian: I feel my heart beating. I pull my eyebrows together. I feel tension in my neck and shoulders. How could he do that?

4. *Connect with the activated client.* The therapist labels the coping behavior and brings the client back into an observer stance:

    Therapist: Can you see what you're doing now? Pause for a moment and become aware of your thoughts and feelings! Can you see how you're sitting and what your hands are doing? What happens if you stop that? Can you feel your alarm system going off? Just stay with what happens.

    You can assess the level of activation using the SUDS. Levels between 6 and 8 (out of 10) are ideal. You might block self-soothing behavior (for example, small body movements) to raise the level of emotional activation. This helps the client to get past the detached protector wall.

5. *Prevent old coping responses and install the observer mode.*

    Therapist: Notice the thoughts running through your head. Can you let them go? Remain nonjudgmental. Be curious. Just notice what happens. Get aware of your emotions and body sensations—just accept them. Just continue breathing in and out slowly. Say yes to everything. Just remain being there, and let everything pass by. What do you notice now?

Brian: Somehow the tension goes down.

Therapist: Try saying "soften, soothe, allow." Remember to say it through the week in the gentlest way you can.

Once the SUDS rating goes down to a moderate level, you can repeat steps 3 through 5 several times. Each time will lead to more habituation, which will limit the level of activation. It is usually a great relief to clients when they realize that all they have to do is shift from their doing mode into a being mode.

6. *Let a healthy solution come up.*

    Therapist: Now that you're more relaxed and can look at the problem, what possible solutions occur to you? How do you feel you should react, or not react? Can you picture yourself doing that? How does it feel?

    Once the client's emotional activation is lowered, it is natural for him to think more clearly. Good options will come to mind. Existing resources are accessible again. Naturally, it is important for the therapist to facilitate this step. Toward the end of therapy, the responsibility for doing this shifts to the client, who is expected to find his own solutions.

7. *Take-home message.* As explained in step 10 in the previous section, try to find a principle to guide your client in the future.

Therapist Tip: It is important for us as therapists to regularly practice mindfulness ourselves. This also applies to other ACT techniques, such as cognitive defusion. There is something artificial about trying to teach our clients what we have not practiced ourselves (and they will sense it). It is also a great benefit for the therapist to develop the ability to conduct therapy in a mindful way.

Summary

In this chapter, we maintained our practical "how to" emphasis. We looked carefully at using mode dialogues on chairs in a variety of ways. While imagery works with interpersonal situations, chair dialogues work with internal representations. Chair dialogues can help clients overcome experiential avoidance and get in touch with and accept painful feelings. They can also teach clients how to keep inner critic modes from taking action, and they strengthen clients' ability to take the lead with the healthy adult mode. Now the stage is set to describe behavior change strategies in detail.

CHAPTER 11

Behavior Change Techniques

In this chapter, we focus on encouraging behavior change through schema therapy. To some extent, imagery rescripting and chair dialogues already include elements of behavior change, such as when clients impeach inner critic modes and care for child modes, but these changes are achieved in the safety of the psychotherapeutic setting. The acid test of any therapy is behavior change in daily life. Schema therapy connects empowering emotional experiences with insights gained in session, leading to new principles and values to guide healthy adult behavior outside of session.

How do we bring about behavior change? The key is to encourage self-efficacy (Bandura, 1977), but we need to get our clients motivated to achieve this. The basic principles are to get active, take small steps leading to successful outcomes, acknowledge the self in bringing change, and provide contingent self-rewarding. These are the core ingredients of successful behavior change in schema therapy, as in other therapies.

When you get to the second half of treatment, do not overly focus on the sessions themselves; instead, prioritize homework. Gradually, schema therapists reduce the frequency of sessions to support clients in taking a more responsible and active role, as we describe in chapter 12 in detail, using all the established behavior therapy techniques (Farrell & Shaw, 2012). For example, some of the chair dialogues described in the previous chapter end in role-play, which can play an important role in preparing clients for behavior experiments.

In the following sections, we describe techniques, tailored to the schema therapy model, to track changes in client behavior. They include mode management plans, schema-mode flash cards, evidence logs, and mode-based diaries.

Emotion Regulation Techniques

Safety first! Before starting experiential work, clients need to learn emotional self-regulation. This cannot be achieved in sessions only. Early in therapy, you will need to establish an emergency plan and train your clients in ways to remain stable between sessions.

The following list of emotion regulation techniques is not exhaustive. You can encourage your clients to add to the list, stressing that the long-term goal is for them to engage in more functional and self-caring behavior. We grouped the skills in three categories that overlap, and each sublist starts with simple techniques—still working with higher levels of emotional activation—leading to progressively more complex ones with a self-caring character.

Cognitive Techniques

- *Self-instructions* (Meichenbaum, 1979): Assign self-statements that clients can repeat to themselves in the coming week.

    Therapist: Just say to yourself "Stay cool, carry on, take one step after the other," "What I'm doing is important," "Slow down," and so on. Such self-talk has a calming effect. To model a good internal dialogue, think about talking with a caring person.

- *Continuous prayers:* This Eastern Orthodox practice can be taken straight from a liturgy; for example, "Lord have mercy, Christ have mercy, Lord have mercy." Or the client can repeat a favorite sacred text: "In the beginning, God…" (Genesis 1:1). This technique has the same therapeutic basis as self-instructions but is more personal and connected to spiritual resources.

- *Counting down numbers:* Count down from 100 by 7s. When you know the result by heart, start counting from 103 or 114.

- *Expressive writing* (Pennebaker, 1997):

    Therapist: Barry, it's a good idea to get an exercise book. This will become your therapy journal. Sit down and start writing whatever comes to mind. Don't reflect, just write. Writing slows down the thinking process.

    As clients write, they will shift from an emotionally driven state to having some perspective. Sooner or later, healthy adult mode will return.

- *Letter writing:* This technique can be used to express feelings toward people who have caused injury. Once the letters are written, read them in therapy. (But do not send them!) Afterward, clients can burn them, a ritual helping them to let go of resentment or bitterness.

- *Body scan* (see chapter 9)

- *Imagery exercises* (for example, see the safe place imagery, in chapter 9)

- *Mindfulness of breath meditation* (see chapter 7)

- *Light ball meditation* (see chapter 9)

- *Watching our thoughts mindfully:* Encourage clients to let "sticky" thoughts go in their everyday life and instead focus on the here and now. This is a step toward developing an ongoing, present inner observer in relation to thoughts.

Perception-Focused Techniques

- *5–4–3 mindful grounding exercise* (see chapter 7):

  Therapist: Barry, start with five things you see, four things you hear, and three things you feel at the surface of your body—for example, your belt, your bottom on the chair, your back against the chair, the shoe around your toes. Shift quickly. Don't remain in one modality. Let interfering thoughts go.

- *Focusing attention:* Encourage clients to describe what they see in detail.

  Barry: I see forty-two layers of bricks in the wall. The wooden ceiling is made out of thirty-eight panels. The window is about forty inches wide and fifty inches high. There are two leather seats with a pillow that has eleven stripes of gray, red, and gold…

- *The ongoing observer stance:* Give clients the homework task to watch their surroundings like a video camera, to describe, and to remain nonjudgmental.

  Therapist: Barry, when walking, do it mindfully. Continually recognize and describe what you see and what you feel.

  Barry: *(The following session, he reported)* I could hear the soles of my shoes slapping on the ground. There was a red car in front of me. The man crossing my way had a beard.

- *Intensive listening:* Encourage clients to listen intently to their surroundings.

  Therapist: Close your eyes. What can you hear? Try to identify the source of the noise and then continue listening. Widen your hearing space. Become aware of the noise architecture of your environment. How does your body react to louder noises?

- *Listening to music:* Barry liked folk music. His therapist encouraged him to use headphones to allow the music to flood him.

- *Mindful tasting:* Barry's therapist gave him the homework assignment to really taste his food.

  Therapist: While eating, focus on the taste sensations of what you eat. Eating spicy food helps.

- *Being in the present moment:* Encourage your client to remain in the present—with what they are actually doing.

  Therapist: Don't let your mind wander. Refocus on what happens in the here and now while you're busy performing other duties.

Physical Activities

- *Intensive body feelings:* Barry's therapist encouraged him to also do some physical activities.

    Therapist: Bend your knees at a right angle and lean your back to the wall. Hold this position for at least thirty seconds, or for as long as you can. Then go back to your activities and remain focused.

- *Inducing light physical pain:* You can use dialectical behavior therapy skills to induce intense physical sensations. Examples include snapping a rubber band on the wrist, rolling a hedgehog massage ball on the skin, and letting ice cubes melt in the hand (but avoid anything that might wound or damage the skin). This can bring clients back to having a sense of their body.

- *Prolonged breathing:* Encourage clients to lengthen their breath.

    Therapist: Count rather quickly when you are breathing in and out and extend the expiration phase. [Note: This stimulates the vagal nerve.] For example, count up to four when breathing in and to eight when exhaling. Or count to four when inhaling, hold your breath for the count of four, and exhale to the count of four. Adapt the rhythm to your needs, but try to follow this ratio.

- *Intensive workout:* Assign mindful physical activities as homework, as Barry's therapist did, to encourage clients to enjoy a sense of vitality and mobility.

    Therapist: Try going for a jog. Can you feel your feet touching the ground, the wind cooling your forehead, or your body moving?

- *Comment on what you are doing:* Have clients, in some form or another, pay attention to regular activities and describe to themselves what they are doing in the moment.

    Therapist: Focus your attention on what you're currently doing. When you wash dishes, just wash each plate. Let every other thought go and keep your mind busy with what you're doing right now.

- *Self-caring procedures:* When you are doing something good for yourself, make use of your observer stance to increase your sense of well-being by focusing more on your activities and perceptions than on the environment.

    Therapist: Lie down for a moment. Feel the ground hold you. Feel the warmth of your body, your heart beating, your breath going in and out. Be aware that your body carries you through your life. Care for it with healthy food and good teeth and skin care!

- *Keep doing things:* Do this to avoid worrying or thought rumination. Barry came to a session concerned about how much time he spent worrying.

Therapist: If you feel low, check your to-do list and start on something. Start with something simple. Stay fully focused on what you are doing and let all interfering thoughts go. Then use your level of activation to proceed with more complex tasks.

We drew these emotion regulation techniques from a variety of sources. When you try to work on clients' emotion regulation skills, first and foremost, we encourage you to be practical. Do more of what works! And, if a particular technique works well, support them to keep doing this technique. Include any healthy coping strategies that your clients used in the past. Make sure that they know how to do the techniques by practicing together in session, and have them use a tracking sheet (figure 11–1) to support this process.

The first homework assignment you offer a client can be to make a hierarchy of skills that he or she commits to applying outside of sessions when triggered. Once emotionally triggered, based on this hierarchy, the client will employ one technique after the other, starting with the easier ones and moving up to the more difficult ones, trying each for about ten minutes. Ask clients to score and record (see figure 11–1) the effect using the subjective units of distress scale (SUDS) ratings before trying the next technique. The main idea is for clients to experience the effect of each technique, to take responsibility for keeping themselves in the emotional tolerance window, and to prepare them for the therapy-specific tasks described in the next section.

Joanne's tracking sheet is typical of what we expect from this homework exercise. The tracking sheet serves two purposes: First, it guides clients through the process and keeps them on track. Second, filling out the sheet is a sign of commitment, and the information offers the therapist opportunities to determine where clients might need more support. (You can download an empty coping mode tracking sheet, along with this book's other online accessories, at http://www.newharbinger.com/40958.)

Schema Therapy Homework Assignments

Therapy works best if clients are actively involved. Create a therapeutic culture in which the client takes an active role from the beginning. Start with small homework tasks. This approach is similar to how a parent gives children small tasks, such as drying dishes, which they carry out successfully and builds up their competence (and an internal locus of control; Rotter, 1966).

Ask clients to create a log in which they put their notes—either a conventional diary or a file on an electronic device. Reviewing homework is an important part of the therapeutic relationship and will help to foster the therapeutic alliance. Compliance with doing homework usually reflects that the client is assuming responsibility for clinical improvement. If homework completion does not reflect this, then why the client is unwilling to assume responsibility for his or her improvement becomes a focus in therapy. If your client remains reluctant to do homework, use empathic confrontation (see chapter 5).

Coping Mode Tracking Sheet Of: Joanne   Date: May 1

Trigger	Emotion	SUDS	Action 1	SUDS	Action 2	SUDS	Action 3	SUDS	Action 4	SUDS	Action 5	SUDS
Home alone	Sad, lonely	8/10	cleaning	8/10	Call sister	4/10						
Husband left for overseas	Sad, lonely	9/10	cleaning	8/10	Scream at children	9/10	Drink wine	2/10				

Figure 11–1. Joanne's coping mode tracking sheet

Listed here are some homework assignments you can use early in therapy:

- Identify triggering situations.

- Monitor modes. Ask, "Which mode am I currently in? Which mode is my partner in?"

- Close your eyes and focus inside when something triggers you during the week. What images arise? Make a list to bring to the next session.

- Detect demanding and punitive critic mode comments. Write them in a list.

- Ask, "What do I need now?" when in a child mode.

- Make a list of pleasurable activities.

- Spend five minutes every day caring for the vulnerable child mode.

- Watch a movie and make a list of any modes that you can identify in the film.

- Talk with your partner or a friend about troubling memories from childhood.

The Schema-Mode Flash Card

The schema-mode flash card (figure 11–2) will help your client do a schema-based situation analysis, and this form can be applied to any kind of schema activation. The flash card can be used in session to reflect an imagery rescripting or chair dialogue session, as a kind of extended inquiry about take-home principles from an experience (as we described in the final step for imagery rescripting, in chapter 9, and putting the mode map on chairs dialogue, in chapter 10). Later in therapy you can also use it to analyze schema activations between sessions. (A blank version of this form, along with this book's other online accessories, is available for download at http://www:newharbinger.com/40958.)

The schema-mode flash card has five steps denoted by the letters A, B, C, D, and E:

1. *Actual scene:* Observe the current emotion and the triggering situation.

2. *Backstage scene:* Connect activated feelings with the schema mode model.

3. *Change perspective:* Identify fused dysfunctional thoughts and make a reappraisal.

4. *Doing:* Shift from maladaptive to functional coping.

5. *Effects:* Look at the actual outcome.

Early in therapy, you usually fill out the flash card with your client, perhaps based on an imagery or chair dialogue exercise. The A, B, C, D, and E initials make learning the steps a bit easier, but initially you should take the lead. Later on, filling out the form becomes a cooperative effort, and finally, the client will be able to fill it out between sessions and bring it to the following session to talk through. Over time, the steps guide clients through the "shifting gear" process. You might ask them to count the steps with the five fingers of one hand as they follow them. Encourage clients to analyze and write down at least two or three situations a week. This will help them to build an "internal therapist," which supports autonomy.

Working with Contingency: Using Diaries

Diaries are a useful tool for clients. They help them to organize and evaluate the success of their behavior experiments, which sustain healthy adult functioning in everyday life. Be creative in helping clients to fit behavior experiments in their daily schedule. It is helpful to offer a variety of tracking tools.

The following suggestions are ranked from simple to more challenging.

The smiley log. The exercise is simple but has a lot of potential impact. It only takes a few seconds. Ask your clients to look back on the day before going to bed and to judge whether it was a good, mediocre, or bad day. Have them record this judgment in a diary using smiley stickers. That's it!

Naturally, clients will begin to ask themselves over the course of each day what kind of day it will be. This increases their awareness of what's going on and the possibility that a client might take some initiative to make it a better day. This warm-up exercise helps to build initial observer skills for the healthy adult mode. After about a month, the log will show a variety of days, which might lead clients to revise their assessment of their quality of life in general and to arrive at a place of greater acceptance. Their assessment will certainly be better than any evaluation made during a "bad mood" day.

The cathartic diary. When clients are weary, ask them to just sit down and start writing whatever comes to mind. Stress that this exercise isn't about reflecting, but just bringing feelings into words. Many people have some experience with writing diaries, perhaps from adolescence. Recall the two memory processes in chapter 9. Writing is a useful way to bring order and sequencing to chaotic feelings by shifting one from episodic to semantic memory processing (Schacter, 1992). Episodic memory operations simultaneously work on parallel tracks. Semantic memory processing crystallizes these processes into linear chains of thoughts. Therefore, this exercise is also useful for slowing down and distancing from what might be causing distress. A lot of research indicates that writing has stabilizing effects on mood (for example, Pennebaker, 1997).

1.	**Actual scene:** What triggered me? What did I feel? What did I do (automatic coping mode)? *I'm alone at home and there's nothing left to clean.*
2.	**Backstage scene:** Childhood memories (schemas) related to the situation? Activated child and inner critic modes? *Being alone in my room as a child, upset that Dad has left and Mom is angry and distracted. (vulnerable/lonely child?).*
3.	**Change perspective:** What are my actual needs, values, and long-term goals in this situation? *My loneliness tells me that I need to do more to connect to others, rather than keep distracting myself with "self-soothers."*
4.	**Doing:** What did I actually do in the situation (functional coping behavior)? *I wanted to drink wine but I called my sister instead to talk about what I'm going through.*
5.	**Effects:** What were the effects of my behavior? *I felt a little more settled after getting some support, but still feel the loneliness. Felt I could tolerate it—that I'm making some positive changes, and it will take some time.*

Figure 11–2. Joanne's schema-mode flash card (modified from Young et al., 2003)

The talking-back diary. Ask clients to track inner critic mode voices and write down what they say on the left side of the form shown in figure 11–3. Then let them try to find a healthy adult response. If they feel blocked, have them try standing up and walking around a little, as you did with them in therapy to induce perspective change. If they remain stuck, work on adequate answers together in the next session. At the beginning of therapy, clients usually identify with inner critic mode voices and regard them as normal. But recording them helps clients to realize what is happening: "My God, they're talking all day!" Clients will also discover that inner critic mode voices tend to repeat themselves.

The diary card. The most complex tool is the diary card (figure 11–4), which covers the full self-regulation cycle according to "plan-do-check-act" (Donabedian, 1966). It oscillates between *cognitive* mental processes (what we intend) and *emotional* situational awareness (what actually happens), with the aim of better connecting explicit left-brain and implicit right-brain processes. Here's an explanation of the form:

- In the first column, next to the time column, clients write their *plans* for the next day. It works best if clients fill out this column before going to bed, because doing so helps to structure the next day.

- In the second column, they insert their observations while following the plan. They could target inner critic mode thoughts, blocked emotions, or issues that interfere with using healthy adult mode.

- The third column shows actual coping reactions, which eventually includes a "shifting gear" movement.

- The fourth column describes the observed effects (ideally, going into healthy adult mode or strengthening happy child mode).

- The fifth column adds a cognitive learning experience that clients draw from this self-regulation cycle.

This form is challenging, and only a few clients will make use of it over an extended period, but it is a powerful tool to introduce and to reinforce self-regulation in the behavior change phase. The diary card is extremely helpful from the therapist's point of view, because it shows clients' capacity for self-organization. This is what counts at the end of the day, not the "storytelling" in sessions. In this way, schema therapy remains a behavior therapy.

Talking-Back Diary

Inner critic thought	Healthy adult comment
He is leaving because of you...	He is leaving to support us!!
You don't deserve him...	Obviously I do, since he married me!!
You don't deserve to be happy...	?? Don't know??
You're just like your mother...	?? Again, don't know??
You are an idiot...	This is simply not true. You struggle with your feelings, not your intellect.

Figure 11–3. Joanne's talking-back diary

It is essential for clients to use *any* kind of tracking tool to increase their mindfulness and their sense of responsibility on a daily basis. This practice strengthens the healthy adult mode. Most clients will only use the more complex diary protocols or the extended diary card for a few weeks or when in crisis. Applied for maybe two weeks on a daily basis, the diaries give clients a motivational push, induce self-efficacy, and keep them on the path toward healing. Include your client in the decision-making process about which diary to use, and for how long. This will help with compliance. Thus, they help in the handover of responsibility for self-care, from therapist to client, and can serve as a starting point for empathic confrontation in case clients remain reluctant to take the initiative. See the following example with Joanne.

Empathic Confrontation Based on a Diary Card

The following transcript shows how the therapist used empathic confrontation after Joanne came into session complaining but not having done her homework.

Joanne: This was a disastrous weekend. I guess the worst since we started therapy. In fact, even worse than before we started therapy. I'm not sure if you can help me at all.

Therapist: Oh, I feel sorry for you having such a hard time, but let's find out what you did to cope with the situation. Let's have a look at your diary card together!

Joanne: Hmm, I don't have it on hand right now...

Therapist: Did you manage to fill it out?

Diary Card

Today's summary:

Date: Friday May 1 Name: Joanne

Time	Planned Activity	Observation	Action	Effect	Learning Experience
6:00 a.m.	Sleep	Sleep	Sleep	Felt energized	Sleep gives me more energy.
9:00 a.m.	Clean	This is good.	Clean	Feel good about myself	
12:00 p.m.	Clean	I'm getting tired.	Clean	Getting exhausted	
3:00 p.m.	Clean	This is too much!	Clean	Exhausted	Cleaning is good, but I need a break sometimes.
6:00 p.m.	Watch TV	I feel alone.	Call my sister	Felt better	I need to plan connection.
9:00 p.m.	Have sister over	I felt anxiety at first, but loneliness settled with time.	Enjoy	Feeling connected	I must take steps to connect.

Figure 11–4. Joanne's diary card

Joanne: Not really.

Therapist: Okay. That's pretty normal when we start trying to use a tool in therapy. However, it's important for our work that you try to take a more active and responsible role. Do you agree that you'll try it again over the next weekend?

Joanne: If you think this will help. Anyway, it can't be worse!

A week later...

Joanne: The weekend was still bad. Not much progress using the diary card! [Note: If the client shows up unimproved the following session, continue working with the diary.]

Therapist: Please let me look at it. Okay, if you take a look yourself, what's your assessment of your effort completing the diary from an observer's perspective?

Joanne: Well, there's not very much on it.

Therapist: Right! Was your idea to abstain from planning some activities over the weekend?

Joanne: I guess I wanted to give the child mode some space for spontaneous activities.

Therapist: Okay, and what was the outcome?

Joanne: Not good!

Therapist: Well, what principle do you draw from that?

Joanne: Maybe making at least some plans for the day?

Therapist: Good. How about planning one activity for Saturday and Sunday, both morning and afternoon? This would leave enough space for spontaneous things and some relaxing.

Joanne: Sounds reasonable.

Therapist: So, shall we give it a try next weekend?

Joanne: Yes.

In this way, the therapist avoids taking over. The responsibility to fill out the diary remains with the client. The focus remains on the diary card, not the therapist, and the diary card itself reveals the problem. Fred Kanfer once observed that something is wrong when the therapist "sweats" more than the client (Kanfer & Scheftt, 1988). Using this tool together later in therapy helps to bring the client into an active role. Increasingly, the therapist steps back and the need for therapy is reduced.

Inducing Behavior Experiments

Once clients have developed sufficient self-regulation skills, it is time to use a behavior experiment to encourage them to overcome experiential avoidance and to face challenging situations that they previously avoided. It is possible that your clients never learned how to deal with difficult situations. Perhaps no one ever explained or adequately modeled such coping skills. If that is the case, they are likely to get stuck in their accustomed coping strategies and need some additional training.

One way to approach difficult situations is with future-directed imagery (see chapter 9). You can use the behavioral activation form (figure 11–5) to support and foster the effects of a future-directed problem-solving imagery. Going through the process facing a situation, step-by-step, in some detail will show potential interactional difficulties. Then you and the client can replay different options in a safe way. This exercise helps your client to develop some sense of self-efficacy by monitoring the increased level of confidence after the imaginary rehearsal. (You can download a blank version of the behavioral activation form, along with this book's other online accessories, at http://www.newharbinger.com/40958.)

Role-plays from conventional behavior therapy are another realistic way to train social skills. There are many variations. As with building up the healthy adult mode, take small steps with these role-plays, too:

1. *Talking to an empty chair first:* The client describes the situation and the expected behavior of the other person. The therapist sits beside the client, supporting him by shaping and eventually modeling behavior. Step-by-step, the therapist connects the expressed behavior with how the client thinks and feels. This will help with reappraisal and habituation until the client feels comfortable.

2. *Talking to the therapist who's embodying the other person's role:* Once the client feels safe in his role, the therapist takes the seat of the other person, giving this person a physical representation. Since it is much more difficult to talk to a real person than an empty chair, this is more like the real situation. The therapist can also give feedback about how it feels to be addressed by the client. This leads to some final adjustments until both are satisfied with the solution.

Behavioral Activation Form Of: Joanne
Date: May 1

1. *Imagine the basic scene:* clearly describe a scene, using as many of your senses as possible, in which you completed the new behavior.

   Joining a local dance class. I have been there many times before but have let it go now for a few years. I can see the route as I drive to the local dance hall in my car, the trees, the houses. I feel nervous and tense in my chest. When I get there I wait in my car until right at starting time so as to avoid any awkward feelings. When I walk inside I can smell the polished hardwood floors and see the girls all chatting, as they know each other.

2. *Getting motivated:* Why is it important for you to make this change now? What value does it move you toward? What will it look and feel like to get closer to this value?

   I need this, I need to bring people and fun back into my life again. Dancing used to be my thing that helped me connect and have fun. It will feel scary, but I hope it will feel happier eventually, once I feel comfortable and start to make connections in the group.

3. *Analyzing obstacles:* What is the biggest single obstacle to you making the change? Now imagine a response that you can make in the scene to overcome it.

   Definitely the biggest obstacle is that awkward feeling if I arrive and I don't know anyone there. I can imagine breaking the ice by introducing myself almost immediately to a few of the girls, and maybe the dance instructor, rather than hiding.

   Rate your level of confidence for completing the new behavior (0/10): 3/10

4. *Playing the scene:* Purposely play through the whole scene. Try to overcome the obstacle you identified. Remember to go slowly, and eventually record the exercise.

   Rerate your level of confidence after you complete the task (0/10): 5/10

5. *Reflection:* How did this exercise feel for me? Does completing this increase my confidence or motivation? What was it like to get closer to my chosen value? Was I able to overcome my obstacle or not? If so, what was that like? If not, how can I rewrite the script to overcome any obstacles next time?

   This felt hard at first, but running through it made me realize that it is normal and I have done this many times before. It also made me think that I can feel more prepared if I pre-prepare some narrative about why I am starting to dance again.

Figure 11–5. Joanne's behavioral activation form

Finally, clients will have to apply skills in real life and observe the outcome. If they show signs of experiential avoidance, ask, "Is your decision to avoid based on experience or on expectations?" Expectations are frequently based on cognitive fusion. It is possible to have an experience only if the client attempts something. Hence, we gently encourage clients to "give it a try." If inner critic mode thoughts still interfere, use chair dialogues until the client can distance from them. If the client's alarm system activates child mode emotions, the emotional resonance sphere technique (described in chapter 10) can be helpful. Whatever technique is used, the goal is to remove the obstacle that is restraining the client. Use a schema-mode flash card or a diary card to monitor the outcome of the executed behavior experiment. You can increase compliance if you ask the client to send you a text message once he or she has carried out the homework or the behavior experiment.

The Good-Night Ritual

The good-night ritual is an exercise for maintaining some mindfulness and self-compassion. It is a useful resource activator, and we recommend doing it with the regularity of a traditional nightly prayer. (An audio recording of this exercise, along with this book's other online accessories, is available for download at http://www.newharbinger.com/40958.) Some of our clients are accustomed to such rituals, which take place at the border between night and day, and so too may yours be familiar. Encourage your client to do the following:

1. Get ready for bed. Turn the lights low. Take a seat on a special chair for the ritual (or place a normal chair in a special position).

2. Take some deeper breaths and let as much tension go as you can while breathing out. Breathe into the stomach. Perform a mini–body scan, and let everything "drop down."

3. Mentally turn to the left and realize how much space you gave to critical thoughts over the day. Just get aware—do not judge! (This is the position we placed the inner critic modes in when we put the mode map on chairs, in chapter 9.)

4. Mentally turn to the right and sense how often you were in touch with your child mode needs. Did you spend at least some moments fully dedicated to realizing a contented or happy child mode? Again, do not judge or beat yourself up. Just acknowledge how it was.

5. Get back into your centered healthy adult mode. How did you balance your attachment and your assertiveness positions over the day? Try to get into some kind of balanced and centered state now. If ruminating thoughts come, let them go.

This ritual serves as a minimal mindfulness-supporting exercise. Done on a daily basis, it can become a self-chosen ritual. Rituals gain their power from repetition, and we propose that this very small exercise can easily be done for a lifetime, reinforcing the healthy adult mode.

Summary

In this chapter, we continued with our practical focus. We brought you into the schema therapy room and described complex therapeutic interactions with very specific steps for changing behavior in clients. The techniques we covered included various ways to develop emotional self-regulation, such as by completing homework assignments and doing role-plays and behavior experiments. We introduced some useful tools, such as schema-mode flash cards, the diary card, various forms to observe and evaluate the day, and the good-night ritual.

CHAPTER 12

Treatment Planning

Therapy is a challenging task, and a lot is at stake. However, as is true with loving relationships, some change in personality is possible (Pearson et al., 1994). Personality change involves leaving accustomed behavioral paths, and the transition can be disruptive. It may involve a transitory reduction in a client's level of functioning before the individual reaches a more functional level again. As when a road is under construction, there can be traffic jams and bumpy lane changes.

Starting Therapy: Stabilization and Building Up Trust

It is understandable then that clients fall back into old behaviors. In the attractor model, which we introduced in chapter 1, this initial hurdle is described as an *aversive fluctuation state* that clients have to cope with. It is a priority for the therapist to deal with this natural source of resistance and to help the client overcome it. Introducing the mode model to the client and building up a reliable and trustworthy therapy relationship are the basic steps, but you might also have to remove other sources of instability.

Stability includes achieving stable:

- *Emotions.* Make the client feel emotionally safe.

- *Life conditions.* Provide a safe and reliable social situation.

- *Symptoms.* Gain control of severe clinical symptoms.

Emotional Stabilization

In schema therapy, there are three elements that aid emotional stabilization in clients.

The therapy relationship. It takes time to achieve control in new situations, which will activate the alarm system, especially if the situation is hard to anticipate or outflanks our set of coping strategies. Then the inner childlike vulnerable state will come to the fore and ask for soothing. The therapist provides the trust and confidence that therapy works and is worth the risk and initial discomfort. This is the core of reparenting.

We want to emphasize that an abstinent therapist cannot fulfill the needs of an activated vulnerable child mode. Some of our clients will need expressions of care, such as those we might show real children. A balance is needed in this reparenting—not extravagant promises but realistic, sensitive care. Remember that your clients have a healthy adult mode along with their activated child mode, so they can soothe their vulnerable child as well.

The schema mode model. During this initial period of transition into therapy, it is also helpful to explain the schema mode model to clients. Understanding schema modes helps to validate their maladaptive behavior as having been the best they could do given their childhood conditions. In addition, what they do is not fundamentally wrong, but a problem usually arises because they either "do too much of a good thing" or neglect alternatives. Their behavioral balance is off, with either excesses or deficits, so the primary goal of therapy for many clients is to work toward a better balance, not completely change behavior. The former is usually much easier to achieve. Using the mode map and the dimensional approach gives clients direction and shows them that all people are alike. By using self-disclosure, therapists indicate that all people—even therapists—have to deal with emotional activations, and that we can only learn to improve our skills gradually.

Skills. Skills compose the third element contributing to emotional stabilization. Many clients have managed to cope with their emotional problems, so it makes sense to ask them what they did before entering therapy. Not everything they do is maladaptive, and a goal should be to encourage them to develop additional skills based on those we presented in chapter 11. Support your client in doing what works best.

> **Therapist Tip:** Ask clients to provide a list of what they did to cope with past negative feelings. Then, together, decide what is still helpful.

Social Stabilization

While some of your clients may live in a reasonably happy social situation, many will not. A few may be too ashamed to reveal the extent of their difficulties to a therapist. They are concerned that the therapist might refuse to work with them. So we need to ask about problems involving work, finances, family members, domestic violence, substance abuse, lack of security in the living situation, children, and other potential difficulties. Such instabilities will drain the energy and reduce the time needed for fundamental changes.

It is usual in the initial phase of treatment for the therapist to give some advice or to actively support the client in resolving severe problems, with the intention of getting therapy started. This advice and support must be limited. Consider whether other professionals or institutions can assist. Once clients are socially stable, schema therapy can continue under more promising conditions.

Reducing Clinical Symptoms

Schema therapy is not always a stand-alone treatment but is often embedded in a broader cognitive behavioral therapy (CBT) treatment approach. Therefore, we can combine the core schema therapy strategies for addressing the personality structure with the symptom-focused interventions successfully used in CBT. In this sense, Samuel Ball developed an approach called dual focus schema therapy (Ball, 1998) to address both clinical foci (personality structure and specific symptoms) while working with addicts.

Ned had inpatient treatment for addiction. He complied with the treatment, behaving in a socially expected way, but failed to work on his avoidant personality. On his way home from therapy he thought about the challenges at home, and he began drinking at the train station. What he lacked was an ability to cope with stress symptoms in real life.

Clients do not usually fit neatly into a specific pattern, as the preceding case example shows. Some have interpersonal problems with a few symptoms, such as depression or anxiety, whereas others shift between many less severe but obvious symptoms. However, some clients suffer from overwhelming clinical symptoms (for example, problem drinking, agoraphobic symptoms requiring a person to accompany them to therapy, severe compulsions that last for hours a day, or anorexia with a very low body mass index). CBT interventions are required first to reduce such symptoms to a manageable level. The more severe and chronic the symptoms, the greater the urgency of bringing the clients to a workable stability. Only then will they be able to cooperate.

The initial goal of therapy is stability. Clients must be stable enough to tolerate changes to their personality structure. We also recommend introducing the schema mode model early in therapy, including a mode map, to clarify the function of the symptoms. When clients appreciate their underlying needs and understand the maladaptive problem-solving function of symptoms, they will comply better with symptom-focused behavior strategies (for example, exposure).

Principle: Exposure therapy works much better when your client understands the function of the symptom and manages to shift into healthy adult observer mode for disidentification.

Once a client has gained enough stability, shift the focus to experiential work to change coping behaviors, but continue monitoring persisting symptoms. Working with a client's inner world and rebalancing coping modes does not automatically make all symptoms disappear. However, we can strengthen the therapy relationship, increase healthy adult mode competencies, and then apply CBT strategies to remaining clinical symptoms. Symptoms tend to recur because we cannot fully erase the underlying attractors. Therefore, clients will have to maintain a degree of self-monitoring and self-regulation more or less for life. *Mindfulness-Based Cognitive Therapy for Depression* provides a good example for how to monitor and deal with depressive thoughts (Teasdale et al., 2002).

Treatment Outline

What does the schema therapy schedule look like? Arntz and van Genderen (2009) provide a detailed outline of what to do, session by session, giving us a useful framework. We separate treatment roughly into five phases:

1. *Initial phase:* Building a therapeutic relationship, stabilization, psychoeducation, and assessment procedures leading to a cognitive case conceptualization

2. *Exploration phase:* Using experiential techniques (especially imagery rescripting or mode dialogues on chairs) to bypass coping modes and access child modes and schema origins, putting flesh on the bones of the case conceptualization, followed by the first corrective emotional experiences

3. *Internal working phase:* Improving self-regulation and increasing the level of healthy adult functioning by using chair dialogues and schema-mode flash cards

4. *Behavior change phase:* Bringing behavioral change to everyday life using role-plays, behavioral experiments, and diary cards in bi-weekly session intervals

5. *Maintenance phase:* Working toward autonomy, reducing therapeutic frequency to monthly, and then initiating termination

Length of phases. The length of the phases varies from client to client. With more functional clients, the initial phase may take only a few sessions. Then, after three to five imagery rescripting sessions exploring the key schema-inducing childhood scenes, the focus shifts to working in the client's inner world with chair dialogues. We have found that healthier clients can learn the basic skills of impeaching inner critic modes and caring for their child modes with ten to fifteen sessions.

The focus then shifts to behavior experiments as the therapist takes a step back. Once the new behavior is stable, we change to the maintenance phase with monthly sessions for up to one year.

While the length of treatment varies, a complete schema therapy treatment with a higher-functioning client can take about thirty to forty sessions over a period of up to two years.

Complex cases. More severely disordered and unstable clients need more time to establish the trust that will allow them to cooperate with imagery work. If a client refuses early imagery work (which is common with severely traumatized, narcissistic, or some cluster-C clients), try to put the modes on chairs to reflect the original schema-inducing experiences. It helps to lay out the chairs according to the mode map and to investigate any reactions using a standing position and by forming a "consultation team." Generally, this process reduces fear in reluctant clients and increases familiarity with the model. Sooner or later, trust will come, and the client will agree to doing chair dialogues. Once clients can tolerate being immersed in their thoughts and feelings, you can shift to imagery work.

Remain flexible, go with the flow, and do what works best. Do not try to break through resistance. Try walking around it. With more challenging cases, you can expect to spend forty sessions (or a year) with a client to make real progress. You can reduce the frequency of sessions to every other week once the client's healthy adult mode has begun to help the therapy. However, expect this phase to last ten to twenty sessions (or up to one more year), and then try monthly session intervals for another year. This adds up to about sixty to eighty sessions over three years or more. This is realistic and in line with the seventy hours Marjon Nadort needed to successfully treat borderline clients in her study (Nadort et al., 2009). Very severely traumatized clients, such as those who suffered sexual abuse in early childhood, might need even more sessions.

How to convey the schedule to the client. Many clients ask about the expected length of treatment. You might postpone your answer until after you finish the exploration phase and have developed a vivid case conceptualization. Then you can give a time frame for therapy:

Maddie had strong traits of borderline personality disorder. Her therapist explained, "You are thirty-seven years old. You had a traumatic childhood and have had many unhappy relationship experiences since then. We can't expect to reverse this easily. Think of it as a huge task, like climbing a Himalayan mountain. It takes years of preparation: getting very fit, learning new skills, and building your endurance. Treatment with schema therapy is for the long haul, meaning years of treatment, but I'll be here to support you through the process."

Most higher-functioning clients are realistic enough to accept that therapy takes time, but some clients with personality disorders seem to believe in magic and hope for a quick cure. Alternatively, some may become frightened if we set a clear limit. For many of them, therapy is the only way they have found for getting their needs met. In effect, we are the best thing that ever happened to them, and they do not want to lose us.

To find a balance when establishing the time frame, you could say something like this:

Therapist: We'll work for about three to four years, in the beginning on a weekly basis, later with longer intervals. I'll do my best to support you. If you do the same, we'll make progress. Along the way, we'll discuss the situation and decide on the next steps. I'll help you build up a healthy adult mode within yourself. Then your healthy adult will take over and will continue doing what I do in the beginning. In this way, I'll be present inside of you, and we'll stay connected.

Again, this parallels the road to autonomy that a child needs to take.

How to extend session intervals. Perhaps the best time to shift to therapy sessions every other week is after a break (for example, a vacation). Usually, clients get along quite well without seeing you every week. You can say something like this:

Therapist: I'm pleased you managed so well over the break. This shows that your healthy adult is getting stronger. Now we have the chance to take the next step toward autonomy by extending the session interval to two weeks. This may make you feel anxious, and I don't want to push too hard. So what do you need to give it a try?

You can assure your client of additional sessions if there is a crisis, and perhaps give permission to exchange emails and make use of audio recordings from earlier sessions as support.

Therapist: So why don't we give it a try for a month. If it doesn't work for you, we can return to weekly sessions. But if we don't try, we won't make progress. Why not record our sessions with your smartphone and listen to the recording in the week in between? That way I'll still be present when needed.

In the maintenance phase, shift to monthly sessions. The focus is on maintaining change and accepting what cannot be changed. Keep the sessions focused on any schema activations. Use brief chair dialogues and work toward integration and acceptance. Resolve any remaining tasks. Double-check to see if initial clinical symptoms have subsided. Once both of you get the impression that your client is remaining stable, you can cease regular sessions and make appointments as needed. This usually marks the end of regular therapy.

Session Planning

We outlined what the course of schema therapy might entail. Now we look at how to structure a single treatment session. There are parallels.

About good timing. Ideally, each session starts with an emotional activation, followed by a phase of clarification and reappraisal, and finally working toward a functional behavioral response. The working phase is the heart of the therapy, so enough time should set be aside for this, usually about twenty minutes in each session, to do it well.

It is best to avoid small talk at the beginning of the session. Think about beginning with either "What have you brought into the session?" or "What do you want to work on today?" Both indicate that the purpose of the session is to work on schema activations. If your client shows signs of emotional activation while presenting a problem, immediately shift into imagery work to access underlying schemas. Nothing works better! Later, start chair dialogues to work with inner critic thoughts or child mode activations you've picked up on. Put them on chairs right away instead of talking things through in the detached protector mode.

Take an active role. Schema therapists are often active at the beginning of a session in order to emotionally turn a spark into a flame. Being able to quickly get to emotional activation is an important skill for schema therapists. Unlike some other therapies, we do not dwell on expressing distress but instead help clients to shift into healthy adult mode. This involves the three steps of the healthy adult mode: perception, reappraisal, committed action. As with any skill, practice makes perfect, which takes time. Carefully apply session activities, such as chair dialogues, according to the client's resources. In the beginning, be a role model and offer emotional support. As soon as possible, pass the responsibility to the client, asking her to find her own solutions.

Watch for hidden inner critic modes. Most clients initially think of their inner critic mode voices as their healthy adult mode. Detecting the underlying beliefs and appraisals requires substantial work, including repetitively sorting out the inner critic modes with an extra chair, taking a distanced observer's perspective, looking at the effects of the inner critic voices on the child mode, reappraising and impeaching the inner critic voices, and developing self-compassion. Do this work carefully. It takes time—usually twenty or more minutes in the middle of the session. Eventually, the client will become familiar with this cycle and take over, ferreting out the inner critic voices on his own.

Do not introduce too much variety to this process, as a consistent approach will help your client to internalize it. This is probably why standardized therapies have tended to show better results, as Schulte (1996) has demonstrated with anxiety disorders.

Care for the end of the session. In the second half of a session, the focus shifts from perception and reappraisal to committed action. Keep in mind that each session should come to a good end. This can take time. If called for, allow your client ten minutes to shift into healthy adult mode at the end of the session.

Change focus over the course of therapy. Developing perception in clients includes going over any activities that occurred between sessions and reviewing flash cards and diaries. Gradually, as therapy progresses, you should spend less time in reappraisal and more time role-playing and engaging in behavior experiments. At some point, clients experience a shift in perception; instead of physically changing chairs to deal with inner critic and child modes, they approach them in more of a mental process, remaining seated on the healthy adult chair. Finally, at some point they will mostly remain in their healthy adult mode during sessions, supported by the therapist, when dealing with challenging life situations and any remaining symptoms. At this point, schema therapy becomes behavior therapy!

Balancing Change and Acceptance over the Course of Therapy

Clients come to therapy seeking change. Even seriously disordered clients desire psychological relief, asking, "Will I ever be normal?" This may be unlikely, since it is rare for low-functioning people to miraculously become high functioning, but a different trajectory can make a big difference in their life. The goal and hope of schema therapy is to change coping strategies and help all clients, high or low functioning, gain emotional flexibility.

Be realistic. False hope is unhelpful in therapy, and being realistic is where acceptance strategies come into play. "Well-being" does not mean remaining free of negative thoughts or feelings. It is about gaining distance from them. Acceptance is a major contribution to the schema model from acceptance and commitment therapy (ACT), and the principles behind acceptance are easy to teach to clients. Acceptance does not mean giving up or resignation; it means understanding that the situation is the way it is, and then being able to focus on remaining options. As described by Linehan (1993) in dialectical behavior therapy, *acceptance* means accepting the unchangeable while committing to working on remaining issues that one can change. Being able to distinguish one from the other remains an important task in therapy.

Acknowledge limitations. Some clients come to therapy with severe limitations, which can include biological traits; deeply entrenched, traumatic early-childhood experiences; lack of empathy (reduced mirror neuron functioning); or limitations in the capacity for mentalization. These can be seen as emotional disabilities, but how do we introduce this idea to clients without damaging their self-esteem? You might say something like this:

Therapist: You asked me if you will ever get rid of this problem. Frankly, that is a very high goal. Looking at the starting point of your life and what you had to cope with, you were burdened with much more than most people. This isn't your fault, of course. You've done a great job carrying this weight and have grown as a person. Comparing yourself with other people isn't fair. You had to work much harder. What you achieved seems like a lot to me, and you can be proud. Unfortunately, some wounds can't be undone, and we'll have to accept the resulting limitations. This doesn't make you a less lovable or worthy person. Looking at what you've gained, I owe you a lot of respect. So let's see what we still can work on, and I'll do my best to help you enjoy your unique life situation.

Such an explanation can relieve clients of the unrelenting expectations of other people. It will certainly supply no further ammunition to inner critic modes. Surprisingly, in our experience, clients do not feel devalued when we're direct in this way. They feel understood! Even ending therapy is much easier when clients can accept what has not changed.

Acceptance is also relevant for clients who have some kind of limitation: old age, limited social and economic resources, or adverse life circumstances. These types of more common limitations also make change harder to achieve. Most of us have an unrelenting standards schema, making it hard to accept limitations. This is an existential challenge for everybody, including therapists. Our training in acceptance helps us to deal with what we cannot change. Thus, we can be good role models. We regard mindfulness, including acceptance, as the air that the healthy adult mode breathes. Creating a mindful and accepting atmosphere in the therapy room equates with practicing what we preach and is an important step in helping our clients.

Termination

In the middle of therapy, we advise shifting to sessions every other week. Naturally, this will depend on the severity of the client's disorder and the progress that you are making. The shift might be between the fifteenth and thirtieth sessions, or sometimes it occurs later. This shift offers a good opportunity to try behavior experiments. It is appropriate to begin using schema-mode flash cards or other homework assignments. By reviewing the flash cards or diaries, you are reducing your level of activity and giving more responsibility to the client.

Here are some useful questions for shifting the locus of control to the client:

- Do you recognize this kind of situation?
- Are you aware of the activated modes and schemas?
- What have you successfully done before in this situation?
- What do other people do in this situation?
- What do you think I would say or do in this situation?
- What would a wise person do?
- How did you get along with the situation on your own?
- What do you think I would recommend you to do?

Many clients will report that between sessions they heard your voice, like the voice of a good parent or friend. This shows that they have integrated you as therapist into their healthy adult mode. This is a sign of maturity. It is also a sign that your client is making progress toward termination.

Conveying the news about termination. How do we discuss the termination of therapy? Ending therapy can be frightening for clients, and clients with dependent traits will find it difficult. Maladaptive schemas might recur when we broach this topic. We have to introduce this step carefully and make it a focus of therapy.

Here's a suggestion for one way to introduce the idea of ending therapy:

Therapist: I have the impression that our job together is mostly done and gains are getting smaller. This is normal in therapy. In the beginning, we don't know what can change and what has to be accepted. I think we've arrived at a point where we have to reassess what we can still work on. I don't want to put pressure on you, but I would like to suggest that you have more time to work on agreed issues between sessions on your own. I suggest we shift to having a session every three weeks [or monthly]. You might think about what we still can work on, maybe making a list of issues. To keep us connected, you can send a text message if there's a crisis. We can also have an emergency session if necessary. I don't want to leave you on your own, but I can see how well your healthy adult mode is functioning. Maybe we can follow this schedule for another year, or maybe a bit more.

Naturally, we want to support our clients in independent self-management. Thus, we have to create a therapeutic setting that both challenges clients and gives them time to adapt. This includes adjusting to less support from us. You might suggest that they record sessions and listen to them at home to feel connected between sessions.

Ethical concerns. Some clients will want to continue sessions even if there is no further progress. They may justify this in terms of being willing to pay. But, unlike many other professional services, therapy is a very personal relationship that you cannot buy with money. You may have to make it clear to the client that therapy is neither a friendship nor a paid service. Therapy is goal-directed and a bilateral contract. We have the right to end therapy if we do not see sufficient progress. This parallels the kind of limit setting used with children to encourage autonomy. There are also ethical concerns about providing therapy that does not lead to any progress.

Balancing these concerns brings us close to contingency management in dialectical behavior therapy (Linehan, 1993): on one hand, we should not "reward" passive clients by offering more sessions; on the other hand, termination is not a punishment. Reducing the intensity of treatment and fading it out is our response to the situation, giving our clients time to react. We extend the intervals while keeping their foot in our door.

Managing termination. For most of our clients, being direct about ending therapy, and reducing the number of therapy sessions slowly, leads to a good outcome. Nevertheless, some may feel disappointed and expect more. How do we deal with them? Keep in mind that the therapist's own schemas, such as unrelenting standards and self-sacrifice (possibly with some entitlement-grandiosity as well), may be affecting the termination process. It's important to remember that we cannot treat *all* clients successfully.

Therapist: It's important for me that you don't blame yourself if you don't make further progress. I am limited as well. And there are limits to what can be achieved in therapy in general. I'd appreciate it if you would allow me to accompany you for a few more sessions to support you in maintaining what we have achieved.

In addition, there is always the risk of clients becoming dependent on their therapist. Being willing to enter an attachment-based relationship is fundamental to successful therapy, but letting go can be painful. Acknowledging our limitations and conveying this to clients in a respectful and not-blaming way supports them as they disconnect from us and strengthens their autonomy. We aren't required to continue therapy endlessly, but we are obliged to act in beneficial ways.

You might also consider including the partner of a client in the termination process. This can help you get additional information about your client's level of functioning and remaining problems. Also, the partner is the person expected to fulfill the attachment needs of the client in the future, so potential benefits of involving this person include providing the partner with information about the client, what triggers the client, what you did in therapy, and how the couple can make use of this knowledge in everyday life.

Termination in the case of Joanne. Let us close by looking at the termination of Joanne's case. Despite many ups and downs, after the first year of therapy, it was clear that Joanne had made several treatment gains. She was relying less and less on her coping modes and was increasingly in touch with her healthy adult mode when her schemas were triggered. She was much more engaged in life areas connected to her personal values and was experiencing a great deal more needs satisfaction. She completed her studies in nursing, started dancing, and her relationships with her husband, sister, and children improved.

Because the therapist was aware that the issue of termination would trigger Joanne's abandonment schema, he introduced it very carefully. He told her that he was proud of her gains and achievements, and he suggested sessions every other week for the next six months or so to give her more opportunity to cope independently of the therapy relationship.

In the following year, Joanne started a job as a nursing assistant and was unable to attend frequent sessions. Nonetheless, she continued to attend monthly therapy sessions for another nine months. After that, Joanne and the therapist together decided to a trial termination of the sessions for about six months. The therapist also reassured her that he would be happy to see her again for booster sessions if things started falling apart.

Summary

In this chapter, we offered an overview of therapy planning, covering the whole course of therapy as well as how to conduct individual sessions. We described session structure and timing, examined the need to balance change and acceptance, and suggested ways to convey to clients difficult messages, such as ending therapy.

CHAPTER 13

Dealing with Difficult Clients

There will always be people who are difficult to treat. This is especially so in schema therapy, since it focuses precisely on what makes a person difficult: personality traits and personality disorders. More and more, schema therapists are often seen as the client's last hope, so it should not surprise us that we see the most challenging cases. While many of the techniques introduced so far work well in practice, we may find ourselves "stuck" with some clients. In those cases, we need additional strategies. How to deal with these challenging clients is the focus in this chapter. We all are limited by our experience and knowledge, so look for additional ideas in the work of colleagues. Nevertheless, we offer the following as a kind of toolkit that might be useful when you find yourself stuck.

Externalizing Clients

If you get stuck with a client, it is best to accept the situation for what it is. Your demanding inner critic mode will put pressure on you, but this is unlikely to help and will probably result in worse performance. It is better to admit that you are stuck and that the situation is difficult. Include your client in the process of evaluating this stuckness by thinking aloud. Voice what options occur to you to get unstuck, and let your client participate in the decision making. This kind of self-disclosure and client involvement is helpful in schema therapy and can relieve you of stress. (Read more about such self-care in chapter 15.)

In chapter 6, we introduced the basic strategy to use with overcompensating clients. However, sometimes disidentification from toxic messages is not easy. Wendy Behary (2013) suggests picturing the child mode by visualizing an eight- or ten-year-old behind the coping mode while the client is acting out. You might also remind yourself that your clients are not seeing you clearly but are driven by a projection based on their schema activations. They are simply acting out what worked best in their childhood. They may also be copying poor family models. Often, your client has changed sides. When they were young, they were victims, but now they act like the offenders who mistreated them. This will help you with your understanding and realistic acceptance.

The Narcissistic Client

The following case example illustrates a narcissistic client.

Barry is a younger brother. His older brother bullied him. This involved holding him down and shaming him (vulnerable child mode). His parents never protected him, instead giving him the message that he had to fight for himself or he would fail in life. Barry thought that this was the way of life and that he would always lose (inner critic mode telling him to swallow his anger, submit, and later detach).

The bullying also happened at school. He was picked on because he was not strong or good at sports, but he realized that he was smarter than his peers. Being smarter became a way for him to cover his own back. He knew things and could impress his teachers (compensation for his defectiveness-shame schema). He thought, Nobody will mess with me anymore!

Then his inner critic mode voices gained an external focus. He became famous as a lawyer who enjoyed belittling those who appeared in court. Not surprisingly, this role change led to relationship difficulties and divorce. This was the reason he came to therapy.

Figure 13–1 shows Barry's mode changes over time. Initially, he was in vulnerable child mode, surrendering to his defectiveness-shame schema. The demanding inner critic mode, based on his unrelenting standards schema, was self-focused, and he went into submission. Then he discovered his intellectual resources, allowing him to make use of his latent anger. This led to compensating for his defectiveness-shame schema. He merged his angry child mode with an externally directed inner critic mode, which he used to great effect in court when overcompensating in self-aggrandizer mode. He became the bully!

One goal in therapy is to bring to the front stage what remains unseen on the backstage. This is not about fighting what we see, but about putting it into context and finally in its place. We validate what we see and acknowledge it as the best solution that the client has found so far with these steps:

- *Stop* the process: "Sorry, it's impolite to interrupt you, but I think there's something relevant going on right now."

- *Explain* this in a "one-down" position (Bateson, 1972): "I see that you're emotionally engaged, and I want to understand better what's actually going on. Therefore, I ask you to stop for a moment because that helps me to get a clearer picture. Could we please both stand up now, to take a look at the situation together?"

In most cases, this process works, and you can continue as described in step 2 in "Dealing Gently with Overcompensatory Modes," in chapter 6. But what should you do when the client is stuck in his anger?

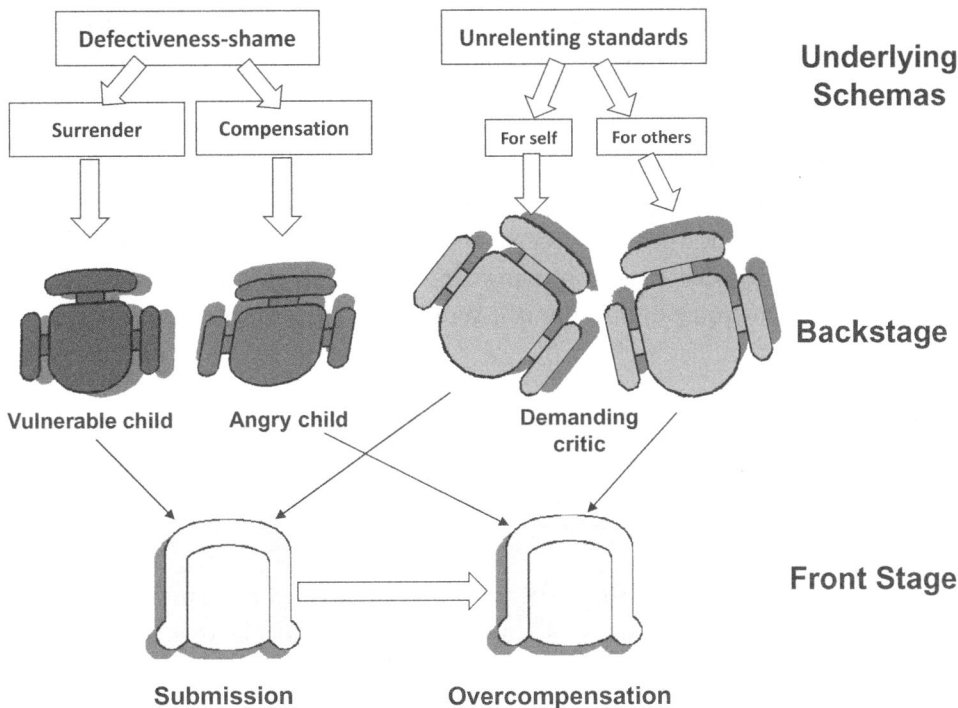

Figure 13–1. Schemas and modes of a narcissistic client

Dealing with Angry Clients

Wendy Behary, an expert working with narcissists, suggested some helpful ways to work with angry clients (Behary, 2013). These methods can be useful, especially if your client refuses to stand up and change to the observer's perspective. The main intention is to keep an emotional connection and retain the client in therapy.

Clarify and validate. "I see you're angry now. That's okay, and I'm sure you have good reasons. Anger is an important driver in life, so let's try to understand what triggered your anger. Even though you're angry at me, this is a chance for us to deepen our understanding, so I'd appreciate it if we could stand up together now to analyze the situation better. This is a good opportunity for learning!"

Ask permission. If you want to say something that your client might hear as critical, ask for permission. This involves the client in the decision: "I have some critical thoughts. Are you interested in hearing them?" You can also anticipate a negative reaction by asking, "You may not like what I'm inclined to say. Nevertheless, do you want to hear it?"

Move from the micro- to the macrolevel. "Something important is happening right now. Maybe this happens to you elsewhere, so we have the chance now to better understand the underlying pattern."

Wind the video back. If there is a sudden turn in the session, stop and say, "Something is happening that I don't fully understand. I can see your anger. So let's rewind the video back to find out when you became angry. Can you identify a trigger? What feelings came up first? What was going on in your mind then?" This works if the trigger was in the session, but you can also use it if your client came to the session in an angry mood.

Talk to an empty chair. If your client is angry at another person, represent that person with an empty chair, and then sit beside the client and encourage her to vent her anger toward the chair. Sometimes having the client close her eyes helps to bring up a more vivid picture of the addressee.

> **Therapist Tip:** If you think your client might be caught in a projection, say, "I'm not sure whether you're really angry with me. Could it be that you're angry at somebody else? Let's see what happens if we both close our eyes and you talk to that person in front of you on the empty chair. Please let all your anger out now."

Vent anger. A client who is angry with you may object to talking to an empty chair. In that case, sit down in front of him, saying, "Okay, I'm here to listen to everything you want to express. What do you want to say? Is there anything more you want to add? What else? I'll comment later, but first speak it all out! Something more?" Don't comment in any way, just stay connected. Look directly at your client. There is no need to smile or nod a lot. Avoid saying too much, because your words will only add fuel to the fire. Usually, your client will soon calm down.

Discriminate. If your client accuses you of not listening, ask, "Okay, I'm sorry that you felt that way, but do you have the feeling that I'm listening *right now*?"

Try a behavior experiment. If your client still resists your intervention, say, "Okay, I understand. You regard my ideas as silly. But please give it a try for ten minutes, then you can call it the most foolish thing you ever tried."

Show personal involvement. If your client wants to leave the session, you can say, "I understand your disappointment and that you want to go. It will make me sad. We have spent time together and I feel some connection to you. You matter to me. Perhaps I've made some mistakes and disappointed or hurt you. I want to do better, so maybe you can help me out a bit. You're already here, so how about giving it a try for the rest of the session and then you can decide whether to go or not."

Split the client up. "Well, I can see your anger, and I'm pleased that you came here to tell me. You could have stayed away! But maybe there are two sides, and along with your anger, there's a small part of you that still hopes we might find something that works for you? How about giving therapy another chance?"

Leave a foot in the door. "Okay, I see your disappointment, and maybe it's better if we stop for now. But I want you to know that I'm still willing to continue, and you can reach me whenever you want to try again."

Accept breaking up. "Maybe you're right: we don't make a good team. Actually, not all therapists match with every client. The limitation may be on my side too. If you want, I can give you the names of some colleagues. I'm sure that one will match better with you and will better help you in dealing with your issues."

Setting Limits on Bullying Clients

Fortunately, it is rare that a client will lose control and engage in bullying in a session. Bullying usually occurs only in couple therapy and is directed toward a partner. Nevertheless, we have to be prepared and have a way of managing such a situation. If you do have a bullying client, consider the following techniques for dealing with the behavior.

Offer self-disclosure. "I have to tell you that I'm a bit surprised about what's happening in our session. I don't feel very comfortable with it. I can't work with you if you speak in this strong way. Could we please stop and change into the observer's perspective by standing up together? This will help us to both understand what's going on."

Split yourself up. "When you treat me this way, there's a part of me that really hates you and would like to kick you out of therapy. But returning to the healthy adult chair, I can see that your bully and attack mode is trying to protect your vulnerable child. This helps me to stay in touch and not take the attack personally."

Set limits. "Please stop now! This is not therapy! Stop—or I'll have to end the session. I want to work with you, but not in this way." It is important to take a firm stance. This includes being physical. So stand up, hold your hands up as if to physically stop your client, put one foot in front of the other, and speak with a firm but not aggressive voice. If you are both standing, we suggest continuing in the standing position, looking down on the chairs, and connecting the situation with the client's mode map.

Leave the room. If the situation continues to worsen, as can happen in a forensic setting or on a psychiatric ward, leave the room. Your client will usually calm down after you leave because you have removed the trigger. If the client clings to you, go to a place where other people are. If you anticipate the situation becoming difficult, take a seat close to the door so the client cannot block your way out of the room.

Empathic Confrontation with Manipulative Clients

You may find inconsistencies in what a client reports in a session. You will need to find some clarification in a nonconfrontational way.

Offer tentative inquiry. "I don't see how this fits. Maybe I'm missing something. Can you help me understand how this makes sense with what you said before? It's hard to help you when I don't have the full picture."

Develop discrepancies. "Okay, I heard your message. But how does that match with what you said about…? Could you please help me understand that?" This usually works best if you only ask questions and avoid taking a personal stance.

Try the Columbo technique. "That's really interesting. Maybe I'm not really getting it, but how exactly did that work if you did…? Why do you think he reacted that way?" Fred Kanfer named this technique of "playing stupid" (Kanfer & Schefft, 1988) after the TV detective played by Peter Falk.

Use time projection. "If I got you right, you want me to do this… You believe that this could help you for the moment. But what will happen in the long run—in a month, next year, in ten years? Would it be better to take a path that might be more difficult for a while but would improve your situation in the long run?"

Split yourself up. "One part of me understands that you're suffering, and I want to help. I can see you somehow trapped in your vulnerable side. Another part of me wants to support the assertiveness side of you and look for a better long-term solution."

Take an observer's perspective. "I see that what you want me to do fulfills your immediate need. But if I take a more responsible role, then I see that other people will have to pay the price. Although I see your point, this is not really fair. So let's stand up and brainstorm. Maybe together we can find a way to solve your problem more fairly."

Self-Harming Behavior

Clients who threaten or do self-harm challenge the therapy relationship. Self-harm is an acid test of the relationship, because the client is taking reparenting to its limits, and the therapist will need to make use of empathic confrontation and limit setting. Dialectical behavior therapy was developed to deal with these self-defeating patterns.

Linehan (1993) uses learning theory, which is a different approach from the developmentally-based schema therapy model. She avoids reinforcing maladaptive behavior. Her approach is to reduce the frequency and intensity of the therapeutic contacts as a reaction to dysfunctional behavior (for example, sending clients into a time-out or ending therapy after two missed sessions back-to-back).

To deal with self-harm, schema therapists constantly connect the displayed behavior with the schema mode model, as a joint reference point, and find a balance of support and confrontation. Arntz and van Genderen (2009) recommend some tolerance of self-mutilating behavior early in therapy for severely troubled clients. But if self-harm limits the progress of therapy, the therapist will have to address it directly. Therapists, as well as our clients, are at risk of avoidance!

Such behavior shows a good deal of aggression. But why don't we see the anger? The inner critic modes prohibit externalizing the anger (toward somebody else). Usually this coping is derived from childhood experiences when open expression of anger was punished. The result is blocked or self-directed anger, and the only remaining object for the aggression is the client's own body. This results in the client being both offender and victim at the same time. The right strategy is to split up the client, get beyond the visible coping mode, and then address both child mode poles and externalize the inner critic voices (as we describe in "A 'Visible' Case Formulation," in chapter 6). While this sounds simple, it is difficult because self-harming clients usually identify more with the inner critic mode voices than their own body.

Accessing the Underlying Anger

Standing and taking an observer's perspective will not usually solve the problem of self-harm. Most self-harming clients are somewhat isolated, so both the extension and substitution techniques are less likely to work. The best option is to directly confront the inner critic mode voices with their inhuman attitude. Consider using strong metaphors. We have used Nazi images, because such figures acted out inhuman behavior in a remorseless way. Be careful not to move too quickly. Take a slow pace and frequently check in with your client, but also remain emotionally connected on a level beyond symptom expression. This is a difficult balance. The two sides are to confront the dysfunctional behavior while keeping an empathic connection with the client. Separating the behavior from the child modes is crucial.

Principle: The approach of accessing underlying anger will work if you manage to emotionally connect clients more to you than to their symptoms.

A therapist's interaction with Angelina, a traumatized borderline client with self-mutilating behavior and suicidal tendencies, may help illustrate this balancing act.

Therapist: I have to admit that it isn't easy for me, but we have to talk about your self-mutilating behavior because it's sabotaging our work together. I understand that you have found that this reduces your inner tension and was the best

	you could do in the past, so I don't want to fight with your "protector." I'd prefer to show you the limitations of this coping strategy, and maybe we can find something better. Could we both stand up to gain a better overview and better understand what's at stake?
Angelina:	Another one of your silly and useless exercises?
Therapist:	Another attempt to increase your flexibility to react to stress.
Angelina:	Okay, but if it turns out to be the same bullsh-- again, I'll step out!
Therapist:	Okay, give me ten minutes! So let's put your self-mutilating coping behavior on the protector chair and put it to one side for now. As you know, the interesting dynamics happen backstage. So we put a chair for your beliefs, or the voices in your head, there.

In this case, the therapist does not ask Angelina to sit on the chair, preferring to have her talk about the chair while standing above it. This allows the therapist to remain standing beside Angelina while giving her room to move, which helps her to feel less trapped or under pressure.

Therapist:	So, what do the voices say to induce or justify the self-harming?
Angelina:	Well, it's her fault. She didn't do what was needed!

It is crucial to adopt a nonjudgmental stance and to try to fully understand how the client sees things, no matter how weird something might seem. Unless you can do this, you will not bypass the coping mode. The questions are basically the same as we described in "Inner Critic Modes," in chapter 6, but you stay in a third-person perspective. This gives the client a bit more distance. Once the beliefs are clear, add an empty chair for the child mode in front of the inner critic mode chair.

Therapist:	Okay. I hope I get your point. So, can we picture another person on the inner critic chair and let the voices speak out their messages? [Note: The therapist repeats some of the core put-down messages.] Is this familiar? Who did you hear talking this way?
Angelina:	*(Feeling uncomfortable and trying to avoid)* But she deserves it!
Therapist:	That's not my point! I just want to know where people talk to other people that way? This usually doesn't happen in daily life between people, face-to-face. It isn't respectful. It can only happen when one person has power over another person. What do you think?
Angelina:	Don't know. Stupid question.
Therapist:	Okay, let's take another step. How do the messages and the behavior affect the other person? What is the point?

Angelina: I don't care.

Therapist: I think that's right. The voices don't care and treat this part as if it's a different person. And you choose sides and try to distance from this vulnerable part, too. But this is as impossible as trying to escape your own shadow. So, on one side it's just kind of silly, but on the other side it makes me angry too. This attitude violates all human values. It's remorseless and amoral—just toxic! Nobody's entitled to treat anybody else that way. This only happens in antisocial settings. The Nazis did that. The Islamic State does it. But I can't accept it! This *is* just inhuman. Nobody who enjoys life does this. People who have been hurt and humiliated themselves do it, changing from the victim to the offender side. Whatever happed to the child down there? I feel connected to her, and I want to try to help her find a way out of this dungeon of despair. Let's break the chain and start a new story instead of endlessly repeating the old violent one. I feel a lot of power inside of you. Instead of letting it go down this destructive path, why not, together, let us find ways to make more productive use of this power. How does that sound?

Angelina: What do you mean by "power"?

Therapist: Well, when I see how much effort and energy you put into this self-defeating behavior, there's no wimp behind it. I actually feel a lot of power deep inside of you, and I'd like to get more in touch with it. I feel a great potential there.

Angelina: Nobody ever saw any "potential" in me.

Therapist: I do. But to make good use of it we should separate the power from the self-injury. I can see that there were roadblocks along your life path that led you to a dead-end street. Let's go back to the main road and find a healthy way for you to live your own life.

Angelina: I don't know what you're talking about.

Therapist: Okay, to be more realistic, let's look at Angelina's mode map. What we see is a self-defeating pattern with some self-harming, binge drinking, suicidal attempts, and bulimia. What's the purpose of all that?

Angelina: Stupid question. I just *have* to do it!

Therapist: What's going on inside of you *before* you do it?

Angelina: I don't know—it feels bad.

Therapist: Exactly! I think all this behavior reduces painful inner tension. Right?

Angelina: Maybe.

Therapist: But I want to understand where this tension is coming from. Any ideas?

Angelina: You're the therapist!

Therapist: I guess it's coming from these put-down voices inside your head, putting pressure on you. How long have these voices existed?

Angelina: They've always been there—and they're right!

Therapist: Does that mean you were born with those voices?

Angelina: No idea. Maybe.

Therapist: Sorry. Can you picture any child born with these voices? No, not at all! These voices come from messages that you heard in childhood that later became part of you. I ask you to put these voices here on the inner critic mode chair.

(Angelina takes a seat on the inner critic mode chair, and the therapist sits down beside her, pointing to the child mode chair in front of her.)

Therapist: Okay, so let's tell that "creep" over there what you think about her!

Angelina starts putting the child mode chair down. The therapist does not allow her to dwell too long on this chair, as he doesn't want to reinforce the inner critic modes. The purpose of this exercise is to fuel the process. After a few sentences, both shift to the child mode chair.

Therapist: How does it make you feel when you hear these voices?

Angelina: I feel paralyzed.

Therapist: Oh, yes! These voices are so toxic! But if you look at your right hand, what's it doing? *(Pointing at Angelina's fists)*

Angelina: Well—I'm hammering on my leg.

Therapist: Exactly. But that's not the vulnerable side of you. What would this fist like to do if everything was possible and nobody would see it? Close your eyes if possible, go back in time, and give me a picture.

Angelina: I want to hit him in the face.

Therapist: How does that feel?

Angelina: Damned good!

Therapist: Exactly! And do you have the right to do it?

Angelina: I never dared to think that. But you're right—he deserves it. And much more.

This transcript presents a different way to enter the rescripting of a traumatic event compared to that described in chapter 9. It works like a preparatory step for Angelina, who wasn't willing to start imagery work because she was caught in her protector mode. Her latent anger was close to the surface, so she and her therapist worked with the activated emotions directly and unblocked them. This only works with clients' cooperation, which we try to gain by not confronting or questioning them directly and by remaining in an inquisitive stance (Fonagy et al., 2004). In this way, it is possible to access the backstage. We regard displayed coping behavior as previously learned behavior that worked to some degree in the past. But if we want to replace it with something more functional, we have to go backstage, detect the toxic beliefs that the client is identified with, and reveal the negative effects on the child modes (as we described in chapter 10, "Putting the Mode Map on Chairs").

Dealing with Suicidal Ideation

Suicidal thinking presents a therapeutic challenge as well. It is essential that you do not allow suicidal protector modes to deflect therapy, and that you always keep in mind the vulnerable child backstage and try to bring it forward. Validate your client's anger, which is a constructive power for good but must be redirected in a functional direction. Being honest and authentic, and indicating that the client means something to you as person, will aid the therapy process when you're confronted by suicidal ideation.

But what if that is not enough? We have to be prepared for an "emergency exit," such as institutionalization, when the client is at risk; however, treatment in a psychiatric inpatient unit does not necessarily mean the end of therapy, so you must be prepared to continue on even in such difficult circumstances.

Angelina found herself in a suicidal crisis.

Therapist: You mentioned that you want to get out of this mess. What does that mean, exactly?

Angelina: Can't we talk about something else?

Therapist: No. Sorry. Excuse me if I'm persistent on this point. I wonder if that means that you're thinking about killing yourself? [Note: Do not use euphemisms, which are avoidant. Clearly name the behavior.]

Angelina: Maybe. Why not?

Therapist: I've known you long enough to know that you need the option of killing yourself as a kind of emergency exit. This is your way out if you can't stand your life anymore. But I'm a professional therapist, and the law expects me

	to send you to a clinic if you're at risk. Sorry, but I don't have a choice. It's in your hands to decide what I have to do.
Angelina:	I guess that's your problem—poor you!
Therapist:	No, it's not just my problem. Looking more deeply, I see two parts to you. One is telling me there's no more meaning in life. This is the more angry and fed-up part. But if that were the only side of you, you wouldn't have come to therapy today. Since you're here, I can assume that there's a part that still hopes for something better than being dead. Your angry part would kill that part of you. I feel responsible to care for this aspect of you and ask you for a moratorium. Please give us four weeks to see whether something can be done besides killing yourself.
Angelina:	My God! You're such a pain in the ass!
Therapist:	If you want to call it that, fine. But I need your commitment, otherwise I must send you to the clinic. I won't abandon you. I'll continue working with you even if you go to the clinic for a few days. It will only be until your current tension goes down a bit and we can then look for ways to improve your situation—at least a bit.

In this case, the schema therapist acted in Angelina's best interest and did what was necessary to care for all of her. We have to be realistic and acknowledge that sometimes a client will be in danger, and we need to be prepared to address that.

Intensive Self-Soothing and Addictive Clients

In this section, we use alcohol abuse as an example of addictive behavior, but the principles apply more widely to other forms of drug abuse and to other impulsive and addictive behaviors, such as gambling, overeating, or excessive Internet use.

Samuel Ball (1998) outlined an integrative approach to treating addiction problems and possible underlying personality disorders in dual focus schema therapy. Schema therapy leads to a greater understanding of personal dynamics but does not remove the symptom itself. Symptom-focused techniques are required besides mode work, which is why Ball emphasizes a dual focus. Though his approach is primarily based on the schema model, it doesn't incorporate more recent work with modes. This may be a reason why it was not a superior treatment compared to an approach solely focused on substance abuse (Ball, Maccarelli, LaPaglia, & Ostrowski, 2011).

In schema therapy, we focus on the function of the excessive self-soothing behavior rather than on the behavior itself. Therefore, the therapeutic alliance is against the behavior. In the mode model, we conceptualize excessive self-soothing behavior as the detached self-soother. We assume that most people with excessive self-soothing behavior simply have no better solution for coping with their emotional discomfort. Given certain traumatic experiences, escaping with excessive self-soothing seems like the least of many evils. The challenge in therapy is to access the underlying triggers of the avoided emotions while reparenting and affirming the client as a person.

As we do mode work, using alcohol abuse as the example here, we address the drinking pattern as a detached self-soother mode. Chair dialogues are a good way to go. Place the use of alcohol on a separate chair (the "drinking chair"), then engage with that chair as described for a detached protector in chapter 6 (see "Bypassing Avoidant or Detached Coping Modes"). Once you better understand the function, you can look for a replacement. If you want to reduce drinking frequency, make a list of possible activities for the client to try before drinking. You may use the coping mode tracking sheet (figure 11–1).

Even though the DSM-5 (unlike the DSM-4) no longer separates substance abuse and dependence, we still think that differentiating the two has an impact on the choice of therapeutic strategy. The core signs that we assume indicate dependence remain being unable to abstain or to control consumption. If there are already signs of dependence, controlled drinking strategies will probably fail. Making a contract with your client to first begin an addiction-treatment program and then to continue therapy will likely be easier than attempting therapy first. Such a commitment will provide some motivation for the client to complete addiction treatment.

We suggest working toward abstinence and suggest the technique of urge surfing, developed by Allan Marlatt and Ruth Gordon (1985). This technique draws on a Buddhist perspective and is a variation of the emotion-surfing exercise described in chapter 7. The basic idea behind urge surfing is that the urge to drink is just a feeling, and all feelings come and go, no matter how strong they appear. Offer this recommendation to your client: "Remain in an observer's perspective, watching your urge to drink. It will come like a wave: it approaches, becomes bigger, peaks, and finally recedes. All you have to do is avoid getting into a *doing* mode and remain in an observing or *being* mode."

Marlatt and Gordon also suggested seeing the urge to drink as an "enemy inside" and as a samurai warrior. He is your enemy. Keep your attention on him. Never feel too confident. He is always there, hidden somewhere, so it is best to keep an eye on him and keep him at some distance. This metaphor highlights that the most dangerous enemy is one you are unaware of!

You can adapt this technique to other substance-related or behavioral abuse. In most cases, the immediate goal will be reduced use rather than abstinence. Managing the difficulty will be an ongoing task for the rest of the client's life.

Ronnie found that he tended to spend hours each night on Facebook and other social media sites. While it was relaxing and he felt some connection to a wide group of people, he wanted to start graduate studies. He thought to himself, I'll try to stay in some contact, but I want to get this degree. It will give me additional opportunities at work.

Ronnie used urge surfing to reduce his Internet use. The goal with urge surfing in schema therapy is more than symptom reduction. We want to build up a strong healthy adult mode that is capable of dealing with a demanding critic mode and engaging in self-compassion. We have found that strengthening the healthy adult instead of "fighting" maladaptive behavior is the best way to build up functional and flexible methods of self-care that can eventually replace maladaptive self-soothing.

Severely Detached Clients

We described ways to work with the detached protector mode in chapter 6. Generally, resistance in therapy is a sign that the client has not yet formed a good enough working alliance with the therapist, but there may be other reasons.

Why does a client refrain from cooperation? Here are some of the most common causes of resistance in therapy.

Lack of understanding. Your client might not understand what you are asking for. Remain patient and clarify. Submissive and dependent clients may feel too insecure to ask about something they fail to understand. They conclude that it must be their fault and that the therapist may punish them, or at least not like them anymore.

Intense fear reaction. In this case, the client remains in an avoidant protector mode because of a fear response. This will occur with severely traumatized clients who were punished for every move they made, and who found that their only remaining control was to freeze and not move at all. If you see this happening, you may have to move from the front stage (protector modes) to the backstage, where the child mode can say what it needs in order to feel more assertive and empowered. You might ask, "What exactly are you afraid of? What's the worst thing that might happen? Did you ever have a bad experience trying something similar?" Usually, this inquiry reveals interfering inner critic mode voices that can disempower the client (as we describe next). The therapist should then soothe and assist the vulnerable child mode: "What could I do to help you feel less frightened?" Do not forget to use childlike language while talking to a child mode.

Competing inner critic modes. Punitive and demanding critic modes may be active at the same time. The client will be afraid to fail, especially when both critic modes are simultaneously active, resulting in a double bind for the client (Bateson, 1972). Whatever he or she does is wrong.

Mandy's demanding critic mode says, "You're getting too fat! You need to go to the gym to exercise." Her punitive critic mode says: "Once more, you'll be the stupidest, fattest person at the gym. You'll act like a jerk and everybody will laugh at you. Don't make a fool of yourself! Forget it!"

In this dilemma, doing nothing is attractive and allows the client to avoid making a mistake. Share this understanding of the double bind with your client. Detect the "voices in the head" from backstage, place them on an inner critic mode chair, and challenge them. If there are two competing inner critic mode voices, place them on *two different chairs*. Then stand up with your client and deal with both of them, one after the other. If these modes are strong or persistent, have the client acknowledge their presence and then try to let them go.

Undisciplined child mode. Some children grow up with insufficient limit setting and develop an undisciplined child mode or, sometimes, an obstinate child mode that is "voting" to abstain from the exercise. We have to detect and then empathically confront them: "I understand that you have to stretch to get this experiment started. Let me make a suggestion: Instead of arguing now, let's give it a try and discuss it later. I'll accept your reservations if you're unhappy with the result. What's the first small step that you can imagine taking?" The idea is to lower the bar to the point that your client can't help but step over it! This strategy also works with depressed clients.

Secondary gain through remaining passive. If, for example, a client is able to leave the house, then a partner might expect the client to return to work. A partner might grow more absent if the client recovers from panic attacks. Or, being less submissive on the client's part might mean taking more responsibility. We have to dismantle the downsides to making gains carefully, clarify the cost-benefit ratio, and develop acceptable alternatives. If there are no serious gains in sight, your clients will stick to old coping behaviors.

Identify passive-aggressive traits. To do this, it helps to try to find out whether the detached behavior of your client is driven more by fear or by sadness (vulnerable child mode backstage) or by blocked anger. Instead of talking with the detached protector, we suggest you bypass that mode by putting a child mode chair behind it. While in detached protector mode, clients are talking from their conceptual self anyway.

It is better take an inquisitive stance and ask the client to try something new. Let him take a seat on the child mode chair behind the detached protector chair as you sit close by. Ask the client what he really feels and needs in an intimate way: "Hey, come on. What do you really want?" If in doubt, offer some thoughts: "This might be a strange thought, but I wonder if you actually want to go to work again…" Carefully watch your client's reaction (including nonverbal signals). For some passive-aggressive clients, for example, a pension or benefits are the only remaining goal to achieve as compensation for the frustrations they had to experience in life. Offer this idea in a validating and respectful way, and try to open the door to look for the pros and cons: "Okay, that makes some sense to me. But what are your goals once you go on benefits?" Remember, for some narcissists who have failed to achieve, secondary anger feels better than getting in touch with underlying sadness.

To work successfully with severely detached clients, we need to fully understand any inner motives. It may be helpful to explore reasons using the mode model. Once the stage is set and all the players are in place, you can be watching for the seemingly best solution. Once you've found it, decide where it makes sense to get active in one way or another, and what limitations the client has to accept. When in doubt, it is better to follow the client's lead rather than a strict agenda. Miller and Rollnick (2002), in *Motivational Interviewing: Preparing People for Change*, noted that clients are always right and it is better to roll with resistance instead of arguing with them, so be sure to leave your clients with a choice. People like having choices. Getting along in life is not a matter of right or wrong, so don't be afraid to experiment. Your clients will be able try something new, draw a personal conclusion, and then take the next step.

Additional Strategies to Deal with Detached Modes

Here, we list additional strategies for dealing with detached modes. They progress from trying to engage more deeply with your client to realizing and accepting what is ultimately unchangeable to finding a way out of therapy.

Introduce the "gate in the wall" metaphor.

Therapist: I understand that the detached protector mode was very important to you in the past. It was the only way to stop hurting. The mode acted like a wall. But if we take the wall literally, there is a downside to it. It keeps you away from people. So how about combining the safety of the wall with a way to get in touch with people again? Picture a big gate in a medieval city wall. It's very thick and robust. If the gate is closed, it almost becomes part of the wall. On top of the gate is your healthy adult mode, deciding when to open and when to close the gate. How do you like this idea?

Validate the detached protector mode and ask for a break. After accepting the function of the detached protector mode in the past and validating its role, you can say the following to the healthy adult mode:

Therapist: Okay, the detached protector did an important job in the past. I want to make a suggestion. You can keep it for difficult situations. But how about learning an additional strategy for safer situations? So, I ask the detached protector to step aside for about fifteen minutes, giving us some time to try something new, and then the mode might come back for the rest of the week until we have our next session. In fact, I feel safer with the detached protector paying attention to your vulnerable child mode, unless your healthy adult mode is strong enough to take over.

Look at photographs from childhood together. Sit alongside your client, looking at photos from her childhood. This creates a warm emotional connection. If the parents paid little attention to your client as a child, you will often see photographs of a sad- or lonely-looking child. Looking at childhood photos will often activate inner critic mode voices about the child, which you can record. In a next step, you can represent these with the inner critic mode chair and let them talk to the child mode chair, thus creating a backstage chair dialogue.

Marilyn brought an album with pictures from her early childhood into the session. Her therapist sat close by her, and they both looked at the pictures. Some showed little Marilyn sitting away from the other children with a sad face. Even worse, there were pictures in which the whole family was laughing and nobody took notice of sad Marilyn. Marilyn and her therapist felt very sorry for the little girl sitting there alone. After the session, Marilyn sent an email to her therapist, writing, "I felt really good being seen but not watched. Thank you!" The session was a breakthrough in their therapy relationship.

Talk to the child mode on the backstage. You can try to access the softer feelings of the client by adding an additional chair behind the detached protector chair to represent the child mode feelings. Note that the client was in detached protector mode at the beginning of the session. Then you, as therapist, leave your original chair in front of the detached protector and encourage the client to take a seat on the child mode chair. Sit close behind the chair (according to the chair positions in figure 6–3) and talk to the child mode directly:

Therapist: I understand that the detached protector was helpful for you in the past. How do you feel, sitting there behind him? I want you to know that I know you're there. I would like to get in touch with you. I like you—you're a very nice child. I think you might feel a bit lonely there behind the wall and want to play with somebody in a safe way. I would like to be the one. Do you trust me? Do you want to give it a try?

Connect with the child mode using a fleece. Farrell and colleagues (2014) described a technique for connecting with the child mode using a fleece or scarf. Seat the client in the child mode chair behind the detached protector. Seat yourself in front of the empty detached protector chair, holding one end of a fleece or a scarf in your hand, and pass the other end to the client, *bypassing* the detached protector. Now slowly tug the fleece and wait for the reaction of the client on the child mode chair. This initiates a nonverbal communication link. Later, leave your chair, sit on another one close by the child mode chair, and ask how your client liked the exercise.

Offer self-disclosure toward the child mode. Have your client sit on the detached protector chair, with you in front but talking to the empty child mode chair behind the client. Lean toward the child mode as if you want to talk to a real child behind the client:

Therapist: I want you to know that I know you're there, even if the "wall" in front of you wants to make me believe that you're not. I like you and I want to get in touch with you. I assume you feel quite lonely sometimes, and I want to be there for you. So if you have any ideas about how you can get in touch with me, please give me a sign.

Offer additional communication channels. Many severely traumatized clients were instructed by their abusers not to speak to anyone about their painful experiences. Some were even programmed to hurt or kill themselves if they dared to do so! But sometimes, there are gaps in the barrier. Maybe the abuser's instructions did not include written information or images, or communicating by email, so offer these methods to your client as a way of getting in touch with you. Another advantage of this technique is that destructive inner critic modes cannot destroy the material before it reaches you.

Allow clients to send email or text messages at night. Another advantage of text messages or emails is that you can send them at any time of the day. Some detached clients have small windows of emotional activation for when they get triggered in life. Make use of them! Especially at night (and maybe after one or two glasses of wine) clients' thresholds are lower than when talking to the therapist in session; thoughts run free, and courage grows, allowing them to be less inhibited.

Mariah had become attracted to her therapist. His warm voice really moved her. His caring eyes rested on her. Recently, in an imagery exercise, he softly held her back to support her. She had never felt so accepted, supported, and cared for. She started thinking about him outside of sessions and pictured meeting him socially. She started to overinterpret his behavior. She read that therapists need to keep some emotional distance from their clients. Wasn't this fact coupled with his behavior proof that he must have some deeper feelings for her? Then one night, listening to romantic music and after half a bottle of wine, she wrote him an email confessing her feelings toward him.

Later, we suggest ways to deal with romantic feelings. But this example illustrates that there are ways to access material that you will probably not get in face-to-face sessions.

Use physical impact. This is a strong technique that might be especially beneficial for male clients. Ask the client to sit on the vulnerable child mode chair, directly behind the detached protector mode chair. Encourage him to sit in a childlike position, with knees close together. Ask him how he feels in that posture. Usually, the client will feel well protected. Then, push the detached protector chair up against the client's knees until he pushes back. Label this gesture, saying, "This is no longer your vulnerable side. There is some power behind it! Make use of this power! Push harder!" Then keep pushing the chair, almost in a mutually competitive way. If the client really engages and gets angry, offer him an additional chair for the angry child mode and ask what he really wants to do to make use of this power.

Offer self-disclosure to the client. If you fail to find the obstacle using multiple techniques, it may be helpful to disclose some frustration and perhaps disappointment, but without accusation. This can be helpful if your client is reluctant to comply with experiential work in the session.

Therapist: I have to admit that I feel a bit frustrated. I think it would be a good idea just to try this exercise out instead of talking about it. In that way, we might gain insight. Experience really helps. I understand that it's a bit frightening for you to do things you've never done before and to show your vulnerable side. I felt the same when I did an exercise like that for the first time. What can I do to reduce your fears or create some trust so we can try it?

Name the therapy-limiting effect. If the client remains avoidant by resisting behavioral experiments or refusing to do homework assignments, explain how she is limiting the potential of therapy.

Therapist: I know that doing this homework might appear silly to you and may remind you of your school days, but we're in a different situation now. Change only happens if you act in a different way. It doesn't just happen by talking about things in therapy. So we have to evaluate; is there something left we can work on?

Reduce the frequency of sessions. If everything suggested above fails to work, you should explain that this is a problem for therapy as a whole. Progress in the second half of therapy requires that between sessions, the client actively contributes to changing behavior.

Therapist: Okay, I see that you have difficulties changing something in your life. We've gone as far as we can just talking things through in sessions. It's time to work on change or accept our limitations. Can we reschedule our sessions to once a month? This might give you more time to try out new behaviors. Let's see what happens.

This is a form of contingency management (Linehan, 1993), which can have the paradoxical effect of encouraging clients to become more active than before because they *feel* the restriction.

Admit our limitations. Instead of continuing to produce new ideas as the therapist, you can go to a "one-down" position (Bateson, 1972). In this way, you show the client your "empty pockets."

Therapist: Well, we have tried many things in therapy. I have to admit I don't know what else to try. But your problems are still there. Are there any ideas from your end?

Work toward acceptance.

Therapist: I see that you've done what you can to cooperate in therapy. Maybe your schemas are too strong and set some limits on how far we can go in sessions. I don't want to force you and make you feel like a failure again. Sometimes schemas are hardwired in the brain. It would be cruel to blame you for having such schemas. This might surprise you, but I suggest accepting them and looking for remaining issues we can work on together in a practical way.

Put the therapy on hold.

Therapist: After all we've tried so far, I still feel we're stuck. It isn't your fault, but it shows some limitations of us as a team. I suggest stopping for maybe three months, which will give you an opportunity to consider the best way forward. Either we leave it this way or we work on some remaining concrete issues. Or we might try to relaunch our therapy and maybe think about taking another approach. Does that make sense?

End therapy.

Therapist: It seems to me as if we've reached a stable place in our therapy. I suggest stopping our regular sessions now. If you find yourself having difficulty with something, you might call me for an appointment so we can look for what you might be able to do. What do you think?

Dependent and Passive Clients

A dependent or passive client can be a therapist's best friend—until you start trying to end therapy!

Kylie appreciated therapy. She was always on time for her weekly appointment, she was never late in paying, and she was extravagant in her praise of the value of therapy. But there were indications that she became stressed when her therapist went on vacation. After two years, Kylie resisted that therapy was drawing to an end. Her therapist insisted on setting a time for the final session, and Kylie attempted suicide.

So how do we avoid such a bind—that is, the seeming ease of working with such clients until it comes time to terminate therapy? Therapy is not a "rent a friend" arrangement. It is by nature time limited and goal directed, so don't promise too much at the beginning of therapy. Stay balanced, even if you really feel for the client. Never say something like "We'll stay together as long as you need me." Some clients will always need you. Kanfer and Schefft (1988) also advised against making client approval a part of your self-confidence, because it can lead to emotionally abusive clients.

With passive clients, it is essential that we move toward behavior change early in therapy. Do not place too much trust in what clients say. Always focus on what they actually do. If your sessions begin to drift, label the problem and refocus on concrete issues. Doing some experiential work in most sessions is preventative. In experiential work, clients have to engage and reveal what is at stake for them. Make use of schema therapy forms. Make reducing the frequency of sessions while increasing the activity of your client a marker of progress, and praise any shifts in that direction. What follows are tips and techniques for working with dependent and passive clients.

Shape the healthy adult mode within sessions. The therapeutic relationship is a very important tool for reinforcing the healthy adult as it emerges in sessions. When the healthy adult emerges, it often does so subtly. When it does show itself, you want to share this with clients so that they, too, can start to recognize their healthy adult mode. This way of reinforcing the mode in session is drawn from a contextual approach called functional analytic psychotherapy (see, for example, Holman et al., 2017). We use this technique with any problematic behavior; when the healthy adult contradicts or counters a maladaptive behavior, we point it out, trying to shape those healthier behavioral patterns.

Joanne's overcontroller mode initially dominated most sessions, analyzing every aspect of her life and ruminating in a way that was largely disconnected from her feelings.

As the therapist began to have more success with helping Joanne attune to and communicate very specific episodes of distress (using the behavioral activation form), he was very quick to point out her success, providing Joanne with interpersonal reinforcement.

Joanne: It was really hard feeling like I was going to be left all alone and abandoned if I didn't cling to my partner. I need a sense of stability from him. But I can also see that the problem is rooted in what happened to me, and that he's not in charge of solving my problems.

Therapist: Wow! I know this has been really hard for you, opening up today. I really appreciate it and feel that I can understand you a whole lot more and can support you in getting more on your assertiveness leg.

Give supportive feedback using technology. Smartphones and the Internet offer us a way to give clients reinforcing feedback quickly and easily. You can ask clients to send you a text message or a short email after they've carried out an assigned exercise, and you can provide instant feedback, which is very rewarding. Even replying with a thumbs-up emoticon or a few approving words can have an impact, so the time spent doing it is well worth it!

Make the therapy relationship itself an issue. Do not hesitate to look objectively at your therapy. Are you making progress? You can split yourself up and speak from a "bad therapist" chair (see "Empathic Confrontation with the Submissive Client," in chapter 6). This creates a space to convey critical messages to clients, which can drive them out of their comfort zone. Sometimes therapy needs to be a less than comfortable place for them! Play the part of an outside observer intruding the cozy intimacy of your therapy sessions, and ask clients to focus on their next step.

How to deal with gifts. Some clients will bring small gifts at Christmas or on a birthday (such personal data is relatively easy to find on the Internet). We usually accept gifts as long as the value is small and it does not happen frequently. On rare occasions, however, a client will have a hidden agenda, perhaps to entangle us in a deeper relationship. Sometimes gifts provide an opportunity to explore hidden feelings.

Rosemary, an elderly lady, suffered from loneliness and was quite isolated. She spent a lot of time in her garden and was meticulous in her housekeeping. She loved making jam and would surprise her therapist with a jar from time to time. She brought one at Christmas and noticed that after the holidays the jar was still on the therapist's shelf—obviously untouched! She felt sad and said to the therapist, "You don't like my jam anymore!" This opened a path to access Rosemary's angry side, which she hid behind her overly submissive behavior. The therapist moved to her side and gently explored her disappointed and angry feelings. This was a turning point in therapy for her.

Define detectable goals on a behavioral level. Ask clients about concrete tasks that are important to them and for which therapy might be helpful, and then set attainable goals. It is not enough for a client to say, "I want to become more self-confident." In what exact situation does the client want to cope better? What steps are necessary? What needs to happen before the client can take the first step? Shift more to the behavioral activation side of therapy when addressing goals. Prepare clients for taking action with role-plays, and insist that they engage in behavior experiments and fill out diary cards to track the effects.

Set time limits. Point out that therapy is time limited. Set a time limit for visible change that is short enough to activate a dependent client (for example, four weeks). Then set the number of sessions that will be needed to reach the goals you have agreed on. Reward clients with more sessions if they achieve the goals. If necessary, indicate that therapy will end one way or the other. Be straight, but remain flexible.

Clients Who Fall in Love with Their Therapists

Clients falling in love with their therapist is an issue that therapists and clients do not often talk about. Nevertheless, it is relevant and happens quite frequently—with both female therapists and male. And do not forget the potential for same-sex attraction.

Developing romantic feelings for a therapist is highly avoidant behavior. In this way, the clients are stepping out of the working alliance. Their brain is flooded by opioid-like hormones as well as oxytocin, resulting in an illusionary state of feeling connected. This wastes time in sessions. It is up to us to read the signals and directly address the problem. Once more, we can use the technique of splitting into a "good" and a "bad" therapist. Let the critical therapist speak out the bad news, and then have the understanding therapist move to the clients' side to support them in accepting the message. The steps to take are as follows:

1. Have the courage to address the issue.

2. Name precisely the behavior of the client that made you suspicious.

3. Point out that attraction is a normal reaction to the emotional intensity of therapy.

4. Do not deny that the client's romantic interest flatters and touches you.

5. Clarify that the therapy relationship has priority, and that you have to avoid any emotional enmeshment.

6. Warn clients that you will have to terminate therapy if they fail to moderate their coping modes.

Simply naming the elephant in the room usually makes things clear:

Therapist: I have to admit that it's no easy task for me to raise this issue, but I regard it as important to do for the sake of our therapy relationship. Sometimes in our sessions, there is a look in your eyes that makes me wonder whether you see me only as your therapist. Is it okay to discuss such feelings openly?

If the client accepts the invitation for discussion, the therapist continues:

Therapist: Therapists are generally understanding, caring, and empathic in session—much more so than in normal life. I have to tell you that I don't behave like this in my private life. This is my role as therapist. This is to some extent artificial, or at least professional. But going into this role creates a very special atmosphere that might cause you to react with romantic feelings.

After the client acknowledges some romantic attraction, the therapist might say something like this:

Therapist: But my professional role and my ethical standards insist that I do not abuse the intimacy of our therapeutic relationship. So I'll ask you to make use of your mindfulness skills to become aware of any romantic feelings and to let them go. I'll support you by staying a bit more detached in our upcoming sessions, until we're on safe ground again. If this doesn't work, my only remaining option would be to refer you to another therapist to continue your therapy. I hope you understand that I can't respond to such feelings. We have to find a way for our interaction to remain therapeutic for you.

Summary

In this chapter, we considered how to work with people who present with a range of problems, including externalizing, self-harm, suicidality, severe emotional detachment, addiction, and falling in love with their therapist. There is no easy way to help difficult clients. The core message we'd like you to take from this chapter is this: don't allow yourself to get stuck or to stabilize a dysfunctional system. Make the stuck relationship itself an issue in therapy, and try some of the specific interventions we suggested. If things remain unchanged, terminate the treatment following the steps we outlined.

CHAPTER 14

It Takes Two to Tango—Including the Client's Partner in Therapy

In this chapter, we look at the important role that your client's partner or spouse can play in schema therapy. Sometimes the partner can be indirectly involved in the therapeutic process, or gradually challenged to contribute to it. Since the well-being of your clients is tightly connected with the quality of their most intimate relationship (Holt-Lunstad et al., 2015), it can be rewarding to include their partner in your work.

Why Is an Interpersonal Perspective Important?

Most of our clients have intimate relationships. Hence, it is more or less impossible to work with one partner in individual sessions without affecting the relationship. From a systemic perspective, there is no doubt that behavior change in one partner induces changes in the other partner as well. Relational systems tend to stabilize themselves (Maturana & Varela, 1998) in this manner. This dynamic can be an advantage, of course, but it can also work against therapeutic progress. The partner may consciously or unconsciously act against changes because they bring him or her into an aversive fluctuating state that may threaten the balance of the relationship.

Indeed, individual therapy has the potential to influence the couples relationship in a strategic way, so you can regard it as a form of couples-focused therapy, a concept that broadens the scope of this book. The mode cycle model can help your client to understand a partner's reactions, including underlying basic emotions. Anticipating such reactions will encourage the client to bring the partner's responses into therapy. Respecting the partner's core emotional needs, too, and including him in the new behavior that therapy is trying to enhance will reduce the client's resistance to therapy.

This interpersonal model can generally be used to describe interactions between any two parties: at work, between parents and children, and even in political affairs. Naturally, it also includes therapy and therapy supervision relationships (see chapter 15). First, we explain how to "entangle" the partner in individual treatment.

Steps for Interpersonal Work

Consider taking the following steps for entangling a client's partner in interpersonal therapy:

1. Think and talk about absent partners in *mode cycle* terms. This may provide clients with a sense that their partner is included in the therapy plan.

2. Put the absent partners on an *empty chair* to bring their perspective into the therapy room. Your clients can then step into their partner's shoes to deepen an understanding of their perspective and increase cognitive flexibility.

3. *Invite* partners to a session for diagnostic reasons. You can ask them to provide a wider perspective. There is a double gain here: you get additional information about your clients and a vivid impression of the partners to balance the viewpoint of your clients in future sessions.

4. Explain a client's *mode model* to his partner using his mode map. We have found that male partners usually like the rationality of the schema mode model, which can help to increase their trust in their partner's therapy.

5. Convey to partners that you respect their needs as part of a balanced and sustainable solution. If they see the long-term gain from positive behavior change, they might be more inclined to *support* the therapeutic change of your clients outside of session.

6. *Develop a mode cycle model* for the couple's interaction. This deepens their mutual understanding. Also, the partner might realize how she may be contributing to your client's pathology. This can be a step into more focused couples work, as described in *Schema Therapy for Couples* (Simeone-DiFrancesco et al., 2015).

Let's return to Joanne. After a few sessions, Joanne's therapist put together the following mode cycle model to help clarify both for him and Joanne the broad dysfunctional patterns in her relationship:

Brandon, Joanne's partner, comes from a high-achieving family. Both of his siblings are very successful in their jobs. As the eldest, he always felt a bit under pressure due to his parents' expectations. He turned out to be a failure in school and later in his working life. He first felt attracted to Joanne because she was successful in her job and appeared strong. Unlike his parents, she accepted him unconditionally, despite his professional shortcomings.

Joanne loved his warm and caring side. He was a bit like her father, whom she missed so much. They looked like a good match, and they got on well.

After giving birth to their kids, she stayed at home while he continued working. Joanne felt a bit abandoned and increasingly responded in overcontroller mode. Brandon felt annoyed and bossed around like he did in his childhood. He reacted by withdrawing and went into detached protector mode. The mode cycle escalated until Joanne went to therapy.

In the following section, we look at how the mode cycle model contributed to working with their interaction pattern.

The Mode Cycle Model

You can use the mode cycle model to understand any two people and their interactions. With the model, you can see both the front stage and backstage levels, which allows you to develop a deeper understanding of the interpersonal dynamic. We act mostly from our coping modes, while our emotional drivers remain mostly hidden backstage. If we want to interact in healthy ways, we need to be aware of our emotional drivers and the needs they express in order to rebalance them. Thus, the model brings our focus to the coping modes and the child mode emotions. Figure 14–1 shows the interacting coping and child modes of Joanne and Brandon.

Schemas bias our perception, appraisal, and reactions; they form our personality. But why did Brandon feel attracted to Joanne and choose her to be his partner? Jeffrey Young sees attraction in terms of "schema chemistry," which is often seen as proof of love. (If it feels right, it must be right!) However, this is emotional reasoning (Arntz, Rauner, & van den Hout, 1995). The true background is that we will see in potential partners similarities to our parents or other significant others who match with our personality structure. If the chemistry does not fulfill the core needs for attachment and assertiveness of both partners (at least in modern Western cultures) in a balanced and flexible way, we can end up feeling trapped in the relationship. Joanne and Brandon initially fit well, but there was no development, no chance for change.

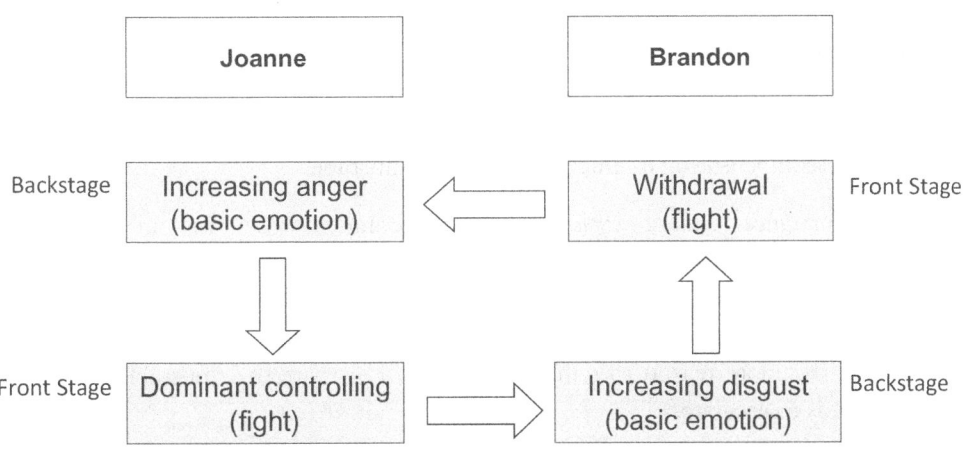

Figure 14–1. The maladaptive mode cycle of Joanne and Brandon

Typical Interpersonal Mode Cycles

Schema chemistry can explain some of the dynamics of attraction in a couples relationship. It also provides some understanding of psychological compatibility in longer-term relationships. Of course, as a therapist, you might observe that such a schema compatibility might not be healthy for a client. However, despite the underlying pathology, the relationship can nevertheless be stable and satisfying for both people if underlying needs fit together sufficiently.

Coping mode interactions lead to a variety of possible dyadic interactions. Each interaction becomes a loop or a cycle because it perpetuates the use of maladaptive coping mechanisms. Consider this example:

Vince had an emotional inhibition schema, which is not unusual in men. Natalie, his partner, was very emotionally expressive, driven by compensating abandonment and emotional deprivation schemas. Vince was a good fit with Natalie, because each relied on the other. He needed some emotional warmth, and she needed his stability.

If both partners show some flexibility in their behavior patterns, they may shift their coping modes, leading to different alternating cycles. This is probably a healthy state, giving the couple the chance to bring their "A team" into play. The situation turns unstable when the mode cycles become more rigid and there is less flexibility in finding adaptive solutions.

Principle: Good relationships have a degree of submissive—or at least cooperative—behavior. The assertiveness side has a cost in terms of inducing fragility in the relationship.

Here are some examples of typical mode cycles:

- *Dominance-dominance cycle:* Both Lee and Stacey went into overcompensator mode to attack each other over an unexpected electricity bill. After they flared up and said some hurtful things, Stacey withdrew. In reaction, Lee went into submission to stabilize the relationship again. Note that the initial mutual overcompensating interaction was highly unstable.

- *Dominance-avoidance cycle:* Jane (an overcompensator acting out of her inner critic mode) criticized Andrew for coming home late from work, which he passively accepted while remaining emotionally detached in his detached protector mode. This made Jane feel entitled to be even more critical, giving Andrew all the more reason to remain detached. This pattern is unstable because it tends to escalate.

- *Avoidance-avoidance cycle:* This cycle has variations in types of detachment, such as simple avoidance or using some sort of soothing behavior. Sandy and Cici live parallel lives under the same roof, with almost no interaction. Sandy spends most of her free time playing computer games, and Cici reads voraciously. This "living together apart" is usually moderately stable unless one partner finds an alternative (Atkinson, 2012).

- *Dominance-submission cycle:* This complementary cycle stabilizes the relationship unless the submissive partner withdraws (cycle 2) or starts to fight back (cycle 1), or the dominant partner gets bored and leaves the relationship.

Reflect: Think about some couples you know well. Can you identify any of these patterns in those relationships? What about the relationship of your parents? And do you see this in your family or romantic relationship?

Toward a Functional Relationship: Bringing the Healthy Adult to the Fore

David Schnarch (2009) described how one partner can fulfill a function for the other. One might well ask, "What do I need a partner for, if I can't rely on him?" The important word in this question is "need." But this need for a partner to function in a certain way indicates dependency, and that the person with the need is not fully in healthy adult mode. What we want to encourage is for both partners to *want* the other, but not to depend on the individual. This requires some autonomy on both sides. Of course, we also have relationships *for* support. Sharing precious moments makes for a richer life, and sharing burdens is a relief, but there is no avoiding the conclusion: we are responsible for our own well-being.

Brad was in a relationship with Colin. Soon after they met, they began to share the same apartment. Brad lost his job and Colin was happy to meet living expenses, but he began to worry when Brad showed no indication that he was willing to begin looking for employment, instead relying on Colin's income.

The application of Schnarch's principles to schema therapy strengthens the healthy adult modes of both partners through mindfulness, by distancing from overwhelming emotions, and by balancing core needs to regain emotional flexibility and negotiate goals in a reasonable way. *Schema Therapy for Couples* (Simeone-DiFrancesco et al., 2015) is another great resource for exploring the application of schema therapy to relationships; it describes the whole process of stopping clashes, rebalancing, emotionally reconnecting in conjoint imagery exercises and chair dialogues, and maintaining a loving relationship.

Both partners should always offer some flexibility when finding a workable solution. Gradual change in the levels of autonomy in a relationship can greatly benefit it, although at the risk of some instability. Usually a partner will appear more attractive with some distance. Sometimes feeling too safe leads to less respect and sensitivity to the other's needs. Balancing our need for a secure attachment with autonomy keeps the relationship alive and flexible.

Issues to Consider When Including the Partner

As noted, integrating partners in schema therapy has innumerable benefits, but it is tricky work. Here are some things to keep in mind.

Protect confidentiality. This is fundamental to treatment, and so it must be discussed if the partner becomes involved. Set ground rules. For example, how much is the therapist permitted to reveal from treatment? We advise you to get permission to be as open as possible about childhood experiences and underlying emotional needs. This will help you to gain the partner's support and to build goodwill. Sharing such experiences helps to bond couples. Remember, good relationships are based on compassion, trust, and faith, and most people respond to openness. As the therapist, you establish the atmosphere!

Prepare the first joint session. Your clients may experience some disappointment in joint sessions. They previously had your full attention, but now they are expected to share. They may feel something like the envy of the firstborn child toward the second born. It is natural for you to focus more on the partner to collect additional information and get a vivid picture of the relationship. To connect with this person, you have to be friendly and validating. Therefore, you should warn your client about possible disappointment before the first joint session.

Keep an eye on your client while listening to the partner. If the client shows signs of distress, check in, as Joanne's therapist did:

Therapist: Joanne, I thought I saw some traces of anger in your face. Are you okay, and can we continue listening to Brandon? You know that this isn't the time to get both sides of the issue. I'm just interested in understanding Brandon's view so we can include it in our work together. Are you fine if we use this time to get his perspective? You'll be able to tell me how you see things in our next session.

The next individual session will also give you an opportunity to emotionally reconnect with your client.

Keep control of the session. Paradoxically, getting an overall picture requires a tight focus. If there is conflict, we tend to keep direct communication between the partners to a minimum. Initially, they will display their conflict pattern (just for a few minutes). Understand this as their favorite mode cycle. We recommend stopping them quickly and asking them to speak only to you, the therapist. Explain the mode cycle to them and reveal that it is dysfunctional. This will keep the process safe and under control. How deeply you can go into the issues beyond analyzing them depends on the readiness of the couple, and losing control of the session will only impede this readiness.

Keep therapy a safe place. Couples are sometimes highly reactive. If the partner starts blaming your client or putting her down, you must immediately "catch the bullet" (Atkinson, 2012) by stopping him and labeling the behavior in relation to the mode cycle model.

Therapist: Sorry, Brandon, but I have to stop you. I can see that you're upset and this is how you see things, but your words are potentially hurting Joanne. I need to keep therapy a safe place for everybody. So, can I ask you to say what you want to say but in a more neutral way? Avoid blame. I want to understand how you see things, but let's agree on some ground rules. The most important is, "Don't hurt!" Thank you for your cooperation.

Give feedback. At the end of the session, ask both partners for feedback. If there is interest, it might be an opportune time to ask them if they are both willing to come in for an occasional joint session. There are potential therapeutic gains from future joint sessions. First, you will receive feedback about your client's activities and progress at home. Second, you can check the impact of therapy on the relationship, possibly leading you to adjust your interventions. Third, you might get a sense of how therapy might be benefiting or harming the partner. Keep this final point in mind if therapy gets stuck. It may be the result of therapy affecting the relationship in a negative way. By having the partner involved, you have the opportunity to remove the obstacle, allowing for progress to continue.

Combine individual and joint sessions in couple therapy. Combining individual and joint sessions in one entire therapy process bears some challenges for the therapist, especially if she conducts individual sessions with both partners. Many colleagues, especially those with a psychodynamic or a systemic background, have reservations about this practice and might even refuse to try it. We acknowledge that you cannot remain neutral as the therapist. You will feel inclined to sympathize with both partners in individual sessions. So the goal is not neutrality, rather it's to balance your attunement in a constructive way. You must step into each person's shoes to understand both perspectives and then subtly convey what you understand to the other partner. It is up to you to bridge the gap. Then, ideally, both partners will be more inclined to follow your lead. The therapist has the opportunity to demonstrate her understanding of both partners and to suggest a helpful balance of autonomy and attachment. A good deal of self-disclosure is a key competence for working with couples, as it helps to show what good attachment feels like and how it works

Pay into the relationship account. If both partners see different therapists, their therapists will usually encourage them to be more assertive, and that might undermine the relationship, because both partners will be more self-centered. That said, you can still regard the relationship as a conjoint enterprise. A successful outcome requires the readiness of both partners to "pay into the relationship account." Conjoint sessions bear the potential to increase both partner's understanding of and willingness to strengthen the attachment leg of the relationship, for the sake of improving it.

Remain flexible. Combining individual and joint sessions in one therapy process is a real challenge for the therapist. It requires a lot of flexibility, self-reflection, and present-moment attunement. Also, you must be willing and able to take responsibility for the overall process. Taking on any blame yourself makes the partners feel more comfortable. Bateson (1972) referred to this as the "one-down" position:

Therapist: I'm sorry if you don't feel understood right now. It's my fault because I have to gain your trust. It pleases me that you've been able to show me your disappointment, giving me the chance to do better. So, what could I do now to make you feel more seen and understood?

> **Therapist Tip:** Obviously, schema therapists need to be familiar with their own schemas and coping styles. If not, they might act out in session.

Start on your client's side. Your clients will profit from the mode cycle model we've detailed in this chapter. They can use it to improve their relationship, even if you do not manage to actively include their partner in therapy. Naturally, it is faster to dig a tunnel from both ends, but you can still get the work done if you start digging from one side only. Your client's learning to step out of a mode clash, while offering the partner a future time to come together and discuss the issue, will have a positive impact on the partner. Learning to remain centered, remaining emotionally balanced in healthy adult mode, will evoke some respect from the partner. Combining autonomy with a warm and caring attitude toward the partner might make the partner feel less rejected or frightened. Even if people react in different and sometimes unexpected ways, generally remaining in healthy adult mode cannot lead them too far off track.

Summary

In this chapter, we introduced the interpersonal perspective to individual schema therapy, based on the mode cycle model, in order to improve individual therapy outcomes. We also described typical mode cycles and offered advice for conducting joint sessions with couples.

CHAPTER 15

Therapist Schemas and Self-Care

Why did you decide to become a therapist? What motivated you? We need to now consider ourselves by looking at some themes we've raised elsewhere in this book. In this final chapter, we apply the mode cycle model to the therapy relationship as a platform for self-reflection and therapy supervision. We also offer some self-care principles to keep your professional life rewarding and fulfilling.

Changing Sides: The Wounded Healer

Schema therapists usually feel a strong resonance with their clients. What is that based on? Psychodynamic therapies use the concept of transference to understand the interaction between therapist and client. Transference is a central principle in psychoanalytic treatment, providing both a window to the past and a present reality. However, it is a two-way reality. If *transference* is transferring feelings about a previously significant person onto the therapist, then countertransference is the same dynamic, but it operates from the therapist's perspective. Schema therapy provides an understanding of these dynamics in terms of schema chemistry (or mutually triggering schemas).

We discussed schema chemistry in chapter 14. It is the natural process or emotional reacting between partners in a relationship or between the client or couple and the therapist. Memory-based likenesses activate schemas, which in turn distort the reception of the current dyadic relationship. To be effective therapists, we need to have considerable awareness of our own schema vulnerabilities to gain an overall perspective on this process.

It is only natural that early maladaptive schemas, including our own, get activated in therapy. Roediger and Laireiter (2013) recently published a schema-based therapy supervision model that provides a systematic view of mode cycle activations that occur in a therapy relationship. Leahy (2001) detected typical schemas among therapists, and more recent research supports his findings (Bamber & McMahon, 2008). These reviews named emotional deprivation, self-sacrifice, and unrelenting standards as the prevailing schemas among therapists. The intensity of the therapy relationship, and the inherent power of the therapist's role, bears the risk of the therapist trying to soothe the schemas of emotional deprivation, abandonment, vulnerability to harm or illness, mistrust-abuse, defectiveness-shame, or dependence-incompetence.

However, having schemas is not necessarily a disadvantage. If we are aware of them and do not act them out in an unreflective way, we can become more sensitive to the subtle emotions of our clients. This will enable us to tune in even more closely, opening up a potentially deeper understanding of our clients' inner worlds and giving them a sense of "feeling felt" (Siegel, 1999). Understanding our schemas can transform our own pain into a resource. Based on Carl Jung's metaphor of the wounded healer, Barr (2006) found that 73.9% of counselors and psychotherapists had experienced one or more wounding experiences that led to their career choice. However, this requires that you, as a therapist, reflect on your own schemas and learn to deal with them in a functional way.

Farrell and Shaw's *Experiencing Schema Therapy from the Inside Out* (2018) is an excellent resource to help you do this in a very practical way. It can help you to identify some of your remaining blind spots. You might also want to get the help of an experienced therapist for either deeper self-reflection or personal therapy. Helpful people sometimes need help themselves! We should apply the same principles to ourselves that we do to clients. It is a question of integrity: we should not preach water while drinking wine.

Mode Cycles and Pitfalls in Therapy

We now want to apply the mode cycle concept to the therapy relationship. Table 15–1 lists all nine possible mode cycles, based on the combination of the three major coping modes and their typical pitfalls. We look at the cycles one by one below.

Table 15–1. Possible mode cycles in the therapy relationship

No.	Client's Mode	Therapist's Mode	Pitfall
1.	Submissive	Submissive	"Friendly" cooperation, but no progress.
2.	Submissive	Avoidant	Client's needs are frustrated again.
3.	Submissive	Dominant	Therapist dominates; client seems cooperative. No autonomy is gained.
4.	Avoidant	Submissive	Therapist "sweats more than the client," but client does not change.
5.	Avoidant	Avoidant	No emotional activation. Therapy gets stuck. Nobody has the courage to end it.
6.	Avoidant	Dominant	Therapist is too demanding or accusatory. There is a risk of client dropping out.
7.	Dominant	Submissive	Therapist allows client to be exploited and devalues the client.

| 8. | Dominant | Avoidant | Therapist lets demanding or devaluing client hit the wall. |
| 9. | Dominant | Dominant | There is a power struggle from the beginning. Usually, therapy doesn't even begin. |

1. Submissive (client)—submissive (therapist). This mode cycle is generally not harmful for the client or therapist. The problem is that not much will happen in therapy. Both people are nice to one another, trying to fulfill each other's wishes and expectations. They probably feel good with one another in session and think that each session was successful. There is a resonance in terms of a mutual understanding. Therapists with an emotional deprivation, abandonment, or social isolation schema will draw a lot from the intimacy and warmth of the therapy sessions. Considering the frequency of these schemas among both therapists and the clients, this mode cycle combination is quite likely. If client and therapist have a good working alliance and they work on specific symptoms guided by good behavior-therapy principles, they might make some progress.

Another downside to this match is that both tend to avoid conflict, and neither is able to make use of constructive anger. They form a good support team, but the client will not easily learn to deal with dominant individuals in life and may remain in a victim role. The inherent risk with this combination is that, when it is time to end therapy, clients might realize that they still lack assertiveness in daily interactions.

2. Submissive (client)—avoidant (therapist). Unlike the first mode cycle, this cycle is potentially harmful for the client, since it might repeat patterns of neglect from childhood. If the therapist remains too detached, she will eventually trigger the client's emotional deprivation schema without any resolution. If in a video-based supervision a supervisor sees this kind of interaction, it needs to be addressed. Such therapist behavior is often based on the therapist's avoidant style of coping with her own schemas, such as emotional deprivation, mistrust-abuse, defectiveness-shame, and dependence-incompetence. If the therapist cannot develop a minimum level of warmth and caring for the client's vulnerable child, she will not be an effective schema therapist. This kind of therapist might gain better results with a more cognitively-oriented treatment, such as cognitive behavioral therapy, or with a behavioral treatment. The emotional focus of schema therapy requires a good deal of emotional resonance on the part of the therapist.

3. Submissive (client)—dominant (therapist). This combination is dangerous for the client. Submissive clients often suffer from having experienced some kind of abuse, and this mode cycle tends to repeat such experiences, especially if the therapist surrenders to an entitlement-grandiosity schema or other-directed schema, such as unrelenting standards or punitiveness. If this cycle is evident, a therapy supervisor must intervene and make the overcompensation a serious subject of supervision to protect the client from harm. This usually requires individual supervision sessions and good skills in empathic confrontation on the part of the supervisor. Ideally, these skills will prevent the supervisee from becoming defensive and quitting supervision.

Therapists who are trying to be perfect are not generally the most helpful for clients. The best way to teach a client how to repair ruptures is to let ruptures occur in therapy in a controlled way. Some transitional overcompensatory traits in the therapist can be helpful, as long as the therapist is aware of them and is able to react flexibly and return to a cooperative stance quickly.

4. Avoidant (client)—submissive (therapist). With this mode cycle, the therapy supervisor has to protect the therapist from sweating more than the client (Kanfer & Schefft, 1988). Almost all therapists have self-sacrifice and unrelenting standards schemas, and many were parentified children accustomed to caring for "hopeless cases." Naturally, there is some danger of doing more of what is not working, or of trying one thing after another, instead of addressing the client's coping modes. Schema therapy offers a model for labeling, contextualizing, and challenging an interpersonal pattern, not for working on the resulting effects or symptoms. With this mode cycle, the therapy supervisor should try to increase the therapist's competence using techniques, including empathic confrontation, to address and bypass the detached protector mode. Not doing so is a waste of the client's time and money.

Sometimes we have to accept that clients, particularly avoidant ones, are doing the best they can and are not able to change further. This is when we recommend changing the focus to acceptance strategies, supporting the client in dealing with remaining symptoms, reducing the frequency of sessions, and finally, ending therapy. Or we can recommend another therapist or another treatment if one or both promises to be a better match. In either case, the supervisor should try to support the therapist in finding a better balance and working toward acceptance and functional distancing. Personal therapy might be needed to weaken the therapist's demanding inner critic modes and to deal with underlying schema such as dependence-incompetence, enmeshment, or self-sacrifice.

5. Avoidant (client)—avoidant (therapist). Detached clients are usually able to protect themselves. That is what they learned in life. Thus, this mode cycle is unlikely to harm them. But detached therapists are not very helpful. They often end up simply talking and avoiding experiential work or any challenges in the therapy relationship. Therapy will tend to go nowhere. It is surprising how often this mode cycle occurs. We really must do frequent experiential work in the internal working phase of schema therapy, because these techniques lead to better outcomes (Bamelis et al., 2014).

6. Avoidant (client)—dominant (therapist). Detached clients should be able to protect themselves against an overcompensating therapist. However, the therapist will need to be persistent to challenge the client's detached protector mode and will need to remain flexible, resonant, and self-reflective. This need for self-reflection is why we think a minimal amount of mindfulness experience is a prerequisite for schema therapists. The techniques we described in chapter 7 can help the therapist balance confrontation and empathy. If a supervisor perceives that the therapist is losing balance and becoming impatient or accusatory, he must intervene with empathic confrontation. It is also helpful if the supervisor acts as a role model, and for the supervisee to understand how empathic confrontation feels from the client's side.

7. Dominant (client)—submissive (therapist). This is the most dangerous mode cycle for the therapist, who faces a high risk of being humiliated or hurt. When therapists surrender to a vulnerability to harm or illness, dependence-incompetence, or defectiveness-shame schema, they can become the victim of an abusive client. While this might be hard to believe, occasionally a therapist will start an intimate relationship with such a client. This results in the enactment of an old interactional pattern in which the therapist is revictimized. Under supervision, the therapist may try to justify his behavior as reparenting. This is false, because he lacks the skills of limit setting and empathic confrontation. Generally, it is not possible to deal with such severe patterns in supervision. The supervisor can encourage the supervisee to get personal therapy or focus on working in settings with less intense therapy relationships that are focused more on content.

8. Dominant (client)—avoidant (therapist). This match potentially hurts the client more than the therapist, who hides behind a wall of detachment. Usually not much progress is made in therapy, and sooner or later the client will either leave or end up in a detached mode along with the therapist. If that happens, there will not be much harm to the client, but there will not be much gain from therapy either. Sometimes, the therapist's detachment results from a lack of alternative therapeutic strategies. If that's the case, it is up to the supervisor to support the therapist by demonstrating and training her in additional skills, such as role-plays. If the therapist's personality and schemas set the limit for progress, personal therapy is required.

> **Reflect:** Think about the mode cycles. Which do you think is most common in your practice?

9. Dominant (client)—dominant (therapist). This combination is rare. Struggles will dominate therapy right from the start. If the therapist is not willing or able to step back into a "one-down" position (Bateson, 1972) to give the client a chance to calm down and engage in therapy, he should say that to the client at an early stage and recommend another therapist. Perhaps this mode cycle offers some potential for mutual understanding, which can assist therapy, but we still encourage the therapist to do his best to functionally deal with his own schema activations. Since schemas can be very powerful, self-reflection is not easy. If a client constantly pushes the therapist's buttons, the therapist dealing with his own schema activations will dominate the interaction and limit therapy. Building a good working alliance will be difficult. We cannot expect all therapists to be equally good at treating every client. Knowing our limitations and accepting them is healthy adult thinking and is much better than following our own demanding critic by trying to get along with every client.

Sue is a psychologist who attended a lecture by a senior clinical psychologist. She sought treatment with him and traveled some distance for therapy sessions. In one session, she talked a lot about her mother, who did not "mirror" her. She expressed some anger. Toward the end of the session, the therapist attempted a summary and a case conceptualization. Sue reacted in an irritated way.

In the next session, she arrived angry and blamed the therapist for acting like her mother by not giving her sufficient attention. The therapist reacted with anger and thought, After this beginning, I'm not going to work with her! He thought about how to convey the message to her without putting her down. He followed the ground rule of don't blame the client, just call it a mismatch.

He said, "Okay, I realize that my understanding of therapy does not meet your expectations. This is fine, and schema therapy is actually more directive than other therapies. You deserve the best therapy available for you. Would it be acceptable if I recommend another therapist for you, who might better match your expectations?"

Sue felt rejected and wanted to give therapy another try. This required self-disclosure from the therapist: "I appreciate your trust in me, but I have to tell you that I feel limited by my own schema activations. This will affect our therapy and won't be helpful for you." The client—a therapist herself—responded, "Do I remind you of your mother?"

The therapist felt some anger coming up inside but was able to take a "one-down" position: "I dislike admitting it, but you're right!"

"Okay, got it! Then it actually doesn't make much sense to go on," said Sue. She then left the office without feeling put down.

The Role of Supervision

Supervision is another interpersonal relationship, so we can apply the mode cycle model to it to better understand the interaction systematically. Just as therapists act as role models for their clients, supervisors act as role models for supervisees. The same principles of support and empathic confrontation are relevant, as we describe below.

For supervisors. Be aware of your own unrelenting standards schema so you aren't overly directive. Allow space for trainees to develop in their own way to be good schema therapists. This form of therapy is very personal, and authenticity is important. Offer your style, but don't make it the gold standard. Let them do it their way!

Video-based supervision. Generally, we like approval more than criticism. Supervisors should blend any critical observations with validation. Start with approval and then shift to anything that needs correction. Face-to-face confrontations are more difficult to take than looking at the issue from a joint reference point, such as by watching a video. (This is another reason to insist on using video material in supervision!) Only video (or, to some extent, audio) recordings of sessions reveal the real interactions in therapy, especially limited reparenting skills. Once a supervisor identifies a rupture or mismatch in a video, she can either try to enhance the therapist's skills in a role-play or dig deeper into the underlying schema activations.

Six of the fourteen rankings of the schema therapy competency rating scale deal with the therapy relationship. This scale, which was developed to rate the recordings required to become an ISST-licensed schema therapist, works quite well. Supervisors use it to shape therapists' behavior to prepare them for the certification procedure. And this is yet another reason why we think video recordings are a must in supervision.

Imagery exercises. Instead of just talking things through in supervision, you can make use of experiential techniques. Here we describe an adaptation of the imagery rescripting technique for a supervisee.

Start with the image of a difficult client. Focus on the therapist's emotions and body sensations. Let her float back into childhood and see whether any images come up. Have her picture the childhood scene in detail, and ask for the child's needs. Bring the therapist's healthy adult into the image, and let it limit the significant other and care for the needs of the child. Ask for the shifted feelings within the therapist, and slowly bring to mind the image of the difficult client. Make sure that the therapist remains in her self-assertive and centered state. After she's faced the client, ask her for her feelings again. End with solution-directed imagery or by role-playing a better interaction with the client.

This exercise usually helps the therapist to become aware of her own underlying schema activations. That knowledge will help her to distance from her emotional reactions, let automatic coping impulses go, and replace them with a more balanced and centered healthy adult mode coping style. You can use the A, B, C, D, and E steps we described for using the schema-mode flash card in chapter 11.

Self-reflection imagery exercises with audio instruction. In addition to the imagery rescripting exercise guided by the supervisor, supervisees can try doing imagery exercises themselves guided by audio instruction. (An audio recording of a self-practice imagery exercise for therapists, along with this book's other online accessories, is available for download at http://www.newharbinger.com/40958.) These allow supervisees to stop the recording and continue at their own pace. A side effect of these practices is that they deepen one's understanding of how imagery exercises feel and work. After such experiential work, the individual's felt sense of energy is higher than before. Surprisingly, working experientially is less exhausting than cognitive restructuring. Try it! Imagery exercises and chair dialogues give us access to reserves of energy to overcome stuck or suffering states.

Self-Care Exercises

Don't treat your clients better than you treat yourself. To be an effective therapist, you need to step out of your self-sacrifice schema and care for your own child modes. Why not do for yourself what we teach clients? We recommend that you try the following self-care exercises.

Mode Awareness

There is no better way to build your mode-identification skills than to work on your own mode activations. Some mindfulness training will help you to build up an internal observer stance. Remembering Kanfer's metaphor of devils on the therapist's shoulder will help you to keep your mode activations, or devils, in mind and replace them with guardian angels.

Here are the steps for identifying and modifying your mode activations:

1. Become aware of your personal level of activation by monitoring your *emotional tension*.

2. Identify *triggering situations* and resulting *coping impulses*.

3. Access your backstage level of *basic emotions* and *activated beliefs*.

4. Identify your underlying *schema activations*?

5. Determine which *"leg" you lean toward* right now. Attachment or assertiveness?

    - How does that relate to your *values*?

    - Can you try to find a better *balance* between assertiveness and attachment?

    - What can you *say to yourself* to get centered again?

6. Think about what a *wise person* would do in your shoes.

    - What would this *behavior* look like in your specific situation?

    - Try to implement this behavior, and then look at the resulting *effect*.

7. What *principles* come from this learning experience?

Once you become better at observing your own mode activations, continue to observe the mode activations of others (besides those of your clients): your partner, your children, your colleagues, and, finally, people out on the street.

Keep Your Own Balance in Life

Track your self-care. We suggest doing the good-night ritual for a month to increase your self-awareness. We also recommend writing in some kind of diary. You will be more confident with your clients if you can talk about your experience using these tools.

If you feel overwhelmed after seeing a client, try a decompression ritual. For example, do a minimindfulness exercise, such as listening to music in the car as you drive home from the office.

Do an environmental audit of your office. How pleasant is it as a workplace? Have a colleague look it over and give you feedback. One idea is to have a "refresh center," a place with fresh fruit, drinks, and maybe energy food to help you deal with that low point in the afternoon.

Consider the following self-care advice, modified from Norcross and Guy's (2007) useful book *Leaving It at the Office: A Guide to Psychotherapist Self-Care*:

- *Think about your values on a regular basis.* Perhaps do a values questionnaire (from acceptance and commitment therapy). Consider writing a personal mission statement.

- *Promote the positive in your life.*

Steven, a psychotherapist, reflected, "I discipline myself to do good things, such as going to a favorite art gallery, attending a concert, or finding a new restaurant. Nothing beats spending quality time with friends."

- Sports or other hobbies give you "quality time." Short vacations or overseas trips may become part of your calendar each year. As therapists, we deal with a lot of ugliness, so we need to balance it by emphasizing the beautiful.

Balance Your Attachment and Assertiveness Needs

Strengthen your healthy adult mode in everyday life. You will be amazed by the impact that balancing assertiveness and attachment can have on you. Once you grasp the concept of the healthy adult mode, you will find that it is effective in all your interpersonal encounters. Try using the mode model in your next argument with your partner and see what happens. Once you have mastered the balance between assertiveness and attachment, you will find it more natural to stay balanced in therapy sessions as well.

Principle: Relationships become difficult when we focus for too long on our need for assertiveness. Reconnection works when both partners can shift back to attachment.

What to Do if You Lose Your Balance

Here are some suggestions about what to do if you lose your balance with assertiveness and attachment. We based these recommendations on suggestions from Norcross and Guy (2007).

Stop to rebalance. Tell your client that you need to go to the restroom. Leaving the situation for a moment, changing body position, and going to a neutral place might help you to rebalance.

Debrief. If you cannot rebalance in the session, debrief as soon as possible after a critical therapeutic incident. Identify a close colleague whom you can call in times of need.

Supervision. Find a peer supervision group, which can offer good additional support alongside individual supervision.

Self-therapy. Consider personal psychotherapy. We think that, at times, self-therapy is absolutely necessary for all practicing therapists. In a time of stress, going to therapy should be our first response, not a reluctant last resort!

Self-care. Seek healthy escapes, exercise, and maintain your physical health. Do not forget what you tell people in treatment about exercise.

Dealing with sleeping problems. If sleeping problems occur, do not go to bed too early. Wait until you get tired, but then go to bed immediately. Once there, relax your body and check all muscles in a body scan. Focus especially on your face and your hands. Now guide your attention on the space in your chest or your stomach. Let all thoughts in your head go. If relaxation works well, a spontaneous deep breath indicates that your autonomic nervous system has shifted into the parasympathetic state. If you do not fall asleep, avoid staying awake in bed. If you cannot get to sleep within half an hour (for example, after waking up during the night), get up and work on something until you get tired again.

Spiritual resources. Use meditation, mindfulness, retreats, or prayer, depending on your personal preferences and values. *Mindfulness for Therapists* (Zarbock, Lynch, Ammann, & Ringer, 2015) is a very helpful resource that includes an eight-week mindfulness-training program.

Self-disclosure. Farrell and Shaw's recent book, *Experiencing Schema Therapy from the Inside Out* (2018), offers additional ideas for deepening self-reflection and self-care. Developing a good road map of your own emotional territory will help you to ride the tides of your activations instead of being lost and acting out. By understanding your own emotions, you will get better at differentiating between your activation patterns and those of your clients. In session, try to remain centered in the emotional tolerance window, making use of your own activations in limited self-disclosure, changing to the reflection level to reconnect with your client, and giving yourself permission to contribute your ideas if your client gets stuck. All this will give you a sense of safety and control about the therapy process and will reduce your perceived stress level.

Schema therapy allows us to act as the real person we are, and that is what we can do best. The challenge for each of us is to continuously transform and develop ourselves, applying the schema therapy model to ourselves and training our healthy adult mode. Our personal growth is an additional reward.

Accept boundaries. There are boundary considerations when treating very difficult clients. Realistically, there is some risk of crossing emotional and sometimes sexual boundaries. Therapists have to be on guard. Reflect on your relationship history. Have you ever dated a psychopathic or borderline partner, or had to deal with a partner with such traits? If you recognize this in your relationship history, you may have some unhealthy patterns of attraction or schema chemistry. Whenever you perceive strong or lasting emotional activations with a client, we suggest that you talk about this with your supervisor. This applies to any negative emotion, such as fear or anger, or feelings of emotional enmeshment or sexual attraction.

Dealing with Sexual Attraction from the Therapist's Side

We discussed the romantic feelings that clients can develop for therapists in chapter 13, but what if you are attracted to a client? Unfortunately, sexual abuse by therapists is not a rare phenomenon. Studies report that during a therapist's career, there is up to a 10 percent chance that he or she will be sexually abusive in one way or another (for a review, see Pope, 1990). Sexual abuse is a violation of our professional standards and is detrimental to the client. However, the relatively high incidence rate indicates that there is considerable risk of becoming enmeshed with a client in an unhealthy way. The therapeutic relationship is by nature emotionally intense, and it can become sexual.

Remember that many therapists themselves suffer from an emotional deprivation or abandonment schema. We are vulnerable to abusing the therapy relationship to compensate for these schemas. This is another example of a devil on the therapist's shoulder. Admit the risk. If you are attracted to a client (and we all will be at some point), we suggest that you consider the following steps.

1. Realize and accept your feelings, but don't give in to them. Training in mindfulness and emotional disidentification can be helpful. Try to distance from pleasurable thoughts, images, and emotions involving the client, and let them go whenever you perceive them. Don't feed them with your attention.

2. Ask the client for permission to record a session. This will increase self-reflection on both sides. Watch the recording, paying close attention to your behavior. Maybe you will see yourself acting silly at times. Watching yourself in a video supports disidentification.

3. Disclose your difficulty to a close colleague. This usually works like turning the lights on after a concert. Once named, emotions tend to cool down.

4. Go for supervision. Ask an experienced supervisor whom you trust for a supervision session, and show this person the video recording of the session with your client. This person may detect traces of persuasion from the client, share your feelings of being attracted, or both. We are all human, but we must remain professional. Receiving supervision can reduce feelings of shame and guilt induced by our own inner critic modes.

5. Disclose your feelings to the client. We have mixed thoughts about disclosing such feelings to clients. If you think doing so would help therapy, carefully plan the way you approach the disclosure with your supervisor. Do not do it impulsively.

One author (Roediger) of this book recommends something like this:

Therapist: I'm really sorry that I have to bring up an issue today that's central for our therapy. I have to admit that, beyond my professional feelings, in the past weeks some additional and somewhat intense feelings have arisen in me. Maybe you already realized this. I tried to keep them down, but I failed. Although it might feel good for the moment, it limits my therapeutic impact. This is why I'm sharing these feelings with you, so that we both—together—might be able to return to a more goal-directed working relationship. I suggest that we cool down the emotional atmosphere in the sessions a bit and focus purely on our working alliance. Does this make sense to you?

However, another author (Stevens) thinks it is too risky to admit to any sexual feelings in therapy and recommends referral.

6. Continue therapy on probation. Agree to a limited number of sessions to find a way back into a balanced professional relationship, and then make time to review the process.

7. Refer the client. If you still find yourself too distracted by sexual attraction, it is best to refer the client to a colleague. It is not the client's fault, but it is *your* problem. When you can't get beyond your feelings, referral is the only way to deal in a professional way with your human limitations, and it is the only way to protect your client.

> **Therapist Tip:** It is a good idea to rate any attraction you have to a client on a 10-point scale. Set an upper limit for your emotional tolerance window. Once you rate yourself at, say, 8, you should automatically refer your client to another therapist.

Summary

In this closing chapter, we looked at the important topic of self-care. It is essential that we take self-reflection as well as self-care seriously, especially when treating difficult clients, who are the norm in schema therapy. Don't preach water while drinking wine. Apply schema therapy principles to yourself first by considering the advice in this chapter. We, the authors, want you to not only be a good schema therapist, but a healthy individual, too. When you are, we all benefit!

Epilogue—Training Opportunities and Resources

Interest in schema therapy is growing worldwide. The International Society of Schema Therapy (ISST), founded in 2008, has more than a thousand members, most of them certified schema therapists, from almost fifty countries.

The ISST has published training guidelines for ISST certification at standard and advanced levels (see http://www.schematherapysociety.org/Resources/Documents/2015 ISST CERTIFICATION REQUIREMENTS.pdf). The training is meant as an add-on to a basic training in cognitive behavioral or psychodynamic therapy, not as stand-alone training. There are also certified training centers in more than thirty countries worldwide. The ISST offers training and supervision to people interested in implementing schema therapy in their countries. If we have piqued your interest, visit the ISST site: https://schematherapysociety.org/Training-Programs.

Free online accessories, including some of the forms we presented and audio recordings of exercises, are available for download at http://www.newharbinger.com/40958. We hope that these resources help you to get the most out of our book!

Afterword

I am so pleased that Drs. Roediger, Stevens, and Brockman decided to write this book. *Contextual Schema Therapy* builds upon the schema therapy approach and fortifies the mainstay of the model: conceptualizing the client's emotional, behavioral, and biologic autobiography, identifying early unmet needs, and healing early maladaptive schemas and coping modes related to current and longstanding emotional suffering.

The authors thoughtfully illuminate how implicit memory activation—informed by early maladaptive schemas and self-defeating schema modes—can hijack the *current moment* where familiar, reminiscent, and even biologically driven conditions can lead to *as-if* self-defeating reactions.

As you've come to appreciate, within the limits of the therapy relationship, the schema therapist is poised in an empathically attuned reparenting role, prepared to connect with vulnerability; confront and negotiate with avoidance; challenge and confront internalized critics, demanders, and punishers; rescript embedded beliefs about self and others; and reimagine maladaptive responses as healthy and adaptive ones.

Drs. Roediger, Stevens, and Brockman offer a comprehensive text that supplies the reader with specific applications of schema therapy for the individual client; share applications of case conceptualization and treatment strategies for challenging populations, including those suffering from narcissism, avoidance, and trauma; and show how to adapt the model for group therapy and couples work, all along recognizing the contributions of leading experts in the schema therapy community, including Arnoud Arntz, Travis Atkinson, Wendy Behary, Joan Farrell, and Ida Shaw.

Consistent with the philosophy of schema therapy, the authors give the reader a clear narrative and descriptive examples of the value of integration. They introduce the reader to methods for weaving strategies—founded in mindfulness models and the acceptance and commitment therapy approach to psychotherapy—into the framework of schema therapy.

As you've gathered from this book, schema therapy is not an eclectic model. Instead, it is an integrative approach, one that carefully selects proven strategies from evidence-based psychotherapies as they relate to addressing schema/mode obstacles that interfere with clients being able to resolve issues emerging from unmet emotional needs and biased cognitive, emotional, and behavioral patterns.

By meeting underlying unmet emotional needs, through the use of a robust conceptual assessment and integrated strategies for change, schema therapy has proven—through outcome studies conducted around the world—to be effective at reducing the intensity of painful emotional experiences; weakening self-defeating coping modes and replacing them with healthy and adaptive ones; and lowering the frequency of triggered reactions often arising from conditions that stir up memorable early childhood experiences.

This book is sure to be an important and valuable resource for practitioners treating some of the most difficult problems in psychotherapy.

—Jeffrey Young
Founder of schema therapy

References

Adolphs, R. (2003). Cognitive neuroscience of human social behaviour. *Nature Reviews Neuroscience, 4*(3), 165–178.

Ainsworth, M. D. S., Blehar, M. C., Waters, E., & Wall, S. N. (1978). *Patterns of attachment: A psychological study of the strange situation*. Hillsdale, NJ: Lawrence Erlbaum.

American Psychiatric Association. (2013). *Diagnostic and statistical manual of mental disorders* (5th ed.). Washington, DC: American Psychiatric Publishing.

Anderson, T. (1987). The reflecting team: Dialog and metadialogue in clinical work. *Family Process, 26*(4), 415–428.

Arntz, A. (2012). Imagery rescripting as a therapeutic technique: Review of clinical trials, basic studies, and research agenda. *Journal of Experimental Psychopathology, 3*(2), 189–208.

Arntz, A., & Jacob, G. (2013). *Schema therapy in practice: An introductory guide to the schema mode approach*. Chichester, UK: Wiley-Blackwell.

Arntz, A., Rauner, M., & van den Hout, M. (1995). "If I feel anxious, there must be danger": ex consequentia reasoning in inferring danger in anxiety disorders. *Behaviour Research and Therapy, 33*(8), 917–925.

Arntz, A., & van Genderen, H. (2009). *Schema therapy for borderline personality disorder*. Chichester, UK: Wiley-Blackwell.

Atkinson, T. (2012). Schema therapy for couples: Healing partners in a relationship. In M. van Vreeswijk, J. Broersen, & M. Nadort (Eds.), *The Wiley-Blackwell handbook of schema therapy: Theory, research, and practice* (pp. 323–335). Chichester, UK: Wiley-Blackwell.

Baars, B. J. (1997). In the theatre of consciousness: Global workspace theory, a rigorous scientific theory of consciousness. *Journal of Consciousness Studies, 4*(4), 292–309.

Ball, S. A. (1998). Manualized treatment for substance abusers with personality disorders: Dual focus schema therapy. *Addictive Behaviors, 23*(6), 883–891.

Ball, S. A., Maccarelli, L. M., LaPaglia, D. M., & Ostrowski, M. J. (2011). Randomized trial of dual-focused versus single-focused individual therapy for personality disorders and substance dependence. *Journal of Nervous and Mental Disease, 199*(5), 319–328.

Bamber, M. (2004). "The good, the bad and the defenceless Jimmy"—a single case study of schema mode therapy. *Clinical Psychology and Psychotherapy, 11*(6), 425–438.

Bamber, M., & McMahon, R. (2008). Danger—early maladaptive schemas at work! The role of early maladaptive schemas in career choice and the development of occupational stress in health workers. *Clinical Psychology and Psychotherapy, 15*(2), 96–112.

Bamelis, L., Bloo, J., Bernstein, D., & Arntz, A. (2012). Effectiveness studies. In M. van Vreeswijk, J. Broersen, & M. Nadort (Eds.), *The Wiley-Blackwell handbook of schema therapy: Theory, research, and practice* (pp. 495–510). Chichester, UK: Wiley-Blackwell.

Bamelis, L. L., Evers, S. M., Spinhoven, P., & Arntz, A. (2014). Results of a multicenter randomized controlled trial of the clinical effectiveness of schema therapy for personality disorders. *American Journal of Psychiatry, 171*(3), 305–322. Retrieved from http://ajp.psychiatryonline.org/doi/suppl/10.1176/appi.ajp.2013.12040518.

Bamelis, L. L., Renner, F., Heidkamp, D., & Arntz, A. (2011). Extended schema mode conceptualizations for specific personality disorders: An empirical study. *Journal of Personality Disorders, 25*(1), 41–58.

Bandura, A. (1977). Self-efficacy: Toward a unifying theory of behavioral change. *Psychological Review, 84*(2), 191–215.

Bargh, J. A. (2014). Our unconscious mind. *Scientific American*, January, 30–37.

Barr, A. (2006). An investigation into the extent to which psychological wounds inspire counsellors and psychotherapists to become wounded healers, the significance of these wounds on their career choice, the causes of these wounds and the overall significance of demographic factors. The Green Rooms. http://www.thegreenrooms.net/wounded-healer.

Bateman, A., & Fonagy, P. (1999). Effectiveness of partial hospitalization in the treatment of borderline personality disorder: A randomized controlled trial. *American Journal of Psychiatry, 156*(10), 1563–1569.

Bateman, A., Fonagy, P. (2009). Randomized controlled trial of outpatient mentalization-based treatment versus structured clinical management for borderline personality disorder. *American Journal of Psychiatry, 166*(12), 1355–1364.

Bateson, G. (1972). *Steps to an ecology of mind: Collected essays in anthropology, psychiatry, evolution, and epistemology.* Chicago: University of Chicago Press.

Beauchamp, T. L., & Childress, J. F. (2001). *Principles of biomedical ethics* (5th ed.). Oxford: Oxford University Press.

Beaulieu, D. (2006). *Impact techniques for therapists.* New York: Routledge.

Beck, A. T. (1967). *Depression: Causes and treatment.* Philadelphia: University of Pennsylvania Press.

Behary, W. T. (2013). *Disarming the narcissist. Surviving and thriving with the self-absorbed.* Oakland, CA: New Harbinger Publications.

Bennet-Goleman, T. (2001). *Emotional alchemy: How the mind can heal the heart.* New York: Harmony Books.

Bernstein, D. P., Nijman, H. L., Karos, K., Keulen-de Vos, M., de Vogel, V., & Lucker, T. (2012). Schema therapy for forensic patients with personality disorders: Design and preliminary findings of a multicenter randomized clinical trial in the Netherlands. *International Journal of Forensic Mental Health, 11*, 312–324.

Berridge, K. C., & Robinson, T. E. (1998). What is the role of dopamine in reward: Hedonic impact, reward learning, or incentive salience? *Brain Research Reviews, 28*(3), 309–369.

Bliss, T. V., Lomo, T., & Blane, H. (1973). Long-lasting potentiation of synaptic transmission in the dentate area of the anaesthetized rabbit following stimulation of the perforant path. *Journal of Physiology, 232*(2), 331–356.

Boston Change Process Study Group. (2008). Forms of relational meaning: Issues in the relations between the implicit and reflective-verbal domains. *Psychoanalytic Dialogues, 18*(2), 125–148.

Botvinick, M. M., Braver, T. S., Barch, D. M., Carter, C. S., & Cohen, J. D. (2001). Conflict monitoring and cognitive control. *Psychological Review, 108*(3), 624–652.

Bowlby, J. (1969). *Attachment and loss.* New York: Basic Books.

Brockman, R. (2013, July). *Schema modes and psychological flexibility processes: An approach to functional integration and initial cross-sectional data.* Presentation at 11th Annual World Conference of the Association for Contextual Behavioral Science, University of New South Wales, Sydney, Australia.

Brockman, R. N., & Calvert, F. L. (2016). Imagery rescripting for PTSD and personality disorders: Theory and application. *Journal of Contemporary Psychotherapy, 47*(1), 23–30.

Buchheim, A., Heinrichs, M., George, C., Pokorny, D., Koops, E., Henningsen, P., et al. (2009). Oxytocin enhances the experience of attachment security. *Psychoneuroendocrinology, 34*(9), 1417–1422.

Cahill, L., Prins, B., Weber, M., & McGaugh, J. L. (1994). Beta-adrenergic activation and memory for emotional events. *Nature, 371*(6499), 702–704.

Cannon, W. B. (1915). *Bodily changes in pain, hunger, fear and rage: An account of recent researches into the function of emotional excitement.* New York: Appleton.

Clark, A., & Chalmers, D. J. (1998). The extended mind. *Analysis, 58*(1), 10–23.

Clarkin, J. F., Levy, K. N., Lenzenweger, M. F., & Kernberg, O. F. (2007). Evaluating three treatments for borderline personality disorder: A multiwave study. *American Journal of Psychiatry, 164*(6), 922–928.

Cousineau, P. (2012). Mindfulness and ACT as strategies to enhance healthy adult mode: The use of the mindfulness flash card as an example. In M. van Vreeswijk, J. Broersen, & M. Nadort (Eds.), *The Wiley-Blackwell handbook of schema therapy: Theory, research, and practice* (pp. 249–258). Chichester, UK: Wiley-Blackwell.

Craske, M. G., Kircanski, K., Zelikowsky, M., Mystkowski, J., Chowdhury, N., & Baker, A. (2008). Optimizing inhibitory learning during exposure therapy. *Behaviour Research and Therapy, 46*(1) 5–27.

Damasio, A. R. (1999). *The feeling of what happens: Body and emotion in the making of consciousness.* New York: Harcourt Brace.

DeCharms, R. C. (2008). Applications of real-time fMRI. *Nature Reviews Neuroscience, 9*(9), 720–729.

De Klerk, N., Abma, T. A., Bamelis, L. L., & Arntz, A. (2017). Schema therapy for personality disorders: A qualitative study of patients' and therapists' perspectives. *Behavioural and Cognitive Psychotherapy, 45*(1) 31–45.

DeRubeis, R. J., Hollon, S. D., Amsterdam, J. D., Shelton, R. C., Young, P. R., Salomon, R. M., et al. (2005). Cognitive therapy vs. medications in the treatment of moderate to severe depression. *Archives of General Psychiatry, 62*(4), 409–416.

De Shazer, S. (1985). *Keys to solution in brief therapy.* New York: W. W. Norton.

Dibbets P., & Arntz A. (2016). Imagery rescripting: Is incorporation of the most aversive scenes necessary? *Memory, 24*(5), 683–695.

Doering, S., Hörz, S., Rentrop, M., Fischer-Kern, M., Schuster, P., Benecke, C., et al. (2010). Transference-focused psychotherapy versus treatment by community psychotherapists for borderline personality disorder: Randomised controlled trial. *British Journal of Psychiatry, 196*(5), 389–395.

Donabedian, A. (1966). Evaluating the quality of medical care. *Milbank Memorial Fund Quarterly, 44*(3), 166–206.

Edwards, D., & Arntz, A. (2012). Schema therapy in historical perspective. In M. van Vreeswijk, J. Broersen, & M. Nadort (Eds.), *The Wiley-Blackwell handbook of schema therapy: Theory, research, and practice* (pp. 3–26). Chichester, UK: Wiley-Blackwell.

Eisenberg, L. (1995). The social construction of the human brain. *American Journal of Psychiatry, 152*(11), 1563–1575.

Eisenberger, N. I., Lieberman, M. D., & Williams, K. D. (2003). Does rejection hurt? An fMRI study of social exclusion. *Science, 302*(5643), 290–292.

Ellis, A. (1969). A cognitive approach to behavior therapy. *International Journal of Psychiatry, 8*(6), 896–900.

Ekman, P. (1993). Facial expression and emotion. *American Psychologist, 48*(4), 384–392.

Ekman, P. (n.d.). Atlas of emotions. http://atlasofemotions.org.

Erskine, R. G. (1998). The therapeutic relationship: Integrating motivation and personality theories. *Transactional Analysis Journal, 28*(2), 132–142.

Farrell, J. M., Reiss, N., & Shaw, I. A. (2014). *The schema therapy clinician's guide: A complete resource for building and delivering individual, group and integrated schema mode treatment programs*. Chichester, UK: Wiley-Blackwell.

Farrell, J. M., & Shaw, I. A. (2012). *Group schema therapy for borderline personality disorder: A step-by-step treatment manual with patient workbook*. Chichester, UK: Wiley-Blackwell.

Farrell, J. M., & Shaw, I. A. (2018). *Experiencing schema therapy from the inside out: A self-practice/self-reflection workbook for therapists*. New York: Guilford.

Farrell, J. M., Shaw, I. A., & Webber, M. A. (2009). A schema-focused approach to group psychotherapy for outpatients with borderline personality disorder: A randomized controlled trial. *Journal of Behavior Therapy and Experimental Psychiatry, 40*(2), 317–328.

Ferenczi, S. (1932/1988). *Ohne Sympathie keine Heilung: Das klinische Tagebuch von 1932*. Frankfurt: S. Fischer.

Foa, E. B., & Kozak, M. J. (1986). Emotional processing of fear: Exposure to corrective information. *Psychological Bulletin, 99*(1), 20–35.

Fonagy, P., Gergely, G., Jurist, E., & Target, M. (2004). *Affect regulation, mentalization and the development of the self*. London: Karnac.

Freud, S. (1915). Instincts and their vicissitudes. In J. Strachey (Trans.), *The standard edition of the complete psychological works of Sigmund Freud* (Vol. 14, 1914–1916, pp. 109–140). London: Vintage.

Freud, S. (1923). The ego and the id. In J. Strachey (Trans.), *The standard edition of the complete psychological works of Sigmund Freud* (Vol. 19, 1923–1925, pp. 1–16). London: Vintage.

Fuster, J. M. (2002). Physiology of executive functions: The perception-action cycle. In D. T. Stuss & R. T. Knight (Eds.), *Principles of frontal lobe function* (pp. 96–108). New York: Oxford University Press.

Gallagher, H. L., & Frith, C. D. (2003). Functional imaging of "theory of mind." *Trends in Cognitive Sciences, 7*(2), 77–83.

Giesen-Bloo, J., van Dyck, R., Spinhoven, P., van Tilburg, W., Dirksen, C., van Asselt, T., et al. (2006). Outpatient psychotherapy for borderline personality disorder: Randomized trial for schema-focused therapy versus transference-focused psychotherapy. *Archives of General Psychiatry, 63*(6), 649–658.

Gilbert, P. (2010). *The compassionate mind: A new approach to life's challenges.* Oakland, CA: New Harbinger Publications.

Goleman, D. (1995). *Emotional intelligence: Why it can matter more than IQ.* New York: Bantam Books.

Grawe, K. (2004). *Psychological therapy.* Cambridge, MA: Hogrefe and Huber.

Greenberg, L. S. (2015). *Emotion focused therapy: Coaching clients to work through their feelings* (2nd ed.) Washington, DC: American Psychological Association.

Haken, H. (1983). *Synergetics: Introduction and advanced topics* (3rd ed.). Heidelberg, Berlin, New York: Springer.

Harris, R. (2009). *ACT made simple: An easy-to-read primer on acceptance and commitment therapy.* Oakland, CA: New Harbinger Publications.

Hawkley, L. C., & Cacioppo, J. T. (2010). Loneliness matters: A theoretical and empirical review of consequences and mechanism. *Annals of Behavioral Medicine, 40*(2), 218–227.

Hayes, S. C., Strosahl, K. D., & Wilson, K. G. (2012). *Acceptance and commitment therapy: The process and practice of mindful change* (2nd ed.). New York: Guilford Press.

Hebb, D. O. (1949). *The organization of behavior: A neuropsychological theory.* New York: John Wiley and Sons.

Heim, C., Shugart, M., Craighead, W. E., & Nemeroff, C. B. (2010). Neurobiological and psychiatric consequences of child abuse and neglect. *Developmental Psychobiology, 52*(7), 671–690.

Holman, G., Kanter, J., Tsai, M., & Kohlenberg, R. J. (2017). *Functional analytic psychotherapy made simple: A practical guide to therapeutic relationships.* Oakland, CA: New Harbinger Publications.

Holmes, E. A., & Mathews, A. (2010). Mental imagery in emotion and emotional disorders. *Clinical Psychology Review, 30*(3), 349–362.

Holt-Lunstad, J., Smith, T. B., Baker, M., Harris, T., & Stephenson, D. (2015). Loneliness and social isolation as risk factors for mortality: A meta-analytic review. *Perspectives on Psychological Science, 10*(2), 227–237.

Ivey, G. (2010). Plying the steel: A reconsideration of surgical metaphors in psychoanalysis. *Journal of the American Psychoanalytic Association, 58*(1), 59–82.

Jacob, G., van Genderen, H., & Seebauer, L. (2015). *Breaking negative thinking patterns: A schema therapy self-help and support book.* Chichester, UK: Wiley-Blackwell.

Jacob, G. A., & Arntz, A. (2013). Schema therapy for personality disorders—a review. *International Journal of Cognitive Therapy, 6*(2), 171–185.

Kabat-Zinn, J. (1990). *Full catastrophe living: Using the wisdom of your body and mind to face stress, pain, and illness.* New York: Delta.

Kandel, E. R. (1989). Genes, nerve cells, and the remembrance of things past. *Journal of Neuropsychiatry and Clinical Neurosciences, 1*(2), 103–125.

Kanfer, F. H., & Schefft, B. K. (1988). *Guiding the process of therapeutic change.* Michigan: Research Press Publications.

Kellogg, S. H., & Young, J. E. (2006). Schema therapy for borderline personality disorder. *Journal of Clinical Psychology, 62*(4), 445–458.

Kliem, S., Kröger, C., & Kosfelder, J. (2010). Dialectical behavior therapy for borderline personality disorder: A meta-analysis using mixed-effects modelling. *Journal of Consulting and Clinical Psychology, 78*(6), 936–951.

Kosfeld, M., Heinrichs, M., Zak, P. J., Fischbacher, U., & Fehr, E. (2005). Oxytocin increases trust in humans. *Nature, 435*(7042), 673–676.

Kosslyn, S. M., Thompson, W. L., Kim, I. J., & Alpert, N. M. (1995). Topographical representations of mental images in primary visual cortex. *Nature, 378*(6556), 496–498.

Lambert, M. J. (1992). Psychotherapy outcome research: Implications for integrative and eclectic therapists. In J. C. Norcross & M. R. Goldfried (Eds.), *Handbook of psychotherapy integration* (pp. 94–129). New York: Basic Books.

Lambert, M. J. (2013). The efficacy and effectiveness of psychotherapy. In M. J. Lambert (Ed.), *Bergin and Garfield's handbook of psychotherapy and behavior change* (6th ed., pp. 169–218). Hoboken, NJ: John Wiley and Sons.

Lazarevic, D., Hough, M., & Brockman, R. (2013) *The relationship between the healthy adult schema mode and psychological flexibility.* Master's thesis, University of Western Sydney.

Leahy, R. L. (2001). *Overcoming resistance in cognitive therapy.* New York: Guilford Press.

Leary, M. R. (2009). The self and emotion: The role of self-reflection in the generation and regulation of affective experience. In R. J. Davidson, K. R. Scherer, & H. H. Goldsmith (Eds.), *Handbook of affective sciences* (pp. 773–786). New York: Oxford University Press.

LeDoux, J. E. (1996). *The emotional brain: The mysterious underpinnings of emotional life.* New York: Simon and Schuster.

Lee, C. W., Taylor, G., & Dunn, J. (1999). Factor structures of the schema questionnaire in a large clinical sample. *Cognitive Therapy and Research, 23*(4), 421–451.

Leslie, A. M. (1987). Pretense and representation: The origin of "theory of mind." *Psychological Review, 94*(4), 412–426.

Lewis, D. J. (1990). The experimental and theoretical foundation of behavior modification. In A. S. Bellack, M. Hersen, & A. E. Kadzin (Eds.), *International handbook of behavior modification and therapy* (pp. 27–51). New York: Plenum Press.

Lieberman, M. D., Eisenberger, N. I., Crockett, M. J., Tom, S. M., Pfeifer, J. H., & Way, B. M. (2007). Putting feelings into words: Affect labeling disrupts amygdala activity in response to affective stimuli. *Psychological Science, 18*(5), 421–428.

Linehan, M. M. (1993). *Cognitive-behavioral treatment of borderline personality disorder.* New York: Guilford Press.

Lobbestael, J., van Vreeswijk, M., Spinhoven, P., Schouten, E., & Arntz, A. (2010). Reliability and validity of the short Schema Mode Inventory (SMI). *Behavioural and Cognitive Psychotherapy, 38*(4), 437–458.

Lockwood, G., & Perris, P. (2012). A new look at core emotional needs. In M. van Vreeswijk, J. Broersen, & M. Nadort (Eds.), *The Wiley-Blackwell handbook of schema therapy: Theory, research, and practice* (pp. 41–66). Chichester, UK: Wiley-Blackwell.

Marlatt, G. A., & Gordon, J. R. (1985). *Relapse prevention: Maintenance strategies in the treatment of addictive behaviors.* New York: Guilford Press.

Maslow, A. H. (1970). *Motivation and personality* (2nd ed.). New York: Harper and Row.

Maturana, H. R., & Varela, F. J. (1998). *The tree of knowledge: The biological roots of human understanding.* Boston: Shambhala Publications.

McAdams, D. P. (2001). The psychology of life stories. *Review of General Psychology, 5*(2), 100–122.

McCullough, J. P. (2000). *Treatment for chronic depression: Cognitive behavioral analysis system of psychotherapy (CBASP).* New York: Guilford Press.

McKay, M., Lev, A., & Skeen, M. (2012). *Acceptance and commitment therapy for interpersonal problems: Using mindfulness, acceptance, and schema awareness to change interpersonal behaviors.* Oakland, CA: New Harbinger Publications.

Meaney, M. J. (2001). Nature, nurture, and the disunity of knowledge. *Annals of the New York Academy of Sciences, 935,* 50–61.

Meichenbaum, D. H. (1979). *Cognitive-behavior modification: An integrative approach.* New York: Plenum Press.

Menninger, K. (1958). *Theory of psychoanalytic technique.* New York: Basic Books.

Merton, R. K. (1948). The self-fulfilling prophecy. *Antioch Review, 8*(2), 193–210.

Messer, S. B. (2001). Introduction to the special issue of assimilative integration. *Journal of Psychotherapy Integration, 11*(1), 1–4.

Metzinger, T. (2000). *Neural correlates of consciousness: Empirical and conceptual questions.* Cambridge, MA: MIT Press.

Miller, W. R. (2000). Rediscovering fire: Small interventions, large effects. *Psychology of Addictive Behavior, 14*(1), 6–18.

Miller, W. R., & Rollnick, S. (2002). *Motivational interviewing: Preparing people for change* (2nd ed.). New York: Guilford Press.

Millon, T. H. (1990). *Toward a new personology: An evolutionary model.* New York: John Wiley and Sons.

Nader, K., & Hardt, O. (2009). A single standard for memory: The case for reconsolidation. *Nature Reviews Neuroscience, 10*(3), 224–234.

Nadort, M., Arntz, A., Smit, J. H., Giesen-Bloo, J., Eikelenboom, M., Spinhoven, P., et al. (2009). Implementation of outcome schema therapy for borderline personality disorder with versus without crisis support by the therapist outside office hours: A randomized trial. *Behaviour Research and Therapy, 47*(11), 961–973.

Nissen, L., & Sturm, M. (2014). Schematherapeutische Strategien bei chronischer Emotionsvermeidung. Zum Konzept des "emotionalen Resonanzraumes." *Verhaltenstherapie and Verhaltensmedizin, 35*(3), 270–286.

Norcross, J. C., & Guy, J. D. (2007). *Leaving it at the office: A guide to psychotherapist self-care.* New York: Guilford Press.

Nummenmaa, L., Glerean, E., Hari, R., & Hietanen, J. K. (2014). Bodily maps of emotions. *Proceedings of the National Academy of Sciences of the United States of America, 111*(2), 646–651.

Panksepp, J. (2011). Cross-species affective neuroscience decoding of the primal affective experiences of humans and related animals. *PLoS One, 6*(9), e21236.

Parfy, E. (2012). Schema therapy, mindfulness, and ACT—differences and points of contact. In M. van Vreeswijk, J. Broersen, & M. Nadort (Eds.), *The Wiley-Blackwell handbook of schema therapy: Theory, research, and practice* (pp. 229–238). Chichester, UK: Wiley-Blackwell.

Pearson, J. L., Cohn, D. A., Cowan, P. A., & Cowan, C. P. (1994). Earned- and continuous-security in adult attachment: Relation to depressive symptomatology and parenting style. *Development and Psychopathology, 6*, 259–373.

Pennebaker, J. W. (1997). *Opening up: The healing power of expressing emotions.* New York: Guilford Press.

Perls, F. S. (1973). *The gestalt approach: Eye witness to therapy.* Palo Alto, CA: Science and Behavior Books.

Piaget, J. (1985). *The equilibration of cognitive structures: The central problem of intellectual development.* Chicago: University of Chicago Press.

Pope, K. S. (1990). Therapist-patient sexual involvement: A review of the research. *Clinical Psychology Review, 10*(4), 477–490.

Porges, S. W. (2007). The polyvagal perspective. *Biological Psychology, 74*(2), 116–143.

Power, W. T. (1973). *Behavior: The control of perception.* New York: Aldine.

Rafaeli, E., Bernstein, D. P., & Young, J. (2011). *Schema therapy: Distinctive features.* New York: Routledge.

Remond, A., Hough, M., & Brockman, R. (2013). *The relationship between self-compassion and schema modes.* Master's thesis, University of Western Sydney.

Roediger, E. (2012). Why are mindfulness and acceptance central elements for therapeutic change in schema therapy? An integrative perspective. In M. van Vreeswijk, J. Broersen, & M. Nadort (Eds.), *The Wiley-Blackwell handbook of schema therapy: Theory, research, and practice* (pp. 239–248). Chichester, UK: Wiley-Blackwell.

Roediger, E., & Laireiter, A. R. (2013). The schema therapeutic mode cycle in behavior therapy supervision. *Verhaltenstherapie, 23*, 91–99.

Roediger, E., & Zarbock, G. (2013). Schematherapie. In T. Heidenreich & J. Michalak (Eds.), *Die "dritte Welle" der Verhaltenstherapie: Grundlagen und Praxis* (pp. 199–218). Weinheim: Beltz Verlag.

Rogers, C. R. (1951). *Client-centered therapy: Its current practice, implications, and theory.* London: Constable.

Rotter, J. B. (1966). Generalized expectancies for internal versus external control of reinforcement. *Psychology Monograph, 80*(1), 1–28.

Ryan, R. M., & Deci, E. L. (2017). *Self-determination theory: Basic psychological needs in motivation, development, and wellness.* New York: Guilford Press.

Schacter, D. L. (1992). Priming and multiple memory systems: Perceptual mechanisms of implicit memory. *Journal of Cognitive Neuroscience, 4*(3), 244–256.

Schnarch, D. (2009). *Intimacy and desire: Awaken the passion in your relationship.* New York: Beaufort Books.

Schore, A. N. (1994). *Affect regulation and the origin of the self: The neurobiology of emotional development.* Hillsdale, NJ: Erlbaum.

Schore, A. N. (2014). The right brain is dominant in psychotherapy. *Psychotherapy, 51*(3), 388–397.

Schulte, D. (1996). Tailor-made and standardized therapy: Complementary tasks in behavior therapy. A contrarian view. *Journal of Behavior Therapy and Experimental Psychiatry, 27*(2), 119–126.

Seebauer, L., Froß, S., Dubaschny, L., Schönberger, M., & Jacob, G. A. (2014). Is it dangerous to fantasize revenge in imagery exercises? An experimental study. *Journal of Behavior Therapy and Experimental Psychiatry, 45*(1), 20–25.

Segal, Z. V., Williams, J. M. G., & Teasdale, J. D. (2002). *Mindfulness-based cognitive therapy for depression: A new approach to preventing relapses.* New York: Guilford Press.

Selye, H. (1936). A syndrome produced by diverse nocuous agents. *Nature, 138,* 32.

Siegel, D. J. (1999). *The developing mind: How relationships and the brain interact to shape who we are.* New York: Guilford Press.

Simeone-DiFrancesco, C., Roediger, E., & Stevens, B. A. (2015). *Schema therapy with couples: A practitioner's guide to healing relationships.* Chichester, UK: Wiley-Blackwell.

Smucker, M. R., & Dancu, C. V. (1999). *Cognitive-behavioral treatment for adult survivors of childhood trauma: Imagery rescripting and reprocessing.* New York: Rowman and Littlefield.

Sterelny, K. (2003). *Thought in a hostile world: The evolution of human cognition.* Oxford: Blackwell.

Stern, D. N. (1985). *The interpersonal world of the infant: A view from psychoanalysis and developmental psychology.* New York: Basic Books.

Teasdale, J. D., Moore, R. G., Hayhurst, H., Pope, M., Williams, S., & Segal, Z. V. (2002). Metacognitive awareness and prevention of relapse in depression: Empirical evidence. *Journal of Consulting and Clinical Psychology, 70*(2), 275–287.

Tronick, E. (2009). "The still face experiment." https://www.youtube.com/watch?v=apzXGEbZht0.

Van Asselt, A. D., Dirksen, C. D., Arntz, A., Giesen-Bloo, J. H., van Dyck, R., Spinhoven, P., et al. (2008). Outpatient psychotherapy for borderline personality disorder: Cost-effectiveness of schema-focused therapy versus transference-focused psychotherapy. *British Journal of Psychiatry, 192*(6), 450–457.

Van der Hart, O., Nijenhuis, E. R. S., & Steele, K. (2006). *The haunted self: Structural dissociation and the treatment of chronic traumatization.* New York: W. W. Norton.

Van der Meulen, M., van Ijzendoorn, M. H., & Crone, E. A. (2016). Neural correlates of prosocial behavior: Compensating social exclusion in a four-player cyberball game. *PLoS ONE, 11*(7), e0159045.

Vansteenkiste, M., & Ryan, R. M. (2013). On psychological growth and vulnerability: Basic psychological need satisfaction and need frustration as a unifying principle. *Journal of Psychotherapy Integration, 23*(3), 263–280.

Van Vreeswijk, M., Broersen, J., & Schurink, G. (2014). *Mindfulness and schema therapy: A practical guide.* Chichester, UK: Wiley-Blackwell.

Weaver, I. C., Cervoni, N., Champagne, F. A., D'Alessio, A. C., Sharma, S., Seckl, J. R., et al. (2004). Epigenetic programming by maternal behavior. *Nature Neuroscience, 7*(8), 847–854.

Wells, A. (2009). *Metacognitive therapy for anxiety and depression.* New York: Guilford Press.

Wieczorek, M., & Brockman, R. (2016). *The schema model and core emotional needs: A self-determination theory perspective.* Master's thesis, University of Technology Sydney.

Winnicott, D. W. (1958). *Collected papers: From paediatrics to psycho-analysis.* London: Tavistock.

Wright, J. H., Basco, M. R., & Thase, M. E. (2006). *Learning cognitive-behavior therapy: An illustrated guide.* Washington, DC: American Psychiatric Publishing.

Yalom, I. D. (1983). *Inpatient group psychotherapy.* New York: Basic Books.

Yang, M., Coid, J., & Tyrer, P. (2010). Personality pathology recorded by severity: National survey. *British Journal of Psychiatry, 197*(3), 193–199.

Yehuda, R., & McFarlane, A. C. (1995). Conflict between current knowledge about posttraumatic stress disorder and its original conceptual basis. *American Journal of Psychiatry, 152*(12), 1705–1713.

Yerkes, R. M., & Dodson, J. D. (1908). The relation of strength of stimulus to rapidity of habit-formation. *Journal of Comparative Neurology and Psychology, 18,* 459–482.

Young, J. E. (1990). *Cognitive therapy for personality disorders: A schema-focused approach.* Sarasota, FL: Professional Resource Exchange.

Young, J. E. (2008). An interview with Jeffrey Young by Eckhard Roediger. https://schematherapysociety.org/Interview-with-Jeffrey-Young-by-Eckhard-Roediger/.

Young, J. E., & Klosko, J. S. (1993). *Reinventing your life: The breakthrough program to end negative behavior…and feel great again.* New York: Plume.

Young, J. E., Klosko, J. S., & Weishaar, M. E. (2003). *Schema therapy: A practitioner's guide.* New York: Guilford Press.

Zarbock, G., Lynch, S., Ammann, A., & Ringer, S. (2015). *Mindfulness for therapists: Understanding mindfulness for professional effectiveness and personal well-being.* Chichester, UK: Wiley-Blackwell.

Zindel, J. P. (2009). Hypnose—eine ganz besondere Beziehung. *Hypnose-ZHH, 4*(1–2), 107–125.

Eckhard Roediger, MD, is director of the Frankfurt Schema Therapy Institute, the first established in Germany. He is former president of the International Society of Schema Therapy (ISST), and board member since its foundation in 2008. He has been a schema therapy trainer and supervisor since 2008, and is author of numerous books, book chapters, and articles about schema therapy in German.

Bruce A. Stevens, PhD, is current Wicking Chair of Ageing and Practical Theology at Charles Sturt University in Canberra, Australia. He is a clinical and forensic psychologist with over twenty years of private practice experience. He has written several books—including two other books on schema therapy—and he has advanced accreditation in schema therapy for both individuals and couples.

Robert Brockman, DClinPsy, is an experienced clinician and academic working out of Sydney, Australia. He is a senior trainer with Schema Therapy Training Australia where he regularly runs ISST-accredited schema therapy training courses throughout Australia, New Zealand, and Asia. Brockman also currently holds a research fellowship with the Institute for Positive Psychology and Education at Australian Catholic University where he researches psychological approaches to well-being. He is currently engaged in clinical research focused on extending the schema mode model into novel clinical populations (e.g., generalized anxiety disorder (GAD), chronic pain, eating disorders, psychosis, HIV sufferers, problem gamblers, and forensic patients).

Foreword writer **Wendy T. Behary, LCSW,** is founder and clinical director of The Cognitive Therapy Center of New Jersey, and a faculty member at the Cognitive Therapy Center and Schema Therapy Institute of New York. She is also a distinguished founding fellow of the Academy of Cognitive Therapy. She maintains a private practice specializing in narcissism and high-conflict couples therapy.

Afterword writer **Jeffrey Young, PhD,** is author of *Schema Therapy*, and founder and director of the Schema Therapy Institute of New York.

Index

A

abandonment schema, 28
acceptance: balancing change and, 222–223; emotion surfing and, 135–136; healthy adult mode and, 133–137; of limitations, 222–223, 246; meditation on practicing, 136–137; older clients and, 135; philosophical background for, 134; psychological flexibility and, 23; rating in clients, 79; realism as form of, 222
accommodation, 12
ACT (acceptance and commitment therapy): rating core processes from, 79–80; schema therapy with, 2, 222
adaptive schemas, 26
adaptive solutions, 165
addictive clients, 238–240
adolescent modes, 51
advice, offering, 103
affect attunement, 10
alarm system, 8, 193–194
alcohol abuse, 239
alienation schema, 28
anger: accessing constructive, 162; dealing with excessive, 171; identifying blocked, 160; underlying self-harming behavior, 233–237
angry child mode, 43, 121, 162; chair dialogues, 188, 189; imagery exercises, 162
angry clients, 229–231
approval seeking schema, 30

Arntz, Arnoud, 171, 275
assertiveness, 7, 8
assessment, 67–69
assimilative integration, 3
Atkinson, Travis, 275
attachment: biology of, 10; coping style of, 8; insecure, 10–11; need for, 6, 7, 10
attention focusing, 199
attention time line exercise, 129–131
attractors: how they work, 13–16; model of, 11–12
attunement, schema, 36–38
audio recordings, 170, 265
automatic processing, 82
autonomy, impaired, 28–29
aversive fluctuation state, 215
avoidance: experiential, 22, 194; schema, 33
avoidant coping modes, 46, 112–114
avoidant–avoidant mode cycle, 254–255, 262
avoidant–dominant mode cycle, 262–263
avoidant–submissive mode cycle, 262
awareness: mindfulness as, 128; schema or mode, 36, 127. *See also* self-awareness

B

backstage motives, 42
balance, maintaining, 267–269
Ball, Samuel, 217, 238
basic emotions, 44, 45
Beck, Aaron, 25

Behary, Wendy, viii, 227, 229, 275
behavior change, 197–213; balancing acceptance and, 222–223; behavior experiments for, 210–212; diaries as tool for, 204, 206–210; emotion regulation techniques for, 197–201; good-night ritual for, 212–213; hierarchies of, 141, 142; homework assignments for, 201–203; imagery for rehearsing, 177–178; processes involved in, 143–148; schema-mode flash card for, 203–204, 205; steps for lasting, 148
behavior change phase, 218
behavior experiments, 210–212, 230
behavioral activation form, 210, 211
being kind to yourself exercise, 137
Bennet-Goleman, Tara, 2
"best day" video exercise, 176–177
biographical scenes, 83, 84
body language, 88–89
body scan, 153, 154, 198
borderline personality disorder (BPD), 2, 97
Boston Change Process Study Group, 89
boundary considerations, 269
brain processes, 16
Breaking Negative Thinking Patterns (Jacob, van Genderen, and Seebauer), 59
breaking up with clients, 231
breath: mindfulness of, 132–133; practicing prolonged, 200
Buddhism, 21, 129, 134
bully and attack mode, 46
bullying clients, 231–232

C

caretaking system, 10
caring for the vulnerable child exercise, 155
case conceptualization, 57–82; case study on, 60–61; comprehensive overview of, 80–82; descriptive mode diagram for, 70–73; genogram for, 59–60, 61; inputs for basing, 58; ISST form for, 62–66; mode map for, 73–79; mode monitoring for, 67–69; rating ACT core processes for, 79–80; schema and mode questionnaires for, 66–67; therapeutic role of, 57–59
cathartic diary, 204
chair dialogues, 179–196; change process and, 145–147; diagnostic process and, 180; emotional resonance sphere and, 193–196; healthy adult mode and, 182–184; historical role-play and, 180–182; mode map as basis for, 184–193; overview of using, 179
chair positions: case formulation, 110–112; emotional activation, 87, 90; empathic confrontation, 116; historical role-play, 181; mode map, 185; overcompensation, 118
challenging clients. *See* difficult clients
changing behavior. *See* behavior change
child modes, 40, 42, 43–45; chair dialogues and, 185–186, 187–188, 190, 192, 243; process of accessing, 119–122, 243
childhood photographs, 167, 243
childhood scenes: methods for accessing, 166–167; picturing in detail, 157, 159
clinical symptoms: coping modes and, 53–54, 55; reducing in clients, 217–218
cognitive behavioral therapy (CBT), 2, 217
cognitive fusion, 22
cognitive processing, 150
cognitive reappraisal, 92
cognitive techniques, 198
Columbo technique, 232
commenting technique, 200
committed action: behavior change hierarchies and, 141, 142; psychological

flexibility and, 23; rating in clients, 80; values as basis for, 138–139, 141
communication channels, 244
compassion: empathy and, 137. See also self-compassion
Compassionate Mind, The (Gilbert), 137
compensatory schemas, 32, 33
compliant surrender mode, 46
conceptual self, 22, 58
confidentiality issues, 256
consistency: acceptance and, 134; theory of, 12
contextual therapies, 21–24
contingency management, 224, 245
contingency theory, 134
continuous prayers, 198
coping modes, 109–119; addressing in clients, 112; bypassing detached or avoidant, 112–114; dealing gently with overcompensatory, 117–119; empathic confrontation with submissive, 114–116; identifying and labeling, 109–110; overview of maladaptive, 40, 43, 45–47; tracking sheet for, 201, 202; "visible" case formulation for, 110–112
coping styles: needs frustration and, 8–9; related to schemas and modes, 51–53
core beliefs, 110
core emotional needs, 5–9
core schemas, 32
counting down numbers, 198
couples-focused therapy. See interpersonal work
creative helplessness, 95
critic modes. See inner critic modes
current scenes, 83, 84, 158

D

decompression ritual, 267
defectiveness-shame schema, 28
defusion: chair dialogues and, 191; psychological flexibility and, 23; rating in clients, 79
demanding critic mode, 48
dependence-incompetence schema, 28
dependent clients, 246–248
descriptive mode diagram, 70–73
detached clients, 240–246; causes of resistance in, 240–241; strategies for dealing with, 242–246
detached coping modes, 46, 112–114
detached protector mode, 46, 112–113, 240, 242
detached self-soother mode, 46
developmental perspective, 50–51
Diagnostic and Statistical Manual of Mental Disorders (DSM-5), 3, 239
diagnostic chair dialogues, 180
dialectical behavior therapy (DBT), 222, 232–233
diaries: cathartic, 204; smiley log, 204; talking-back, 206, 207
diary card: empathic confrontation based on, 207–210; explanation and example of, 206, 208
difficult clients, 227–250; addictive clients, 238–240; angry clients, 229–231; bullying clients, 231–232; dependent or passive clients, 246–248; excessively self-soothing clients, 238–240; externalizing clients, 227; manipulative clients, 232; narcissistic clients, 228–229; romantically-interested clients, 248–250; self-harming clients, 232–238; severely detached clients, 240–246
disactualization, 36, 91
Disarming the Narcissist (Behary), viii
disciplined personal involvement, 98
disconnection and rejection domain, 28
dissociation, dealing with, 168–169
dominance/overcompensation modes, 46–47

dominant–avoidant mode cycle, 254, 263
dominant–dominant mode cycle, 254, 263–264
dominant–submissive mode cycle, 255, 263
downstream engineering, 22
dual focus schema therapy, 217
dual-focusing exercises, 13–15

E

ego-dystonic sentences, 122
eightieth birthday imagery exercise, 140
email messages, 244
emotion regulation techniques, 197–201; cognitive techniques, 198; perception-focused techniques, 199; physical activities, 200–201
emotion surfing, 135–136
emotional activation, 86–96; case vignette on, 91–92; change process and, 145–147; distancing from, 95; gestures and body language in, 88–89; imagery work related to, 166; increasing the level of, 88; inducing in clients, 87–88; mentalization and, 95–96; perspective changes and, 89–95; primary and secondary, 121–122; sitting positions for, 87, 90
emotional deprivation schema, 28
emotional inhibition schema, 30
emotional learning, 16–19
emotional processing, 143–145, 150
emotional resonance sphere, 193–196
emotional stabilization, 215–216
emotional tolerance window, 17–19, 167–168
emotion-focused therapy (EFT), 44
emotions: acceptance of, 135–136; basic vs. social, 44–45; improving access to soft, 88; needs connected to, 8–9; perspective changes for cooling, 89–92; poles in the spectrum of, 45

empathic confrontation: balancing reparenting and, 85, 86, 96–99; case example of using, 101–102; chair positions for, 116; diary card as basis for, 207–210; manipulative clients and, 232; submissive clients and, 114–116
empathy: expressing to clients, 103, 104; schema attunement and, 36–38
empty chair dialogue, 191, 210, 230
ending sessions, 221
enmeshment schema, 29
enraged child mode, 43
entitlement-grandiosity schema, 29, 32
environmental audit, 267
ethical concerns, 224
Experiencing Schema Therapy from the Inside Out (Farrell and Shaw), 260, 268
experiential avoidance, 22, 194
experiential work: behavior change related to, 143; healing process in, 173
exploration phase, 218
exposure therapy, 217
expressive writing, 198
extension technique, 93
externalizing clients, 227

F

fact checking, 163
failure (to achieve) schema, 29
family genogram, 59–60, 61
Farrell, Joan, 47, 275
fear networks, 22
fear reactions, 240
feedback, giving, 103, 247, 257
fight coping style, 8
5-4-3 mindful grounding exercise, 131–132, 199
flash card, schema-mode, 203–204, 205
fleece/scarf technique, 243
flight coping style, 8
floating-back process, 157, 159

focusing attention, 199
follow coping style, 8
forgiveness, 175, 176
FRAMES acronym, 103–104
freeze coping style, 8, 47
front-stage coping modes, 42
future-directed imagery, 151, 176–178, 210

G

gate in the wall metaphor, 242
genogram, 59–60, 61
gestures, 88–89
gifts from clients, 248
Gilbert, Paul, 137
global workspace theory, 42
goal setting, 83, 248
good-night ritual, 212–213, 267
Good Parent mode, 49
Gordon, Ruth, 135, 239
Grawe, Klaus, 134
grief, imagery for, 172–176
guilt, imagery for, 172–176

H

happy child mode, 44
Harris, Russ, 138
healthy adult mode, 2, 40, 49–50, 125–142; acceptance in, 133–137; ACT core processes related to, 79–80; chair dialogues for strengthening, 182–184, 186, 190–191; committed action in, 141, 142; explanation of, 125–126; identifying strengths in, 126–127; mindfulness in, 128–133; self-awareness in, 127–128; self-compassion in, 137; shaping in sessions, 247; steps for shifting into, 82; values connection in, 138–140
here-and-now interaction, 113
historical role-play, 180–182

homework assignments, 201–203
hypercriticalness schema, 30

I

imagery exercises, 149–178; emotion regulation and, 198; future-directed, 176–178, 210; introducing to clients, 149–151; for loss, grief, and guilt, 172–176; purposes served by, 151; rehearsal and behavioral activation, 177–178; rescripting process using, 156–172; resource imagery, 151, 152–156; supervision using, 265; for traumatic events, 167–172
imagery exercises (specific): "best day" video, 176–177; body scan, 153, 154; caring for the vulnerable child, 155–156; eightieth birthday, 140; farewell imagery, 174–176; light ball meditation, 153, 154–155; positive affect imagery, 139; safe place imagery, 152–153
imagery rescripting, 156–172; audio recordings of, 170; change process and, 145–147; dealing with dissociation in, 168–169; details on process of, 158–165; emotional tolerance window and, 167–168; monitoring using SUDS, 170; overview of steps in, 157–158; purposes served by, 151; sexual abuse and, 171–172; traumatic events and, 151, 167–172
impact techniques, 92
impaired autonomy and performance domain, 28–29
impaired limits domain, 29
impulsive child mode, 43
infant modes, 50–51
inflexible attention, 22
information processing systems, 150
inhibition, emotional, 30
initial phase of treatment, 218

inner critic modes, 40, 43, 47–49; chair dialogues and, 185, 186, 187, 189–190; dealing with competition between, 240–241; process of working with, 122–124; watching for hidden, 221
inquisitive stance, 159
insecure attachment, 10–11
instability schema, 28
insufficient self-control schema, 29
integrative approach, 3
intensity adjustments, 167
intensive body feelings, 200
intensive listening, 199
interactional patterns, 83–85
internal working phase, 218
internalization process, 48–49
International Society of Schema Therapy (ISST), 62, 273
interpersonal work, 251–258; involving partners in, 252–253; issues to consider for, 256–258; mode cycle model of, 253–255

J

joint perspective, 90
Jung, Carl, 260

K

Kandel, Eric, 12
Kanfer, Fred, 232
kindness exercise, 137
Klosko, Janet, vii

L

labeling coping modes, 109
learning, emotional, 16–19
learning theory, 233
Leaving It at the Office (Norcross and Guy), 267
LeDoux, Joseph, 16

letter writing, 198
light ball meditation, 153, 154–155
limitations, acknowledging, 222–223, 245
long-term potentiation, 11
loss, imagery for, 172–176
loyalty conflicts, 161

M

macrolevel patterns, 83–85, 230
maintenance phase, 218
maladaptive coping modes, 40, 43, 45–47. *See also* coping modes
maladaptive schemas, 26
manipulative clients, 232
Marlatt, Allan, 135, 239
McCullough, Jim, 98
meditation: acceptance of emotions/sensations, 136–137; light ball, 153, 154–155; mindfulness of breath, 132–133
mentalization: explanation of, 19–20; improving in clients, 95–96
metaphors: gate in the wall, 242; theater, 42; two-minds, 144
microlevel patterns, 83–85, 230
mindfulness: attention time line exercise, 129–131; breath meditation, 132–133; building skills in, 131; daily maintenance of, 133; 5-4-3 mindful grounding exercise, 131–132; healthy adult mode and, 128–133; psychological flexibility and, 23; rating in clients, 79; schema therapy and, 21, 129; tasting food with, 199; therapist practice of, 196, 268
Mindfulness for Therapists (Zarbock et al.), 268
Mindfulness-Based Cognitive Therapy for Depression (Teasdale et al.), 218
mirror neurons, 10
mistrust-abuse schema, 28, 32

mode cycle model: interpersonal work and, 253–255; therapy relationship and, 260–264
mode dialogues. *See* chair dialogues
mode flipping, 20, 79
mode map, 73–79; chair dialogues based on, 184–193; mode recognition and, 77–79; purposes served by, 74; working with, 74–77
mode monitoring form, 67–69, 128
modes, 1, 39–55; awareness of, 266; child, 40, 42, 43–45, 119–122; clinical symptoms and, 53–54, 55; coping, 40, 43, 45–47, 109–119; descriptive diagram of, 70–73; developmental view of, 50–51; explanation of, 39–40; healthy adult, 40, 49–50; inner critic, 40, 43, 47–49, 122–124; integrating schemas and, 51–53; monitoring of, 67–69; recognition of, 77–79; types of, 40–42. *See also* schemas
motivation, 147, 197
motivational interviewing, 102–104
Motivational Interviewing (Miller and Rollnick), 242
music listening, 199

N

Nadort, Marjon, 219
narcissistic clients, 228–229
needs: emotions connected to, 8–9; poles of human, 6–7; systems of, 5–6
Neff, Kristen, 137
negativity-pessimism schema, 30
neurobiological perspective, 11–12
Nissen, Lukas, 193

O

observer mode, 195–196, 199
one-down position, 258
other-directed internalization, 48

other-directedness domain, 29–30
outline of treatment, 218–220
overcompensatory coping modes, 34, 46–47, 117–119
overvigilance and inhibition domain, 30
oxytocin, 10

P

pain, inducing light, 200
parent modes. *See* inner critic modes
parentification, 163
passive clients, 246–248
passive-aggressive traits, 241
perception-focused techniques, 199
performance, impaired, 28–29
personality change, 215
personality disorders, 1–2
perspective changes: chair dialogues and, 189; cooling emotions using, 89–92; extension and substitution techniques for, 92–95; imagery rescripting and, 157, 159–160; making progress by bringing, 104–106
phases of treatment, 218
photographs, childhood, 167, 243
physical activities, 200–201
physical impact technique, 244
planning treatment. *See* treatment planning
positive affect imagery exercise, 139
posture changes, 89
prayers, continuous, 198
present-moment contact: emotion regulation and, 199; psychological flexibility and, 23; rating in clients, 79
primary emotions, 121–122
psychodynamic therapies, 259
psychological flexibility, 2, 23
psychological rigidity, 22
psychosomatic symptoms, 110
punitive critic mode, 47–48
punitiveness schema, 30

R

rational processing, 144–145
realism, 222
reappraisal, 128, 157, 161
recognition seeking schema, 30
rehearsal and behavioral activation imagery, 177–178
Reinventing Your Life (Young and Klosko), 34, 59
rejection and disconnection domain, 28
relational frame theory (RFT), 21–22
relationship work. *See* interpersonal work
reparenting, 3; balancing empathic confrontation and, 85, 86, 96–99; fine-tuning the process of, 99–100; principle of limited, 96–97; therapeutic need for, 98
rescripting process. *See* imagery rescripting
resistance, causes of, 240–241
resonance, 37–38, 161
resource imagery, 151, 152–156
responsibility, 103, 191
rewinding the video, 230
rigid truths, vii
rituals: decompression, 267; good-night, 212–213
role-plays: healthy adult mode, 191; historical, 180–182; social skills, 210
romantically-interested clients, 248–250
ruptures, therapy, 92

S

safe place imagery, 152–153, 164
schedule of treatment, 219–220
schema chemistry, 253, 259
Schema Mode Inventory (SMI), 67
schema model, 1, 34–36; limitations of, 34; relevance of, 34–36
schema theory, 36
schema therapy, 1–3; attunement in, 36–38; case conceptualization in, 57–82; contextual approach and, 23–24; essential components of, 59; hallmark elements of, 3; including partners in, 251–258
Schema Therapy for Couples (Simeone-DiFrancesco et al.), 252, 255
Schema Therapy: A Practitioner's Guide (Young, Klosko, and Weishaar), vii, 2–3
schema-mode flash card, 203–204, 205
schemas, 1, 25–34; attractors as, 12; coping styles for, 33–34; core and compensatory, 32; descriptive list of, 27; domains of, 28–30; explanation of, 25–26; integrating modes and, 51–53; process of changing, 16–17; recognition of, 31; responses to, 33–34. *See also* modes
Schnarch, David, 255
second wave therapy, 2, 21
secondary emotions, 121–122
self, constitution of, 20
self-actualization, 85, 86
self-aggrandizer mode, 46
self-as-context, 23, 80
self-awareness: healthy adult mode and, 127–128; mode monitoring form for, 67–69, 128
self-care exercises: for emotion regulation, 200; for therapists, 266–269
self-compassion: activation of, 163–164, 195; attachment and, 11; healthy adult mode and, 137
self-directed internalization, 48
self-disclosure, 98–99, 231, 243–244, 245, 268–269
self-efficacy, 103–104, 197, 210
self-harming behavior, 232–238; accessing underlying anger in, 233–237; dealing with suicidal ideation and, 237–238
self-instructions, 198
self-reflection, 3, 85, 86, 128

self-sacrifice schema, 29
self-soothing clients, 238–240
self-symbols, 137
self-therapy, 268
sessions: planning process for, 220–221; reducing the frequency of, 245
sexual abuse: reprocessing of, 171–172; by therapists, 269
sexual attraction issues, 269–270
Shaw, Ida, 47, 275
shift gears step, 82
shift into step, 82
shift out step, 82
short diagnostic imagery, 151
sitting positions. *See* chair positions
skills: emotional, 216; mindfulness, 131; social, 210
sleeping problems, 268
smiley log, 204
social emotions, 44–45
social isolation schema, 28
social stabilization, 216–217
socialization, 20
spiritual resources, 268
stabilizing clients, 215–218; emotional stabilization, 215–216; reducing clinical symptoms, 217–218; social stabilization, 216–217
standing position, 189, 191
STEP acronym, 128
"still face" experiment video, 44–45
strengths, identifying, 126–127
structural dissociation model, 171
Sturm, Michael, 193
subjugation schema, 29
submissive–avoidant mode cycle, 261
submissive–dominant mode cycle, 261–262
submissive–submissive mode cycle, 261
submissive clients, 46; empathic confrontation with, 114–116; mode cycles involving, 261–262
substance abuse, 239

substitution technique, 94–95
SUDS ratings, 13, 170, 195, 201
suicidal ideation, 237–238
supervision, role of, 264–265
supportive feedback, 247
surrendering to schemas, 33
symbolization, 137

T

take-home messages, 165, 186, 192–193
talking-back diary, 206, 207
tasting, mindful, 199
tentative inquiry, 232
termination, 223–225; conveying the news about, 223–224; ethical concerns about, 224; managing with clients, 224–225
text messages, 244
theater metaphor, 42
theory of mind, 19
therapy planning. *See* treatment planning
therapy relationship, 83–107, 259–271; balancing act in, 85–86, 100–102; conflicts related to, 166; dealing with ruptures in, 92; emotional activation in, 86–96; gestures and bodily changes in, 88–89; improving mentalization in, 95–96; interactional patterns in, 83–85; looking objectively at, 247–248; mode cycles and pitfalls in, 260–264; motivational interviewing in, 102–104; perspective changes in, 89–95, 104–106; reparenting process in, 96–98, 99–100; role of supervision in, 264–265; romantically-interested clients in, 248–250; self-care for therapists in, 266–269; sexual attraction toward clients in, 269–270; stabilization of clients in, 215–218; therapist self-disclosure in, 98–99; wounded healer in, 259–260
therapy scenes, 83, 84

third wave therapies, 2, 21
tilted images, 15
time limits, 248
time projection, 232
transference, 259
traumatic event rescripting, 151, 167–172; audio recordings for, 170; dealing with dissociation in, 168–169; emotional tolerance window in, 167–168; monitoring using SUDS, 170; overview of working with, 170–172; sexual abuse and, 171–172
treatment planning, 215–225; balancing change and acceptance, 222–223; basis for starting therapy, 215–218; outline of treatment, 218–220; session planning, 220–221; termination process, 223–225
triggering situations, 195
Tronick, Edward, 10, 44
trust, 215, 218–219
two-minds metaphor, 144

U

undeveloped self, 29
undisciplined child mode, 44, 241
unrelenting standards schema, 30
urge surfing, 239–240

V

validation: of angry clients, 229; of coping modes, 109, 242
values: committed action based on, 138–139, 141–142; eightieth birthday imagery exercise, 140; healthy adult mode and, 138–140; pathological disruption of, 22; positive affect imagery exercise, 139; psychological flexibility and, 23; rating clarity of, 80
values road map, 141, 142
venting anger, 230
video-based supervision, 264–265
vulnerability to harm or illness schema, 28
vulnerable child mode, 43, 121; chair dialogues, 188; imagery exercise, 155–156

W

watching thoughts, 198
Weishaar, Marjorie, vii
willingness, 135
working phase, 218
wounded healer, 259–260
Wright, Jesse, 26

Y

Young, Jeffrey, vii, 1, 2, 3, 25, 39, 125, 167, 253, 276
Young Atkinson Mode Inventory (YAMI), 67
Young Compensation Inventory, 67
Young Parenting Inventory, 67
Young-Rygh Avoidance Inventory, 67
Young Schema Questionnaire (YSQ), 34, 66, 67

MORE BOOKS *from* NEW HARBINGER PUBLICATIONS

ACT MADE SIMPLE
An Easy-To-Read Primer on Acceptance & Commitment Therapy
978-1572247055 / US $39.95

HANDBOOK OF CLINICAL PSYCHOPHARMACOLOGY FOR THERAPISTS, EIGHTH EDITION
978-1626259256 / US $59.95

PROCESS-BASED CBT
The Science & Core Clinical Competencies of Cognitive Behavioral Therapy
978-1626255968 / US $69.95
CONTEXT PRESS
An Imprint of New Harbinger Publications

ACT FOR PSYCHOSIS RECOVERY
A Practical Manual for Group-Based Interventions Using Acceptance & Commitment Therapy
978-1626256132 / US $49.95
CONTEXT PRESS
An Imprint of New Harbinger Publications

CFT MADE SIMPLE
A Clinician's Guide to Practicing Compassion-Focused Therapy
978-1626253094 / US $49.95
CONTEXT PRESS
An Imprint of New Harbinger Publications

FUNCTIONAL ANALYTIC PSYCHOTHERAPY MADE SIMPLE
A Practical Guide to Therapeutic Relationships
978-1626253513 / US $49.95

newharbingerpublications
1-800-748-6273 / newharbinger.com

Follow Us

(VISA, MC, AMEX / prices subject to change without notice)

QUICK TIPS *for* THERAPISTS
Fast and free solutions to common client situations mental health professionals encounter every day

Written by leading clinicians, Quick Tips for Therapists are short e-mails, sent twice a month, to help enhance your client sessions. **Visit newharbinger.com/quicktips to sign up today!**

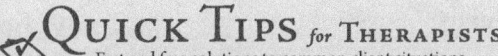

Sign up for our Book Alerts at **newharbinger.com/bookalerts**

Register your **new harbinger** titles for additional benefits!

When you register your **new harbinger** title—purchased in any format, from any source—you get access to benefits like the following:

- Downloadable accessories like printable worksheets and extra content

- Instructional videos and audio files

- Information about updates, corrections, and new editions

Not every title has accessories, but we're adding new material all the time.

Access free accessories in 3 easy steps:

1. Sign in at NewHarbinger.com (or **register** to create an account).

2. Click on **register a book**. Search for your title and click the **register** button when it appears.

3. Click on the **book cover or title** to go to its details page. Click on **accessories** to view and access files.

That's all there is to it!

If you need help, visit:

NewHarbinger.com/accessories